Juridicum – Schriften zur Rechtsphilosophie

Die Schriftenreihe will eine Gelegenheit zur Auseinandersetzung mit theoretischen, methodischen und politischen Grundfragen des Rechts bieten, um der Verständigung über die Grundlagen moderner Rechtsordnungen zu dienen. Angesichts einer gesteigerten gesellschaftlichen und rechtlichen Dynamik und der durch Globalisierung und Technisierung immer komplexer werdenden sozialen Umwelt des Rechts ist die Beschäftigung mit eben diesen Grundlagen besonders wichtig. Zentrale Anliegen der Rechtsreflexion der Gegenwart wie Versuche zur Begründung der Menschenrechte, von Verfassungsstaat und internationaler Rechtsordnung oder der Beantwortung der unterschiedlichsten Fragestellungen der Medizinethik kommen ohne eine Rückbesinnung auf die Grundlagen des Rechts nicht aus. Dies ist die klassische Aufgabe der Rechtsphilosophie, die gleichermaßen eine Teildisziplin der Praktischen Philosophie wie der Rechtswissenschaft ist und in ihrer ganzen Vielfalt in der Schriftenreihe gepflegt werden soll.

Carolina Esser

Recognized Women:

A Theory of Recognition of Women and Case Studies

Springer

Carolina Esser
Legal Theory, International
and European Law
Paris-Lodron Universität Salzburg
Salzburg, Austria

ISSN 2945-9826 ISSN 2945-9834 (electronic)
Juridicum – Schriften zur Rechtsphilosophie
ISBN 978-3-658-46848-4 ISBN 978-3-658-46849-1 (eBook)
https://doi.org/10.1007/978-3-658-46849-1

This Springer imprint is published by the registered company Springer Fachmedien Wiesbaden GmbH, part of Springer Nature.
The registered company address is: Abraham-Lincoln-Str. 46, 65189 Wiesbaden, Germany

Homo sum: nihil humani a me alienum puto.
I am a human being; nothing human is alien to me.[1]

(Publio Terêncio Afro)

[1] Free translation.

Acknowledgment

This book is my doctoral thesis in philosophy of law, developed at the Paris-Lodron University of Salzburg, Austria. I am deeply grateful to my advisor, Professor Stephan Kirste, for his generosity in welcoming my research and for his brilliant insights on human rights and democracy. My heartfelt thanks to my colleague Kristin Albrecht, for her unwavering support, sorority, and loyalty throughout my research, as well as for the empowering conversations that I will always cherish.

My research on women's rights, particularly with women from non-Western and non-democratic countries, was inspired by the transformative experience of working at the Centre Batha in Morocco, with women survivors of violence. I am indebted to Professor Azelarabe Lahkim Bennani for inviting me to conduct research at Sidi Mohamed Ben Abdellah University in Fès, as a visiting scholar. I also extend my gratitude to Vechta University, where I first embarked on my studies in the philosophy of law in Germany.

This book would not have been possible without the courageous women who shared their stories with me—most of them survivors of violence and misrecognition. To those Chinese and Moroccan women who spoke to me and entrusted me with their experiences, I owe the deepest gratitude. The vulnerabilities you revealed have become the strength that fuels our collective struggle for our recognition as women.

Lastly, as a woman, I feel recognized and empowered, particularly by the remarkable men who have been part of my journey. The recognition of women can and should be supported by all genders, and I am grateful for the men in my life who exemplify honesty, kindness, empathy, and intelligence. To my husband, Mateus; My father, Sérgio; My uncles Daniel and Paulo; My teacher and friend, Lucas Gontijo: thank you for contributing for my recognition as a woman.

Introduction

Despite the attempt to build a theory of recognition based on private and public aspects of life, Axel Honneth did not sufficiently take into consideration discussions on gender equality, specifically regarding the recognition of women and how the patterns of recognition (*Muster intersubjektiven Anerkennung*) could be interpreted from a gender equality perspective. Furthermore, Honneth did not clarify how cultural differences can influence recognition, and how culture plays a role in the building of female identity. I intend to analyze and assess Axel Honneth's theory of recognition from gender and intercultural perspectives.

According to Honneth, the *recognition* of a person as a self-confident, self-respected, and self-esteemed individual happens through three dimensions of personality: needs and emotions (primary relationships of recognition), moral responsibility (legal relations of recognition), and traits and abilities (community of value)[2]. In other words, it occurs within three perspectives: a private sphere of life including family and friendships—*pattern of love*, where the person is recognized as a family member and as part of private relationships of love and care; and two public spheres of life—*pattern of law*, where the person is recognized as a legal person, being the addressee and author of rights; and *pattern of solidarity*, where a person is recognized as a member of a community of value through empathy and solidarity within the group[3]. Each pattern

[2] Honneth 1995, 129.

[3] "The only way in which individuals are constituted as persons is by learning to refer to themselves, from the perspective of an approving or encouraging other, as beings with certain positive traits and abilities. The scope of such traits—and hence the extent of one's positive relation-to-self—increases with each new form of recognition that individuals are able to apply to themselves as subjects. In this way, the prospect of basic self-confidence is inherent in the experience of love; the prospect of self-respect, in the experience of legal

of recognition must follow certain conditions to allow an individual to reach self-esteem, self-confidence, and self-respect.

During the process of identity formation of an individual, she may experience offenses to the patterns of recognition, and then struggles should begin to recover her recognition.

In the context of discussing how recognition can be achieved, Honneth indicates that *struggles* always accompany recognition[4]. There is no recognition without struggling for it.

The primary agents of struggle are the human beings themselves. Honneth does not adopt the law or the state as the central agents for recognition and justice. Despite his premise of democratic life, he still believes that recognition is reachable through individuals' actions, such as through struggles for recognition.[5]

Nevertheless, Honneth does not clarify how exactly individuals should struggle for recognition, especially in contexts where their freedom to develop their identity may be limited—for instance, I could mention a non-democratic country, where the freedom of expression for women does not exist at all.

Besides the lack of sufficient proposals and clarifications about the struggles, Honneth does not approach a more specific dimension: a struggle for gender equality and the recognition of women. Women, mainly in the pattern of love, are more vulnerable to experiencing disrespect and misrecognition[6]. Honneth's theory of recognition does not allow women's complete and reasonable achievement of recognition. An analysis of the patterns and other elements of recognition may show that it is not possible to build a model of recognition of women yet. Considering that, I first ask:

a) Why is Axel Honneth's theory of recognition not reasonable for women's recognition?

As a second step, I would inquire:

b) How can his theory be modified to fully include the recognition of women?

---

recognition; and finally the prospect of self-esteem, in the experience of solidarity." (Honneth 1995, 173)

[4] Honneth 1995, 168.

[5] "(...) we as human beings have a permanent demand imposed on ourselves, a demand to make things better." (Honneth 2013, 217)

[6] Okin 1999, 5.

These two problems will be hypothesized in this work.

Chapter 1, then, analyzes the Honnethian theory of recognition, his approach of morality, ethical life, and formation of human identity. The study begins from the most prominent work of Honneth *"The struggle for recognition: the moral grammar of social conflicts"* (1995, referred to as "Struggle for recognition" below) and, through an analysis of his other productions, clarifies the concept of recognition and its patterns. Each pattern of recognition will be criticized and assessed as well.

Recognition will be better understood if one analyzes the denials of recognition. The institute of *disrespect* in Honneth's theory has a crucial role, and it is necessary to study disrespect mainly from the perspective of an individual's private life. *Chapter 2* analyzes these offenses to the patterns of recognition, which Honneth denominates practices of "disrespect." I understand that recognition is measurable as soon as one focuses on its offenses. It is also a methodology adopted by most of the Critical Theorists, who advocate that a philosophical concept turns out to be realizable and definable if one looks at the society's issues—which Habermas calls as social pathologies, for instance, at the offenses and social limits to this philosophical entity[7]. Recognition is definable and measurable if one analyzes the current situation of society, from the perspective of offenses to recognition.

In *Chapter 3,* I will, then, introduce the Honnethian solution to situations of disrespect: the necessity to struggle for recognition. This chapter introduces my hypothesis for problem (b): How can Honneth's theory of recognition be modified to fully include the recognition of women?

---

[7] Forst lists three main objectives of a critical theory: "Hence a critical theory of (in)justice has to be above all a critique of the existing *relations of justification* (or of 'justificatory power'). Such a critique, speaking in 'diagnostic' terms, has three essential aspects. First, by way of critical social analysis it aims at *exposing unjustifiable social relations*, not just political ones in a narrow sense, but also those of an economic or cultural nature, that is, all those relations, in more or less institutionalised form, that fall short of the standard of reciprocal and general justifiability and are marked by forms of exclusion or domination. Second, it implies a discourse-theoretical (also in part genealogical) *critique of 'false'* (possibly ideological) *justifications* for such relations, that is, justifications that veil asymmetrical power relations and traditions of exclusion (say, along gender or class lines). And third, it implies an account of the *failure (or non-existence) of effective social and political structures of justification* to (a) unveil and (b) change unjustifiable social relations." (Forst 2011, 314)

A model of recognition of women may be built through specific *struggles* for the recognition of women, with support coming from the pattern of law. The concept of *struggle* is studied, and also the critiques of Honneth's idea of *struggle*. The work stresses these critiques and provides its position regarding some interpretations of the Honnethian theory.

Chapters 4 to *7* present my proposals for struggles for recognition in the patterns of love, law, and solidarity, with a highlight of the role of law for the recognition of women.

In *Chapter 4,* I will inquire as to which struggle is able to exist in all three patterns of recognition. This struggle is the one against indifference. The work will clarify that indifference can be interpreted as a behavior and a feeling; being neutral, positive or negative; intentional or unintentional. I comprehend struggles against indifference as a negative intentional feeling and behavior.

Indifference is a major motivating factor of disrespect of women, offending practices of solidarity, and damaging the recognition. The work argues that the individuals should confront the indifference they feel inside themselves. The first struggle to happen is the one inside oneself, when feelings of indifference are replaced by solidarity, compassion, affection, and care.

Chapter 5 proposes struggles in the pattern of love, inside the contexts of family and friendship. Within these contexts, individuals should struggle for the emancipation of the family member and for the open revisability of a culture.

After proposing struggles in the pattern of love, I will then focus on the struggle inside the second pattern of recognition, namely the pattern of law. I interpret the pattern of law as a primary support for all the patterns of recognition, promoting the preservation of the necessary elements of women's recognition. In Chapter 6 I introduce my hypothesis for problem (a): Why is Axel Honneth's theory of recognition not reasonable for women's recognition?

Honneth's theory of recognition is not sensible for a theory of recognition of women because his approach does not place the pattern of law in a principal position in comparison with the other patterns—namely, love and solidarity. It is necessary, then, to rearrange the patterns of recognition in such a way that law would be the fundamental pattern maintaining the other dimensions of recognition, especially love in the context of women's recognition.

Chapter 6 will analyze the role of legal recognition, especially through human rights. A society cannot reach social freedom by either only meeting public ethical requirements related to material resources or to the participation in deliberative private and public spaces, meeting successful private experiences of love and care such as family and friendship, for instance. Instead, both must exist. The formation of human beings' identity comes from psychological—more precisely, emotional—individual claims, and shared public ethics—specific provisions related to material resources, the inclusion in a public deliberative space, and the fulfillment of individual emotional needs within the entire community. Considering that, all societies should comply with recognition in both perspectives: public and private, supported by legal recognition.

Commonly, theorists focus just on public dimensions of justice. They forget to consider the private spheres of recognition as well, related to the private life of individuals, in their family and friendship circles. Furthermore, the primary agents of justice should be the human beings themselves, and not the commonly discussed legal institutes or state institutions. Additionally, justice should be analyzed from an intercultural perspective, in order to promote the philosophy of law as a more fruitful and realistic science, instead of studies based mainly on Western paradigms.

To turn recognition into real practices of justice and respect of women, I will highlight some human rights, which would facilitate the identification of recognition and disrespect in different cultures, including the non-Western societies.

Sequentially, *Chapter 7* proposes struggles in the pattern of solidarity. It will be relevant to detail the concept of solidarity and its relevance to the theory of recognition. The struggles in this pattern hold a confrontation of indifference as a social pathology. Besides my interpretation of indifference as a feeling and behavior, I also comprehend it as the most influential social pathology that nowadays damages social justice and recognition. If the members of society continue to ignore that other human beings are being victims of exploitation and violations of fundamental human rights, they will never be able to guarantee the realization of justice. If they let social justice be a task only for lawyers, philosophers, and government, they neglect to develop the most significant power worldwide: the power of people's actions.

Furthermore, in the pattern of solidarity, I advocate for struggles for metanoia, honoring difference, and accountability. Additionally, I will highlight the Honnethian struggles for voluntary practices and democracy.

Whereas *Chapters 1* to *7* study Honnethian recognition from a theoretical perspective and also propose my modifications to the theory, *Chapters 8* to *11* illustrate recognition and struggles through case studies. The case studies will illuminate how the pattern of law relates to the achievement of women's recognition, taking it from an intercultural approach[8].

Chapter 8 intends to identify how to build women's recognition especially through the role of law, adopting then case studies. First of all, the chapter highlights the influences of Hegel in the work of Honneth, and how law can be understood *as recognition* and *as a struggle.* Furthermore, the French influences in Honnethian thought, as well as the role of Critical Theory for the building of his theory are also described. After these discussions, the chapter then justifies the adoption of the case studies.

As liberal democracy plays an important role in the discussions of recognition, I choose case studies from different contexts that are not part of the ones currently discussed by Honneth. Unquestionably, democratic societies provide more pathways for citizens to express themselves. Their dissatisfaction with offenses to patterns of recognition can be brought to public debates with the support of the law. There, people have freedom of expression and freedom of speech, for instance.

Nevertheless, to make recognition universal, applicable to different cultural contexts and achieving the recognition of women, one of my objectives is to find forms of implementing struggles for women even in authoritarian regimes with a low level of liberal democracy and where the pattern of law is still not fully developed.

The work then adopts case studies from two different countries: China, in *Chapter 9,* and Morocco, in *Chapter 10,* and analyzes them from a perspective of similarities, regarding offenses to women, and the conditions for struggles for recognition there.

Although China and Morocco are vastly different, the offenses to the recognition of women there make the demographic distinctions not necessarily significant. Case studies show that Chinese and Moroccan women usually keep their family and love relationships private, and when they experience some offense to recognition—for instance, domestic violence, usually these practices are not denounced or sanctioned as a result of social indifference. Furthermore, although both countries are examples of a system of rights under constant development within their regional contexts, the recent reforms in their legislation do not contribute to the achievement of women's recognition at all. I will evaluate

---

[8] "Interculturalism makes a comparison between cultures (extra group analysis). On the other hand, multiculturalism examines a specific culture, country, city, or community, with a focus on the minorities, that live inside there—intragroup analysis—". (Kymlicka 1995, 18)

why the legal reforms in both countries have not been sufficient to guarantee women's recognition.

Regarding China and Morocco, I will adopt the collection of scientific data, namely legislation and secondary literature, such as institutional reports, articles, and books. The study of China and Morocco will contemplate their legal norms and constitution during their history with a focus on human rights. I will analyze international reports—such as the ones from the United Nations—as an official data source.

The research has a unique relevance, as access to sources regarding China and Morocco is limited because of state restrictions on research and documentation. Nevertheless, the study will introduce unpresented data from observations experienced by the author through her research, relationships, interviews, and conversations with Chinese and Moroccan people. I can mention, for instance, an interview with a Chinese activist in Shanghai, which provided a lot of unprecedented information on the historical-legal background of gender equality activism in China. Furthermore, in Morocco, the author has worked on observations and collection of data during a voluntary internship at Centre Batha, a multifunctional center sponsored by Unesco, for the support and empowerment of women victims of gender-based violence.

Additionally, the research will include articles and books written by Chinese and Moroccan authors.

The last chapter of the work, *Chapter 11,* demonstrates that, despite several impediments for reaching the recognition of women in these countries, there are struggles for recognition happening there. I will collect data about social and private movements for the recognition of women there, as well as clarify how the conditions, elements, and patterns of the theory of recognition are illustrated within these societies.

The possibility to analyze the Honnethian theory of recognition contributes, firstly, to the improvement of the legal-philosophical paradigm, expanding it from Western to non-Western contexts. The research intends to break the tradition of legal-philosophical studies, which usually do not effectively approach societies outside the West.

Axel Honneth's theory of recognition has been relevant to the philosophy of law, as it relates freedom and justice to building one's identity. Nevertheless, the theory has not sufficiently considered the recent changes in law, especially regarding gender equality and how it would be possible to achieve women's recognition within different cultural contexts.

My work would contribute to a reinterpretation of the theory of recognition from the perspective of gender equality, analyzing each element and pattern of recognition, and proposing forms of overcoming the shortcomings that the theory still holds.

I will see that Axel Honneth focuses on the *struggle for recognition* that, in his view, results from the denial of recognition, which is even more fundamental than injustice. Nevertheless, Honneth does not sufficiently explain the impacts on identity formation caused by an absence of democratic and deliberative public spaces in some societies, especially if one considers the pattern of law. It is, then, important, to interpret his theory and modify it to include different cultural contexts. It would contribute to the philosophy of law, expanding its studies from the commonly adopted democratic contexts to non-democratic ones, and interpreting it from a gender equality perspective.

Furthermore, Honneth's approach to the *struggles for recognition* does not sufficiently propose forms of struggles that are feasible for different cultural contexts especially regarding women's recognition.

Finding ways to increase *recognition* of women would reduce a shared *indifference* that interferes with all patterns of recognition. It would be sustained by specific human rights, which correlate with forming women's identity through love, law, and solidarity. Instead of relying only on changes in the form of government, regime, rule of law, or division of powers, individuals should take more active accountability in achieving women's recognition. The work contends that struggles are more than just public movements, especially in dealing with case studies in societies where public protests and political marches are limited—for instance, in China and Morocco.

In the end, the work will reach the objectives of clarifying why Honneth's recognition is not yet ready to allow a complete model of recognition of women; and to propose the necessary changes to his theory, to promote gender equality from an intercultural point of view, with support coming from legal recognition.

The elements of Honneth's theory of recognition contribute to a theory of legal recognition of women, but not sufficiently. It needs further elaboration of the following aspects: how the pattern of law sustains the other patterns of recognition, especially love; how the pattern of law may embrace gender equality, specifically in non-democratic and non-Western countries; how culture plays a role in female building of identity; and determination of their mutual relationship.

This work represents an attempt to comprehend recognition from different perspectives, different countries, different cultures, different disciplines, and different genders[9].

[9] This work adopts the ethnological efforts to interpret alien cultures, without any intention of judging them, but rather comprehending their social contexts and studying them from the Honnethian perspective. Lévi-Strauss was part of this ethnological approach, condemning structuralist criticism:

"With this set of conditions, ethnology poses itself a problem that is, so to speak, one of scientific strategy, and that Claude Lévi-Strauss has formulated with exactitude (Lévi-Strauss, 1974): how can ethnology study an alien culture, its ideas of rationality which are obviously completely unknown to the ethnologists, without destroying them by taking from them by theoretical means their fear-awakening strangeness? This key question of ethnology is a source of much instruction for structuralism, for in this situation the structuralist decision consists in allowing the alien culture to remain the 'Other', to remain hermeneutically incomprehensible, by setting the ethnological researcher the sole task of investigating the anonymous rule-governed processes and events of this culture. […] The structuralist criticism of the various ethnological efforts to understand alien cultures asserts that every interpretation of an alien culture that seeks to understand the meanings of the actions expressing that culture implicitly contains the destruction of those meanings—for the rationality that is proper to the alien plexus of social relations is allegedly transposed into the ethnologists' own horizon of rationality and in this manner pulverized, so to say". (Strauss *apud* Honneth 1988, 132)

In the same direction, see Taylor:

"In short, exclusive reliance on an acultural theory unfits us for what is perhaps the most important task of social sciences in our day: understanding the full gamut of alternative modernities that are in the making in different parts of the world. It locks us into an ethnocentric prison, condemned to project our own forms onto everyone else, and blissfully unaware of what we are doing". (Taylor 1992, 93)

Contents

Abbreviations

CEDAW	Convention on the Elimination of All Forms of Discrimination against Women
Centre Batha	Centre multifonctionnel Batha pour la autonomisation des femmes victimes de violence basée sur le genre
Chinese Anti-Domestic Violence Law	Chinese National Law on Domestic Violence
Democracy as reflexive cooperation	Democracy as reflexive cooperation: John Dewey and the Theory of Democracy Today
Disrespect	Disrespect: the Normative Foundation of Critical Theory
Freedom's Right	Freedom's Right: the social foundations of democratic life
HDI	China's Human Development Index
IMF	International Monetary Found
IPDF	Initiative pour la protection des droits des femmes
Moroccan Law on the Elimination of Violence against Women	Law 103.03 on the Elimination of Violence against Women
NPC	China's National People's Congress
PRC	People's Republic of China
Reification	Reification: a Recognition-Theoretical View
Struggle for recognition	The struggle for recognition: the moral grammar of social conflicts
UN	United Nations

UN Women	United Nations Entity For Gender Equality And The Empowerment Of Women
UNDP	United Nations Development Programme
UNICEF	United Nations Children's Fund
VPN	Virtual private network
WF	Shanghai's Women Federation
Women's Federation	All China Women's Federation

Part I
Theory

1 What is Recognition?

The core of Axel Honneth's social theory lies in recognition. In the following, I will clarify the Honnethian concept of *recognition*, its relationship with social freedom, and the importance of *struggles for recognition*. According to him, recognition cannot be achieved without struggles for it.

Furthermore, this Chapter will analyze the critiques addressed at Axel Honneth's theory of recognition and assess them.

I understand that a re-elaboration of struggles for recognition is useful for achieving women's recognition. It is relevant to extend it to contexts not located in the West, and for democracies in a very early stage of development.

1.1 Honnethian Recognition

The book *Anerkennung: eine europäische Ideengeschichte* is one of the most recent works of Axel Honneth. In this book, he inquires if the concept of recognition changes according to different countries, that means, if the socio-cultural conditions influence the formation of the concept of recognition[1]. The author makes a historical comparison between recognition in Germany, France, and the United Kingdom.

For Honneth, the development of bourgeois society in the three countries above was different, and it has reflected in the way the reflections about recognition developed there[2].

[1] Honneth 2018, 17.

[2] Honneth 2018, 23.

C. Diamantino Esser Santana, *Recognized Women:*, Juridicum – Schriften zur Rechtsphilosophie, https://doi.org/10.1007/978-3-658-46849-1_1

The French idea of recognition comes from the concept of *amour propre*, developed by authors such as Rousseau, Sartre, and Lacan[3].

Honneth states that Hobbes' theory also was a strong influence on French recognition. The social contract has worked as a guarantee for people to be physically safe inside the monarchical state. The subject respects the social contract and demands the appreciation of others, because she wants to feel either preferable in comparison with the others, or because he wants to obtain the fortune of social appreciation and safety[4].

Nevertheless, what these citizens were experiencing is not a recognition related to affective feelings and psychological attachment[5]. Because of that, in France, any mention of recognition used to have a negative meaning. The search for attending to the expectations of the other makes the subject lose his own identity. Furthermore, it creates the risk that the others, who are interacting with the one "recognized", are just playing roles without exercising their true selves[6]. When comparing Rousseau and Sartre, Honneth sustains:

> Beide gehen, wenn auch aus unterschiedlichen Gründen, davon aus, dass das Anerkannt werden eine negative, nicht wünschenswerte Konsequenz hat: bei Rousseau die einer Verunsicherung über das eigene Selbst, bei Sartre die eines Verlustes des Für-sich-Seins und damit der eigenen Freiheit.[7]

In the context of France, for Honneth, only Durkheim has touched a positive recognition, when it was related to social integration[8].

On the other hand, in the United Kingdom, recognition used to have a positive meaning. Adam Smith has highlighted the necessity of taking oneself to the place of an "external observer"[9]. The basis for recognition pretends to detach the subject from an egoistic position and makes him see the reality of the other, from a sympathetic point of view. In the same way, David Hume has approached concepts such as sympathy and compassion[10]. When comparing Rousseau and Hume, Honneth has claimed:

---

[3] Honneth 2018, 14 and Honneth 2018, 19.

[4] Honneth 2018, 43.

[5] Honneth 2018, 26.

[6] Honneth 2018, 28 and Honneth 2018, 55.

[7] Honneth 2018, 69.

[8] Honneth 2018, 62.

[9] Honneth 2018, 14.

[10] Honneth 2018, 87.

> Vergleichen wir diese abschließende These Humes mit dem, was Rousseau zur amour propre gesagt hat, so zeigen sich zwei nahezu entgegengesetzte Auffassungen der Funktion und Wirkungsweise der zwischenmenschlichen Anerkennung: Wird der Mensch bei Rousseau dadurch, dass er nach sozialer Wertschätzung strebt, in einen unheilvollen Strudel des epistemischen Zweifels über sein eigenes Selbst gerissen, so wird er bei Hume durch dasselbe Streben heilsam dazu angetrieben, seine Absichten fortan zugunsten des allgemeinen Wohls dem Richtspruch eines unparteilichen Beobachters zu unterziehen.[11]

Smith goes in the same direction. For him, there is a kind of affectional recognition when someone aspires to connect with others in feeling and experience[12]. It happens, usually, within people who share similar circumstances. However, Smith goes further and sustains that it is necessary to widen the perspectives of recognition, making the subject relate to different subjects who are part of completely different circumstances, thus creating a generalized Other[13]. As a result, recognition in the United Kingdom was positive[14].

Finally, when discussing the German concept of recognition, Honneth clarifies that despite the influences of the French and English contexts, the first time the word "recognition" was used was in Germany[15]. There, Hegel had begun to deal with the dimensions of recognition, a model that has influenced Axel Honneth.

Whereas in France recognition was related to *amour propre* and in the United Kingdom to sympathy, in Germany recognition relates to respect[16].

The Honnethian concept of recognition was introduced in *Struggle for recognition*, which defines it from three different patterns: love (*Liebe*), rights (*Recht*), and solidarity (*Solidarität*).

In 2013, when questioned about the book *Struggle for recognition*, Honneth stated during an interview that, since the publication of this book, there have been many developments in his theory, but he would try to keep the inspiration from the early Hegel in order to develop a kind of social theory.[17] Furthermore, he would keep his understanding of the organization of the societies from certain patterns of recognition.[18] Nevertheless, Honneth said that he would better clarify

---

[11] Honneth 2018, 97.

[12] Honneth 2018, 144.

[13] Honneth 2018, 144.

[14] Honneth 2018, 84.

[15] Honneth 2018, 14.

[16] Honneth 2018, 133.

[17] Honneth 2013, 210.

[18] Honneth 2013, 210.

that the patterns are not stable forms of recognition, but rather that they are historically developed.[19] Finally, Honneth has stated that he would also be clearer regarding the interdependence between recognition and institutions.[20]

Honneth is endorsing that the division between three patterns of recognition is still useful for the achievement of recognition, but it is important to consider that they have a historical perspective. I come from this premise and I try to consider the patterns of recognition from the perspective of different cultures, pretending to historicize recognition.

In "*Disrespect: the Normative Foundation of Critical Theory*" (2007a, referred to as "*Disrespect*" below), Honneth keeps this same view, arguing that recognition has three modes of existence, and their denials influence an individual's self-relation and morality[21].

For Jacques Rancière, Honnethian theory of recognition represents a construction of the self through three elements—self-confidence, self-respect, and self-esteem—mediated by a so-called "other." Honneth's theory relates to the community, and community is a result of intersubjective relationships, which are not utilitarian, but rather a combination of relations of confidence, respect, and esteem with other persons[22], so that:

> The tripartite division of love, rights, and solidarity is grounded in a similar principle. A common element can be found in a multiplicity of relationships: the child with his mother, the lover with the loved one, the juridical subject making contracts, the civil subjects obeying the common law, or the political subject constructing a world of mutual recognition.[23]

Following Honneth's methodology of three patterns of recognition, the next sections of Chap. 1 analyze the patterns of recognition separately and also highlight their private and public dimensions.

---

[19] Honneth 2013, 210.

[20] Honneth 2013, 210.

[21] Honneth 2007a, 133.

[22] Rancière 2016, 86.

[23] Rancière 2016, 86.

1.2 The Three Patterns of Recognition and their Private and Public Dimensions

I comprehend as private life when the subject relates to her family and friends. Relationships with relatives and friends are generally related to the intimacy of a person, and they usually happen inside the home.

The Honnethian pattern of love occurs mainly in an individual's private life. Relationships developed in an individual's intimacy can become publicly formalized, for instance, marriage. Nevertheless, the nature of relationships of love is still intimate and private.

On the other hand, each individual experiences a public life when she is in public spaces. There, a person is seen by other persons; there, she needs to comply with social norms of behavior. The patterns of law and solidarity have more public characteristics. In law, the person, in comparison with other persons, realizes that she is equally respected and protected by the legal norms. In solidarity, the person realizes that she has worth for her community, and she cooperates with her community.

It is relevant to clarify that all patterns of recognition may have public and private nuances, nevertheless I understand that love, law, and solidarity are more attached to one or the other perspective.

After clarifying my interpretation of the classification—public or private—of the patterns of recognition in an individual's life, I will now analyze each pattern separately.

1.3 The Honnethian Pattern of Love

As soon as the human being is born, normally he will first interact with his parents. Later, this person will have relationships with friends and other relatives. Honneth refers to Winnicott's psychological thesis and explains that at this stage, mother and child have a symbiotic relationship; the baby is entirely dependent on his mother. He is not able to communicate his physical and emotional needs, requiring the mother's dedication. In this phase, there is no individuality, and both subjects feel like a unit[24].

This relation becomes the feeling of love when the inevitable experience of separation disappoints the baby's needs. At this time, the child recognizes the

[24] Honneth 1995, 96.

mother as an independent person and, hence, the child begins to develop his self-confidence[25]. The sphere of love, therefore, enables the self-confidence of the subject.

These experiences of love must occur appropriately. The person should have her needs and free-will taken into consideration, as well as respectfully and reasonably satisfied.

In relationships with relatives and friends, the fulfillment of needs and desires, for Honneth, is necessary for the full development of an individual's identity. "*Only where two people mutually agree to support each other's personality development, even when it takes a direction that cannot be anticipated, can we speak of an intersubjective relationship that earns the moniker of 'love'.*"[26]

The pattern of recognition called "love" occurs in the context of an individual's primary relationships in family, friendship, and passion:

> Love relationships are to be understood here as referring to primary relationships insofar as they—on the model of friendships, parent-child relationships, as well as erotic relationships between lovers—are constituted by strong emotional attachments among a small number of people.[27]

In the pattern of love, the individual has relations of affection and care with some people, such as parents, some relatives, some friends, and partners. Intimate love relationships are normally few in a person's life.

Regarding friendship, for instance, Honneth has sustained that social freedom can be fully exercised in the context of friendship, because the individuals eliminate boundaries required in everyday communication, giving to their friends privileged access to their emotions and experiences[28].

The book *Disrespect* clarifies that the pattern of love is the enjoyment by the individual of care and love, making possible the development of his self-confidence (*Selbstvertrauen*). Honneth claims that "self-confidence" should derive from E. H. Erikson's theory (1980)[29].

For Erikson, individuals have eight psychosocial stages of development. In each psychosocial stage, human beings experience different challenges, which contribute to the development of their characteristics, such as self-confidence. The eight stages are: trust vs. mistrust; autonomy vs. shame and doubt; initiative

---

[25] Honneth 1995, 111.

[26] Honneth 2014a, 146.

[27] Honneth 1995, 95.

[28] Honneth 2014a,139.

[29] Honneth 2007a, 136.

vs. guilt; industry vs. inferiority; identity vs. confusion; intimacy vs. isolation; generativity vs. stagnation; and integrity vs. despair.[30]

Erikson does not refer directly to the development of self-confidence in a specific stage. Nevertheless, many scholars locate the "confidence" in one or more phases, such as in the period of identity vs. confusion, when the individual is an adolescent. At this time, a person develops her own identity within the context of many personal reflections and doubts about life goals and personal characteristics. Adolescence is a moment of a variety of doubts for the person, and it has a crucial role in the formation of an individual's personality. There, confidence begins to exist.

On the other hand, different scholars understand that confidence develops in the first six stages of an individual's life—namely trust vs. mistrust; autonomy vs. shame and doubt; initiative vs. guilt; industry vs. inferiority; identity vs. confusion; and intimacy vs. isolation.

I understand that self-confidence develops during the entire life of individuals, which can aggregate many psychosocial stages of life. I do not agree with theorists who understand that it stays in just some of them.

Considering that, when Honneth states that his conception of "self-confidence" comes from Erikson, I interpret it inside the theory of eight stages of psychosocial life as an element continually growing during an individual's life.

Later on, during an interview in 2010, Honneth assumed that his mention of love and care in the pattern of love was attached exclusively to the mother/father/caregiver-infant relationship: "*That comes from the fact that when I was talking about love and care, I was really talking about the very early mother/father/caregiver-infant relationship. [...]*"[31]. Now, it seems that Honneth recognizes the fact that these feelings continue developing during an individual's life, in regards to her experiences with friends and relatives, as I will further see.

1.3.1 The Role of Love in Recognition

Love is the first dimension of recognition that a person experiences when she is born. The love is maintained by relationships that have begun at the beginning of an individual's life and then maintained by new relationships that happen during her life.

---

[30] Erikson 1993, 247.

[31] Honneth 2010a, 160.

The love experiences promote self-confidence, and love has a crucial role in recognition.

Furthermore, considering that love relationships are intimate, a person is more open-hearted when living her private life. When she is among friends and family, a person feels typically safe and relaxed; she feels "at home." It may result in a kind of vulnerability of a person within this pattern. Inside love, a person does not expect offenses or denials of recognition, coming from private partners and relatives. An offense in the pattern of love represents a significant offense to the individual's expectations.

For Honneth, self-confidence is the prerequisite for all types of self-realization, and the experience of love is the core of all ethical forms of life. Because of that, love should be protected from external forces and influences, and law makes the integrity of love possible.[32]

Therefore, love has an important role for recognition, as it comes at the beginning of the individual's formation of identity.

Nevertheless, Honneth has been criticized because of his approach to the pattern of love, as I will see further.

1.3.2 Critiques of the Honnethian Pattern of Love

First of all, Honneth is criticized for attaching recognition to a primary relationship, which can be unequal. Authors such as Iris Young, Amy Allen, and Johanna Meehan accuse Honneth of a naive interpretation of the mother-infant relationship. For them, this relationship is not equally enjoyed by child and mother, as the former is hierarchically submissive to the latter.[33]

---

[32] Honneth 1995, 176.

[33] Petherbridge 2011, 24. See also Meehan (2011):

"Even when parents bond intensely with their newborns, the period of symbiotic intoxication that Honneth describes seems like a fantasy, to be criticised both for its anti-feminist implications (must women experience the loss of subjectivity that Honneth claims to value so highly in order to successfully relate to their infants?) and because it issues in a problematic account of self/other relationships. Even if symbiotic unity were psychically possible and desirable, most people's lives do not allow for the exclusive and intense union between child and caregiver that Winnicott and following him, Honneth, describe. [...] Honneth's description of infant-maternal relationships does not recognise even the economic and political conditions of middle-class women, but even more dramatically, it does not recognise the reality of truly impoverished women's lives where bonding with infants at all can be impossible." (Meehan 2011, 95)

And:

Later on, Honneth assumed that this primary relationship can be interpreted as unequal because, inevitably, the child is submitted to the ones who are taking care of her. Nevertheless, I understand that the love experienced in childhood is still fundamental to an individual's formation of identity.

During an individual's life, the elements experienced in childhood can be continually endorsed by the family and culture, that means, the care process is influenced by socialization. Honneth assumes that, in the child's first experiences of love, not just hierarchy between child and caregivers exists, but also a cultural influence coming from parents and caregivers.[34] This topic is relevant to this work, as I am concerned with the application of the theory of recognition[35] in different cultures and societies.

The pattern of love is the moment when the individual mostly receives influences from the cultural traditions of her community, and it is usually endorsed in domestic relationships. This is one more reason why the pattern of love must acquire more relevance in the theory of Honneth[36], especially if I focus on the recognition of women.

Indeed, family influences can turn out to be oppressive. Parents or caregivers can influence their modes of behavior and practices—such as the choice of their religion, limiting their freedom of expression, consciousness, and self-determination.It may be intentional or non-intentional.[37]

"The attachment-disordered child's affective damage and the social problems it results in demonstrate that moral forms of life are vulnerable even in early infancy. Without empathy or whatever we might call the caring orientation to another person that a loved child "naturally" brings to relationships throughout life, the intersubjective bonds required for moral engagement cannot be formed, or are not formed strongly enough." (Meehan 2011, 117)

[34] "Thus, if one concentrates only on that element of care, there is a certain invitation to describe it as reciprocal—as a reciprocal dependency—this is Winnicott's description, I think. If one takes a broader view of care and is attentive to the element of socialization in the care-giving, then your point, Amy, makes sense. However, in that case, one probably takes a different perspective on the care process; one views the care and love given in infancy and childhood as already having an element of socialization in it, and then it becomes evident that the mother or father or other caregiver unintentionally uses her or his own power, which she or he has because of the helplessness of the child, to reproduce certain regimes, let's say cultural regimes." (Honneth 2010a, 160).

[35] As our theoretical framework is Axel Honneth, when we use the term "theory of recognition" we are considering specifically his theory.

[36] Julie Connolly states that Honneth has privatized the sphere of love and it is necessary to defetishise love in the Critical Theory. (Connolly 2010, 430).

[37] "I deliberately do not use the word 'domination'. This is a non-intentional process. It is not part of the intentions of the parents to reproduce a certain picture of femininity or, at least, a

Some theorists state that the mother-infant relationship is not as romantic as Honneth defines it. The woman has the ultimate responsibility as a mother, and it can be damaging and problematic. The argument turns out to be substantial if one considers underprivileged people experiencing unfavorable economic and political conditions. Motherhood, in such conditions, is not as harmonious as Honneth presupposes.

In spite of all of the above critiques, I understand that to build his theory and to arrive at the definition of recognition, Honneth needed to divide the aspects of an individual's life into three perspectives. As a matter of methodology, he decided to theoretically describe the patterns of recognition, considering them dynamic and adaptable to different situations in real life. As a sociologist, Honneth is aware that studying human behavior and social practices has historical and cultural dimensions.[38]

The fact that the relationship between mother and infant varies according to cultures and time does not damage the description of the Honnethian pattern of love. It is essential to highlight as well that the pattern of love does not limit itself just to the mother-infant relationship. As Honneth describes it, the pattern of love begins at the time a person is born, and it keeps developing during an individual's life, in her relationships with friends and relatives.

Even if there is no mother-infant relationship caused by, for instance, situations of poverty and child abandonment, it may be possible that this child will experience love in her childhood, youth, or adulthood, coming from other kinds of intimate relationships.

If the individual does not experience love at all, then she will not attain the element of self-confidence in recognition. In this context, it is relevant to study how the pattern of love could be affected, how the individual is not recognized in this dimension. According to Honneth, the pattern of love is affected in cases

---

certain subordinating concept of femininity, but simply by the way in which the parents care for their child, subordinating power is reproduced." (Honneth 2010a, 156)

[38] See, for instance, Honneth's statement in 2010: "When I wrote, Struggle for recognition (Honneth 1995 [1992]), I definitely had a completely unhistorical concept of love and care. That was a mistake. At least later on, I try to see love and care as social forms. I now see love and care as taking on a specific social form in each historical period; this means that they include and entail certain elements of enabling that are taken from the overall societal-historical system, let's say from our cultural system of social esteem; however, they are evidently taken in such a way that they become a constitutive part of the social forms of love and care. In other words, love and care do not appear neutrally but rather in historically specific forms, which are mirrored in the overall cultural system of recognition." (Honneth 2010a, 157).

when physical integrity is violated, such as physical abuse, torture, and rape.[39] In these cases, the victim is forcibly deprived of freely disposing over her own body.[40] It represents the most fundamental sort of personal degradation, because it causes humiliation and reflects on other forms of a person's practical relation-to-self.[41] The victim experiences not just purely physical pain, but rather the combination of this pain with the feeling of being defencelessly at the mercy of another subject[42]. "*Physical abuse represents a type of disrespect that does lasting damage to one's basic confidence (learned through love) that one can autonomously coordinate one's own body.*"[43] As a consequence, the victim experiences social shame and the loss of trust in herself and the world.[44]

The most critical effect of an offense in the sphere of love is the loss of confidence in oneself, caused by the feeling of being a victim of some compelled act. Offenses in the pattern of love should also be extended to mental integrity. Honneth speaks about physical abuse, but psychological abuse also injures a person's self-confidence and affects the pattern of love.

The offenses to the pattern of love are relevant, this pattern influences the other two modes of recognition, namely law, and solidarity:

> In our context, to speak of 'love' as an 'element' of ethical life can only mean that, for every subject, the experience of being loved constitutes a necessary precondition for participation in the public life of a community. This thesis becomes plausible when it is understood as a claim about the emotional conditions for successful ego-development: only the feeling of having the particular nature of one's urges fundamentally recognized and affirmed can allow one to develop the degree of basic self-confidence that renders one capable of participating, with equal rights, in political will-formation.[45]

If there are offenses in the sphere of love, it means that the individual is not ready to take part in the other patterns of law and solidarity.

Nevertheless, Honneth lately has sustained that the offenses in love relationships do not necessarily represent a moral offense able to motivate a struggle for recognition:

---

[39] Honneth 1995, 132.

[40] Honneth 1995, 132.

[41] Honneth 1995, 132.

[42] Honneth 1995, 132.

[43] Honneth 1995, 132.

[44] Honneth 1995, 132.

[45] Honneth 1995, 38.

> Every love relationship does, to be sure, involve an existential dimension of struggle, insofar as the intersubjective balance between fusion and ego-demarcation can only be maintained through the overcoming of resistance on both sides. But the goals and desires connected with this cannot be generalized beyond the circle of primary relationships, at least not in a way that would make them matters of public concern. The forms of recognition associated with rights and social esteem, by contrast, do represent a moral context for societal conflict, if only because they rely on socially generalized criteria in order to function.[46]

I disagree with this statement of Honneth. Offenses located at the pattern of love have relevance for the achievement of recognition, indeed in the other two patterns as well. Offenses to the sphere of love relate to social morality. Therefore, they motivate struggles for recognition. Furthermore, they can be generalized, as they represent offenses of esteem and respect as well.

Many years after the statement made above, in *Struggle for Recognition*, Honneth has assumed that social freedom and moral freedom may happen only if personal relationships are individually decided, without any external constraints against the individual. As an example, he mentions the arranged marriage of seventeenth century Europe. I will show in the following chapters that, to this day, arranged marriage happens in countries such as China and Morocco. Honneth states:

> For the propertied classes in Europe all the way up to the seventeenth century, it was taken for granted that the heads of the family were to arrange the marriage of their daughters or sons; in no way were emotional harmony or individual happiness taken into account, only the long-term advantages for the relatives. Hence it would be misleading and highly problematic to use the term 'intimate relationship' during this era, which, after all, implies a measure of freedom to mutually explore individual feelings.[47]

---

[46] Honneth 1995, 162.

[47] Honneth, 2014a, 142.

"In the philosophy of a 'unity of opposites' [Vereinigungsphilosophie] that can be traced back to Hölderlin, we even find the notion that it is only in love that human freedom is fully realized, for only here do individuals offer each other a chance for free self-realization. In the sober everyday reality of marriage at the time, however, this idealistic enthusiasm was hardly to be found; due to predominant gender ascriptions, women had little opportunity to articulate their needs in a free and unforced manner." Honneth, 2014a, 143.

Honneth clarifies that, nowadays, in Europe, intimate relationships turned out to be freer, but people have been experiencing a decreased capacity for self-restriction in long-term relationships, and it results in an increasing number of divorces and single households, prejudicing the pattern of love:

> Therefore, the institution of 'pure' intimacy linked to the reciprocal acceptance of certain role obligations, which had just recently been fully democratized and made available to the entire population, now seems to be in crisis once again. In any case, the rising divorce rate, the growing number of single households and the many reports of the increased susceptibility of personal relationships to conflict indicate subjects' decreased capacity for the self-restriction so crucial for long-term attachments.[48]

Honneth also discusses the parents-children relationship in adulthood nowadays. For him, the element of affection is necessary for the younger generations, who are supposed to take care of their parents. Children, nowadays, should feel love and affection for their parents, in order to contribute to their care and support. If these elements do not exist at all, then it may be possible that the children will not feel the moral obligation to take care of the elders.[49]

All these examples endorse the fact that the pattern of love has strong relevance in the formation of the individual's identity. Sequentially, I will continue analyzing the patterns of recognition, and the next section examines the dimension of law.

---

[48] Honneth 2014a, 152.

On the other hand, Honneth makes other interpretation of this social phenomenon. The increase in the number of divorces represents a higher capacity of people to decide by themselves about their lives, using affection, without being constrained to agree on long and eternal traditional family's conformations, such as marriage, when there is no more love between the couple: "The rising divorce rate could also be interpreted as a sign that attachments based purely on affection are taken much more seriously today than in the past; the fact that individuals stay single longer can be interpreted as a desire to explore subjects' own need for attachment; and the increasing conflicts found in personal relationships can be viewed as an indicator of the everyday difficulties, especially for men, of implementing the principle of equality that has already been normatively accepted." (Honneth 2014a, 153.)

[49] Honneth 2014a, 165.

In the next chapters, we will see that these Honnethian examples of recognition and freedom inside the pattern of love are not the same in societies such as China and Morocco. Although there are some movements and struggles for the emancipation of individual and social freedom, these countries are still influenced by cultural traditions, exercised especially into the pattern of love.

1.4 The Honnethian Pattern of Law

In 2014, Honneth published the most relevant work for his studies on the pattern of law. In "*Freedom's Right: the social foundations of democratic life*" (2014, referred to as "*Freedom's Right*" below), Honneth proposes a normative reconstruction, in order to comprehend the current societies, their struggles for recognition, and the achievement of justice, from a dual perspective. In 2020, the book "*Die Armut unserer Freiheit*" attached more studies on the pattern of law, specifically regarding the role of freedom in the theory of recognition.

On the one hand, subjects are addressees of rights, as they can enjoy their lives with the certainty that law assures them freedom and autonomy. On the other hand, they are also authors of rights, being respectful to other subjects in the public space, being cooperative, having responsibility for the social requirements[50].

Therefore, an egalitarian legal order would be divided through two freedom-guaranteeing spheres[51]. Firstly, a space for private autonomy must exist, retreating the person from role obligations and attachments, exploring the aims of her individual life.[52] Secondly, a space for collective autonomy, where a person deliberates in civil cooperation and experiences socialization.[53] This social space is sustained through democratic attitudes.[54] For Honneth, it is necessary to comprehend freedom not just from a individual and singular point of view, but also from a conceptual meaning in social contexts.[55] For instance, there is a difference between the freedom of political opinion, the freedom to contract in the labor market, and the freedom of spontaneous relationships within love.[56]

In this sense, Honneth acknowledges that a pattern of law holds an individual and a collective autonomy, although it relates to a private life of a person (represented mainly by the pattern of love) as well as to a social life (represented mainly by the pattern of solidarity).

The Honnethian normative reconstruction endorses a form of freedom more appropriate to recognition: the social freedom. Claims for democratic attitudes support the reaching of social freedom. The pattern of law guarantees not just

---

[50] Honneth, 2014a, 72.

[51] Honneth, 2014a, 72.

[52] Honneth, 2014a, 72.

[53] Honneth, 2014a, 72.

[54] Honneth, 2014a, 72.

[55] Honneth, 2020, 38.

[56] Honneth 2020, 38.

democracy as a political regime, but also democracy as an ideal and attitude, as a practice in an individual's private and social life[57].

A social freedom based on a more expanded comprehension of democracy results in the detachment of Honneth's theory from the studies on law which do not take into consideration the relevance of social theory and sociology for the pattern of law. "*Nothing has been more fatal to the formulation of a concept of social justice than the recent tendency to dissolve all social relations into legal relationships, in order to make it all the easier to regulate these relationships through formal rules.*"[58]

The second pattern of recognition, then, is called "*law*" (*Recht*). In law, the person is morally responsible for her acts and at the same time, she knows that the other persons are also responsible for their actions, in the same proportion. All individuals have moral accountability; they are all equally accountable for their actions and consequences. Honneth states that this mode of recognition guarantees the "self-respect" (*Selbstachtung, Selbstrespekt*) conceptualized by Dillon[59].

According to Dillon, self-respect is a complex entity, which holds different emotions. The core of self-respect is a deep appreciation of one's morally significant *worth* (Dillon 1997, 228). In his words:

> More specifically, self-respect is better understood as comprising all those aspects of cognition, valuation, affect, expectation, motivation, action, reaction, and interaction that together constitute what we might call "an appreciative mode of being toward and with oneself and the world with regard to one's worth." On this view, pride, shame, and resentment are among the elements constitutive of being a self-respecting person.[60]

Dillon also states that self-respect exists beyond private, public, and social dimensions. Self-worth relates to sociopolitical contexts of life[61]. Although Honneth connects self-respect with the pattern of law, the facts that happen in the spheres of love or solidarity are also related to self-respect and, as a consequence, the pattern of law permeates all patterns of recognition. Law makes possible

---

[57] Chap. 7 will further explore this topic.

[58] Honneth, 2014a, 66.

[59] Honneth 2007a, 136.

[60] Dillon 1997, 228.

[61] Dillon, 1997, 244.

the existence of the spheres of love and solidarity[62]. If individuals were not legally accountable for their acts, then it would be hard to reach the elements of recognition in private—the pattern of love—and public life—the pattern of solidarity.

Legal recognition enables that a person become recognized in the other patterns of recognition as well. For instance, the private and intimate relationships in the pattern of love contribute for the building of a person's self-confidence just if she is primarily addressee of rights. In the sphere of solidarity, when experiencing cooperation within social public spaces, the person also must be primarily legally recognized. The certainty of a legitimate legal protection allows that a person perform not just in the pattern of law, but also in the patterns of love and solidarity, which implies on the permeability between Honnethian law and ethics.

In Honneth's theory, the meaning of self-respect comes from its denials:

> The reason why it is so difficult, in the case of self-respect, to demonstrate the reality of the phenomenon is because, to a certain extent, it acquires a perceptible mass only in a negative form—specifically, only when subjects visibly suffer from a lack of it. The actual presence of self-respect can therefore be inferred only indirectly each time, by making empirical comparisons involving groups of people, from whose general behaviour one can draw conclusions about the forms in which the experience of disrespect is symbolically represented.[63]

It is relevant, then, to evaluate how self-respect is denied. Van den Brink holds that law's disrespect has two sides in Honnethian theory: "*First, it consists in the legal restriction of one's personal autonomy and moral responsibility. Second, and perhaps even more fundamentally, it consists in comparative inequality with other citizens who do not have their personal autonomy restricted.*"[64].

[62] "Patterns of recognition based on law extend into the inner sphere of primary relations, because individuals must be protected against the danger of physical violence that is structurally inherent in the precarious balance of every emotional bond. Today, the intersubjective conditions that enable personal integrity include not only the experience of love but also legal protection against the injuries that can be causally connected with love. Modern legal relations have a different influence, however, on conditions of solidarity. Here, they establish normative limitations to which the formation of community-generating value-horizons must generally be subject. The question, therefore, as to whether solidarity is to be included as a further element among the conditions for post-traditional ethical life cannot be settled without some reference to legal principles". (Honneth 1995, 177)

[63] Honneth 1995, 120.

[64] Van den Brink, 2011, 167.

Honneth clarifies that self-respect is denied in cases of deceit, fraud, and legal discrimination against whole groups of people[65]. For him, varieties of discrimination or disrespect arise when the underlying principles of recognition are interpreted one-sidedly, in favour of a certain social group.[66]

Although he does not mention which are the offenses in the pattern of law from an isolated individual perspective (for instance, a case of domestic violence against a woman), I understand that self-respect may be offended by violations not just against whole groups of people, but also against isolated individuals. Self-respect, then, may germinate from situations of disrespect and violations to the pattern of law, being recovered through struggles for recognition.

Honneth clarifies that, over time, the pattern of law is getting wider, as the individuals, in each community, expand their capacities as human beings. Nowadays, legal recognition encompasses a social standard living that guarantees a minimum of cultural education[67] and economic security[68].

---

65 "We have initially construed the term 'rights', only roughly, as referring to those individual claims that a person can legitimately expect to have socially met because he or she participates, with equal rights, in the institutional order as a full-fledged member of a community. Should that person now be systematically denied certain rights of this kind, this would imply that he or she is not being accorded the same degree of moral responsibility as other members of society. What is specific to such a form of disrespect, as exemplified by the denial of rights or by ostracism, thus lies not just in the forcible restriction of personal autonomy but also in the combination with the feeling of not enjoying the status of a full-fledged partner to interaction, equally endowed with moral rights." (Honneth 1995, 133)

66 Honneth 2022b, 17.

67 In Chap. 5 we will introduce the Honnethian interpretation of an "emancipated family member" as someone with the right to discuss about her own culture, being also open to other cultural perspectives. Coming from this context, we interpret that "cultural education", for Honneth, would be the building of an individual's capacity to recognize the meaning of her own culture and, also, to valorize the importance of considering differences inside her culture and in regard to different cultures. In other words, it signifies respect of intragroup differences and choices, as well as the cultural differences of those outside the group. Individuals culturally educated comprehend that their identity has influences from their culture, but, at the same time, they have autonomy for in making choices within a cultural context. A cultural education, then, should relate to interculturalism.

68 Honneth 1995, 117. See also: "In being legally recognized, one is now respected with regard not only to the abstract capacity to orient oneself vis-à-vis moral norms, but also to the concrete human feature that one deserves the social standard of living necessary for this." (Honneth 1995, 117)

For Honneth: "*It became clear from this that, on its own, legal recognition holds a moral potential, one which can be developed via social struggles in the direction of an increase on both generality and context-sensitivity.*"[69]

Honneth endorses the necessity of a change coming from the Kantian tradition of an individual's autonomy to a new conception of autonomy, which is related to an individual's moral sensitivity to contexts. In the Kantian tradition, the autonomous individual should obey the categorical imperative and, in this way, be guided by practical, rational principles. Instead of just considering rational principles, the autonomous subject should also be morally sensitive to contexts[70].

Following this, Honneth, in *Struggle for recognition,* states that the pattern of law should consider the particularity of each community, as legal recognition presupposes a moral knowledge of legal obligations, as well as an empirical interpretation of the situation.[71] The next sections will further clarify the role of law for recognition, and how the Honnethian pattern of law represents a change in the tradition of Critical Theory.

---

[69] Honneth 1995, 176. See also: "Unlike modern legal recognition, social esteem is directed, as we have seen, at the particular qualities that characterize people in their personal difference. Thus, whereas modern law represents a medium of recognition that expresses the universal features of human subjects, this form of recognition demands a social medium that must be able to express the characteristic differences among human subjects in a universal and, more specifically, intersubjectively obligatory way. [...] The cultural self-understanding of a society provides the criteria that orient the social esteem of persons, because their abilities and achievements are judged intersubjectively according to the degree to which they can help to realize culturally defined values. [...] This form of mutual recognition is thus also tied to the presupposition of a context of social life, whose members, through their orientation towards shared conceptions of their goals, form a community of value." (Honneth 1995, 122).

[70] See Honneth: "Kant therefore assumes, just like Hegel, a teleology concerning directed progress; but he does not deliver it over to the anonymous process of an unfolding of spirit. Instead, he takes this teleology as a construction that the subjects acting in the sense of enlightenment must achieve, in order to gain a clear consciousness of the historical place of their own projects. The combination of these two system-bursting elements leads therefore to the consequence that the thought of a learning process spanning generations must be understood as a construction that necessarily shapes the historical self-understanding of the supporters of the Enlightenment: all those who actively side with the moral achievements of the Enlightenment are thus forced to see the history preceding them as a conflict-ridden learning process, which, as heirs of this process, they have to continue in their own time. Such a hermeneutic reduction of the idea of progress, in all probability, represents the only possibility for making Kant's philosophy of history fruitful again for the present." (Honneth 2007c, 16)

[71] Honneth, 1995, 113.

1.4.1 The Role of Law in Recognition

The pattern of law guarantees that a person is equally respected by the members of her community in the public space, as well as respected in her intimate relationships. As a result, she will be able to enjoy recognition in private and public life, enjoying social, moral, and legal freedom.

Since Hegel and Mead, the pattern of law has had a special role in the process of struggles for recognition. The dynamics of struggle expand the rights an individual already holds:

> Like Hegel, Mead considers the motor of these directed changes to be a struggle in which subjects continually strive to expand the range of their intersubjectively guaranteed rights and, in so doing, to raise the level of their personal autonomy. For both thinkers, then, the historical liberation of individuality occurs in the form of a long-term struggle for recognition.[72]

Struggles for recognition in the pattern of law do not just contribute to an expansion of rights, but also to their transformation according to new individual and social claims. For instance, Honneth mentions that private relations of recognition expand as soon as they need to be protected against offenses such as physical violence. "*Today, the intersubjective conditions that enable personal integrity include not only the experience of love but also legal protection against the injuries that can be causally connected with love.*"[73]

I understand that the pattern of law holds not just a positive system of rights, but actually the necessary normativity that permeates recognition. The next section will discuss how legal and moral norms exist within recognition and how Honneth's theory interprets it.

1.4.2 Critiques of the Honnethian Pattern of Law

a) Law and the ethics of recognition

In 2013, Honneth sustained that his theory is not an ethics of recognition. He defends that it is not a moral obligation for human beings to recognize each other. It would culminate in an empty moralism[74]. Honneth advocates for a social

[72] Honneth 1995, 84.

[73] Honneth 1995, 177.

[74] Honneth 2013, 213.

theory with a certain moral-practical intention. He clarifies that one needs to analyze the existing accepted norms and assess why people do not engage and do not comply with such norms.[75] For him, recognition is based on principles, and these principles are institutionalized in specific spheres.[76]

Despite these statements during this interview in 2013, I understand that Honneth has interpreted recognition as ethics at different moments in his work, for instance when he proposes universal principles, conditions, and elements inside each pattern of recognition. Furthermore, the author has argued more than once that moral feelings and behaviors represent recognition, so that recognition turns out to be not just a moral obligation but also a sort of human virtue to be honored.

In *Struggle for recognition*, Honneth approaches morality when he debates the traditions of Kant and Hegel. Honneth emphasises that the original Hegelian concept of ethical life and its implications in the conception of a good life are useful for the theory of recognition.

Furthermore, Honneth also adopts the Kantian notion of moral autonomy[77], attaching to it the conditions for human beings' self-realization. For Honneth, morality is one of the protective measures to enable a good life. The concept of good, nevertheless, should not be attached to notions of substantive values of concrete tradition-based communities. Rather, it should come from the plurality of all particular forms of life[78], which are guided by the universality of the three patterns of recognition[79].

If one understands that recognition is not ethical, then the whole model of recognition would be incoherent. Deranty sustains that "*Recognition has become a moral concept in an institutional sense; it is an "ethical" concept, in the Hegelian acceptation of the term.*"[80]

[75] Honneth 2013, 213.

[76] Honneth 2013, 213.

[77] Honneth 1995, 172.

[78] Honneth 1995, 172.

[79] "The only way in which individuals are constituted as persons is by learning to refer to themselves, from the perspective of an approving or encouraging other, as beings with certain positive traits and abilities. The scope of such traits—and hence the extent of one's positive relation-to-self—increases with each new form of recognition that individuals are able to apply to themselves as subjects. In this way, the prospect of basic self-confidence is inherent in the experience of love; the prospect of self-respect, in the experience of legal recognition; and finally the prospect of self-esteem, in the experience of solidarity." (Honneth 1995, 173)

[80] Deranty 2016, 45.

b) The ethical principles of recognition

Honneth endorses Hegelian ethical life, in a way that the theory of recognition bases itself on ethical principles, which are theoretical, permanent, universal, and normative.[81] The human activity, then, does not sustains itself through any rules whatsoever, but rather through normative principles that allow the participants to mutually comprehend each others as authors and addressees.[82]

For Honneth, social justice[83] is related to the principles of love/need, law/equality, and merit/achievement[84]. Genel argues that:

> There are thus three normative principles that express something about the moral demands that modern individuals can legitimately raise: the principle of love, of juridical equality, and of performance. Those established principles of modern societies constitute standards for "immanent" social criticism. From this perspective, justice is the outcome of the transformation of the orders of recognition: the result of the back-and-forth movements and tensions between institutionalized principles and unsatisfied claims for recognition expressed by individuals.[85]

The principle of love states that the stereotypes practiced by the current society in the context of love should be progressively eliminated, promoting different possibilities of relationships and behaviors in regards to love[86]. When the person is experiencing love, she should be open to different contexts and conformations of love.

---

[81] Honneth 2014b, 819.

[82] Honneth 2014b, 819.

[83] "Our conception of justice is thereby implicitly extended by the addition of a link to the future, which, in the political praxis at least, had never been used before in this way." (Honneth, 2010b, 15)

[84] Honneth 2004b, 355. In the article "*Recognition and Justice: Outline of a Plural Theory of Justice*", Honneth uses the denominations: *principle of merit*, *principle of doing justice to achievements*, and *principle of achievemen*t as synonyms.

Furthermore, *Principle of law* is used as a synonym of *principle of equality*. (Honneth, 2004b, p. 352). Markle denominates the Honnethian principle of achievement as *principle of accomplishment* (P.386), whereas Genel denominates it as *principle of performance*. The Honnethian *principle of law* is denominated by Genel as *principle of juridical equality* (Genel 2016, .22).

[85] Genel 2016, 22.

[86] "Thus a moral progression in the sphere of love might mean gradually eliminating those role clichés, stereotypes and cultural attributions that structurally stand in the way of the possibility of mutual adaptation to the needs of others". (Honneth 2004b, 262)

The principle of law/equality is related to the pattern of law, and it states that each person has the same obligations and rights. When a person experiences the pattern of law, she is aware of the equality shared with the other members of her community, especially concerning their legal claims and duties.

The principle of merit relates to cooperative relationships, in which the person acquires merit by contributing to her society[87]. Every person is responsible for cooperating with her society, thus respecting the principle of merit.

They are the general principles of recognition. To comprehend such ethical principles in the moral practices of recognition, Honneth clarifies that they should be normatively interpreted by considering the particular aspects of *need*, the *situation of life*, and *contribution* respectively:

> Within each sphere it is always possible to launch a moral dialectic between the universal and the particular by calling upon the general principle of recognition (love, law, achievement) to appeal to a particular aspect (need, situation in life, contribution) that had not yet been adequately considered in the previously practiced conditions of application.[88]

For Honneth, each principle is distinguished by the particular needs of the interaction partner, in relations of reciprocal affection (needs); by the accountability of the individual in the legal contexts of a society (situation in life); and by the specific qualifications and competences of discrete social members, in what John Rawls called 'social cooperation' (contribution).[89] To this extent, Honneth holds that his theory of recognition sees injustices in the form of three shapes of disrespect: bearing on natural needs in intimate and familial relations, on accountability in relations between legal subjects, and on individual capacities in cooperative working relationships.[90]

---

[87] "In order to be actually able to make use of their individual autonomy, single subjects have just as much right, according to the kind of social relationship, to be recognized in their needs, in their legal equality, or finally in their contributions to society. As can be recognized from such a formulation, the content of what we call 'just' is here to be measured according to the respective kind of social relationship that subjects maintain with one another. If the concern is with a relationship shaped by an appeal to love, then the principle of need has priority, whereas in legally shaped relationships the principle of equality takes priority, and in cooperative relationships the principle of merit. [...] Because we live in a social order in which individuals owe the possibility of an intact identity to affective care, legal equality and social esteem, it seems to me appropriate in the name of individual autonomy to make the three corresponding principles of recognition the normative core of a conception of social justice". (Honneth 2004b, 358)

[88] Honneth 2004b, 261.

[89] Honneth 2022b, 15.

[90] Honneth 2022b, 15.

Petherbridge argues that Honneth creates a two-level order of recognition. First of all, recognition relates to an elementary form at a socio-ontological level. Secondly, it relates to three normatively derived forms of recognition, namely love, law, and achievement. For him, the Honnethian existential mode of recognition is the foundation for all the other substantial forms of recognition.[91]

To adapt such ethical principles to an individual's life and to the differences between cultural contexts, Honneth calls for a criterion of progress. "*To pick out from the multitude of such particularizations typically appealed to in social struggles for recognition those which are morally justified now requires, additionally, the application of a criterion of progress, no matter how explicitly formulated.*"[92]

When Honneth states that the general principles of recognition must be applied for each situation, concerning the need, the life's condition, and the achievements of each person, he is trying to relate an ethical life with recognition as a moral act[93]. Because of that, struggles are something in construction, which will be continually developed by people, in each context, e.g., in each different culture.

Furthermore, he holds that to observe social justice, one must take into consideration the substantiality of ethical institutions in society, which grant the participation of individuals in practices of recognition—institutions such as legal security, state authority, civil support[94]. I understand the importance of comprehending state institutions—including law—as part of the structure, which permits the achievement of recognition. Nevertheless, it is necessary to reiterate that some societies have institutions, which do not collaborate for recognition but damage the achievement of social justice.

Honneth argues that to build a conception of justice, one must adopt the premises of his "normative reconstruction". Firstly, one must assume that individuals from a community share universal values and ideals. Secondly, it is necessary to understand that these social values directly influence the conception

---

[91] Petherbridge 2011, 27.

[92] Honneth 2004b, 361.

[93] "Within each sphere it is always possible to launch a moral dialectic between the universal and the particular by calling upon the general principle of recognition (love, law, achievement) to appeal to a particular aspect (need, situation in life, contribution) that had not yet been adequately considered in the previously practised conditions of application." (Honneth 2004b, 361).

[94] "What we now call 'just' can no longer merely be measured by whether and to what extent all members of society enjoy negative or reflexive freedoms, rather justice must entail granting all members of society the opportunity to participate in institutions of recognition. This means that certain normatively substantive and thus 'ethical' institutions requiring legal security, state authority and civil support shift to the centre of our idea of social justice." (Honneth 2014a, 61).

of justice in a way that justice embraces shared goods. Thirdly, one must then identify the institutions and practices that allow the realization of those social values. Fourthly, normative reconstruction identifies that institutions, traditions, and social values are not static; they represent communal ethics, which is changeable over time and depending on the society itself[95]. It demonstrates Honneth's historicist approach[96]. One must not just identify the institutions that endorse shared goods, but also the ones that do not contribute to their increase.[97]

Stephan Kirste states that *"[...] there is no value without form in law, but also that form is valuable in law. The form is an expression of values. Gustav Radbruch called justice the value of law"* (Kirste 2019, 53). Accordingly, the normative reconstruction proposed by Honneth is a methodology to promote recognition

[95] "The attempt to develop a conception of justice on the basis of social analysis must, as a first premise, assume that the given form of social reproduction in society is determined by shared universal values and ideals. The aims of both social production and cultural integration are ultimately regulated by norms that are ethical in the sense that they embody conceptions of shared goods. The second premise claims, as a first approximation, that the concept of justice cannot be understood in isolation from these overarching social values; social practices and institutions are 'just' to the extent that they are capable of realizing generally accepted values. Only with the third premise do we have a more detailed definition of what it means to develop a theory of justice on the basis of an analysis of society: Out of the diversity of social reality, we select—or to put it in methodological terms, we normatively reconstruct—those institutions and practices that are truly capable of securing and realizing general values. Finally, the fourth premise should guarantee that in applying this methodological procedure we do not merely affirm existing instances of ethical life. If we strictly follow the procedure of normative reconstruction, we will have to develop the latter to a point that clearly demonstrates the extent to which ethical institutions and practices do not represent the general values they embody in a sufficiently comprehensive or perfect fashion." (Honneth 2014a, 10).

[96] "Historicism is the methodological position which holds that key moral and political principles, or, as Honneth says, the normative fabric of a given epoch, change substantially over time, so that any relationship drawn between the past and the present, in either direction, is unwarranted. Critical analyses of the present do not apply to the past". (Deranty 2016, 74)

[97] "Ins Zentrum der Idee sozialer Gerechtigkeit wandert damit die Vorstellung, dass jene normativ gehaltvollen und daher von Hegel»sittlich« genannten Institutionen der rechtlichen Sicherstellung, der staatlichen Obhut und der zivilgesellschaftlichen Unterstützung bedürfen, um den ihnen zugrundeliegenden Anspruch auf soziale Freiheit auch tatsächlich realisieren zu können—nur im arbeitsteiligen Zusammenspiel von Recht, Politik und solidarischer Öffentlichkeit können die institutionellen Gebilde am Leben erhalten werden, denen die Gesellschaftsmitglieder die verschiedenen Facetten ihrer ineinandergreifenden Freiheiten und wir damit im Ganzen eine Kultur der Freiheit verdanken". (Honneth 2020, 58).

through the pattern of law. Law allows universal social values to reach the appropriate form through the appropriate institutions, eventually culminating in the achievement of recognition.

Honneth is claiming that there is no way to define justice and social values from a definitive perspective. Following his Hegelian influences, he understands that justice changes depending on the society and time. Morality is understood as a totality of norms accepted in a relevant way, characterized by a historical revisability and openness.[98] A group appropriates a socially practised norm, just if the persons jointly conceive this norm as desirable for their self-realization.[99] Individual inclinations change over time, so that this norm must be historically open..[100] What is possible for a theory of justice is to analyze it for a particular society for a specified period. Nevertheless, the principles of recognition should always be respected.

c) International law and the ethics of recognition: liberal or communitarian?

Coming from these discussions on the pattern of law and how normativity permeates all the patterns of recognition, I will now situate Honneth within the political-philosophical categories of either liberalism or communitarianism.

Liberalism focuses on the individual. The state should act to just the minimum extent necessary to promote individual freedom through her autonomous decisions. Different theories approach liberalism from various perspectives, but all of them bases on the freedom of the individual as a member of society[101].

On the other hand, communitarians have a social interpretation of an individual's identity, thus understanding that the formation of an individual's goals and behaviors is always influenced by her culture and shared values. Winfried Brugger describes different variations of communitarian theories, but all of them come for the fundamental questions: what do all individuals and groups have in common? What should unite them?[102]

---

[98] Honneth 2014b, 822.

[99] Honneth 2014b, 822.

[100] Honneth 2014b, 822. See also: "My goal is to argue for the continuing relevance of Hegel's theory of ethical life by showing that it supplies us with a normative vocabulary that we can use to assess the respective value of the various freedoms we practice". (Honneth 2016, 167)

[101] "Der Liberalismus will also die Freiheit des Einzelnen oder, um sich vom Libertarismus abzugrenzen, die Freiheit des Einzelnen als Mitglied der Gesellschaft in den Fokus seiner Betrachtungen stellen […]" (Rieß 2012, 7).

[102] Brugger 433,2003.

Generally, communitarians understand that human beings have 'constitutive' ends, and every individual, in the end, is guided by these shared goals[103]. They accuse liberals of proposing an atomistic view of human relationships.

Max Pensky holds that Axel Honneth is not a communitarian, because he does not limit individuals' morality. On the contrary, in his theory, morality is adaptable from society to society.[104] Coming from this, I will inquire if Honneth could then be seen as a liberal.

Will Kymlicka is one of the leading liberal authors of the present day, and he believes that individual rights should have more relevance than a shared value of common good. According to him, liberalism advocates for the importance of being free to revise one's ends.

Kymlicka believes that individual rights sustain social relationships, and he gives an example: "*Indeed, the most basic liberal right—freedom of conscience—is primarily valuable for the protection it gives to intrinsically social (and non-instrumental) activities*".[105]

Kymlicka accuses post-war liberals of misunderstanding the meaning of citizenship, which should not be viewed as something uniform and undifferentiated[106]. It is crucial to understand the culture from plural and diverse perspectives.

Honneth assumes that each culture or generation has different moral attitudes and practices of recognition, which are temporal and cultural. More than that, Honneth clarifies that solidarity—one pattern of recognition—represents the appreciation of an individual and her culture, assuming that culture varies according to the context. Honneth states many times that recognition and justice are attached to the particularity of communities, thus assuming the historicism within recognition. For instance:

---

[103] Kymlicka 1995, 91.

[104] "For Honneth, what is important is the phenomenon, from the rise of feminism, gay and lesbian rights, environmentalism and even contemporary anti-globalisation movements, of the expansion and pluralisation of numerous and not-always compatible secondary interpretations. This surely raises the question of what our cultural 'value horizon' must be like, to be capacious enough to accommodate them all, without simply admitting, like Rawls, that it must consist simply of an overlapping consensus regarding the right and the wrong ways of disagreeing how to live, or like Habermas, that it can consist of nothing more than the bonding effects of successful communicative rationality to remain true to itself." (Pensky 2011, 148).

[105] Kymlicka 1995, 26.

[106] Kymlicka 1995, 173.

> To avoid the danger of merely applying immanently derived principles of justice to given reality, we must not assume that we have already sufficiently analysed social reality itself; instead we must throw into relief the essential features and particularities of that society by demonstrating the contribution that each respective social sphere makes to securing and realizing the values that have already been institutionalized in society.[107]

Additionally, when discussing the institute of disrespect, Honneth comprehends that the feeling of being hurt or ashamed has a moral-political background, because it depends on the cultural-political context where the victim is inserted. As a consequence, only where the articulation of a social movement is possible, can disrespect trigger political resistance and struggles.[108]

On the other hand, if Honneth is categorized as a classical liberal, his theory would tolerate cultural disparities, accepting cultural practices not necessarily accorded to the conditions, elements, and principles of recognition. Bonni Honig makes a critique against the classical liberal political philosophers.[109] The author argues that some liberals attribute the responsibility to injustices to a specific culture, forgetting that the problem resides in the human beings themselves.[110] For this author, liberal discussions should focus more on the individual himself, on the human moral values and practices. For instance, in United States and China, "*culture*" has been used as an excuse for human rights' violations and cruelty. "*My culture made me do it*" may be used to justify the violation of human rights.[111]

---

107 Honneth 2014a, 7.

108 Honneth 1995, 138.

109 Honig 1999, 28.

110 Honig 1999, 28.

111 Honig 1999, 28. See also:

"And, contra Okin, culture is something rather more complicated than patriarchal permission for powerful men to subordinate vulnerable women. There are brutal men (and women) everywhere. Is it their Jewish, Christian, or Muslim identity that makes them brutal or is it their brutality?" (Honig 1999, 28).

Additionally:

"'Culture' is a way of life, a rich and timeworn grammar of human activity, a set of diverse and often conflicting narratives whereby communal (mis)understandings, roles, and responsibilities are negotiated. As such, 'culture' is a living, breathing system for the distribution and enactment of agency, power, and privilege among its members and beyond. Rarely are those privileges distributed along a single axis of difference such that, for example, all men are more powerful than all women. Race, class, locality, lineage all accord measures of privilege or stigma to their bearers." (Honig 1999, 31)

Honneth does not make any exception; he does not relativize the conditions for the formation of human identity within the patterns of recognition[112]. It is problematic to categorize Honneth as a classical liberal, because the theory of recognition is not unlimitedly flexible, relative, and adaptable to different contexts.

Petherbridge argues that Honneth, then, is between liberalism and communitarianism. For him, Honneth attempts to adopt a middle path between communitarian and Kantian models.[113] In contrast to communitarian approaches, Honneth accounts for structures of identity-formation.[114] Nevertheless, Honneth questions Kantian-based theories, considering them too weak to account for the motivational source for morality and to establish a connection to a pre-theoretical emancipatory interest.[115]

I understand that Honneth is closer to a liberal view of society, based on self-realization and autonomy, but limited by ethical principles, which are universal and that follow normative reconstruction.

In spite of his vast discussions on normative reconstruction, Honneth unfortunately does not interpret the pattern of law from either a multiculturalist or interculturalist approach. Brincat argues that although Honneth states that international relations must be moralized, he does not sufficiently link his theory with international affairs.[116]

Van den Brink agrees on that:

> For instance, will Honneth's ideas concerning the centrality of autonomy, pluralism and egalitarianism be reinforced by aboriginal peoples and non-Western immigrants in modern societies who struggle for the recognition of their cultural identity as opposed to their identity as workers and equal citizens? Their second nature as social beings seems to be split between Western and non-Western life-worlds.[117]

[112] Rancière criticizes the struggles for recognition, as would not be possible to relativize recognition from intercultural perspectives:

"In Muslim countries in particular, the argument was as follows: they are Muslims, and in Islam, there is no distinction between civil law and the religious law so we cannot impose a form of personality that contradicts the way they construct their individuality and their social relations. As we know, this colonial argument has often been taken up in recent times as a valid multicultural argument. This shows all the ambiguity of recognition". (Rancière 2016, 91)

[113] Petherbridge 2011, 15.

[114] Petherbridge 2011, 15.

[115] Petherbridge 2011, 15.

[116] Brincat 2013, 227.

[117] Van Den Brink 2011, 162.

I also understand that Honneth, as well as other authors of Critical Theory, does not sufficiently apply his theory regarding international relations, meaning political macro discussions and conflicts between countries as legal parts in a global context. More than that, Honneth does not directly discuss challenges of recognition on cultures that are not European and not democratic. Intragroup cultural conflicts (inside the same social group—for instance, between different generations) as well as extragroup cultural conflicts (identity's differences between different communities) relate to recognition and should be included in the discussions.

d) Ethics of recognition: normativity and discourse

Coming from these discussions on the pattern of law, it is relevant to analyze it from the perspective of intersubjectivity, commonly represented by the theory of communication of Jürgen Habermas.

Honneth states in the conclusion of the book "*Pathologies of Reason: On the legacy of Critical Theory*" (2007)[118] that the classical Critical Theory, despite some problems, is the only one capable of analyzing the current society. To reinterpret Critical Theory nowadays, one should consider the developments realized since its foundation, mainly the work of Habermas and the reflections of social psychology. This dialogue between Honneth and Habermas has brought to light some critiques of Honneth's interpretation of the pattern of law. Nevertheless, for Honneth, the work of Habermas should be reviewed in a variety of forms, for instance throught including a proper practical critique of the opposition between groups or classes.[119]

Axel Honneth does not focus on the public sphere of deliberative communication, but instead on the struggle for recognition that, in his view, results from the denial of recognition, which is even more fundamental than injustice. Nevertheless, Honneth does not sufficiently explain the impacts on identity formation caused by an absence of democratic and deliberative public spaces in some societies, especially if one considers the pattern of law.

Intersubjectivity, according to Honneth, results in a constitution of individuals' selves, which build their own identity in contact with each other. Now, this process does not begin with the struggle for recognition, to which Honneth devotes

[118] Honneth, A. 2007b. Pathologies of Reason: On the Legacy of Critical Theory. Translated by James Ingram. New York: Columbia University Press.

[119] Honneth 2020, 301.

his first major monography, but instead, it starts from the birth of the human being, even when she is not yet able to communicate.

In later stages of the formation of the identity, two further spheres of recognition emerge: the sphere of solidarity and the sphere of rights, which are relationships established among subjects that make possible the formation of an identity endowed with self-esteem and self-respect.

In comparison to Habermas, Honneth builds his concept of intersubjectivity differently. For Honneth, it is not the communicative action, but the struggle for recognition that is decisive, for preserving the identity formation of human beings, thus ensuring the freedom of the person.

In *Freedom's Right*, Honneth deepens the discussion on freedom and its relationship with the autonomy of the subject guaranteed by the recognition resulting from struggles for recognition. Honneth asserts that freedom should be interpreted as the individual's striving for autonomy, whereby justice will be recognized in modern society[120].

Honneth criticizes and tries to improve the theory of Habermas by taking as a first step the analysis of the offenses to the spheres of recognition, namely the feelings of disrespect[121]. Honneth holds that all communicative action should have as a presupposition the achievement of social recognition. In other words, during the communicative action, the subject should enjoy the feeling of being recognized as a moral person. The opposite of recognition is moral injustice, which Honneth calls "feelings of social disrespect."[122]

The communication paradigm should be seen not in terms of a theory of language but of a theory of recognition[123]. For Honneth, Habermas is the best scholar, when one thinks of the functioning of society in the face of the structures

120 Honneth 2011, 34.

121 Honneth 2007a, 72.

122 Honneth 2007a, 71.

123 "But Habermas is mistaken when he too hastily identifies the fundamental structure of intersubjectivity with speech. It is, ontogenetically speaking, beyond all doubt that the acquisition of the ability to identify one's objectual-instrumental body as properly one's own clearly precedes the 'practical acquisition of an understanding of the system of personal pronous'. Similarly, it cannot be maintained that the demarcation from each other of communicative and propositional content of utterance is prerequisite for the human being's consciousness of his bodiliness under the twofold aspect of his organismal bodiliness and his objectual-instrumental bodiliness." (Honneth 1988, 85)

See also:

"Honneth considers communication to be irreducible to linguistic exchanges because it has corporeal and broad material dimensions, which necessitate an analysis of the nondiscoursive, social signs of contempt and of social invisibility". (Genel 2016, 15)

of power globally damaged by capitalism. Nevertheless, the discourse-theoretical approach is not the ideal for the theory of recognition. In 2021, Honneth has reasserted that other forms of access to phenomenological consciousness exist, which do not require that language itself be the sole object of analysis. For example, he believes that it is possible to give a relatively accurate description of certain emotional reactions, without necessarily focusing the analysis of their linguistic representation.[124]

According to Habermas, on the other hand, intersubjectivity is a communicative interaction between subjects, in their *Lebenswelt*, which follows an argumentative procedure to reach the "*understanding*". "In other words, the communicative act allows subjects to interact with each other, seeking consensus on claims of universal validity"[125].

It becomes possible when these human beings act in a participatory manner, using the argumentative procedure and contributing and looking forward to mutual understanding.[126] "*According to Jürgen Habermas, private and political autonomy are in a necessary connection and are of equal origin. Accordingly, the granting of rights should be an expression of the political autonomy of citizens*" (Kirste 2019, 46).

The first problem in Habermas' theory is that he argues that communicative practices presuppose democratic conformations. Secondly, although Habermas admits that there is a variety of *Lebenswelt*—which influences the public sphere and, therefore, the validity claims of each community naturally differ from those of the others -, he does not satisfactorily explore how subjects develop different demands, goals, values, and norms of individual and social recognition.

The *Lebenswelt* represents the immediate experiences of any human being in his daily life. We live everyday experiences of communication and interaction with other subjects to reach an understanding. Culture, society, and our personalities coexist in our *Lebenswelt*.

---

[124] Honneth; Bankovsky 2021c, 12.

[125] "The perspectival character of perception and interpretation, which is linked with the communicative roles of the first, second, and third person, is decisive for the structure of an action situation. The members of a collective count themselves as belonging to the lifeworld in the first-person plural, in a way similar to that in which the individual speaker attributes to himself the subjective world to which he has privileged access in the first-person singular. Communality rests, to be sure, on consensual knowledge, on a cultural stock of knowledge that members share." (Habermas 1992b, 131).

[126] "Coming to an understanding [Verständigung] means that participants in communication reach an agreement [Einigung] concerning the validity of an utterance; agreement [Einverständnis] is the intersubjective recognition of the validity claim the speaker raises for it." (Habermas 1992b, 120).

Lebenswelt contrasts with the *Systemwelt*. The *Lebenswelt* is surrounded by *Systemwelt*, which consists of institutions guided by strategic action and by individual interests. Politics and economy belong to these institutions. There is a colonization of the *Lebenswelt* by the *Systemwelt*, since interests determined by artificial systems, which may result in social pathologies, influence subjects' actions[127].

In *The Theory of Communicative Action*, Habermas deals with the colonization of *Lebenswelt* and the emergence of social pathologies. In this book, the law is within the *Systemwelt*, as a means of colonization of *Lebenswelt*, guided by strategic action. Approximately one decade later, in *Between Facts and Norms: Contributions to a Discourse Theory of Law and Democracy*, Habermas develops another view about law and the relationship between *Lebenswelt* and *Systemwelt*. He understands that it is possible to combine both worlds through the integrating role of speech and language, and institutions such as law.

Habermas goes on to consider that law makes possible the transfer of mutual validity claims to the public space[128]. The subjects, authors of the validity claims, need public institutions that validate their requirements because otherwise, they could not realize them concretely. There are necessary efficient state institutions of the *Systemwelt* that promote discussion between subjects. One of them is the law, which enhances the deliberative quality of the decision-making process.

Law has an essential role in the construction of intersubjectivity. For Habermas, it is a tool, which enables the validity claims—developed in the social environment by legal rules and decisions—to achieve the deliberative public space. Nevertheless, the interpretation of intersubjectivity and its relationship with the pattern of law makes better sense within the theory of recognition of Honneth, as it comprehends democracy wider than just a political regime, and it also includes in the processes of recognition different kinds of nuances which do not necessarily touch communication in the sense discussed by Habermas.

For Honneth, if one takes Habermas' theory of freedom from a deconstructive ethic point of view, then mutually recognized norms will only succeed in expressing the freedom of participating subjects if these norms allow subjects to present

---

127 "The key issue in Habermas' 'colonization thesis' is that everyday realms of action are increasingly organized, not on the basis of the norms we have mutually agreed ('principles of social integration') but on the basis of the money and power that already drive our political and economic system ('principles of system integration') (Habermas, 1987). His concern is that the 'system' in this respect, is growing in advanced capitalist societies through the extension of state administration and legal bureaucracy into everyday life". (Edwards 2004, 116)

128 Habermas 1996, 29.

themselves in intersubjective structures of public life without shame.[129] In this context, it is not enough to be able to participate through egalitarian rights, but also through affective relations of love and friendship, which are unilateral and related to unconditional care.[130] In other words, Honneth places care within the pattern of solidarity, essential for the reaching of recognition.

1.5 The Honnethian Pattern of Solidarity

The pattern of recognition called "solidarity" (*Solidarität*) is formed when the subject realizes that his capabilities have worth to his community. This section will study the Honnethian comprehension of solidarity, also considering the influences, which Honneth assumes from Hegel, Durkheim, Dewey, Heidegger, Tugendhat, and Lukàcs. First of all, Honneth states that Hegel has considered solidarity as a synthesis of love and law:

> At the point where Mead brought in the model of the functional division of labour for this form of recognition, we found in Hegel's early work the outline of an idea of relationships based on solidarity. 'Solidarity' is, however, only one possible title of the intersubjective relationship that Hegel aimed to designate with the concept of 'reciprocal intuition' [*'wechselseitige Anschauung'*]. For Hegel, it represents a synthesis of both preceding types of recognition, since it shares with 'law' [*Recht*] the cognitive point of view associated with universally equal treatment, but shares with 'love' the aspect of emotional attachment and care.[131]

For Hegel, then, solidarity has two essential elements: to treat people equally and to practice emotional attachment and care.

In Honnethian theory, the sphere of solidarity also represents a union between the other two spheres: love and law. In the dimension of solidarity, relationships and individuals themselves are considered valuable.

Comparing Hegel's and Mead's ideas of solidarity, Honneth argues that in Hegel it relates to ethical life, and in Mead it relates to labor. The relevance of this comparison rests on the fact that, although Hegel recognizes the importance of solidarity as a synthesis of law and love, he does not explain how the individuals build reciprocal feelings of respect based on solidarity. For Honneth, then, when

---

[129] Honneth; Bankovsky 2021c, 16.

[130] Honneth; Bankovsky 2021c, 16.

[131] Honneth 1995, 91.

discussing practices of solidarity, it is fundamental to discuss shared goals and values of a community of individuals.[132]

In the dimension of solidarity, there is a sharing of social ethics, a sharing of values, which makes the individual feel self-esteemed. More than self-esteem, solidarity also promotes social esteem.

There is a public, social, and collective meaning of solidarity, and Honneth relates it to the role of the individual in his community. He bases this notion on Hegelian ethics, which interprets solidarity from the perspective of the ethical (*sittliche*) state. Huttunen clearly explains the meaning of *Sittlichkeit* in Hegel. The instances of family and civil society, for Hegel, must be accompanied by the ethical state:

> Hegel calls for a value community called the sittliche (ethical) state which is ruled by rational feeling. This rational feeling surpasses the contradiction between loving one's family and the egoistic reason of civil society. For Hegel, the sittliche (sitte means custom or habit) state is a sphere of reciprocal good behavior and caring for each other. In the sittliche state, people feel solidarity and compassion toward the "abstract other", toward another citizen of the state. In the level of the state, familial love is extended towards all citizens and is cultivated into rational feeling which ties up the individuals into a reciprocal ethical community. Citizens of the sittliche state are in a certain sense sisters and brothers to each other. The state is a kind of extended family.[133]

According to Hegel, then, solidarity is practiced in the ethical state, in a way that the familial love experienced in the family is transformed into a rational feeling at the community level, making people see each other as worthy of ethical behavior and caring.

---

[132] Honneth 1995, 91. See also:

"As is clear from the foregoing, our formal conception of posttraditional ethical life would be incomplete if it were unable to indicate the position occupied by substantive values. For the attempt to start out from the intersubjective conditions for personal integrity in order to reach the normative universals of a successful life must, in the end, also include the pattern of recognition associated with social solidarity, which can only grow out of collectively shared goals. The fact that these, for their part, are subject to the normative restrictions set by the legally sanctioned autonomy of all subjects sterns from the fact that these aspirations are situated within a relational network and need to coexist with the two other patterns of recognition, that is, love and rights." (Honneth 1995, 178).

[133] Huttunen 2011, 241. See also:

"[...] in the affective relationship of recognition found in the family, human individuals are recognized as concrete creatures of need; in the cognitive-formal relationship of recognition found in law, they are recognized as abstract legal persons; and finally, in the emotionally enlightened relationship of recognition found in the State, they are recognized as concrete universals, that is, as subjects who are socialized in their particularity." (Honneth 1995, 25).

Honneth explains that for Hegel—and also for Durkheim, even the market and economic activities presuppose solidarity, as the contracts and relations which occur in these scenarios must be fair and just for people to trust in each other[134].

In *Disrespect,* Honneth clarifies that when he uses the term "community," it means that people inside this group appreciate each other, based on the shared common values and shared mode of life. People give worth to each other, according to their qualities and capacities as particular individuals or as a group. It means mutual recognition.

Honneth proves that solidarity is more than respect and tolerance[135]. Solidarity, for him, is more than tolerance, because individuals share the same values, they are not just accepting the culture of others, but more than that, they agree on the same values.

Regarding *respect*, I already studied that, in the pattern of law, individuals attain self-respect as soon as they enjoy equal treatment related to autonomy, moral responsibility, and social worth. Solidarity is different from respect because there is an emotional element in solidarity; it exists when one individual cares about the other. Being respected, on the other hand, means enjoying the personal autonomy to live and make choices, without interferences coming from other persons. Solidarity presupposes more interaction and appreciation between individuals, whereas respect relates more to the individual's freedom and autonomy, not necessarily a sharing interaction.

Furthermore, in "*Reification: a Recognition-Theoretical View*" (aforementioned as "*Reification*") Honneth, when discussing recognition, analyzes the elements of "practical involvement," "engaged praxis," and "care," coming from Dewey, Lukàcs, and Heidegger, respectively[136]. Honneth is not directly discussing solidarity, but instead discussing reification and recognition. I understand that these

---

[134] Honneth 2014a, 181.

[135] Honneth 2007a, 257.

[136] "For the moment, I merely want to emphasize the fact that our actions do not primarily have the character of an affectively neutral, cognitive stance toward the world but rather that of an affirmative, existentially colored style of caring comportment. In living we constantly concede the situational circumstances of our world a value of their own, which brings us to be concerned with our relationship to them. On this elementary level, the concept of "recognition" thus shares a fundamental notion not only with Dewey's concept of "practical involvement" but also with Heidegger's "care" and Lukàcs's "engaged praxis"—namely, the notion that the stance of empathetic engagement in the world, arising from the experience of the world's significance and value [*Werthaftigkeit*], is prior to our acts of detached cognition. A recognitional stance therefore embodies our active and constant assessment of the value that persons or things have in themselves". (Honneth 2005, 111)

concepts are not just more than the opposite of reification, but also a fundamental influence for the Honnethian pattern of solidarity.

From Dewey, "practical involvement" should occur when individuals experience interaction with the world. Instead of a self-centered practice, the practical involvement by human beings makes them involved with the world and its various elements, for instance, emotional, cognitive, and volitional aspects[137].

Lukàcs argues that "engaged praxis" is necessary for human beings, as a way to make individuals free of the mere relation of subject-object. An individual should experience reality from an existential point of view, giving to it a qualitative significance, more than just an objective vision of a subject-object schema[138].

The perspective of recognition related to caring, to empathy, exists mainly in the pattern of solidarity. Solidarity promotes so-called "self-worth" (*Selbstwertgefühls)*—a concept developed by Tugendhat[139].

According to Tugendhat, the feeling of self-worth comes from recognition by other individuals. The one recognized is seen as someone who practices the good inside a community[140].

As mentioned, in *Disrespect,* Honneth states that solidarity promotes *self-worth.* Nevertheless, some years before he claimed—in *Struggle for recognition*—that the pattern of solidarity promotes *self-esteem (Selbstschätzung) and social esteem,* in that time he does not adopt the expression "self-worth." In *Disrespect,* besides using the term self-worth, at the same time, he writes: "*Therefore, every form of solidarity, understood as mutual esteem, is based on the existence of a shared intersubjective horizon of value.*"[141] Here, he mentions *mutual esteem.*

---

137 Honneth 2005, 110.

138 Honneth 2005, 105.

139 Honneth 2007a, 136.

140 "The specifically moral motivation is when the agent "die soziale Ächtung fürchtet" (Tugendhat 2007b, p. 155). People want to be recognised as good, and that implies respecting the reciprocal wants in the community. But this is an external restraint; morality is not something one genuinely wants, rather an impediment to take into account in order to stay socially afloat. So the motivation is social recognition, it is not directed at moral goodness itself. One is not moral because one has identified with the practice. But this implies that one has no reason to be moral when it comes to actions that can be performed in secret. Morality could then in principle consist of "freeriders", people that give the impression to have a moral character but in reality fake the moral sentiments (cf. Tugendhat 1997a, 43 f.)." (Eriksen 2009, 53)

141 Honneth 2007a, 257.

Despite the Honnethian variety of terms, it does not change the core meaning of what solidarity promotes to the individual. The result of solidarity is an individual's feeling of having worth in her private life—self-esteem or self-worth—and inside her community—social esteem or mutual esteem[142].

It is relevant to note that solidarity can be interpreted from two directions: the one who receives solidarity—as discussed above—and the one who practices solidarity. Taking into consideration the last one, according to Honneth, solidarity is the capacity to appreciate someone and her culture, to respect it, and to tolerate it. The individual's capabilities are considered valuable to a concrete community. Solidarity, then, means the recognition of someone's qualities as something worthwhile for a shared life. Van den Brink argues: '*The point of a post-traditional conception of solidarity, Honneth claims, is that members of society recognise each other as persons who value "freely chosen life-goals."*'[143]

Solidarity is related to cultural appreciation. In "*Redistribution or Recognition? A Political-Philosophical Exchange*" (2003), Honneth states that recognition affects three contexts: rights, love, and cultural appreciation[144]. Instead of mentioning *solidarity* as the third context, Honneth uses the term *cultural appreciation*. Despite such denomination, for the sake of clarity, this work will keep adopting "solidarity" as the third pattern of recognition.

According to Honneth, in modern societies, solidarity claims for symmetrical esteem between individualized and autonomous subjects.[145] In other words, the individuals view one another as holders of significant values for shared praxis.[146] These relationships inspire a passive tolerance, but also an active sense of care for the other one.[147]

Cases of solidarity, according to Honneth, are situations in which persons are free to choose their ways of life, without external restrictions. Honneth states that

---

[142] "As we saw, a person's 'honour', 'dignity', or, to use the modern term, 'status' refers to the degree of social esteem accorded to his or her manner of self-realization within a society's inherited cultural horizon. If this hierarchy of values is so constituted as to downgrade individual forms of life and manners of belief as inferior or deficient, then it robs the subjects in question of every opportunity to attribute social value to their own abilities. [...] For individuals, therefore, the experience of this social devaluation typically brings with it a loss of personal self-esteem, of the opportunity to regard themselves as beings whose traits and abilities are esteemed" (Honneth 1995, 134).

[143] Van Den Brink 2011, 161.

[144] Honneth 2003b, 3.

[145] Honneth 1995, 129.

[146] Honneth 1995, 129.

[147] Honneth 1995, 129.

different cultures focus on different forms of recognition. Moreover, even inside the same community, the difference is fundamental:

> Once love for persons is separated, at least in principle, from legal recognition and social esteem, three forms of mutual recognition have emerged that are geared towards specific developmental potentials as well as distinct types of struggle. [...] The breeding-ground for these collective forms of resistance is prepared by subcultural semantics in which a shared language is found for feelings of having been unjustly treated, a language that points—however indirectly—to possibilities for expanding relationships of recognition.[148]

As I already discussed, when analyzing different cultures and values, Honneth could be seen as a liberal philosopher, as he comprehends that forms of self-realization vary between communities and historical cases. Nevertheless, he does not advocate for full toleration of any cultural difference, stating just that there is permanent tension and struggle within different groups.[149]

Considering the importance of solidarity and self-worth, Honneth clarifies that it can be denied in different situations, such as a simple case of not greeting another person, or severe cases of stigmatization[150]. Now, it is important to highlight the role of solidarity for recognition.

1.5.1 The Role of Solidarity in Recognition

The pattern of solidarity relates to the experiences of a person inside her community. When someone feels social- and self-esteem, this individual can cooperate with her community, contributing to the achievement of shared goals and complying with social norms. Honneth comprehends that solidarity comes much more

---

[148] Honneth 1995, 170.

[149] Honneth 1995, 126.

[150] Honneth 2007a, 136.

According to the psychological theories regarding stigmatization:

"According to Goffman, stigmatization is a process of global devaluation of an individual who possesses a deviant attribute. Stigma arises during a social interaction when an individual's actual social identity (the attributes he or she can be proved to possess) does not meet society's normative expectations of the attributes the individual should possess (his or her virtual social identity). Thus, the individual's social identity is spoiled, and he or she is assumed to be incapable of fulfilling the role requirements of social interaction." (Kurzban; Leary 2001, 187).

from the shared experiences of disrespect within a community, then from a historical background of practices of engagement and empathy. For him, the biggest misconception underlying the regeneration of European solidarity today is the belief that feelings of togetherness only come from the memory of positive commonalities and glories.[151] For Honneth, just if one look at the ordinary sources of family cohesion, then what motivates family members to work reciprocally for each other's welfare is actually a chain of collectively survived crises and disasters, be they deaths, illnesses, quarrels, or personal defeats.[152]

From a public perspective, struggles for solidarity require engagement and people's actions. The ones who are struggling are making claims for the recognition of themselves or their general community, struggling then for different persons. From a private perspective, the struggles can also relate to the individual herself and to someone related to her in private life. In both cases, the relevant point is that the struggles themselves require solidarity.

The pattern of solidarity, then, has a role in making the struggles for recognition possible.

Honneth has been criticized regarding his conception of solidarity, as I will further see.

1.5.2 Critiques of the Honnethian Pattern of Solidarity

Max Pensky criticizes Honneth, arguing that he does not confront situations of offenses to solidarity, and that the liberalization of different forms of life, permitting individuals to appreciate themselves and their cultures indiscriminately, could imply on a potent offense to solidarity[153].

For Pensky, if solidarity can vary according to different societal values, then one cannot consider a permanent notion of solidarity, but on the contrary, a continuous struggle for recognition called solidarity. For him, there is one aspect that remains constant: the feeling of low self-esteem, being denigrated or invisible,

---

[151] Honneth 2020, 324.

[152] Honneth 2020, 324.

[153] "It is not entirely clear in *Struggle for Recognition* what Honneth would suggest as a remedy to a situation of widespread denigration of ways of life, the psychological pathologies of low self-esteem arising from it, and the crisis of recognition that seem to be generated, in turn, by such pathologies. [...] And would such a *success* in the liberalisation of cultural models of self-realisation projects not then precisely undermine the possibility of solidarity by making *any* form of life valuable, simply by definition?" (Pensky 2011, 148)

marginalized and worthless.[154] This feeling keeps existing whereas the individual constantly experiences her project of self-realisation failing through a lack of recognition.[155]

Anderson disagrees with Pensky and states that the openness of solidarity is necessary, transforming solidarity in an environment where persons can attain social esteem. For him, the social conditions for esteem are determined by the prevailing sense of what is to count as a worthwhile contribution to society. Anderson comprehends the sense of esteem in the horizon of values of a particular culture. Thus, Honneth's notion of solidarity is opened to the possibility of placing conditions of self-esteem as a field of contestation and cultural struggle for the recognition. For Anderson: "*'Solidarity' is the term Honneth uses for the cultural climate in which the acquisition of self-esteem has become broadly possible*".[156] Accordingly, Honneth makes his point when he understands solidarity as a tool for allowing different practices inside a culture or between different cultures, and the possibility of transformations.

After the critiques of Honneth's solidarity, it is necessary to question if he states a minimum content for solidarity, to universalize solidarity, and avoid an openness that can result in cultural practices of disrespect. If Honneth understands that solidarity represents whatever each community wants to adopt as social values, then it could culminate in situations of misrecognition. Solidarity, in some cases, would allow practices of disrespect, of offenses to recognition—for instance, societies which practice female genital mutilation. If a community has this practice inside their shared values of respect to the tradition, then people would participate in the ritual of mutilation. They feel they are being solidary, helping each other, contributing to the maintenance of traditional value, and having worth from others. However, in the end, they are all ending in disrespect. It is relevant, then, to inquire which are the limits to the element of solidarity, to make it coherent with recognition itself.

Nancy Fraser understands that recognition should be related to justice, and not necessarily to solidarity. She does not interpret recognition in the same way as Honneth does. For Fraser, recognition always relates to a view of the

[154] Pensky 2011, 145.

[155] Pensky 2011, 145.

[156] Anderson 1995, xvii.

subjects inserted in their community, considering their cultural values[157]. Nevertheless, she does not believe that recognition has a variety of dimensions, such as economic, moral, and legal ones.

According to her, recognition must include the parity of participation[158]. Parity of participation has two conditions. Firstly, the "objective condition", meaning that the participants should be economically equal; they should have an equitable distribution of material resources. Societies cannot hold institutions which tolerate significant differences in incomes and wealth conditions.

The second condition of parity of participation is the "intersubjective condition", meaning that all people should have equal opportunities to reach their social esteem, without denigrations of recognition. The institutions should not promote the depreciation of some categories of persons.

Fraser, for instance, criticizes affirmative strategies, as they induce the minority groups to see themselves as better than other groups, and they generalize characteristics of different behaviors and life inside the same group (she will later call it "the problem of reification"). The affirmative strategies can culminate in separatism and generalization.

As a solution, Fraser proposes that the group should participate in general debates in the same way as other individuals. She is against communitarianism. In her words, usually misrecognition is interpreted as depreciated identity.[159] As a result, politics of recognition means identity politics, affirming a given group identity.[160] This interpretation is problematic, because it encourages separatism and downplays intragroup domination.[161] For Fraser, misrecognition should be understood as status subordination caused by institutionalized patterns of cultural value.[162] As a solution, parity-fostering alternatives should be responsible of guaranteeing the parity of participation.[163]

Fraser makes a critique of communitarianism, arguing that it advocates that groups of individuals should stay within their community, adoring and venerating their own culture. Communities would be isolated groups of people, without inclusion and without valorizing the individual's autonomy.

---

[157] Fraser mistakes, as she is not allowed that, for Honneth, solidarity and culture are closely related. Then, it is mistaken to think about culture appreciation without touching solidarity.

[158] Fraser 2003b, 36.

[159] Fraser 2003b, 87.

[160] Fraser 2003b, 87.

[161] Fraser 2003b, 87.

[162] Fraser 2003b, 87.

[163] Fraser 2003b, 87.

Honneth, in turn, contends that recognition is not just a question of justice, but also a way of self-realization and development of identity, in a way that "*terms of recognition must represent the unified framework for such a project [of justice]*".[164]

Social justice, for Honneth ("*The Political Identity of the Green Movement in Germany: Social-Philosophical Reflections*," 2010), should consider integrity, and not just equity. For him, the tendency nowadays to comprehend social justice from a social-economical perspective should be reviewed. Enough material resources are necessary, but they should be accompanied by immaterial goods, such as education and social esteem. It signifies conditions of equal opportunity. Nevertheless, more than equity, the integrity of social life is also a necessity:

> In view of the growing tendencies towards social exclusion, it will become once again increasingly important to remind ourselves of the original intentions behind this concept of justice. But strangely enough, this way of defining social justice has always remained blind to forms of disadvantage and harm that are not directly linked to the socio-economic class position or to the reality of working class life. For these types of deprivation only come into view, once the criterion for social justice is not defined as equal opportunity in the narrow sense, but as the integrity of the social life form as a whole.[165]

Honneth states that subordinated persons and groups suffer not only from a lack of material goods and opportunities for action, but also, and perhaps more severely, from the limited respect and esteem they receive from those enjoying social power.[166]

Furthermore, Honneth understands that the conception of social justice nowadays should include cultural pluralism and the importance of concern about future generations[167]. As a result, social justice means not just positive rights, "*but also in the shape of appropriate attitudes, modes of comportment and behavioural routines.*"[168]

Recognition promotes the autonomy and self-determination of the individual, and these represent the bond between the individual and her social community, "*The enormous gravitational force exerted by the notion of autonomy derives from the fact that it manages to form a systematic link between the individual subject*

[164] Honneth 2003b, 111.

[165] Honneth 2010b, 14.

[166] Honneth 2022b, 12.

[167] Honneth 2010b, 16.

[168] Honneth 2014a, 67.

and the social order."[169] It is precisely the notion of individual self-determination that Honneth puts in the center of modern conceptions of justice: "*That which is 'just' is that which protects, fosters or realizes the autonomy of all members of society.*"[170]

It is possible to conclude that the book "*Freedom's Right*" (2014a) makes the connection between the theory of recognition and the Honnethian theory of justice[171]. The discussions on recognition places law as a key facet on the building of one's respect and dignity. Therefore, Honneth must properly explore the role of law for recognition, in order to comprehend how the reaching of justice and equality would then affect recognition.

I agree that recognition itself relates to justice, as justice, for us, is more than a compliment of legal norms, living standards, or well-being. Justice also encompasses the certainty of taking part in an equal society, having worth inside one's community, and being free to live with self-confidence, self-esteem, and self-respect. Forst goes straight to the point arguing that "*Justice, according to this view, is not primarily about what you have (or do not have), rather, it is about how you are treated.*"[172]

Another point of discussion between Fraser and Honneth concerns the capitalist economic order and cultural values. Honneth and Fraser question how capitalism should relate to recognition. Firstly, capitalism could be a social system that differentiates itself from other social systems, totally without regard to cultural values. On the other hand, capitalism could be a consequence of cultural values, connected to many forms of recognition.

Honneth comprehends capitalism from the second point of view, endorsing that capitalism has not just an economic dimension, but also cultural, legal, and moral aspects. Because of that, for Honneth, the experiences of disrespect inside the capitalist system affect more than just cultural and economic dimensions, but also legal and moral perspectives. It also justifies the fact that recognition relates not only to justice, but also to moral and legal dimensions.

Nevertheless, for Fraser, there is a separation between the capitalist system and culture, in a way that cultural aspects involve recognition, and, on the other hand, economic and capitalist issues involve claims of redistribution. In other

---

[169] Honneth 2014a, 15.

[170] Honneth 2014a, 18.

[171] For G. Markle, Honneth derives a theory of justice from social theory, following a Hegelian methodology and going beyond, as Honneth recognizes "the potential for transforming and transcending existing social roles within contemporary society." (Markle 2004, 383).

[172] Forst 2011, 308.

words, the denial of recognition inside the capitalist system is not necessarily a denial of justice. Situations related to economic affairs, which need to be solved through redistribution, do not involve recognition claims. A situation requiring recognition does not necessarily require redistribution and vice versa.

Honneth, on the other hand, understands that each situation of injustice represents an instance of social disrespect[173]. Also, all social disrespect motivates struggles for recognition. Because of that, if one tries to think about a situation exclusively related to a redistribution solution, one isat the same time dealing with injustice, a form of social disrespect.

I agree with Honneth and disagree with Fraser. For me, if someone is in need of redistribution, she is at the same time experiencing offenses to patterns of recognition. A person in need does not have her pattern of law and solidarity preserved, as she is not inserted in the dynamic of her community, not having self-respect and self- and social esteem.

Discussing Honneth's solidarity results in a question about recognition itself. To recognize someone through a solidary action may signify a *feeling* of recognizing someone—with compassion, care, and empathy—or maybe just a *behavior*: "to recognize someone".

1.5.3 Recognition as a Feeling

In *The I in We: Studies in the Theory of Recognition* (2012), Honneth has stated that recognition comes from four premises. Firstly, recognition consists always in positive feelings, which someone experiences for another person or group.[174] Secondly, recognition is represented by modes of behavior coming together with words and symbolic expressions. When regarded as intersubjective relationships, recognition is also a 'stance' (*Haltung*), an attitude.[175] Thirdly, it is an intentional act, not just a side effect. Fourthly, recognition contains many forms, feelings, and relationships.[176]

---

[173] In this direction, see Forst:

'Approaches like Fraser's thus are doomed to remain bound to conventional paradigms of thinking about justice, especially to "goals that have already been publicly articulated" thereby neglecting "everyday, still unthematized, but no less pressing embryonic forms of social misery and moral injustice".' (Forst 2011, 306)

[174] Honneth 2012b, 79.

[175] Honneth 2012b, 79.

[176] Honneth 2012b, 79.

Honneth states that additionally to these four premises, recognition should embrace various forms of practical attitudes whose primary intention consists in a particular act of affirming another person or group.[177] It would not be interpreted as ambiguously or ideological, but rather as an intersubjective prerequisite for the ability to fulfill one's life goals autonomously.[178]

For Honneth, recognition is what makes it possible for the human being to see herself as someone valuable to herself, to her community, relatives, and friends. Recognition is a positive feeling, as it gives the subject self-confidence, social-esteem, and self-respect.

> As in other contexts, a negative approach provides a preliminary justification: unless one presupposes a certain degree of self-confidence, legally guaranteed autonomy, and sureness as to the value of one's own abilities, it is impossible to imagine successful self-realization, if that is to be understood as a process of realizing, without coercion, one's self-chosen life-goals. With regard to such a process, 'lack of coercion' and 'freedom' cannot be understood simply as the absence of external force or influence, but must rather signify the lack of inner barriers as well as psychological inhibitions and fears.[179]

More than that, recognition relates to honor. Clifton D. Mark (2014), for instance, compares the Honnethian theory of recognition with the one of Charles Taylor, relating it to the idea of the feeling of honor and analyzing a division between categorical recognition and comparative recognition. Charles Taylor proposes a social political theory related to recognition, very attached to discussions on multiculturalism and the necessity for the rule of law to consider the diversity of life forms, respecting the authenticity ideal of person in the modernity.

For Taylor, non-recognition, that is, disrespect, results on a paralyzing feeling in individuals, which makes respect a vital human need[180]. According to Taylor, the notion of identity combined with recognition has changed over time, and

[177] Honneth 2012b, 79.

[178] Honneth 2012b, 79. Althusser understands that not just the state apparatus but also other instances of individuals life—family, for instance—can provoke ideology. In that way, the processes of recognition could be interpreted, by Althusser, from a negative perspective. For Honneth:

"Althusser calls ideologies forms of addressing people. In that sense ideologies are forms of false recognition of groups, and what I have to do is to preserve the conceptual means to make a distinction between these false forms of recognition which are definitely there and forms of justified recognition, in that sense correct recognition." (Honneth 2004b, 388)

[179] Honneth 1995, 174.

[180] Taylor 1994, 46.

nowadays it means: "*the one that is specifically mine, the one that I discover in myself*", what Taylor calls a contemporary interpretation of the ideal of *authenticity*[181]. This ideal faces challenges nowadays, as the so-called "self-realization" does not properly consider individual's connections with other human beings in social relationships. For Taylor, in fact, a wrong idea of self-realization may be self-destructive whereas not allowing one to achieve true authenticity[182]. Nevertheless, for him, recognition is not a sufficient solution. As Taylor dedicates himself for the study on multiculturalism, he holds that not just recognition perspectives should be took in consideration, but also new conceptions of equality and diversity, whereas cultural diversity should be seen as a value itself.

Mark interprets the theories of Honneth and Taylor from the perspective of honor.

Mark understands that honor is a crucial aspect of the theory of recognition, and it should be studied from a categorical and comparative approach. The categorical perspective considers honor between different groups in society, assuming that between different groups, there is always an immanent inequality. People from different groups know that there are privileged persons who occupy higher positions in a social hierarchy. It may signify financial hierarchy, social hierarchy, or others. According to Mark, Honneth's theory adapts itself just to a categorical approach, as Honneth admits that different groups have differences regarding honor.

On the other hand, the comparative perspective analyzes honor inside the same group. Mark argues that even if individuals share the same hierarchical level, one individual will always try to reach higher positions, leapfrogging the other subjects in the same group. The conflicts, which come in this context, are more complex, and, from Mark's point of view, Honneth is not aware of it: "*Honneth and Taylor begin their histories of recognition with a serious error. Captivated by the view of a great hierarchical class-system and its differential categories of recognition, they lose sight of the sharply competitive nature of recognition between equals.*"[183]

Mark states that, for Honneth, there is solidarity intragroup and, supposedly, equal relations of honor would come.[184] Nevertheless, any relationship of equal individuals may incur in competition between them. These individuals, then, would engage in an anxious struggle for distinction, trying to eliminate any

[181] Taylor 1994, 48.

[182] Taylor 2011, 45.

[183] Mark 2014, 28.

[184] Mark 2014, 21.

risk of being consider categorial inferior.[185] As a result, it is only by ignoring honor's comparative aspect that Honneth would be able to comprehend intra-group relations under honor as solidarity' relations.[186]

Mark's main argument is that both authors—Honneth and Taylor—do not consider recognition from the comparison between different people inside the same group: "*Honneth and Taylor do not see the present state of recognition as sui generis but rather as the result of the historical transformation of earlier honor-systems.*"[187] This problem affects Honneth's objective to reach a "full-recognition", a moment when subjects enjoy an egalitarian honor inside their groups, by way of acts of solidarity: "*The first reversal is the move from inegalitarian to egalitarian recognition. Under modernity, all individuals must be recognized as 'full members of society.*'"[188]

More than that, for Mark, honor presupposes differences between the individuals. Quoting Miller, he holds that, if there is no difference, there is no honor: "*The comparative character of honor is a formal, rather than substantive property.*"[189]

Mark comprehends that honor in the categorical level promotes some conflicts, but these conflicts are smoother than the disputes related to comparative honor: "*This structure of relationships led to relations between equals that are usually described as tense, anxiety-ridden and verging perpetually on open conflict.*"[190]

Joel Anderson agrees with Mark, whereas the former argues that Honneth fails to consider the conflicts between individuals—in the same group—and institutions located in the same structure:

---

[185] Mark 2014, 21.

[186] Mark 2014, 21.

[187] Mark 2014, 16.

[188] Mark 2014, 21.

[189] Mark 2014, 18.

[190] Mark 2014, 19. For more about recognition and anxiety, see Honneth:

"On the theoretical level, it appears to me extremely useful to follow Neumann in trying to understand neurotically intensified mass anxieties as a kind of social pathology that can deeply interfere with the individual's ability to participate in democratic will-formation. In order autonomously to form an opinion and be able to articulate it publicly, freedom from anxiety is indispensable, since anxiety impairs self-esteem, limits deliberative powers, and allows ego-estranging idol substitution to take effect. With this initial idea, Neumann goes far beyond the agenda of the central representatives of the Frankfurt School, since he is interested in a normatively grounded diagnosis of a social pathology that coheres with the presuppositions of a democratic public sphere. Socially produced anxieties are significant for him not simply because they violate the preconditions for the development of a free subjectivity, but rather because they in turn destroy the conditions of uninhibited will-formation in the public sphere". (Honneth 2003, 253)

> Honneth's account of 'the social' focuses on the central role of conflict between social groups, rather than between individuals (as is assumed by Hobbesian and rational choice theorists) or between structural entities (as systems theorists, structuralists and even post-structuralists assume).[191]

I do not agree with Mark's interpretation of recognition. When Honneth develops his patterns of recognition, he allows for the possibility that relationships are naturally conflicting. In the models of love, rights, and solidarity, individuals will deal with differences. It is part of the process of formation of their identity. Furthermore, any sort of competition between individuals for having more honor than others do not correspond to an ethics of recognition, which holds a moral value.

Indeed, when discussing the change from the idea of social honor to social prestige, Honneth states:

> The individualization of achievement is inevitably accompanied by the opening of societal value-ideas for differing forms of personal self-realization. From this point on, it is a form of value pluralism—albeit one defined in class-specific and gender-specific terms—that constitutes the cultural framework of orientation within which individuals' level of accomplishment and thus their social worth are defined. It is in this context that the concept of social honour gradually becomes watered down into a concept of social prestige.[192]

Honneth does not presuppose a consensus of individuals before they begin to struggle for recognition. People can be struggling, together, based on different reasons. The objective of the struggle must be the same: looking forward to recovering recognition.

For Honneth, people do not have to feel equal in all the characteristics of their personalities or lives. What makes people be together to engage in struggles is the offense to a pattern of recognition and also the feeling that they are taking part in the same community. Honneth comprehends recognition and solidarity from the perspective of care and compassion.

The critiques from Mark and Anderson show that they see practices of solidarity without regard to the ethics of recognition. The authors come from utilitarian approach. Whereas Honneth believes that individuals should practice solidarity based on an ethical life, attached to worth, Mark and Anderson seem to think that people tend naturally to compete and to feel honored in detriment of others

---

191 Anderson 2011, 48.

192 Honneth 1995, 125.

who are different, trying to reach the best for themselves, no matter the impacts on others. For Honneth, human beings do not have these moral tendencies.

Van den Brink criticizes Honneth, arguing that he does not consider possible conflicts between the patterns of recognition:

> If I understand Honneth correctly, then his account of morality implies that a moral attitude that is appropriate for one form of recognition cannot in itself conflict with an attitude that is appropriate for another. [...] At the same time, however, claims that spring from one of the three basic modes of recognition may conflict with one another *in concrete situations*, for example a situation in which loyalty to a friend one wants to protect from trouble with the law, conflicts with obedience to the law. Here, Honneth refuses to define a "superior vantage point".[193]

I also understand that the theory of recognition should have more elements to make it possible for individuals to handle potential situations of conflict between patterns of recognition. This work will propose in the next chapters some modifications to the theory of recognition, to avoid conflicts between the spheres of recognition.

In this section, it was possible to verify that recognition is also represented by positive feelings shared by individuals. For the one who recognizes, it represents an intention of giving worth to the other, guaranteeing respect, esteem, and confidence for the one being recognized. The former, then, experiences recognition from feelings of self-esteem, self-respect, self-confidence, as well as from a general feeling of being respected and appreciated. According to Honneth, recognition always relates to the achievement of self-realization.

Sequentially, I will inquire if recognition can also be understood as a behavior.

1.5.4 Recognition as a Behavior

In "*The I in We: Studies in the Theory of Recognition*," Honneth makes a semantic interpretation of "recognition." He clarifies that in English, French, and German, the word can be interpreted with different nuances, but in all of them, it indicates a speech act *"in which one admits or acknowledges a point, in which case 'recognition' has a primarily self-referential sense."*[194]

Besides this semantic meaning, Honneth holds that recognition is a moral act and functions as a performative response to another person. He states that

---

[193] Van Den Brink 2011, 159.

[194] Honneth 2012b, 79.

recognitional behavior is a moral act. The subjects should avoid and recriminate egocentric behaviors and always look at the intentions, free-will, and needs of the other subjects. The consciousness that the other subject has worth provokes recognitional behavior[195].

It is essential to highlight that, before the publication of *The I in We: Studies in the Theory of Recognition*, Honneth had already connected his three patterns of recognition with the moral in *Struggle for Recognition* (1995). Additionally, in 1997, in the article *Recognition and Moral Obligation*[196], it was advocated that all individuals have to struggle through moral aspects of daily life, following moral obligations.

Furthermore, Honneth holds that the communicative action practiced by the subject should have as a presupposition the achievement of social recognition; the subject has expectations of being recognized as a moral person.

Instead of representing just an ethical principle and a feeling, recognition should be represented by daily actions focused on respect and solidarity. These representations culminate in struggles for recognition.

Recognition always comes accompanied by the struggles, a dynamic process that does not has its beginning and end clearly defined. Struggles for recognition are permanent, and they work as a dialectic movement towards better conditions of formation of identity.

The struggles for recognition are necessary when disrespect compromises the processes of an individual's identity formation, as I will further see.

1.6 Conclusion of Chap. 1

In Chap. 1 "*What is Recognition*?" I have studied that recognition is a moral act, consisting of positive feelings towards the one being recognized. The act of recognizing has an intention, and it includes a variety of attitudes. More than that, I also interpret recognition as an ethical process, which influences individuals in their moral behaviors.

Coming from a more detailed study on recognition, I also comprehend it from three different dimensions.

The pattern of love gives self-confidence to the individual. There, she experiences private relationships with parents, friends, and relatives during her entire life. These relationships must contribute to her self-realization, authenticity, and

[195] Honneth 2012b, 84.

[196] Honneth, 1997.

communicative freedom. As a result, the pattern of love endorses individual freedom.

For Honneth, the dimension of love is damaged when physical abuses occur. Nevertheless, I understand that mental abuse and other kinds of violence in the private life of individuals are also offenses against love, and they interfere in their development of self-confidence.

I understand that Honneth gives more attention to the pattern of solidarity, and it is more evident in the book "*Freedom's right*", when he sustains that social freedom, located in the pattern of solidarity, is the one to be amplified to all the dimensions of recognition.

Nevertheless, I advocate for a focus of Honnethian theory on the pattern of law, especially regarding women's recognition. The formation of recognition comes precisely from the analysis of its opposite: disrespect, offenses to the patterns of recognition. The recovery of recognition comes firstly from legal recognition. Because of that, this pattern turns out to be very fundamental to women's recognition.

According to Honneth, in the pattern of law, individuals experience the achievement of self-respect. There, he proposes a normative reconstruction of ethical life, arguing that modern law should not be as dogmatic as in the past, and it is necessary to consider the pattern of law from a sociological and social theoretical approach. That means, instead of interpreting the law as a formal condition of achieving recognition, one should consider two spheres of freedom-guaranteeing, for the achievement of self-respect and self-worth.

Firstly, individuals should have freedom and autonomy to make choices in their lives. Secondly, they should have civil cooperation and responsibility, adopting democratic attitudes in public spaces. Only if the law is interpreted from this dual perspective, can the pattern of law work.

In this context, I have also analyzed that the theory of recognition could adopt some elements from the theory of communicative action of Habermas, in order to improve the pattern of law. The last author has a focus on a theory of socialization and language, but he forgets to comprehend the particular dimension of the individual. Honneth, on the other hand, focuses on the individual himself, and he just considers the public spaces when discussing the normative reconstruction. If one connects both theories, the result would be a theory of recognition able to go further than traditional democratic premises, and include the formation of validity claims in different contexts, protected by the pattern of law.

The pattern of law, as discussed in this Chapter, can be offended by deceit, fraud, or legal discrimination. Whereas the pattern of love represents the primary relationships of individuals, the pattern of law makes the maintenance of all the patterns in Honneth's theory.

Finally, Chap. 1 has also discussed the pattern of recognition called "solidarity." This pattern has a crucial role in Honneth's theory, as he comes from Hegel's interpretation of solidarity as a synthesis of law and love. In this pattern, individuals reach self-esteem, social esteem, and self-worth. The individual has more than respect and tolerance, but also a real appreciation for others in his community, with emotional attachment.

Honneth adopts Dewey's concept of practical involvement as an interaction of the individual and his world. More than that, he introduces Lukács' engaged praxis, meaning that the individual in the pattern of solidarity adopts a qualitative significance in his life. Finally, for Honneth, practices of solidarity also hold Heidegger's care, meaning that the individual is not just a mere observer but also a participant in the dynamic of solidarity, having empathetic attitudes.

All these dimensions are useful because I understand that the aspects developed in the pattern of solidarity mainly motivate the struggles for recognition. Although the struggle comes from the offenses to recognition, I will see that the tools and the possibilities for struggling for recognition are located in the pattern of solidarity.

The chapter has shown that Honneth was also criticized for his conception of solidarity.

For Pensky, Honneth errs when he may permit some cultural models that disrespect recognition. I understand that it is possible to minimize these risks as I will propose in subsequent chapters.

Nancy Fraser criticizes Honnethian solidarity because, for her, Honneth should include the parity of participation when considering the achievement of recognition. I understand that the second condition of parity of participation—intersubjective condition—would endorse the pattern of solidarity, as it means the achievement of equal opportunities for the individuals to reach their social esteem. Nevertheless, I disagree with Fraser when she criticizes the Honnethian approach to capitalism. For her, discussions regarding capitalism do not affect recognition, but instead redistribution. For me, as well as for Honneth, the impacts of capitalism in an individual's life go beyond just economic conditions, equally affecting moral and individual dimensions of life.

Mark has criticized Honneth from another approach. For him, the theory of recognition does not consider the comparative dimension of honor, as people inserted in the same group naturally compete with each other. Nevertheless, I understand that, for Honneth, individuals do not compete, but rather are involved by affection and compassion. They usually act in a solidary way because they receive the conditions for the practice of recognition. More than that, it seems that Mark presupposes a consensus between individuals who are going to struggle for recognition. On the contrary, Honneth does not advocate for consensus or elimination of cultural differences, even inside the group.

Additionally, I have studied the critique made by Van den Brink against Honnethian recognition, concerning the possibility of conflicts between the patterns of recognition. The theory of recognition needs some premises and limitations to avoid potential conflicts between the patterns. This work will propose some of these limitations.

The chapter has also stated that recognition may be included in normative ethics, being represented by positive feelings and behaviors.

Sequentially, it is essential to follow my methodological explanation regarding the theory of recognition. I have firstly discussed the three patterns of recognition and shown the primary offenses against them. As a second step, it is crucial to clarify the forms of denials—called disrespect—and how they can be solved—employing struggles for recognition.

This work understands that it is very relevant to focus on the offenses to the patterns of recognition. First of all, if one identifies the ways in which the dimensions of social freedom are denigrated, then it is possible to inquire how to recover the recognition. Secondly, it is precisely the experiences of offenses to recognition that begin the processes of struggles for recognition. Considering that, disrespect is what provokes the struggles for recognition, promoting this dual relationship "struggles for" with the "achievement of recognition" in the end.

After describing what recognition means, the next chapter will explain how the patterns of recognition are exposed to offenses, which Honneth calls "disrespect."

2 What is Disrespect?

Assuming that achieving recognition is the ideal of Honnethian ethics, the institute of disrespect represents the opposite of recognition.

2.1 *Disrespect* means an Offense to Recognition

When the patterns of recognition suffer offenses, this may signify disrespect. The experience of disrespect is what makes the subject engage in struggles for recognition. "*What the term 'disrespect' [Mißacthung] refers to is the specific vulnerability of humans resulting from the internal interdependency of individualization and recognition, which both Hegel and Mead helped to illuminate.*"[1]

The theory of recognition is not just related to the concept of recognition, but also to the concept of struggle. For Honneth, recognition has struggles as its premise, and, in order to struggle, the individual should be affected, her patterns of recognition must be violated.

> Honneth justifies the abandonment of the paradigms of the exploitation of labour, the total administration of society through instrumental reason, and the colonisation of lifeworlds, always by the one exigency: to be true to the hermeneutics of injustice, that is, the full range of experiences of social suffering.[2]

Deranty uses "hermeneutics of injustice" to describe all the experiences of suffering, disrespect, and misrecognition in the theory of recognition. It is not possible

[1] Honneth 1995, 131.

[2] Deranty 2011, 72.

C. Diamantino Esser Santana, *Recognized Women:*, Juridicum – Schriften zur Rechtsphilosophie, https://doi.org/10.1007/978-3-658-46849-1_2

to conceive what justice and recognition mean without considering the disrespect to patterns of recognition.

In the same direction, Petherbridge evokes that in the theory of recognition, the opposition between justice and injustice, recognition and misrecognition, are necessary tools for understanding them:

> As Rainer Forst enumerates in his discussion of the debate between Honneth and Fraser, contexts of justice are always primarily contexts of injustice, even though for Forst, they also presume a specific context of justification. For Honneth, social domination can only be adequately critiqued if we begin from the experience of injustice, that is, normativity can only be derived negatively, not on the basis of ideality.[3]

For Petherbridge, recognition presupposes an undamaged intersubjectivity. The subject-formation during ethical life should be successful, and he calls this phenomenon "*normative foundation of recognition.*"[4]

More than paying attention to the damage to the individual, Brincat highlights the importance of considering the harm against individual autonomy, affecting human vulnerabilities:

> Yet whereas the notion of harm has been typically restricted to the protection of negative liberties for the individual's exercise of will, recognition theory shows that we also need to account for the various threats to individual autonomy that occur through damage, distortions or pathologies in the social relations that support individual autonomy.[5]

---

[3] Petherbridge 2011, 18. In the same direction, see:

"According to Honneth (and this is perhaps the point of closest affinity with fellow Hegelian Charles Taylor), it is with our inchoate feelings, and at the margins of traditions, and more generally in the encounter with the *conflicted* and the *unresolved* that the needed innovative resources for Critical Theory are to be found". (Anderson 2011, 50).

[4] Petherbridge 2011, 13.

[5] Brincat 2013, 245. See also Salonia: "This negative experience of the individual indicates, consequently, a normative dimension: the individual perceives its own suffering as a social injustice; it feels the injustice of a society that cannot fulfill its normative expectations of recognition. With respect to this Honneth remarks: If the adjective 'social' is to mean anything more than 'typically found in society', social suffering and discontent possess a normative core. It is a matter of the disappointment or violation of normative expectations of society considered justified by those concerned. Thus, such feelings of discontent and suffering, insofar as they are designated as 'social', coincide with the experience that society is doing something unjust, something unjustifiable (Fraser; Honneth, 2003, p. 129)." (Salonia 2008, 133)

This section focuses on the offenses against patterns of recognition, to clarify how individuals can struggle against it. According to Honneth, "*In this sense, the distinctions between three patterns of recognition gives us a theoretical key with which to separate out just as many kinds of disrespect.*"[6]

First of all, it is necessary to identify some denominations used by Honneth. In Honneth's literature, he uses different terms to characterize practices against the patterns of recognition. In *Struggle for recognition*, Honneth denominates all forms of offenses to recognition with the term "*disrespect*" (*Mißachtung*).

I consider that the Honnethian denomination of disrespect is a synonym of misrecognition. Both mean the opposite of recognition: when a pattern of recognition is damaged according to Honnethian theory, there is disrespect/ misrecognition. This work will adopt more the term "disrespect" because Honneth uses this term much more than misrecognition.

2.2 Disrespect vs. Injustice

Injustice is another denomination used by Honneth. I interpret it, coming from his theory, as a category of many species—social injustice, legal injustice, moral injustice, for instance.

Honneth argues that the opposite of recognition is *moral injustice*, defined by "*feelings of social disrespect.*"[7] In this sense, injustice is also a form of disrespect.

2.3 Disrespect vs. Social Pathology

Social pathology is a form of disrespect, which affects all the patterns of recognition—love, law, and solidarity.

It is necessary to analyze the Honnethian conceptualization of social pathology. First of all, Honneth assumes that the analysis of social pathologies must consider the empirical research, a look at the society itself, going beyond the conceptual work:

> I think the only thing that empirical research can do is to prepare empirical indications about pathological effects, and empirical research can definitely show in what direction the concrete institutionalization of *Sittlichkeit* always would have to go. At the moment in which *Sittlichkeit* is no longer seen as an already institutionalized fact,

[6] Honneth 1995, 132.

[7] Honneth 2007a, 71.

> then one needs some indication as to how to institutionalize *Sittlichkeit* always again, and there empirical research can help.[8]

According to Honneth, a social pathology demonstrates that people are not able to take part rationally in forms of social cooperation. He differentiates social pathologies from social injustice, because the later restricts participation in social processes of cooperation, whereas social pathologies impair reflexive access to primary systems of actions and norms.[9]Social pathology is one or a range of negative consequences experienced by society in the form of symptoms in their daily life. A group of individuals suffers the effects of some specific context, which affect them negatively and result in different symptoms, in the same way as a disease, a pathology.

For instance, when discussing disrespect in the pattern of love, Honneth has stated that torture causes a psychological death in the individual:

> These metaphorical allusions to physical suffering and death articulate the idea that the various forms of disregard for the psychological integrity of humans play the same negative role that organic infections take on in the context of the reproduction of the body. The experience of being socially denigrated or humiliated endangers the identity of human beings, just as infection with a disease endangers their physical life.[10]

Considering that, experiences of disrespect can cause symptoms in the victims.

Honneth introduces examples of symptoms of social pathologies. For him, the *rigidity* of the society leads to depression or loss of orientation as symptoms. It relates to the social pathology called *social shame.* Honneth understands that the feeling of shame is the most open of our moral feelings.[11] It includes not just the shyness of an exposed body, but also the violation of a continuation of an action.[12] The person has either a real or an imaginary interaction partner, whom witnesses the injured ego.[13] Social shame comprehends a feeling of denying oneself ego ideal, and also a feeling of low self-esteem coming from one's

[8] Honneth 2004b, 386.

[9] Honneth 2014a, 86.

[10] Honneth 1995, 135.

[11] Honneth 1995, 137.

[12] Honneth 1995, 137.

[13] Honneth 1995, 137.

interaction partner[14]. In any case, from Honneth, shame leads to disrespect and, as a consequence, to the impetus for a struggle for recognition.[15]

For Gwynn Markle, Honneth connects "*a theory of justice with the diagnosis of social pathologies and how such a method differs from, for example, contemporary Kantian methods such as Rawls's own strictly political approach to a theory of justice and even Habermas's recent work.*"[16]

The tradition of Critical Theory has been analyzing different social pathologies—for example Adorno and Horkheimer's approach of alienation, or Habermas' colonization of lifeworld -, and Honneth, following this tradition, intensely discusses the disrespect experienced by human beings in their processes of recognition. The disrespect can be represented by social pathologies.

Honneth recognizes that to identify a situation of social pathology, one must pay attention to social manifestations and sentiments, which sometimes are not easily identifiable.[17] For instance, it can be identified through diffuse moods of depression, loss of orientation, and 'reflexive consternation' (*reflexive Betroffenheit*).[18] For Honneth, empirical investigations rarely are able to perceive these diffuse moods and collective sentiments.[19] Therefore, based on Hegel and the

---

[14] Honneth 1995, 137.

[15] Honneth 1995, 137.

[16] Markle 2004, 383. In the same direction:

"This combination of a theory of social integration with the diagnostic of the social forms of individual pathology is in fact Honneth's idiosyncratic definition of social philosophy." (Deranty 2011, 66)

[17] Honneth 2014a, 87.

Regarding depression and recognition, see:

"The French sociologist Alain Ehrenberg, in an impressive study bearing the title La Fatigue d'être soi (Ehrenberg, 1998), arrived at the conclusion, after having sorted through the clinical evidence, that we are currently faced with a rapid rise in the frequency of depression; not merely a growing number of therapeutic findings but also the unprecedented sales of pharmaceutical anti-depressants show that, to a horrifying degree, full-blown depression is displacing the symptoms of neurosis. As a key to explain how this kind of illness has become a mass phenomenon Ehrenberg makes use of the idea that individuals have as it were been psychically overburdened by the diffuse but widespread demand that they must be themselves; the permanent compulsion to draw the material for an authentic self-realization from their own inner lives requires of individuals an ongoing form of introspection which must sooner or later leave them feeling empty; and the point at which inner experience no longer marks out the path for one's own life, even given a strong resolution that it do so, signals in Ehrenberg's view the moment when a depression begins (for conditions in Germany, see Frommer et al., 1999)". (Honneth 2004a, 475)

[18] Honneth 2014a, 87.

[19] Honneth 2014a, 87.

young Lukács, a better way to identify social pathologies is through the analysis of artistic manifestations in the communities.[20]

This work highlights the definition of social pathology because identifying a social pathology makes it possible for one to consider how to confront it, how to struggle for the recovering of her recognition[21]. Social pathology is also a form of disrespect.

2.4 Social Disrespect vs. Individual Disrespect

While I comprehend *social pathology* as an example of Honnethian *disrespect*, not all forms of disrespect can be called social pathologies.

It is justified by experiences of disrespect that happen individually. As a result, not all forms of disrespect are social pathologies, but all social pathologies are forms of disrespect.

As examples of individual disrespect, Honneth mentions individual harm, mental harm, and moral injury. Salonia clearly defines that "*For the Critical Theorist, suffering counts as the original form of an emancipatory interest, that is, an impulse to transform those social relations that cause this suffering.*"[22]

Honneth understands that stigmatization and all other forms of denials of recognition are forms of individual *mental harm* and *moral injury*[23]. Honneth analyzes the moral damage analytically and contends that the victim—the one not being recognized—must hold three conditions, which will make her vulnerable to suffering a moral injury.

First of all, the human being should be reflexively conscious of her condition, well-being, and moral vulnerability. If the subject is not conscious of her well-being and vulnerability, she would not feel injured.

I disagree with this prerequisite. Some societies and countries have part of the population not reflexively conscious of their individuality, a phenomenon caused by their cultural, political, or religious background. These contexts influence the individuality of persons, culminating in the absence of reaction. It was discussed by the first generation of the Frankfurt School—for instance, Max Horkheimer,

[20] Honneth 2014a, 87.

[21] It will be seem in the following chapters that, nowadays, there is a social pathology which prejudices recognition in its varied patterns: the social pathology of "indifference".

[22] Salonia 2008, 125.

[23] Honneth 2007a, 136.

Theodor Adorno, Herbert Marcuse, and Walter Benjamin. These authors called this phenomenon "alienation."

Herbert Marcuse states that alienation affects the relation of the person with herself, as well as with others. It is something that exists in the economic sphere and also in other life's dimensions[24].

Additionally, Theodor Adorno introduces the concept of *verwaltelte Welt*, a world permeated by different kinds of alienation. People are alienated at work as well as in their leisure time. The human being submits herself to homogeneous lifestyles and behaviors; there is no space for a full and individual formation of one's own identity. The individuals should act in the same way, the way defined by the structures of power, which alienate them all[25].

Whether, according to Honneth, there is a moral injury just in case the victim is conscious of his situation, then alienated subjects would not suffer from moral damage. If there is no moral injury, then there is no disrespect and injustice. Because of that, the first requisite of Honneth turns out to be wrong. If there are individuals who are not conscious of their situation, it already represents a concrete and primary offense: alienation is the first—and, nowadays, maybe one of the most prominent—form of moral injury.

My critique of Honneth could be further endorsed, if one thinks, for instance, of the case of child abuse. When a child suffers abuse, probably she is not fully aware of the crime—consider, for example, a child subjected to illegal labor; probably, this child does not know that "child labor is forbidden" in her society. This situation is a moral injury, independent of the fact of her being aware of her vulnerability or not.

Honneth goes further and holds that the second requisite for a moral injury is the violation of moral expectations. I agree with that, but I also think that disrespect can also limit the development of moral expectations. If one thinks about moral expectations being violated, one should also consider the ones who do not have the chance to develop their moral expectations freely.

Each person, according to the limits of her culture, develops moral expectations, makes plans about the future, and has expectations regarding individual and social behaviors. Nevertheless, some cultures limit an individual's expectations regarding, for instance, studies, work, family, and leisure. In some societies, disrespect does not just violate moral expectations, but also influences the origin and development of these expectations. Consider, as an example, a Muslim woman,

---

[24] Marcuse 1972, 17.

[25] Adorno 2008, 78.

who could decide not to marry, or to marry a non-Muslim man. Inserted in Islamic culture, she will not be allowed even to develop this kind of expectation.

I contend that disrespect, a social injustice or a moral injury do not presuppose that the victim should be "reflexively conscious" of the damage and that she will necessarily have violated moral expectations. It may be that she will not have the consciousness of her own moral expectations at all.

Honneth argues that moral injury results necessarily in the mental shock of the victim. I do not agree on that, as the alienation makes individuals not self-conscious of their situation. If they suffer a moral offense, they may not feel a mental shock instantly. The alienation suffered during their lives already injured them.

One could ask how these subjects should struggle for their recognition if they are not conscious of the situation and not directly mentally shocked. I will see in subsequent chapters that the subject directly injured is not necessarily the one to exercise the struggles for recognition. In cases like this, the ones who are not entirely alienated should struggle for the others. After the process of struggle, recognition will be recovered in this community, and they all will be conscious of their own identities.

Thirdly, Honneth states that in the situation of a moral injury, individuals share intersubjective presuppositions; they wait for the same affirmative reactions. When some response is very different from the expectation, it provokes a mental shock in a conscientious individual; there is a moral injury, which prejudices recognition[26]. A minimum of intersubjective presuppositions should exist inside a community of individuals. Nevertheless, I argue that, because of the alienation of some individuals, alienated ones do not necessarily share all the same intersubjective presuppositions as the ones that are reflexively conscientious.

2.5 Conclusion of Chap. 2

Chapter 2 has explained the relevance of considering the offenses to recognition, as they represent different forms of limiting the possibilities of the subject to achieve social freedom and autonomy.

I have discussed the difference between individual disrespect—which can happen within all patterns of recognition, but especially in the pattern of love -, and social disrespect—when affecting the community.

[26] Honneth 2007a, 134.

Furthermore, the institute of disrespect was related to injustice and social pathology. Social pathologies are forms of disrespect and moral injustice. The analysis of them, inside the hermeneutical context of injustice, is essential for beginning struggles for recognition.

Chapter 2 has criticized Honneth's premises regarding disrespect. I do not agree with the author when he states that moral injury presupposes an individual's consciousness of his well-being and individuality, as well as moral expectations and shared intersubjective presuppositions. I have demonstrated that alienation and other kinds of social pathologies interfere in the formation of moral expectations, and sometimes individuals do not have consciousness of their role as victims of disrespect and, as a consequence, agents of struggles for recognition.

For Honneth, every time a person suffers disrespect, it is fundamental that this situation is confronted by struggles for recognition. Recognition is a moral act, and it can be preserved through struggles for recognition.

The struggles are a crucial element of Honneth's theory. Whereas recognition works as a moral ideal, struggles for recognition are empirically possible and necessary. They can represent public movements, strikes or protests, as well as private actions, which try to confront disrespect and restore the patterns of recognition. All these kinds of struggles are fundamental. Each person and each community should be aware of the accountability to confront practices of disrespect. The next chapter will demonstrate the role of struggles for recognition.

3 What are Struggles for Recognition?

Chapters 1 and 2 have studied what *recognition* and *disrespect* mean for Axel Honneth. Now, Chap. 3 will analyze the third element of Honneth's theory: the struggles for recognition. First of all, the chapter will indicate why recognition and struggles work dynamically. Struggles are actions which make recognition possible, and an analysis of the struggles of a community identifies the claims of these persons.

The chapter studies the concept of struggle for Honneth and presents the foremost critiques against it. I understand that struggles should have a private dimension, not just a public one. It seems that Honneth focuses on the public patterns of recognition—namely law and solidarity, as he states that all struggles presuppose a minimum of deliberative democratic attitudes. Nevertheless, it is also necessary to review the concept of struggle for societies with a low level of democracy, considering the possibility of also adopting democratic attitudes into one's private life.

Additionally, the chapter will demonstrate who is responsible for engaging in struggles for recognition. It will be argued that the struggles for recognition should be practiced not just by the one offended, but also by the ones who witness a situation of disrespect. More than that, although individuals tend to engage only if they are related to some case of disrespect, I argue that the agents of struggle are not necessarily acquaintances of the victim of disrespect. Struggles for unknown persons are also necessary.

3.1 Struggles against Disrespect and for Recognition

Recognition, according to Honneth, does not exist separately from struggles.

C. Diamantino Esser Santana, *Recognized Women:*, Juridicum – Schriften zur Rechtsphilosophie, https://doi.org/10.1007/978-3-658-46849-1_3

Honneth states that the concept of struggles should come mainly from the theories of Hegel and Mead. He assumes that there are vast discussions on the concept of struggle from Marx to Sorel, and Sartre[1]. Nevertheless:

> None of the three authors was able to contribute to the further systematic development of the conception founded by Hegel and deepened by Mead. Although, in empirical contexts, they often made virtuoso use of the model of recognition, its normative implication remained too opaque, too alien even, for them to be able to move it to a new level of explication.[2]

Honneth follows Hegel, considering that ethical life is formed from conflicts and struggles for the recovery of human beings' recognition: "*In this way the history of an ethical sphere can be thought of as a conflictual process whereby a certain validity surplus initially inherent in every ethical norm is gradually stripped away*".[3]

In *Freedom's Right*, Honneth argues that the current claims of justice must be analyzed from the perspective of struggles for recognition of individuals. The analysis of struggles for recognition is fundamental to the study of social justice, to identify what kinds of claims future generations and societies are going to demand:

> We will only be able to get a clear sense of the future requirements of social justice if we recall, by addressing the struggles that have been fought on the normative foundation of modernity, the claims that have not yet been redeemed in the historical process filled with social demands for the realization of institutional promises of freedom.[4]

He endorses that an ethical relation to the idea of freedom requires an analysis of social reality. The institutions that make individuals experience recognition in the

---

[1] Honneth 1995, 146.

[2] Honneth 1995, 159.

[3] Honneth 2014b, 824.

[4] Honneth 2014a, viii.

interaction with others have relevance for the achievement of freedom.[5] Considering that recognition relates to justice, it is necessary, according to Honneth, to struggle for the preservation or recovery of recognition. Now I will first clarify what Honneth understands by struggles for recognition.

3.2 Definition of "*Struggle*"

In the conclusion of *Struggle for recognition*, Honneth states that, over time, the struggles for recognition will be the ones responsible for showing to what extent recognition presupposes modifications in the capitalist society or a turn to political republicanism, ecologically based asceticism, or collective existentialism[6]. Struggles carry the claims of a specific community. Struggles are always in construction, dynamic; they are a living organism, a process:

> According to Honneth, although some social struggles are driven by self-interested conflicts over resources, once the ideology of instrumentalist reason is undermined, we can see these struggles as also giving expression to moral claims that can serve as normative standards.[7]

Different communities or countries experience different offenses in their patterns of recognition:

> Empirically, whether the cognitive potential inherent in feeling hurt or ashamed becomes a moral-political conviction depends above all on how the affected subject's cultural-political environment is constructed: only if the means of articulation of a social movement are available can the experience of disrespect become a source of

[5] Honneth 2014a, 65. See also:

Meine Lösung der damit umrissenen Aufgabe bestand in dem Vorschlag, zwei Erkenntnisleistungen zu unterscheiden, die die um Emanzipation kämpfenden Gruppen gleichermaßen zum Zweck der Sicherstellung der praktischen Erfolgsaussichten ihres Handelns vollziehen können müssen: Einerseits sind sie darauf angewiesen, sich entgegen der Tendenz zu deren Naturalisierung die ständige Deutungsoffenheit der etablierten Normen zu Bewusstsein zu bringen, andererseits müssen sie die Interessen zu durchschauen lernen, die die Fixierung auf die gegebene, institutionell verkörperte Deutungspraxis zu erklären helfen. Beide Erkenntnisleistungen repräsentieren Wissensformen, um es zu wiederholen, an deren Erwerb die um ihre soziale Einbeziehung kämpfenden Gruppen deswegen ein Interesse haben müssen, weil sie damit die Erfolgsaussichten ihrer Bemühungen erhöhen. (Honneth 2020, 318).

[6] Honneth 1995, 179.

[7] Anderson 2011, 53.

> motivation for acts of political resistance. The developmental logic of such collective movements can, however, only be discovered via an analysis that attempts to explain social struggles on the basis of the dynamics of moral experiences.[8]

For Honneth, there is a feeling experienced by individuals or communities, which begin the majority of struggles for recognition. This feeling is shame.[9]

When discussing feelings and emotions which motivate struggles, Honneth adheres to John Dewey's conception of human emotions, coming from his pragmatist psychology[10]. For Dewey, human emotions are attached to the experiences the subject has during her life. She can have either positive or negative feelings, but first she should experience different moments in her life, to form a variety of feelings. On the other hand, the tradition of psychology used to state that the emotions first exist in the inner human beings, not being attached to the experiences itself.

For Dewey and also for Honneth:

> According to this conception, negative feelings such as anger, indignation, and sorrow constitute the affective side of the shift of attention towards one's own expectations that inevitably occurs as soon as one has difficulty making the step one planned to make upon completing an action. Positive feelings such as joy or pride, by contrast, arise when one is suddenly freed from a burdensome state of excitement, because one has been able to find a suitable, successful solution to a pressing action problem.[11]

As a result, when experiencing these emotions, the human being realizes that her own person depends on the recognition of others[12]. "*In the context of the emotional responses associated with shame, the experience of being disrespected can become the motivational impetus for a struggle for recognition.*"[13]

I understand that not just social struggles, observed in the public spaces, can indicate society's claims. The private life of individuals also carries struggles, which sometimes cannot be publicized. One should also consider the private struggles for recognition.

Honneth begins his analysis on the concept of "struggle" from Machiavelli and Hobbes. More than the Hobbesian model of struggle based on self-preservation,

---

[8] Honneth 1995, 139.

[9] Honneth 1995, 137.

[10] Honneth 1995, 136.

[11] Honneth 1995, 136.

[12] Honneth 1995, 138.

[13] Honneth 1995, 138.

for Honneth the conflict that triggers the struggle for recognition has an ethical nature, and it relates to the ethics and intersubjectivity of human individuality.[14]

Many other thinkers, such as Marx and Hegel[15], further developed the concept of struggle.

Taking Hegel into consideration, Honneth understands that the Hegelian struggle aims at different claims. The first are claims to the subject's subjectivity. The second are claims for social respect for property rights[16].

For Hegel, the struggle has a positive dimension, because it makes the subject aware of the relations of recognition, with a consciousness-forming function[17].

For Honneth, struggles must be interpreted as a variety of actions, but also a manner of defending moral roles[18]. Social struggles are always tentative to improve a social situation. There is no recognition without a prior struggle.

Considering that the individual and his society are always subjected to offenses to the patterns of recognition, the existence of struggles is necessary. Nevertheless, I understand that people do not comprehend their role in the dynamics of struggling, in a way that they usually transfer the accountability for the recovery of recognition to the state or the law, as I will further see.

3.3 Critiques of the Honnethian Definition of "*Struggle*"

Some authors, such as Pensky, criticize Honneth, arguing that struggles necessarily need public institutional intervention to be finally solved:

> The *Struggle for Recognition* is not entirely clear in its explanation of how cultural struggles over 'secondary interpretations' of esteem correspond to social and political institutions. Such struggles after all become visible as moments in a story of the changing modes of social integration in modern societies only insofar as they are *resolved*, and such resolutions are invariably institutional ones.[19]

---

[14] Honneth 1995, 17.

[15] "With this reinterpretation of the Hobbesian model, Hegel introduces a virtually epoch-making new version of the conception of social struggle, according to which practical conflict between subjects can be understood as an ethical moment in a movement occurring within a collective social life." (Honneth 1995, 17).

[16] Honneth 1995, 21.

[17] Honneth 1995, 26.

[18] Honneth 1995, 168.

[19] Pensky 2011, 149.

Pensky commits two errors. First of all, he understands that struggles can be finished and solved once and for all. On the contrary, Honneth—following Hegelian historicism—considers that the processes of struggling are continuous, and the patterns of recognition will be continuously violated, leading to constant and dynamic struggles. Over time, the community will acquire more conditions to achieve more recognition, but it is almost utopic to imagine a society without any disrespect.

Secondly, Pensky understands that the solution for situations of disrespect generally will require the intervention of public institutions—for instance, law or state. This work advocates precisely the opposite: there are forms of struggling for women's recognition that do not require such institutions, and these are the necessary actions for improvement of a recognition, especially in non-democratic societies.

Rancière goes beyond these discussions and holds that Honnethian struggles do not strive for recognition, but for places, identities, and parts:

> Because if recognition is not merely a response to something already existing, if it is an original configuration of the common world, this means that individuals and groups are always, in some way, recognized with a place and a competence so that the struggle is not "for recognition", but for another form of recognition: a redistribution of the places, the identities, and the parts.[20]

Rancière misunderstands the amplitude of the concept of recognition. Struggles for places, identities, parts, and other perspectives are part of recognition. It culminates in the formation of an individual's identity, coming from a complex process of affirmation and emancipation.

Mark, on his part, argues that Honneth's theory is not clear in why groups would engage in struggles for recognition, and how it would be practiced between people with social differences:

> The struggle for recognition, for Honneth, is a process whereby ignored groups educate the wider public regarding how the general norms accepted by all apply to their particular cases. Without further elaboration, it is difficult to see why such attempts should meet with any resistance, because it provides no account of what other groups would stand to lose from the recognition of previously ignored kinds of achievements. Honneth allows that there will be no conclusive end to the efforts of groups to raise the social value of their abilities and achievements just because there is 'no adequate way of anchoring [the valuation of activities] in something like a value-neutral, purely

[20] Rancière 2016, 90.

> "technical" functional order'. Yet this prospect does not seem to worry Honneth too much as he never develops the point.[21]

Mark questions what would motivate people to struggle? What would make people engage in the struggles of others? Coming from an ethics of recognition, social differences do not interfere in the practices of struggle, because human beings would feel morally responsible for struggling against disrespect. I have seen that solidarity relates to compassion and care, and human beings have the moral obligation to struggle for the recognition of themselves and other subjects in the same way.

To make it clearer, I will inquire about who should struggle for recognition.

3.4 Who should Struggle?

It is relevant to evaluate who are the subjects who begin the struggle. I argue that, in any situation of disrespect, struggles must always begin. It should occur even if a victim of disrespect begins struggles inside herself for the recovery of recognition. When someone suffers a disrespect, the first step toward the recovery of recognition occurs when this person identifies which nuances of her own self-respect, self-confidence, self-esteem are being damaged, and how she could confront the practices of disrespect against her. In other words, she acknowledges that she was victim of a misrecognition and that she may begin struggles inside herself. Nevertheless, although this necessary consciousness of a disrespect and a first self-centered struggle for recognition is required, sometimes it may not be sufficient.

Let me present an example of spousal abuse. It is clear that, sometimes, the female victim of disrespect does not have the conditions to free herself. She cannot engage in a struggle for her recognition precisely at the moment of suffering disrespect. In these cases, I understand that each person in her community who witnesses the disrespect is a necessary agent in the dynamic of ethical life, having the accountability to struggle for her and, as a consequence, for her community.

It may be that a situation of disrespect occurs in a woman's private life, and there is no witness at the time of disrespect. In this case, I argue that she should try to find support and care afterward, as soon as possible. Even if she chooses not to request official assistance—for instance, going to the police, she could at least share her story with some friend or relative, to feel cared for and appreciated.

---

[21] Mark 2014, 27.

If the woman shares her story of disrespect with someone, this person, then, is a witness of a situation of disrespect, and he is responsible for supporting this woman and trying to recover, at least, her pattern of love.

I am not encouraging witnesses of situations of disrespect to act on behalf of the victims necessarily in public instances. I am aware that, in particular, cases involving violence against women may require their exclusive complaint—for example filing a police report or the legal requirement for divorce. I argue that a struggle for recognition can happen in different forms, such as the support of victims' self-confidence. The simple act of listening to this woman, caring for her, telling her that someone cares about her is a form of endorsing that her recognition is not completely damaged.

Additionally, from the point of view of the witness of an instance of disrespect, the situation of disrespect can involve two species of victim: (i) an unknown person, a woman whom the witness does not know at all; or (ii) an acquaintance, a friend, a relative, or a colleague, someone whom the witness knows. I argue that struggling for recognition is a moral obligation, and the one who witnessed disrespect should struggle, independently of knowing the victim in advance. Struggles for recognition should occur in every situation of disrespect.

According to Honneth, individuals achieve or maintain their recognition by social confirmation. That means, their personality is confirmed by individualization and inclusion. By doing so, societies can increase their social integration and guarantee equal participation for the citizens[22].

I will see in the next chapter that, nowadays, there is a social pathology called indifference, which reduces the struggles for recognition and compromises the protection of recognition. Usually, people do not take action for the recovery of patterns of recognition of individuals whom they do not know—and, sometimes, even of individuals they know. Societies experience isolation of individuals, in a way that sometimes people do not mind about injustices and disrespect committed against other human beings. Indifference occurs in different societies and cultures.

It will be further explained that practices of indifference should be confronted by collective solidarity. If we struggle against indifference, then women's recognition would be achievable. I understand that each culture has its own patterns of recognition and practices of disrespect. Nevertheless, I think that it is possible to

[22] "If these background convictions are now retrospectively made explicit, then two criteria result which, taken together, can justify the talk of progress in recognition conditions. On the one hand we are dealing with a process of individualization, i.e. with increasing the chances of legitimate articulation of personality portions; on the other hand with a process of social inclusion, i.e. with growing involvement of subjects in the circle of full members of society." (Honneth 2004b, 360).

increase recognition for all of them if I focus the struggles on the indifference, especially on the private sphere of recognition.

Honneth has stated, in an article published in 2012, that, in the West, struggles for recognition are seen as negative and violent. People who are struggling for a minimal inclusion in society, striving for minimal economic or political recognition—further referred to as "invisibles" by Honneth—, are seen as savages.

> One part of the struggle for recognition, namely that conducted from below by the members of the so-called 'underclass', therefore now takes place in the brutalized form of merely battling for public visibility or compensatory respect: because one is no longer included in the official, societally sanctioned arenas where respect can be acquired, the focus is on wresting social recognition outside the entrance gates by non-normed means.[23]

There is a tendency nowadays to dramatize conflicts, and the movements for a recovery of recognition turns out to be misinterpreted: "*Social conflict has thus been barbarized in the sense that the struggle for recognition in past decades has so emphatically lost its moral basis that it has been turned into an arena of decidedly rampant self-assertion.*"[24]

This discussion brings me to the comprehension of struggles as a public or a private instance.

3.5 The Struggles for Recognition and their Private and Public Dimensions

Taking the definition of Honneth into consideration, many interpreters[25] see social struggles as necessarily public acts with a political background—for instance, labor strikes. Nevertheless, the societies with restrictions regarding public manifestations also need to protect their moral necessities, "*The 'grammar' of these struggles turns out to be 'moral' in the sense that the feelings of outrage and indignation generated by the rejection of claims to recognition imply normative judgments*

[23] Honneth 2012a, 17.

[24] Honneth, 2012a, 18.

[25] For instance, Van den Brink states that the political culture is conducive in permitting struggles for recognition and giving tools for people to struggle, specifically if people are able to organize themselves in social movements (Van den Brink 2011, 168).

about the legitimacy of social arrangements."[26] I contend that struggles should not be only public acts, but also private actions.

Honneth and many other Western authors—for example, Habermas—fail to evaluate their theories without reference to democratic models.

I argue that the achievement of social justice and women's recognition must be studied especially for countries with limitations on public struggles for recognition. It is relevant to find forms to increase practices of struggling in such countries, to increase their levels of social justice and women's recognition.

In the article "*Democracy as reflexive cooperation: John Dewey and the Theory of Democracy Today*" (1998, referred to as "*Democracy as reflexive cooperation*"), Honneth concludes that democracy is not just a political concept, but also a social ideal. The public spheres of discussion and communicative action are possible if all the participants have the same access and rights to be in a pre-political situation, which makes them able to insert themselves in the public debate, meaning that they are allowed to develop public struggles. This idea of pre-political conditions comes from John Dewey.

Honneth holds that intersubjective cohesion and solidarity are possible in societies which have the normative conditions of liberal democratic societies. Nevertheless, Honneth does not clarify what he understands as "normative conditions of liberal democratic societies"[27].

Unquestionably, democratic societies hold more conditions for citizens to express themselves. Their dissatisfaction with offenses to patterns of recognition can be brought to public debates. There, people have freedom of expression and freedom of speech, for instance. Nevertheless, to achieve women's recognition, applicable to different cultural contexts, one of my objectives is to study the theory of Honneth, finding forms of implementing struggles for recognition also in authoritarian regimes, with a low level of liberal democracy.

I argue that it is possible to create normative liberal democratic conditions in authoritarian societies, to guarantee the achievement of recognition for those communities. To make it possible, one should focus on the population, and not on the state—governmental instances. Here, I need to reiterate that Honneth mentions the democratic attitudes to be adopted by individuals, without any necessary relation with the state.

The work does not advocate that struggling means necessarily going against the law or the state. In some societies, citizens are not allowed to confront the authorities.

---

[26] Anderson 2011, 53.

[27] Honneth 2007a, 254.

On the contrary, I understand that the concept of struggles for recognition should be expanded in a way that individual and potentially trivial actions are viewed as struggles. I call them 'potentially trivial,' as they may seem to have no significance.

For instance, one should consider the pattern of love, the private relationships between lovers, relatives, and friends in their daily lives. In a situation of disrespect in the pattern of love, for instance, it seems that Honneth would suggest a struggle located in the patterns of law and solidarity, coming from the cooperation and public engagement in the process, turning the disrespect into something public. If the state and the law can help, they would also be included in the process of struggle.

Although Honneth recognizes that solidarity relates to care, practical involvement and engaged praxis, the author at the same time presupposes the existence of normative deliberative democracy, allowing people to publicly struggle for recognition. For me, to achieve women's recognition, the first elements are more important than the focus on democracy. The increase of democratic attitudes is always necessary and should be taken into consideration, but, firstly, his theory should analyze the forms of struggling in a private dimension of life, without necessary public support.

According to Honneth, recognition is related to self-confidence, self-respect, and social/self esteem. A victim of misrecognition in the sphere of love, for instance, has her self-confidence violated. The struggle of someone else in her name could at least reestablish her social confidence.

Evidently, the theory of recognition presupposes the achievement of the three patterns of recognition—love, rights, and solidarity –and the reestablishment of recognition regarding this woman should involve the other two patterns, namely the patterns of rights and solidarity. Nevertheless, my work contends that the recovery of just one pattern of recognition—for instance, the pattern of love—is a significant step for a future restoration of other patterns of recognition of the society in question.

To be recognized means that a person has the opportunity to enjoy her personal life (pattern of love) and her social relations (as a holder of rights and duties—pattern of rights—and as a participant citizen—pattern of solidarity).

Struggles for unknown persons are necessary, as misrecognition affects not just the one directly being offended, but also the community[28]. When a woman is being abused, for instance, and no one takes action, the community where she

---

[28] Honneth 1995, 162.

lives is also being abused. Struggles against disrespect will always contribute to the recognition of the offended woman and her community.

The full enjoyment of the patterns of recognition results in a satisfactory formation of human identity, reflecting in the ethical life[29]. A person with a self-determined identity is more capable of being ethical and behaving in a solidary manner. Struggles are always a way to expand the pattern of rights, in a way that Honneth endorses Hegel's and George Mead's[30] defenses of it:

> Like Hegel in his treatment of the formative process of the 'collective will', Mead views the moral development of societies as a process in which the meaning of legal recognition is gradually broadened. Both thinkers agree that, historically, the potential for individuality is only unleashed via an increase in legally enforced freedoms. Like Hegel, Mead considers the motor of these directed changes to be a struggle in which subjects continually strive to expand the range of their intersubjectively guaranteed rights and, in so doing, to raise the level of their personal autonomy. For both thinkers, then, the historical liberation of individuality occurs in the form of a long-term struggle for recognition.[31]

Honneth has argued in a recent interview that struggles should be seen as a productive force in the human life-world:

> And it takes thousands of forms. It starts with the young baby, who is struggling against his or her parents. It's what's happening in classrooms in different forms. It slowly changes the way we understand the principles of recognition, the way we understand ourselves, and it slowly helps to make our societies normatively better.[32]

Every society should find ways of struggling in their private sphere, in their intimacy, even in small communities and family situations. *"(...) we as human*

---

[29] "The point of departure for a social theory of this sort has to be the basic claim on which the pragmatist Mead and the early Hegel are agreed in principle: the reproduction of social life is governed by the imperative of mutual recognition, because one can develop a practical relation-on-self only when one has learned to view oneself, from the normative perspective of one's partners in interaction, as their social addressee". (Honneth 1995, 92).

[30] It is important to highlight that, according to Jean-Philippe Deranty, Honneth comes from the tradition of Georg Mead, but, at some point of his studies, he abandoned it:

"In "Postmodern Identity and Object-Relations Theory: On the Seeming Obsolescence of Psychoanalysis", published in 1999, Honneth continued to use the parallelisms between the American behaviourist and the English psychoanalyst's models of ontogenesis to underpin his intersubjectivistic subject-theory. However, in texts after 2000, the reliance on Mead has been abandoned." (Deranty 2011, 82).

[31] Honneth 1995, 84.

[32] Honneth 2013, 217.

beings have a permanent demand imposed on ourselves, a demand to make things better."[33] Honneth assumes that struggles for recognition are a moral obligation of human beings.

Struggles for recognition are, then, private and public. Private struggles for recognition may exist within personal relationships of love, for instance in the family context or friendship. Public struggles for recognition may happen through different forms, such as public debates, protests, or political engagement. Both nuances of the struggles—private and public—may be better exercised if the individuals have democratic instances, not just in a political form, but also through democratic attitudes and opportunities to discussion, debate, and exercise of autonomy, even within family and private contexts.

Considering that, this work will propose different forms of struggle in subsequent chapters. When one sees a situation of disrespect, one should develop ways of confronting it, putting aside indifferent behavior and turning into an active struggler.

3.6 Conclusion of Chap. 3

Chapter 3 has stated that, firstly, Honnethian struggles for recognition should clarify how to guarantee normative deliberative democratic conditions for different societies, especially the ones with low level or no democracy at all.

Secondly, struggles should be more than public movements and, in the case of women's recognition, focus on the pattern of love as well, where the majority of offenses to women's recognition occur. As Honneth comes from a public paradigm of struggling for recognition, he appears to consider as necessary the struggles especially in the patterns of law and solidarity. However, it is not possible for this to occur in authoritarian states, for instance. Considering this context, struggles should also be addressed to the pattern of love, including also "potentially trivial actions," more than just public social movements or petitions at public instances.

Thirdly, Chap. 3 has defined that the agents of struggles must be anyone who witnesses situations of disrespect, and not just the victim or her acquaintances.

Finally, the connotation of struggles nowadays should also be reviewed, as societies tend to brutalize them, considering struggles as practices of disorder. On the contrary, struggles are, first of all, moral attitudes.

---

[33] Honneth 2013, 217.

The chapter has also identified critiques of the concept of struggles. For Pensky, Honneth errs, because, for him, struggles usually presupposes the presence of public institutions. Rancière, on his part, understands that Honnethian struggles are searching for identity and other aspects of an individual's life, and not for recognition. Mark questions the motives, which make individuals struggle. He also asks why people would engage for the ones who are located in different social categories. Some of these critiques are solved utilizing my proposal of struggles, which will be studied in the subsequent chapters.

Part II
Proposal

4 How to Struggle in the Three Patterns of Recognition?

> Martin Luther King Jr. believed that the greatest tragedy of his era was the "appalling silence of the good people."[1]

The first chapter has studied the definition of *recognition*. Sequentially, Chap. 2 has described the offenses to recognition, which are called *disrespect*. When recognition is denied by disrespect, then it is necessary to struggle for recognition. Chapter 3 has analyzed that there are different forms of *struggling*; for instance, struggles should come from different agents, and not just necessarily from the direct victims of disrespect.

After the assessment of Honnethian theory from the elements of *recognition, disrespect,* and *struggles for recognition*, now I will inquire how to struggle in each pattern of recognition.

I understand that the theory of recognition does not sufficiently explore struggles, especially for societies that do not have all the democratic elements supposedly necessary for the achievement of recognition. The theory of recognition is based on a minimum of political democratic institutions and democratic attitudes, but I understand that it is crucial to create forms of struggles for women's recognition detached from it.

The work proposes, then, different forms of struggling for recognition, following the division of love, solidarity, and law.

Before analyzing each pattern separately, this chapter focuses on a struggle useful for the three patterns of recognition.

---

[1] Peters 2014, 9.

C. Diamantino Esser Santana, *Recognized Women:*, Juridicum – Schriften zur Rechtsphilosophie, https://doi.org/10.1007/978-3-658-46849-1_4

4.1 The Struggle against Indifference

Indifference is a term with different connotations in philosophy and psychology. This work interprets indifference from three different perspectives: as a negative emotion, intentional behavior, and social pathology. My approach to indifference is justified by several reasons.

First of all, coming from the Honnethian theory of recognition, I have already proven that any situation of disrespect damages recognition; that every person who witnesses a situation of disrespect is an agent responsible for struggling for recognition; and that the achievement of recognition is possible only if people struggle for it. On these grounds, the presence of indifference—either as an emotion, behavior, or social pathology—results in the absence of struggles. Any interpretation of indifference as a neutral or a positive institute is erroneous, because in the context of recognition, it is fundamental that people not behave neutrally, people should struggle.

Secondly, indifference as a behavior spreads in different cultural contexts and societies. As a result, it damages the achievement of recognition from a macro perspective, as people generally do not engage in struggles.

More than an emotion, indifference is inserted in a shared ethics, from the moment when human beings adopt it as a principle of their actions. Indifference comes from an individual psychological perspective and turns out to be socially shared—it is not just individually practiced anymore. I will see that, in the end, indifference may be a social pathology.

Indifference damages the patterns of love, law, and solidarity. As a consequence, struggles against indifference should happen in all of them.

Although I reject the interpretations of indifference as a neutral or a positive feeling, for the sake of accuracy, I will briefly assess these perspectives.

4.1.1 Neutral Indifference

For the stoics, someone "indifferent" is neither virtuous nor vicious, the one indifferent is neutral.[2]

[2] Ferrater Mora 1964, 929. See, for instance, Marcus Aurelius: "XV. To live happily is an inward power of the soul, when she is affected with indifferency, towards those things that are by their nature indifferent." (Marcus Aurelius, Eleventh Book. 2013, 19).

If a neutral life is exercised in a vicious or in a virtuous way, then this life is not indifferent anymore[3]. I do not agree with the stoic definition of indifference because, in the context of the theory of recognition, a neutral life may be vicious when it damages recognition and the moral obligation to struggle. If the individual finds situations of disrespect during her life, then it is necessary for her to engage in struggles. If she stays neutral in a situation of disrespect, the indifference as a neutral feeling results in a neutral and apathetic behavior, damaging the achievement of recognition through struggles.

4.1.2 Positive Indifference

Some authors understand indifference as an expression of free will. Indifference would mean the freedom not to act, not to do anything, a kind of negative freedom[4]. To be indifferent, according to these authors, is guaranteed by the human right to freedom.

I reject such an interpretation of indifference, because an ethics of recognition presupposes people's engagement in struggles. In a situation of disrespect, it is fundamental to struggle.

Michael Walzer interprets *toleration* in different forms. First of all, toleration may be seen as a *benign indifference*[5]. *Toleration* means an absence of actions, willing to respect different cultures or minorities—a resigned acceptance of difference for the sake of peace—. It turns to be a *benign indifference* when the acceptance is passive, relaxed, benignly indifferent to difference.[6]

Nevertheless, for Walzer, toleration is not enough to appreciate an individual or a community. He states that mutual respect is also necessary: "*To tolerate someone else is an act of power; to be tolerated is an acceptance of weakness. We should aim at something better than this combination, something beyond toleration, something like mutual respect*".[7]

---

[3] Ferrater Mora 1964, 929.

[4] Ferrater Mora 1964, 929.

[5] Walzer 1997, 10.

[6] Walzer 1997, 10. For Walzer, toleration may be also represented through a kind of moral stoicism that comprehends that the "other" has rights to exercise even in unattractive ways (Walzer 1997, 10). It could be understood as a kind of curiosity and openness to the others (Walzer 1997, 10). Finally, toleration could also be understood as an enthusiastic endorsement of difference, either from an asthetic endorsement of the diversity of God's creation or of the natural world, or from a necessary condition for human flourishing. (Walzer 1997, 10).

[7] Walzer 1997, 52.

According to him, difference should be twice tolerated, on a personal and a political level. It holds different feelings such as resignation, indifference, stoicism, curiosity, and enthusiasm.[8]

Nevertheless, I understand that toleration should have limits. I do not agree with the blind toleration of cultural practices of disrespect. I agree with the respect of cultural differences if the cultures adhere to the ethics of recognition. In the case of Honnethian disrespect in a cultural manifestation, then individuals should not tolerate it anymore. On the contrary, individuals are responsible for struggling for the recognition of this community.

Paul Dumouchel also has a positive interpretation of indifference. For him, in the context of capitalism, there is a change of perspective from solidarity to scarcity. Scarcity means a contract of mutual indifference[9].

Dumouchel explains that, on the one hand, formalists understand that the market, by definition, is fair, and the agents are rational and do not prejudice each other at all[10]. On the other hand, substantivists claim that the market economy is destructive and the bonds of solidarity have been damaged[11]. The substantivists, then, consider the institute of indifference as a negative result of this process.

Dumouchel classifies himself from the perspective of mimetic theory, believing that neither formalists nor substantivists are right. He advocates for a positive meaning of indifference, as it frees the human beings of obligations of solidarity, which will result in violence[12].

The author sees obligations of solidarity as negative, because they will always result in violence and duties of revenge. When people create strong bonds of solidarity between each other, they cannot accept any threats to their peers, and they will incur violent acts for the benefit of the members to whom they are

---

[8] Walzer 1997, 91.

[9] Dumouchel 2003, 155.

[10] Dumouchel 2003, 159.

[11] Dumouchel 2003, 159.

[12] "The substantivists on the contrary will claim that modern market economy has historically been destructive of traditional bonds of solidarity; it has instituted indifference to the suffering of others as a way of life. [...]Mimetic theory suggests that we can share neither of these points of view. The destruction of sacred bonds of solidarity periodically strengthened by sacrificial rituals cannot be such a bad thing. Substantivists also fail to see that our indifference, which they condemn, protects us from our own violence, and that by condemning it they condemn own violence but fail to renounce it. [...] Justice as fairness is justice amongst those who are indifferent. Yet we should not condemn it, for until everyone has renounced his or her own violence, it is what protects each individual against all those who are not indifferent. The ambivalence of scarcity is our own ambivalence." (Dumouchel 2003, 159)

solidary. In the end, solidarity will result in a conflict for protection, in a dispute for space, and acts of violence.

For Dumouchel, solidarity was replaced by scarcity, which has resulted in practices of indifference. Nowadays, there is no obligation of solidarity and bondedness anymore.[13] In his words:

> Traditional bonds of solidarity impose obligations of violence and duties of revenge. [...] Scarcity isolates conflicts. Just as it allows us not to help those whose basic needs are not satisfied, it allows us, "not to get involved" in other people's conflicts. Scarcity generates, to borrow an apt phrase from Norman Geras, a "contract of mutual indifference".[14]

The interpretation of Dumouchel is the opposite of the ethics of recognition. Solidary acts are necessary for the recovery of recognition of people and the formation of struggles for recognition. Struggling for recognition is a moral obligation for all human beings—regardless of being a direct victim of disrespect—, and the human being's relationships are based on active feelings such as compassion, care, and affection.

4.1.3 Negative Indifference

> For this village, even were it incomparably more remote and incredibly more primitive, is the West, the West onto which I have been so strangely grafted. These people cannot be, from the point of view of power, strangers anywhere in the world; they have made the modern world, in effect, even if they do not know it. The most illiterate among them is related, in a way that I am not, to Dante, Shakespeare, Michelangelo, Aeschylus, Da Vinci, Rembrandt, and Racine; the cathedral at Chartres says something to them which it cannot say to me, as indeed would New York's Empire State Building, should anyone here ever see it. Out of their hymns and dances come Beethoven and Bach. Go back a few centuries and they are in their full glory – but I am in Africa, watching the conquerors arrive. (1953: 635)[15]

The theory of Honneth had addressed elements of indifference when he discussed invisibility, individualization, reification, the freezing of society, and autonomization. I will analyze all these institutes and contend that their characteristics can be

[13] Dumouchel 2003, 155.

[14] Dumouchel 2003, 155.

[15] James Baldwin *apud* Stichweh 1997, 12.

summed up in the institute of indifference as a negative emotion and intentional behavior. I will prove that indifference is the opposite of Honnethian solidarity.

Honneth's first approach to this topic occurred in 2001 when he discussed "*invisibility.*"

In "*Invisibility: on the epistemology of 'recognition',*" Honneth quotes the book "*The Invisible Man*" by Ralph Ellison. In this story, invisibility means non-existence in a social sense. It is not related to a physical non-presence, but, more than that, with someone being made invisible[16]. People who suffer acts of invisibility eventually have social meaninglessness, "*as a result 'invisibility' here cannot designate a cognitive fact but rather must mean a kind of social state of affairs*"[17]. For Honneth, social invisibility is a form of moral disrespect because the subject makes the other invisible and with no worth[18].

To make someone invisible is to "look through" this person, without even seeing her as a human being. There is no perception of this person at all[19].

Invisibility is different from prejudice, because in prejudice someone is seen, and then "seen as" inferior. There is a difference between "looking through" someone and "seeing someone as"[20].

Making someone invisible also has a performative aspect because it is represented by human behaviors and gestures. There is an intentionality "in looking through" someone. For Honneth, invisibility has an intention of the one who acts; it is not accidental behavior[21].

If the conditions of visibility are not accomplished, then "*their absence is normally considered an indicator of a social pathology that can end in a condition of 'invisibility' for the person affected*"[22].

To clarify the invisibility, Honneth, then, analyses what visibility means, in such a way that, for me, it eventually represents recognition.

---

16 Honneth 2001, 111.

17 Honneth 2001, 112.

18 Honneth 2001, 123.

19 Honneth 2001, 112.

20 Honneth 2001, 115.

21 Honneth 112, 2001. See, for instance, Honneth's comments of the novel of Ellison:

"In the latter cases, the protagonists, specifically the white masters, intentionally seek to make clear to blacks, who are physically present, that they (the blacks) are not visible to them. The colloquial expression for such active forms of intentional invisibility is 'looking through' someone". (Honneth 112, 2001).

22 Honneth 2001, 119.

First of all, visibility is related, by Honneth, to the Kantian concept of "respect." Acts of giving worth to someone are part of human beings' intelligibility. It represents the renouncing of egocentric inclinations[23]:

> Once again, with Kant, we must keep hold of the idea that all these assessments of worth can only be the evaluative aspects of a property that he designates the "intelligibility" of the person: whether we consider another human being to be loveable, worthy of respect, or worthy of solidarity, what is displayed in each case in the experienced 'worth' is merely a further aspect of what it means for humans beings to lead their lives in rational self-determination.[24]

In this context, for Honneth, morality coincides with recognition, because when a person assumes that the other person has worth, it represents a moral attitude.

It is possible to identify visibility in observing people's actions, behavior, gestures, expressions. As Honneth states, there are specific ways of reacting that represent a positive attitude with the other person, being open to her and seeing her properly—emphatic forms of expression[25]. More than representing the rationality of a human being's act, visibility comes from two different orders: cognizing (*Erkennen*) and recognizing (*Anerkennen*)[26].

The first order, cognizing, is related to perception. It involves a spatiotemporal framework, where the visible individual has situationally relevant properties[27]. It is an elementary form of individual identifiability[28].

After cognizing, the person is, then, recognized, if she acquires visibility in a non-visual sense, as a positive meaning of an affirmation, making the subject gain social 'validity.' Recognizing is related to public expression: "*In contrast to cognizing, which is a non-public, cognitive act, recognizing is dependent on media that express the fact that the other person is supposed to possess social 'validity'*"[29]. Both can also have private aspects; for instance, when experiencing domestic violence, a woman is neither cognized nor recognized, even in her intimacy.

Gestures and expressions, then, turn out to be very important in human beings' interactions, because they symbolically show to the addressee if he can expect a benevolent attitude from the person who performs the act. Expressive gestures

---

[23] Honneth 2001, 121.

[24] Honneth 2001, 122.

[25] Honneth 2001, 115.

[26] Honneth 2001, 113.

[27] Honneth 2001, 113.

[28] Honneth 2001, 113.

[29] Honneth 2001, 115.

are meta-actions, "*by making a gesture of recognition towards another person, we performatively make her aware that we see ourselves obligated to behave towards her in a certain kind of benevolent way*"[30].

Honneth exemplifies the "*recognizing*" through the relationship experienced by a child with her caregivers. Smiling and other facial expressions are reciprocal forms of love, devotion, sympathy, and care:

> These expressive responses do not articulate a cognition of just any type, but rather express in abbreviated form the totality of the actions that are supposed to be accorded to the small child on the grounds of his situation. To this extent, recognition possesses a performative character because the expressive responses that accompany it symbolize the practical ways of reacting that are necessary in order to 'do justice' to the person recognized. In the felicitous formulation of Helmut Plessner, one could say that the expression of recognition represents the 'alegory' of a moral action.[31]

Honneth clarifies that the child-caregiver relationship can be extended to relationships in adulthood:

> By way of a differentiation of the perception by which he originally sees in the facial expression of his caregiver a reflection of his own potential as an intelligible being, the growing child learns to infer from his partners in interaction different assessments of worth that are always perceptions of his intelligible nature.[32]

It is relevant to highlight the fact that the public expressions which imply the feeling of being visible and, then, recognized, depend on each culture. The range of gestures, expressions, and behaviors, which represent people receiving worth and positive empathy, varies according to context[33]. For instance, the public expression required for Chinese to be recognized in China is not the same as the public expression in Morocco. Individuals expect to be treated according to their culture. If they are not, then they can become invisible.[34]

---

[30] Honneth 2001, 120.

[31] Honneth 2001, 120.

[32] Honneth 2001, 125.

[33] "Of course, all these forms of expression vary considerably between different cultures; nonetheless, their constitutive function for interpersonal communication remains constant. By replacing or enhancing speech acts, or independently of them, these expressive responses are supposed to make clear publicly to the person in question that she has been accorded social approval, or possesses social validity, in the role of a specific social type (friend, cleaning lady, fellow traveller)". (Honneth 2001, 199).

[34] Honneth 2001, 116. And also:

Honneth's study of "*invisibility*" should be reviewed under two aspects. First of all, it seems that the first order *cognizing* presupposes a real physical contact between the two individuals, the one who cognizes and the other to be cognized:

> The subject can only claim of another person that she looks through, ignores, or overlooks him if he has already ascribed to that person the achievement of a primary identification of him. To this extent, invisibility in the figurative sense presupposes visibility in the literal sense.[35]

Nevertheless, nowadays, there are several situations of *cognizing*, which occur, for instance, in virtual spaces—such as social media. I understand that cognizing and recognizing can occur without physical contact or physical presence. More than that, I have seen that struggles do not presuppose a necessary connection between the agent and the addressee of recognition. If Honneth argues that to recognize one first needs to cognize the one receiving the worth, then it would not be possible to practice it with human beings outside social contact. Nowadays, we need precisely the opposite: people fighting for the recognition of others, even without knowing them[36].

The digital revolution and the prominence of social media, as well as the plurality of forms of life, make it necessary to conceive recognition independently of a spatiotemporal perception. People should be able to struggle for each other without presupposing any prior contact. Nowadays, the phase of cognition does not have the same role as in the past[37].

"The act of recognition is, as we have seen, the expressive demonstration of an individual decentering that we carry out in response to the worth of a person: we make known publicly by means of corresponding gestures and facial expressions that we concede to the other person a moral authority over us, on the basis of their worth, that sets limits to the realization of our spontaneous impulses and inclinations." (Honneth 2001, 126).

[35] Honneth 114, 2001.

[36] Our work, for instance, intends to struggle for Moroccan and Chinese women, even considering that the author is Brazilian.

[37] "Für jeden aufmerksamen Zeitgenossen dürfte gegenwärtig außer Frage stehen, dass die digitale Revolution der Kommunikationsverhältnisse nicht nur die Formen der Anbahnung und Aufrechterhaltung privater Beziehungen, sondern auch die Wege der politischen Meinungsbildung nachhaltig verändern wird; mit dem Internet, das den Einzelnen in die Lage zugleich einer Enträumlichung und Beschleunigung seiner Interaktionen versetzt, entstehen heute mit wachsendem Tempo eine Vielzahl von Netzöffentlichkeiten, deren Außengrenzen und Themen in ständigem Fluss begriffen sind." (Honneth 2020, 205)

See also, O'Lemmon: "Despite the tremendous advances brought about by this revolution, there is today a rapidly expanding gulf within and between societies along technological lines; alarming effects on sociality and cognition due to a persistent online presence; and a

Secondly, after building a complete explanation regarding the process of recognition, coming from cognizing and arriving at recognition, at the end of his text, Honneth seems to change the order, explaining that the emphatic forms of expression performed in a spatiotemporal dimension represent, for the addressee, recognition itself. Nevertheless, he does not clarify sufficiently how the pattern of cognizing keeps existing, what is the importance of this pattern in the process of recognition:

> At least genetically, recognizing precedes cognizing insofar as the infant infers from facial expressions the "worthy" properties of persons *before* he is in a position to grasp his environment in a disinterested way. [...] Corresponding to the priority of recognition in our social form of life is the prominent status of gestures and facial expressions with which we demonstrate to one another in general a motivational readiness to be guided in our actions by the moral authority of the other person.[38]

Honneth's "invisibility" relates to my concept of "indifference," especially regarding the element of intentionality.

Nevertheless, I understand that the term "invisibility" is not the proper one to define the nature of the institute. "Invisibility" concerns just the perspective of the victim: the one being made invisible. The term "indifference" concerns the two sides of the same institute: the perspective of the one practicing indifference, "to be indifferent"—the agent –, and the victim, the one suffering it—"the one disrespected."

In 2004, in the article "*Organized Self-Realization: Some Paradoxes of Individualization,*" Honneth directly mentioned the institute "indifference." In that instance, he uses Georg Simmel's approach to the term, when indifference represents an impoverishment of social contact. Based on Simmel's book *The Philosophy of Money*, Honneth holds that individualization may lead to the tendency of individuals to become ever lonelier as the network of anonymous social contacts expands.[39] This observation, from Honneth, comes from an observer

---

concentration of power in the form of wealth and data within a handful of tech companies, the likes of which has never been seen before." (O'Lemmon. 2022. The worst mistake 2.0? The digital revolution and the consequences of innovation Available at https://link.springer.com/article/10.1007/s00146-022-01599-5#citeas. Access on 08.05.2023).

[38] Honneth 126, 2001.

[39] Honneth 465, 2004a.

viewpoint, and it would be even stronger if I consider process of increasing loneliness and isolation felt or suffered on one's own interests alone, independently of other people.[40]

Honneth relates the various aspects of *individualization*. Whereas it represents an opportunity for human beings to exercise their autonomy, at the same time, societies experience an excess of selfish behaviors coming from individualization. Simmel calls it "mutual indifference":

> The result of this paradoxical reversal, where the processes which once promised an increase of qualitative freedom are henceforth altered into an ideology of deinstitutionalization, is the emergence in individuals of a number of symptoms of inner emptiness, of feeling oneself to be superfluous, and of absence of purpose.[41]

The process of mutual indifference is experienced in the metropolis, because, there, the principle of money[42] is active and endorsed. People develop a *blasé metropolitan attitude*:

> This incapacity to react to new stimulations with the required amount of energy constitutes in fact that blasé attitude which every child of a large city evinces when compared with the products of the more peaceful and more stable milieu. [...] The essence of the blasé attitude is an indifference toward the distinctions between things. Not in the sense that they are not perceived, as is the case of mental dullness, but rather that the meaning and the value of the distinctions between things, and therewith of the things themselves, are experienced as meaningless.[43]

People also begin to act with excessive discretion and in isolation—called by Simmel as "*mutual reserve*".[44] For this author, in the metropolis, people experience a slight aversion, a mutual strangeness and repulsion that, in a close contact

---

[40] Honneth 465, 2004a.

[41] Honneth 463, 2004a.

[42] For Honneth as well, the current economic global context does not endorse solidarity and cooperation, but actually incentives people to behavior in the opposite way:

"Like Hegel, Durkheim believed that the sphere of the market can only be grasped as an 'ethical' relationship that ensures freedom if it can be described as a system of economic activity founded on pre-market relationships of solidarity. Therefore, both authors had to search for mechanisms within the market that could motivate individual economic actors to be more sensitive to the interests of other actors and thus take into account the underlying principles of their cooperation". (Honneth 2014a, 194).

[43] Simmel 1900, 14. See also: "There is perhaps no psychic phenomenon which is so unconditionally reserved to the city as the blasé outlook". (Simmel 1900, 14)

[44] Simmel 1900, 15.

that has arisen any way whatever, can break out into hatred and conflict.[45] Simmel defines it as a sphere of indifference.[46]

Such social problems are a result of the politics of money. All emotional relationships between persons—which used to rest on their individuality—become intellectual relationships, transforming people into numbers, endowing them with an indifferent significance. They will have worth as soon as they offer something objectively perceivable.[47] The intellectualistic person is indifferent to personal things, which are not purely rationally perceptible. It is the result of a society submitted to the principle of money[48].

For Simmel, then, individualization has the effects of mutual reserve and mutual indifference, a result of the principle of money dominating an individual's life[49]. The definition of indifference coming from Simmel does not present the element of intentionality. The intellectualistic person is not interested in emotions because he is alienated by capitalism and the principle of money.

The study on the process of alienation was developed some years later by the first generation of the Frankfurt School. The alienation, the blasé attitude, and the mutual indifference all describe an absence of attitude from the individuals. Nevertheless, such an absence of actions is not necessarily intentional. The agent does not act indifferently necessarily because he wants to. On the contrary, he is influenced by the principle of money, and his rational capacity to choose his actions is lost. He can recognize the other subjects and things, only if they represent some rational result or some interest.

4.1.4 Unintentional Indifference

According to Lillehammer, there are two kinds of indifference. The first occurs when the individual agent does not know about some situation, practicing, then, an involuntary and unintentional indifference. It results from the ignorance of

[45] Simmel 1900, 15.

[46] Simmel 1900, 15.

[47] Simmel 1900, 12.

[48] "The purely intellectualistic person is indifferent to all things personal because, out of them, relationships and reactions develop which are not to be completely understood by purely rational methods—just as the unique element in events never enters into the principle of money". (Simmel 1900, 12)

[49] Simmel 1900, 16.

the facts; the individual does not have knowledge and awareness of the case[50]. Reification and autonomization are also results of involuntary actions of people.

On the other hand, there is the voluntary indifference: a voluntary feeling, when the person is aware of the situation, she knows what is happening and then voluntarily chooses not to give importance to it, to ignore it[51]. Voluntary and intentional indifference damages recognition.

Heidegger also has an interpretation of indifference, as negative and unintentional. He talks about indifference as boredom[52], i.e., as a situation in which things are covered by a veil of indifference when the individual experiences a lack of interest in things and a presence of anguish.

Axel Honneth has also mentioned a kind of unintentional indifference in his work "*Reification.*" In this instance, he mentions that reification is a kind of *ossified behavior* of human beings.[53] Individuals lose their capacity for empathetic engagement, and their world loses its qualitatively disclosed character[54]. Arguing against such reification, Honneth endorses that care attitudes should have not just a genetic priority but also a conceptual priority over a neutral cognition of reality[55]. In the end, his aim is to prove that a recognitional stance has a genetic and categorical priority over all attitudes regarding the self and the world.[56]

Reification does not have intentionality. A human being loses his capacity to act, to engage, to perform empathetic behavior, but he does not choose to behave indifferently. Human beings do not objectify their lives and those of others from an instance of liability and guilt.

Honneth bases his analysis on the work of Georg Lukács. According to Honneth, Lukács intended to interpret reification as a mental habit, which makes persons lose their empathetic engagement. People transform themselves into neutral spectators. For Lukács, *reification* is a process and a result.[57]

Honneth states, further, that the process of reification occurs not just between persons, but also regarding all elements which surround the individual..[58] This process, from my point of view, is also encouraged by alienation.

---

[50] Lillehammer 2017, 18.
[51] Lillehammer 2017, 18.
[52] Ferrater Mora 1964, 929.
[53] Honneth 2005, 109.
[54] Honneth 2005, 109.
[55] Honneth 2005, 109.
[56] Honneth 2005, 109.
[57] Honneth 2005, 125.
[58] Honneth 2005, 132.

In 2012, in the article "*Brutalization of the social conflict: struggles for recognition in the early 21st century*", Honneth analyzes Parsons' theory and argues that, unfortunately, the solidary and active human behaviors expected by Parsons' theory had not happened at all. Nowadays, struggles for recognition seem to be frozen, as human beings are not in the mood to do something.[59] For Honneth, there has not been moral indignation when social recognition is denied, and public outcries are not expressive[60]. Instead, the struggles for recognition are frozen as an external perspective of individual's life, and he does not comprehend it as part of his own interiorized self[61]. Honneth mentions an oppressive silence experienced by the current societies and asks—without further answering to it -: "*What shapes has the struggle for recognition since assumed?*"[62]

Two years after the article mentioned above, Honneth introduces another concept related to indifference: the autonomization of the human being. Autonomization signifies that people's actions are fixed and rigid, making them socially isolated and implying a loss of communication. Lifeworld interaction is damaged.[63] In this time, Honneth argues that there is a personal lack of interest in the private spheres of life, as well as in the public spaces. They are not just disinterested in public affairs, but also they do not consider the infringements of the private life of other members of the community. It seems to me that autonomization is also a consequence of alienation, in the same way as reification and freezing. There is no intentionality in autonomization.

4.1.5 Intentional Indifference

Until now, I have seen that Honneth mentions the freeze of struggles, reification, and invisibility, as attitudes, which interfere in the achievement of recognition. From my point of view, they are all examples of behaviors with some elements of indifference.

Nevertheless, I comprehend that the indifference that affects recognition is the one with intentionality. The practices of reification, the freeze of struggles, autonomization, and invisibility have no intentionality from the perspective of the human being, because people are generally alienated. On the other hand, I

[59] Honneth 2012a, 16.
[60] Honneth 2012a, 16.
[61] Honneth 2012a, 16.
[62] Honneth 2012a, 16.
[63] Honneth 2014a, 114.

contend that, in indifference, there is a human being's intentionality, he sees some situation requiring solidarity, and he chooses to ignore, to make it invisible, to not engage, to not act. For me, human beings are immersed in this social pathology of indifference.

Nowadays, practices of indifference affect the dynamics of social struggle. It is argued that the collective feeling of *indifference* damages the achievement of recognition.

Lillehammer mantains that the feeling of indifference can be carried out by individual persons, as well as by social groups, institutions, or any other locus of agency[64]. My focus is on individuals' indifference, because I advocate that the struggles for women's recognition should be more related to individuals' private lives, and practices of individual indifference are widespread in such pattern by friends, relatives, or partners.

First of all, I inquire: who should struggle? Either the victim or the witnesses are responsible for struggling. Nevertheless, many situations of disrespect do not allow the victim herself to engage in struggles for recognition. She needs someone to struggle, to engage, to act. It is at this moment that indifference manifests. People, in general, do not participate in struggles for the recognition of other people, and people may sometimes not engage in struggles for recognition even for themselves.

Indifference manifests either as an emotion or as a behavior. In the first case, it must be confronted by struggles within oneself—as I will further see. In the second case, indifference should be confronted by struggles in the pattern of love, law, and solidarity.

If I inquire for whom one should struggle, it can be for a friend or a relative; for a person whom one does not know at all; or for oneself. In the Section 3.4 "*Who should struggle?*" of this work, I have argued that the agents of recognition are responsible for struggling even for people they do not know at all. Furthermore, although a victim of disrespect has the conditions for struggling for herself, other individuals could also be agents of this struggle, contributing for the reaching of recognition. The engagement in struggles for recognition is a moral obligation.

In all situations of disrespect, indifference should be confronted. The symptoms of invisibility, autonomization, freezing, and reification occur inside the dynamic of disrespect, affecting the achievement of recognition.

---

[64] Lillehammer 2017, 24.

> Are there moral limits to corporate profits? Are there moral ceilings and floors that we should place on wages and salaries? Why is it that so many people in our country who work two and three jobs still can't get out of poverty? Why are the products at Walmart so cheap? What is the environmental impact of the food that I buy? Why is it that we have so much and our lives are so comfortable when one-third of the world, or 2.4 billion people, live in poverty? How much is enough, and when does our consumption become morally obscene?[65]

Any struggle against indifference, even if potentially trivial, can contribute to the achievement of recognition.

Axel Honneth and some other philosophers develop deep and complex theories that touch real life. Generally, they propose ideal theoretical models, containing elements, premises, and objectives. Nevertheless, they do not go straight to the method of application of this approach in reality. When studying recognition, Honneth mentions some situations of recognition and disrespect, but he does not explain how to come from the struggles and recover recognition again. The key to Honneth is the struggle, but the author does not clarify how to struggle in a variety of societies worldwide.

The next section will demonstrate that, first of all, the individual should struggle inside herself, confronting feelings and beliefs which make her apathetic and indifferent. This may happen in all the patterns of recognition. She should struggle against feelings of indifference. The section studies the struggles inside oneself, in order to explain how I understand the relation between indifference and recognition.

4.2 Struggles inside Oneself

Considering that indifference compromises recognition, I advocate for a struggle against feelings of indifference that all individuals are able to experience. According to Honneth, recognition is a voluntary act. The one who decides to struggle should have a motivation to abandon a neutral position and to engage in the struggle for recognition.

---

[65] Peters 2014, Preface "Seeing with New Eyes".

As a consequence, it is necessary to evaluate which kind of emotion could impair the engagement of this individual, damaging the beginning of the struggles. I argue that the fundamental emotion which makes an individual not begin to struggle is the emotion of *indifference*[66].

From a psychological interpretation of indifference, it is a mental state, in which a person feels that she cannot act, that it is impossible to act, to decide, to do something[67].

A person who witnesses a situation of disrespect may experience the feeling of indifference, in a way that she will be apathetic, not beginning any struggle for the recovery of recognition. Under this circumstance, it is necessary to identify how to struggle against the indifference within oneself.

I understand that the struggle against indifference should focus on the transformation of the emotion of indifference into solidarity. For Honneth, solidarity relates to appreciating someone else and the community as a whole. It is necessary, then, that people cultivate feelings of solidarity and cooperation.

The cultivation of feelings and values relates to the nature of recognition. I have seen that, recently, Honneth has avoided affirming that "to recognize someone" is a moral obligation. I disagree with him, and, for a guarantee that recognition is an ethical model, I understand that the theory of recognition could be linked to an ethics of care. Then, the transformation of feelings of indifference into feelings of solidarity could happen.

In regards to the ethics of care, Honneth has clarified that a solution for reification would be the understanding of recognition as a prior moral value for human beings, instead of the Heideggerian notion of care (*Sorge*)[68]. Heidegger states that individuals should adopt a position of a participant, and not just of a mere observer, in experiencing his shared life. Caring for each other means that individual will look to the other individual, trying to understand her position, necessities,

---

[66] In the above sections, it was advocated that, for us, indifference is a negative emotion, an intentional behavior, and a social pathology.

[67] Ferrater Mora 1964, 929.

[68] "With the expression 'care' we have in mind a basic existential-ontological phenomenon, which all the same is *not simple* in its structure. The ontologically elemental totality of the care-structure cannot be traced back to some ontical 'primal element', just as Being certainly cannot be 'explained' in terms of entities. [...] In defining 'care' as 'Being-ahead-of-oneself—in Being-already-in...—as Being-alongside...', we have made it plain that even this phenomenon is, in itself, still structurally *articulated*." (Heidegger 1962, 241).

and feelings, with an empathetic attitude[69]. Nevertheless, for Honneth, Heideggerian care is not appropriate for recognition, as it does not contain a fundamental element of sentimentality.[70]

There are interpretations of care, such as the one from Carol Gilligan, which could be seen as fundaments for practices of solidarity.[71] Gilligan understands that the dimension of care has a feminine perspective of responsibility for the care of other persons. For the feminist author, an ethics of care is emotional and involves different positive feelings from the one who engages in actions of caring. I understand that to care about someone is to be solidary, and it means, in the end, to cherish recognition.

White's interpretation of "care" is also useful for recognition. Care is understood as a counteracting to the insensivity to the unique particularity of the other.[72] White proposes a comprehension of care from a generalisation of the Heideggerian attitude of *Gelassenheit*, and a disengagement of compulsion to act, leaving space for more sensitive awareness of the particularity of the other.[73] It would be understood as a postmodern virtue ethics of care (*Fürsorge*), oriented towards the cultivation of modes of conduct, such as the ability to listen and to become emotionally involved.[74]

In this sense, care means a sensitivity to the situation of other persons and emotional involvement.

On these bases, I understand that the subject can struggle against her feelings of indifference through an ethics of care, feeling that she is responsible for the achievement of recognition of other persons, being motivated by a moral sensitivity, emotional involvement, love, protection, and compassion. In the end, indifference is transformed into solidarity through care.

Now, the struggle inside oneself will make it possible for this individual to engage in other struggles in the context of her private life.

---

[69] Honneth 2005, 107.

[70] Honneth 2005, 107.

[71] Gilligan 1982, 10.

[72] Sinnerbrink 2011, 195.

[73] Sinnerbrink 2011, 195.

[74] Sinnerbrink 2011, 195.

4.3 Conclusion of Chap. 4

The theory of recognition is lacking in objectively indicating the necessary actions to achieve recognition, especially if I take into consideration women's recognition. Although the patterns of recognition vary from society to society, I already have seen that they have core elements and moral values. What is missing in Honneth's theory is a way to increase women's recognition, especially considering the struggles.

The struggle against indifference should be a method to increase recognition and diminish practices of disrespect in all the patterns of recognition. If we confront indifference, then struggles for recognition happen, and it will trigger feelings of inclusion and solidarity between people.

Chapter 4 has explained that struggles against intentional and negative indifference are necessary for the achievement of recognition. Despite different interpretations of the institute of indifference, I understand that Honneth interprets it from a negative perspective, related to invisibility, individualization, reification, the freezing of society, and autonomization.

When discussing invisibility, Honneth contends that people should take other individuals into consideration from the dual perspective of cognizing and recognizing. In this context, I have argued that recognition does not presuppose a physical contact between individuals in the act of cognizing. On the contrary, the moral obligation to struggle does not depend on previous contact between the victim of disrespect and the agent of struggle.

When discussing individualization, Honneth mentioned the term *indifference* for the first time, through the theory of Georg Simmel. The indifference in this theory is considered negative and unintentional.

The Honnethian elements of *reification* and *freezing of society* are also not necessarily intentional. Alienated people do not realize that they are being indifferent with other persons, they do not have intentionality when ignoring a situation of disrespect.

I understand that intentional indifference is the most relevant for struggles, and in some societies intentional indifference has become a social pathology.

I have seen that other authors interpret indifference as a neutral behavior, for instance the stoics. On the other hand, Walzer and Dumouchel understand that indifference is a positive institute, freeing people of the obligation to care and to be solidary with others. For Walzer, benign indifference relates to toleration.

After advocating that the general struggle, which can happen in all patterns, is the struggle against intentional and negative indifference, I will now evaluate which specific struggles are able to happen in the patterns of love, law, and solidarity.

5 Struggles for Recognition in the Pattern of Love

I understand that the pattern of love has a crucial role for recognition, especially with my focus on women's recognition.

First of all, love relationships are intimate, and usually, the relationship occurs privately between the subject and a partner, who is a friend, a relative or a life partner.

In case of disrespect practiced by the partner against this person, probably she does not have people around to help her. There is a range of possibilities regarding disrespect in the private context of love. Inside an intimate relationship, different cases of abuse can happen and the victim is alone and fragile. The perpetrator, on the other hand, feels that the privacy of love protects him, and no one is witnessing his actions.

Okin states that the majority of practices of gender discrimination—a form of Honnethian disrespect, occurs inside families and the private life of the individual. For instance, she mentions that the home is where much of culture is practiced, preserved, and transmitted to the young, and the distribution of power inside the home impacts participation in the public patterns of life[1]. According to her, "*The more a culture requires or expects of women in the domestic sphere, the less opportunity they have of achieving equality with men in either sphere.*"[2]

More than gender discrimination, the pattern of love can also hold situations of disrespect against children: "*The family is a place where illiberal things happen*

[1] Okin 1999, 5.

[2] Okin 1999, 5.

C. Diamantino Esser Santana, *Recognized Women:*, Juridicum – Schriften zur Rechtsphilosophie, https://doi.org/10.1007/978-3-658-46849-1_5

not only because of male superordination over women but because of adult superordination over children."[3] Children can suffer disrespect not just because of gender inequality, but also because of an excess of hierarchical superordination.

Secondly, according to Honneth, the experiences of love are the first in an individual's life, and she develops her primary relationships in her private and intimate life with her relatives and friends. This pattern begins at an individual's birth, and the relationships of family and friendship can last for the whole life of a person[4].

The experiences of love influence the other two patterns of recognition: law and solidarity. The feeling of self-confidence reached in love stimulates an individual's participation in her community.

On this basis, I advocate that the preservation of the pattern of love is also very relevant to the achievement of recognition in the public patterns. The dialectics between recognition and struggles is a dynamic process, a constant movement, which can begin in love and keep going in the spheres of law and solidarity.

Additionally, the pattern of love has a critical role in the formation and preservation of a culture. According to Walzer, national culture is better preserved in private and domestic settings than in public ones. Moreover, generally, the ones responsible for the maintenance of traditions are the women[5]. In his words: "*Tradition is transmitted in the lullabies that mothers sing, the prayers they whisper, the clothing they make, the food they cook, and the domestic rites and customs that they teach.*"[6]

Walzer draws a model of toleration focused on immigrant families living in a new country.[7] He argues that, nowadays, the traditional paradigms of cultures

---

[3] Halley 1999, 92.

[4] Once this misdirected concretization is removed, an idea remains, which has been developed here using the example of psychoanalytic object-relations theory: in the tense balance between fusion and ego-demarcation, the resolution of which is part of every successful form of primary relationship, subjects mutually experience themselves to be loved in their individuality only insofar as they are not afraid of being alone. This mode of basic self-confidence represents the basic prerequisite for every type of self-realization in the sense that it allows individuals to attain, for the first time, the inner freedom that enables them to articulate their own needs. Accordingly, the experience of love, whatever historical form it takes, represents the innermost core of all forms of life that qualify as 'ethical' [sittlich]. (Honneth 1995, 176).

[5] Walzer 1997, 64.

[6] Walzer 1997, 64.

[7] Walzer 1997, 64.

tend to be challenged by new perspectives created by the new generations.[8] Children and youths who are born into a mixed family find a cultural paradigm shift. These families will have a mixture of their traditional cultures with the culture of the country they are living in.[9]

Such families and friendships, now, may practice a new model of toleration in their private life. This toleration model is drawn as "a postmodern project", where people experience a life without clear boundaries, secure, or singular identities.[10] Difference, then, seen to be encountered everywhere and every day, whereas individuals mix freely with members of the majority.[11]

Walzer highlights a very relevant challenge that the first generation of mixed families face. Now, they deal with tolerance at home, where ethnic, religious, and cultural debates happen within spouses, in-laws, children, and "*with our own hyphenated or divided selves*".[12]

Whereas the old generation of the family brings the traditional values, the new generations raised in a new country have different life perspectives. From this conflict, recognition is necessary, through respecting the autonomy of each member of the family, as I will further see. In the pattern of love, I identify struggles to be developed inside the contexts of family and friendship.

5.1 Struggles Inside Family and Friendship

After confronting the inner indifference, the person, then, should engage in struggles in the pattern of love, as follows.

5.1.1 Struggles for the Emancipation of the Family Member

In 2014, Honneth stated that: "*Free market participants, self-aware democratic citizens and emancipated family members—all of whom correspond to the ideals institutionalized in our society—mutually influence each other, because the properties of the one cannot be realized without those of the other two*".[13]

---

[8] Walzer 1997, 64.

[9] Walzer 1997, 64.

[10] Walzer 1997, 64.

[11] Walzer 1997, 64.

[12] Walzer 1997, 87.

[13] Honneth 2014a, 330.

I understand that the idea of an *emancipated family member* is relevant to the pattern of love. The role of a family member influences the achievement of recognition. A person must feel that she can trust in her family and that her self-realization is respected within the family context.

Honneth does not clarify the exact meaning of an emancipated family member, but I understand that it is influenced by the Hegelian idea of the ethical dissolution of the family that results in emancipation.

For Hegel, the ethical dissolution of the family happens when the children learns the freedom of personality, becoming recognized as persons in the eyes of the law. The old family, then, falls into the background, as a merely initial ground and origin.[14] Furthermore, for Hegel, there is also the natural dissolution of the family by the death of the parents, particularly the father.[15]

Coming from that, an emancipated family member is someone with freedom of personality, who has the voice and freedom to manifest her opinions, to talk, and to debate ideas with her relatives. According to Honneth, private relationships should be democratic, in such a way that all participants have the right to deliberate, to choose their life goals, and to practice democratic attitudes. An emancipated family member can discuss the expectations of her parents and relatives from the older generation, and at the same time she will be heard by them. A person should not comply with all her family premises and traditions. It is necessary to have a previous moment of sharing of ideas, life goals, and authentic feelings. Within the family context, individuals would achieve recognition through constant struggles for emancipation. This struggle could be better implemented if individuals also reach a revisability of their own culture inside private life.

5.1.2 Struggles for the Open Revisability of a Culture

Will Kymlicka argues that individual freedom presupposes the feeling of belonging to a national group, but what is more important is the possibility for the person to question her own societal culture[16]. There are endless definitions

[14] Hegel 2008, 175, pp. 177.

[15] Hegel 2008, 175, pp. 178.

[16] "The sort of culture that I will focus on, however, is a societal culture—that is, a culture which provides its members with meaningful ways of life across the full range of human activities, including social, educational, religious, recreational, and economic life, encompassing both public and private spheres. These cultures tend to be territorially concentrated, and based on a shared language". (Kymlicka 1995, 76).

of autonomy[17], but I understand that, from the perspective of the theory of recognition, Will Kymlicka's comprehension of autonomy is useful for the proposal of struggles for recognition able to happen in different cultural contexts. Kymlicka interprets autonomy from a multicultural perspective, which faces the challenges imposed by different contexts of life—for instance, non-democratic and non-Western countries cover individual's autonomy in a different form.

Kymlicka's definition of autonomy states that the individual has autonomy when she can rationally revise her own identity and role in her cultural community.

> The defining feature of liberalism is that it ascribes certain fundamental freedoms to each individual. In particular, it grants people a very wide freedom of choice in terms of how they lead their lives. It allows people to choose a conception of the good life, and then allows them to reconsider that decision, and adopt a new and hopefully better plan of life.[18]

I understand that Kymlicka's autonomy amplifies the possibilities of struggles for recognition within private relationships, such as family and friendships. His definition of rational revisability encompasses an essential interest in identifying and revising one's current beliefs about mistaken values[19].

The revisability of a culture must be a premise for the emancipated family member. Struggles in the pattern of love for the emancipation of an individual inside a family requires struggles for the revisability of her culture as well.

The pattern of love has a role in the formation and maintenance of a culture, as the traditions are practiced daily in the private and domestic spaces. I have also shown that sometimes a person does not attain self-confidence in the pattern of love, because her cultural traditions are not freely discussed, and she cannot attain her emancipation as a family member.

According to Kymlicka, the meaning of a good life should come from the inside, from people's experiences, values, and beliefs. More than that, this concept should always be open to revision and questioning. Individuals have the right to build their meaning of the good life and also to have education, freedom of

---

[17] For instance, Stephan Kirste makes a compilation on that. For him: "Die Neigung, in dieser Situation ergebnisorientiert zu agieren und sich dabei an Maßstäben zu orientieren, die nicht diejenigen des „Begünstigten“ sind, und so den Willen des anderen zu seinem vermeintlichen Vorteil zurückzustellen, wächst mit der funktionalen Ausdifferenzierung der Gesellschaft. Alle hier vorgestellten Arbeiten vereinigt das Anliegen, unter diesen Bedingungen die Autonomie des Einzelnen bestmöglich zu sichern.“ (Kirste 2010, 585).

[18] Kymlicka 1995, 80.

[19] Kymlicka 1995, 213.

expression, and association, to judge what is valuable, what they understand as the good life. Furthermore, she should have access to other ways of life[20].

5.2 Conclusion of Chap. 5

Whereas Chap. 4 proposed a struggle useful for all the patterns of recognition, Chap. 5 contended that in the pattern of love the individuals should focus on the struggle for the emancipation of the family member; and the struggle for the open revisability of a culture.

The ethics of care, especially the one developed by Carol Gilligan, can help the person to conceive solidary feelings from the honor of caring for others, having compassion for and emotional attachment to other individuals.

After confronting the inner indifference, the individual then, in the pattern of love, should conceive herself as an emancipated family member in her private relationships of love. That means, although the family holds traditional cultural values, individuals should have a voice with their relatives; they must be able to share their life goals freely. Autonomy and freedom of expression should occur inside the family.

Additionally, the emancipated family member struggles also for the open revisability of her culture, being able to choose the cultural practices which she is going to follow or not.

In conclusion, in love, an individual should struggle inside himself, confronting feelings of indifference through a morality based on care, compassion, and solidarity. Secondly, the person should also fight for her emancipation as a family member, as well as for the open revisability of her culture.

All these aspects should be integrated into the pattern of love, so that this dimension of recognition can finally be achieved. Individuals will thus be able to attain self-confidence, being prepared to experience recognition in the next two public patterns of law and solidarity.

[20] Kymlicka 1995, 81.

6 Struggles for Recognition in the Pattern of Law

6.1 Struggles for Recognition and Human Rights

I understand that the struggles in the pattern of law relate to human rights. Struggles for recognition and human rights are two institutes that, from the perspective of legal theory, share similar characteristics, as follows.

Chapter 3 detailed what struggles for recognition mean. I have seen that struggles are a living organism, aiming for the achievement of moral claims of an individual and her community. As quoted in Chap. 3, Honneth has stated that struggles express moral claims that may serve as normative standards[1].

On the other hand, I understand that human rights are continuous, living, historical, and dynamic as well. Kirste argues that the history of human rights has proven the Hegelian "progress in the consciousness of freedom".[2]

Human rights may be not just legal rights, but carry a moral form as well. Kirste clarifies that a human right has a moral form when it obliges all human beings and institutions. Additionally, a human right has a legal form when it obliges public authorities (legal rights)[3]. For the theory of recognition, depending

---

[1] Anderson 2011, 53.

[2] Kirste 2019, 24.

[3] Kirste 2020, 361.

This comprehension of the moral and legal forms of human rights relates to the discussions on *Drittwirkung* (the third party effect of fundamental rights):

"Rights which are given Drittwirkung are constitutive of the general legal order (i.e., the economic constitution); they are rights which must be generally observed and may be used by the judge as interpretative guides to the private rights and duties of individuals. (2009) It is one of the methods liberalism uses to channel political struggles, protecting fundamental rights and limiting the strength of government." (Engle 2009, 166). Nevertheless, Engle

C. Diamantino Esser Santana, *Recognized Women:*, Juridicum – Schriften zur Rechtsphilosophie, https://doi.org/10.1007/978-3-658-46849-1_6

on the society one is considering, the rights to women's recognition[4] may have more of a moral than a legal form. I know that there are societies without legal norms embracing human rights, such as states with a low level of democratic instances or without a democratic political regime at all. For these societies, struggles for recognition could embrace human rights as a moral instance. It does not mean that in non-democratic contexts there are no human rights at all, but actually that these legal systems are incomplete, and human rights there did not reach the legal form yet.

Kirste states that democracy as a political regime supports the achievement of legal human rights[5]. Some legal regulations such as the Millennium Declaration, the Universal Declaration of Human Rights, as well as the Convention on the Elimination of All Forms of Discrimination endorse the political autonomy of people and the equal opportunity to participate[6].

I argue that rights to women's recognition should always be carried by the struggles for rights, either in a moral or legal form. Rights to women's recognition in the form of legal human rights are guaranteed through legal regulations. On the other hand, rights to women's recognition in the form of moral human rights are spread and still being build inside a woman's community.

This interpretation of the struggles for rights to recognition contribute for the reaching of recognition in general, but especially for the reaching of women's recognition. It is justified by the fact that women experience a variety of forms

argues that the methods of Drittwirkung are not free of mistakes. First of all, it seems to be polysemic, relating to who holds the right against whom (private parties, inter se) or, instead, on how may the right be enforced (must the state intervene to enforce the right or may the private parties themselves somehow enforce it?). (Engle 2009, 172). Secondly, third party effect seems to protect a purely economic constitution and fundamental human rights are universal and inalienable values, in that sense prior and superior to economic rights. (Engle 2009, 171)

[4] We adopt the plural term "women's recognition" and not "woman's recognition", because the recognition of an individual woman also represents the achievement of the social recognition's conditions for women as a group. Any case of a female individual recognition contributes for the reaching of women's recognition as a category of addressees of rights.

[5] "For a discourse on the justification of rights to be an expression of human rights, i.e., the political autonomy of people in the status activus, participants must have a free and equal opportunity to participate. In the so-called Millennium Declaration it is then also stated that "democratic and participatory governance based on the will of the people best assures" human rights, especially dignity, freedom and equality. Art. 29 II of the UDHR also speaks of democratic society as the ideal condition for the realization of human rights. The preamble of the Convention on the Elimination of All Forms of Discrimination against Women (CEDAW) of 18 December 1979 therefore consistently states that a worse position of women in elections or even their exclusion violates their human dignity." (Kirste 2019, 48).

[6] Kirste 2019, 48.

of disrespect—theoretically discussed in the above chapters of this work and also to be further discussed in the upcoming chapters—, which, predominantly, are not totally embraced by the legal system they are inserted. It requires, then, that the struggles come not just under a universal legal protection guaranteed, for instance, by general human rights—and namely women rights—, but also through subjective rights carring recognition within their specific scope.

Donnelly, when discussing the relative universalism of human rights, affirms that the implementation and enforcement of universal human rights is relative, depending on where one has the (good or bad) fortune to live[7]. He mentions the systematic violation of positive (legal) human rights by several states, although they do not lose their legitimacy in international law at all[8]. This is easily exemplified by the atrocities recently committed by the Russian government against Ukraine[9]. Nevertheless, I understand that a moral form of human rights would be the first step in all cultures for the future achievement of legal and effective human rights.

It it is important to mention the phenomenon called *regionalization of human rights*, as over time, different cultural societies have been creating their own human rights declarations. There is a discussion whether such regionalization of human rights damages their universalism[10]. I contend that, especially in the context of women's recognition, if one accepts the regionalization of human rights, it must fulfill the moral conditions for the achievement of respect, freedom, and self-realization of the human beings, in other words, the reaching of recognition.

Human rights relate to recognition as they also have not just an individual facet, but they relate to the community in which one is embedded. According to Kirste,

> [...] the image of men in human rights declarations in international law is not one of an isolated individual self. Although the independence of the individual self is a goal

[7] Donnelly 2007, 283.

[8] Donnelly 2007, 289.

[9] BBC News. 2022. Ukraine, the UN and history's greatest broken promise. Available at: https://www.bbc.com/news/world-europe-61021862. Access on: April 14th, 2022.

[10] "The 'regionalization' of human rights appears to be closely connected with the different cultural areas. This is simply a fact that must not be neglected. The debate on human rights and the creation of Declarations is particularly intense in the Islamic-Arabian world. [...] It is an open question whether the 'regionalization' of human rights as is illustrated by the numerous declarations and conventions works against the claim for universal validity or whether it constitutes a stage on the way to universalism". (Schmale 1993, 7)

of these declarations and charters, the individual human being develops in exchange with others and has to be recognized by others.[11]

Human rights are, then, individually and socially spread. This being the case, they are always universal. '*The 1993 World Human Rights Conference, in the first operative paragraph of the Vienna Declaration and Programme of Action, asserted that "the universal nature of these rights and freedoms is beyond question"*'.[12]

Donnelly argues that human rights are commonly confused with values or with matters that require a human rights debate[13]. They are not values themselves. Actually, they seek to realize social values. Human rights are entitlements of all individuals that may be exercised against the state and society, being equal and inalienable[14].

There is universality in human rights, even if this universality has nuances of relativity. Donnelly makes a distinction between the "concept" and the "conceptions" of a human right. He advocates that the concept of a human right, as its general idea, must be universal. On the other hand, according to each specific situation and cultural context, it may be that a conception of a specific human right, as the way its main concept will be perceived, may have different implementations[15]. For him, it is possible to consider a "certain prima facie tolerance"[16] regarding the conceptions of human rights, but it does not mean a problematic normative cultural relativism at all[17]. Donnelly calls this phenomenon "relative universality of human rights".

The universalism of human rights is another characteristic that the struggles for recognition carry. Although Honneth stayed noncommittal between liberalists and communitarians within political philosophy, he has always been decisive in arguing that recognition involves universal values defended through struggles in the pattern of law.

Considering that human rights and struggles for recognition are related, I focus, then, on the struggles for rights to women's recognition. Rights to women's recognition, in turn, are human rights.

---

[11] Kirste 2020, 362.

[12] Donnelly 2007, 288.

[13] Donnelly 2007, 285.

[14] Donnelly 2007, 284.

[15] Donnelly 2007, 299.

[16] Donnelly 2007, 301.

[17] Donnelly 2007, 296.

6.2 Rights to Women's Recognition are Human Rights

"*By attributing a right to someone or something, the law becomes subjective and the subject achieves an objective legal validity as a legal person. Thus, already in the form of an individual right, objectivity and subjectivity are basically mediated*"[18]. Honneth's interpretation of intersubjectivity and the relevance of the pattern of law for recognition endorse the fact that the attribution of a right to someone implies on her recognition. Honneth has discussed it when proposing the methodology of normative reconstruction. Nevertheless, Honneth does not objectively point out which are the rights related to recognition, which I will denominate "rights to recognition". In the context of this work, the proposition of rights to specifically women's recognition is relevant.

Human rights claims spread through the private life of an individual, as well as through her social and public life. For communities where human rights are neither legally recognized (legal rights)[19]; nor, although legally recognized, duly implemented, the patterns of recognition prepare the ground for demanding rights to women's recognition. It happens through different forms of struggle, for instance either private or public debates, individual or group actions in private and public spaces.

The discussions on the pattern of law have demonstrated that law promotes the subsistence of love and solidarity. Without rights to recognition, namely legal recognition, it will not be possible for the person to reach recognition either in love or in solidarity.

I argue that rights to recognition are ultimately human rights. It is possible to find rights to recognition either in legal human rights, in the moral conformation of human rights, or as human rights in formation. In any case, I understand that all human right carry a moment of recognition.

First of all, I understand that some legal human rights already in the so-called international Bill of Rights[20] are definitely related to the recognition of women and, in this way, they are, in the end, rights to women's recognition. For

[18] Kirste 2020, 361.

[19] The form of human rights as individual rights and as positive, discursively legitimized human rights is not value-neutral, but is itself an expression of human dignity, not of the flesh and blood human being, but of the human being as the (international) legal order itself reconstructs him by rights and duties. Human rights thus present themselves as a dialectical development of the formal and material meaning contained in the concept of human dignity. (Kirste 2019, 53)

[20] These four groups of human rights—the rights of the human being vis-à-vis public authority, rights through public authority, rights of participation in public authority and the right to

instance, the right to human dignity embraces the conditions for the achievement of women's recognition and, in this sense, it may also be called a right to women's recognition:

> What "fundamental" means is expressed by the preambles of the UN Charter or the UDHR. They express the idea that all human rights are based on the fundamental right of human dignity. All other human rights are concretizations of this basic human right to be permitted to make oneself the person one wants to be.[21]

On the other hand, there are human rights that are not legal yet, there are human rights with a moral form, and these ones may be called rights to women's recognition as well.

A third category would then be human rights that already do not exist, but are being demanded based on the disrespect experienced by women worldwide. As already mentioned, human rights are also a constant insurgence of new claims from individuals. For instance, in the beginning, women and non-European citizens were not considered worthy of human rights:

> One can call such usage of a word "meristic", from the ancient Greek meros, meaning "part". Meristic usage of a word is characterized by the fact that part of a whole is given a label to which actually only the whole is entitled. The first period of human rights, in other words, is characterized by a highly meristic concept of the human being. One said "human being" but only meant "European male".[22]

Years later, especially in the so-called "second generation of human rights," after the publication of the Universal Declaration[23], human rights have begun to consider all human beings as legitimate parts.

---

recognition of the legal capacity of the human being—have been concretized by further declarations and conventions under international law and recognized as binding for the states, so that they result in an "international Bill of Rights". (Kirste 2019, 28)

[21] Kirste 2020, 361.

[22] Von Senger 1993, 286.

[23] "1.The period in which the theory—and thus, inevitably, the practice—of human rights was non-universal, with discrimination according to sex, race, etc. This period lasted up to the Universal Declaration of Human Rights of 1948.

2.The period in which at least an attempt has been made to base human rights on the principles of universalism, without discrimination according to sex, race, etc. (but with discrimination against the unborn human child). This period is characterized by universalism in theory and in international law, but by no means automatically in practice, and was inaugurated by the Universal Declaration of Human Rights of 1948." (Von Senger 1993, 287)

6.3 The Foundation of the Rights to Women's Recognition

In the context of women's recognition, it is relevant to inquire which would be the foundation of the rights to women's recognition.

There are several discussions on the foundation of human rights, such as a historical (either evolutionary-continuous or historical-eventful) and anthropological approaches.[24] I understand that, in the theory of recognition, the foundation of the rights to women's recognition rests on disrespect, in the offenses to recognition. Honneth understands that the dialectic of recognition comes from the struggles that persons begin when confronted with some kind of disrespect against patterns of recognition. In this sense, the rights to women's recognition arise from the several offenses that women suffer in several contexts of their lives.

Kirste states that some philosophers consider the origin of human rights from experiences of injustice.[25] He mentions, for instance, the "sad and sentimental stories" from Richard Rorty, which made significant contributions to human rights culture.[26]

For Kirste, there is a risk in justifying human rights based on the exemplary experiences of injustice, because a person must, first of all, have a feeling for a human right before she experiences its violation as an injustice.[27] This position is similar to the one advocated by Honneth when discussing *disrespect*. In Chap. 2, I have seen that Honneth presupposes a reflexive consciousness of an individual before he realizes that she was a victim of a moral injury, of an instance of disrespect.

Nevertheless, I keep questioning this premise from Honneth and I also question the risk discussed by Kirste. Alienation, for instance, may not allow that an individual has the chance even to build moral expectations and the understanding of her position as an addressee of human rights. Experiences of injustice may surpass an acknowledgement of legal recognition, so that the rise of human rights come exactly from the experiences of disrespect.

---

[24] Kirste 2019, 31.

[25] Kirste 2019, 34.

[26] Kirste 2019, 35.

[27] Kirste 2019, 35.

6.4 Cases of Rights to Women's Recognition

Several human rights include the achievement of gender equality, although they may not mention it directly. For instance, I can mention the right to equality[28].

Furthermore, human rights are women rights as well, placing men and women as their addressees. I argue that human rights are not just women's rights—in the sense of women being their addressees—, but actually they are also rights to women's recognition. All human rights hold conditions for the recognition of a person. The comprehension of human rights from this perspective will clarify how human rights may be achieved through struggles for recognition.

I will, then, present some examples of human rights that also constitute rights to women's recognition.

6.4.1 The Right to Recognition

Article 6 of the Universal Declaration of Human Rights states: "*Everyone has the right to recognition everywhere as a person before the law*"[29]. This right relates to the *status subjectionis* defined by Jellinek *apud* Kirste, "*[...] there is the status subjectionis as the status of subjection of all persons to the law, or rather, the status of the recognition of the legal capacity of man*".[30]

Kirste mentions also the "right to rights" from Hannah Arendt, as "*[...] a right that recognized all people as having legal capacity*"[31]. The right to recognition stated in the Universal Declaration is a right to women's recognition, allowing all women to be addressees of rights and duties.

6.4.2 The Right to Freedom of Movement and Residence

Following the numeric order of the articles in the Universal Declaration, article 13 declares the *right to freedom of movement and residence*:

---

[28] Article I: All human beings are born free and equal in dignity and rights. They are endowed with reason and conscience and should act towards one another in a spirit of brotherhood. (United Nations 1948, Universal Declaration of Human Rights).

[29] United Nations 1948, Universal Declaration of Human Rights.

[30] Kirste 2019, 27.

[31] Kirste 2019, 34.

Article 13

1. Everyone has the right to freedom of movement and residence within the borders of each State.[32]

If I compare it with my analysis of Honneth's theory, focusing on the pattern of love, I can observe that the limitations on the freedom of movement directly damage women's legal protection of their possibility to move. Women are addressees of the right to move and to go across the borders of their hometown, in order to experience their own life goals, respecting their authenticity and freedom. It is relevant for the formation of an individual's identity that she moves to wherever she decides, without limitations imposed by either public instances such as the government, or private relationships such as familism[33]. In this sense, if this right is not fulfilled, then women's recognition is also compromised.

The right to freedom of movement and residence also relates to the next human right that I shall discuss, namely, to marry and to found a family.

6.4.3 The Right to Marry and to Found a Family

Article 16 of the Universal Declaration declares the *right to marry and to found a family*:

Article 16

1. Men and women of full age, without any limitation due to race, nationality or religion, have the right to marry and to found a family. They are entitled to equal rights as to marriage, during marriage and at its dissolution.
2. Marriage shall be entered into only with the free and full consent of the intending spouses.
3. The family is the natural and fundamental group unit of society and is entitled to protection by society and the State.[34]

[32] United Nations 1948, Universal Declaration of Human Rights.

[33] Familism can be defined as situations when "[...] family members are expected to bring glory to their paternal family lineage; [...]" (Ting & Chiu, 2002 *apud* Leung 2017, 769).

[34] United Nations 1948, Universal Declaration of Human Rights.

The critical aspect of this human right is the guarantee of gender equality in the moment of getting married, and also in cases of divorce. More than that, marriage should be an institute chosen by both intending spouses.

There are offenses to recognition when cultures set unequal conditions for men and women regarding marriage—especially in cases of divorce. For instance, if a woman is not able to choose freely if she wants to get married and how her relationship will be structured in her familiar context, then she may not enjoy feelings of self-confidence, self-esteem, and self-respect. In such cases, this woman may be treated as an object, being submitted to her husband's commands in a patriarchal and hierarchical relationship. It gets worse if she decides to divorce, whereas in some cases, she will not receive the equal division of property between the consorts, and sometimes even children custody may not be equal and fair. More than that, there are cultural practices in which the parents of the intending spouses arrange their marriage, without respecting their own choices.

In theses cases, men and women are being disrespected and their recognition is damaged as well. All situations of disrespect related above will be dully exemplified in the upcoming chapters regarding case studies in China and Morocco.

6.4.4 The Right to Freedom of Thought, Conscience, and Religion

The Universal Declaration declares in article 18 the *right to freedom of thought, conscience, and religion:*

> Article 18
>
> Everyone has the right to freedom of thought, conscience and religion; this right includes freedom to change his religion or belief, and freedom, either alone or in community with others and in public or private, to manifest his religion or belief in teaching, practice, worship and observance.[35]

I understand that this human right is one of the most disrespected by some United Nations signatories and it violates women's recognition directly. The Moroccan constitution, for instance, institutes the Islamic religion as official, and Moroccans are not supposed to change their religion or manifest different beliefs.

[35] United Nations 1948, Universal Declaration of Human Rights.

Kymlicka endorses Kukathas' expression of "*right to exit*", meaning that people should be allowed to go out of their cultures if they want to do so.[36] Nevertheless, Kymlicka criticizes the ingenuity of Kukathas, who argues that this exit is possible in all situations in which people are willing to be at a market society, theoretically having economic conditions to exit.[37] Undoubtedly, this is not the only requirement for people to go out of a culture. For Kymlicka, Kukathas mistakes when he believes in a substantial freedom even if a person does not have enough conditions of literacy, education, or the freedom to learn about the outside world.[38]

Kukathas errs when he does not realize that individuals born into poor socio-economic or cultural conditions do not have substantial freedom. There is no real freedom when the circumstances do not allow the subject to choose another community. In the end, she does not have real possibilities to exit, and she is not substantially free.

The right to exit relates to the *right to freedom of thought, conscience and religion.* I agree on the fact that individuals should have the right to develop their own life goals, respecting the principles of recognition, and having the right to change their lifestyles, their beliefs, their religion. The right to exit a culture does not mean the negation of one's tradition, but rather the opportunity to enjoy different ways of life, in different places and cultures. I have seen in the above chapter that Kymlicka calls it *rational revisability* of a culture[39].

Donnelly has also stated that culture is not destiny, it is a repertoire of practices and meanings, with which members of a society handle daily relations (Donnelly 2007, 296). It creates a feeling of fixed perpetuity of a culture, but people are always able to transform it.

Recognition encompasses the feelings of self- and social-esteem, whereas a person comprehends her as part of a community, being someone necessary for the achievement of common values. This social recognition is possible just if, on the other hand, the person also has the individual feeling of self-respect and

[36] Kymlicka 1995, 234.

[37] Kymlicka 1995, 234.

[38] Kymlicka 1995, 234. More than individual freedom, Kymlicka advocates that his liberal view includes the principle of equality: "A liberal democracy's most basic commitment is to the freedom and equality of its individual citizens. This is reflected in constitutional bills of rights, which guarantee basic civil and political rights to all individuals, regardless of their group membership. Indeed, liberal democracy emerged in part as a reaction against the way that feudalism defined individuals' political rights and economic opportunities by their group membership". (Kymlicka 1995, 234)

[39] Kymlicka 1995, 213.

self-confidence, for example, being free to elaborate and choose her religion. A previous subjective enjoyment of freedom of thought, conscience, and religion makes possible that a person occupies her role within the society. Therefore, she is able to advocate for her own individual goals, being able to freely deliberate in the private and public instances. This is related to the human right next discussed: to freedom of opinion and expression.

6.4.5 The Right to Freedom of Opinion and Expression

In article 19 of the Universal Declaration, there is the *right to freedom of opinion and expression*:

> Article 19
>
> Everyone has the right to freedom of opinion and expression; this right includes freedom to hold opinions without interference and to seek, receive and impart information and ideas through any media and regardless of frontiers.[40]

The *right to freedom of opinion and expression* is affected by cultural traditions. Similarly, as already mentioned, the *right to freedom of thought, conscience and religion* also suffers influences of cultural values. If a person does not have the chance to build her own opinion and to hold it either in private or public spaces, then she will not become fully respected and recognized.

6.4.6 The Right to Family Planning

In 1968 at the United Nations International Conference on Human Rights in Tehran, the right to family planning was discussed. It relates to the strengthening of health systems, gender equality, and access to sexual and reproductive health care and reproductive rights (United Nations Population Fund, 2018).[41]

In 2018, the United Nations Population Fund endorsed the 1994 International Conference on Population and Development and the 2030 Agenda for Sustainable

---

[40] United Nations 1948, Universal Declaration of Human Rights.

[41] United Nations Population Found. Family planning is a human right. Message for World Population Day by Dr. Natalia Kanem, Executive Director. 11 July 2018. 06 Jul 2018. Available at https://www.unfpa.org/press/family-planning-human-right. Access on 12.04.2022.

Development, committing governments, parliamentarians, the private sector and civil society to support family planning, especially in developing countries.

It means the guarantee to a reliable supply of a full range of modern contraceptives, strengthening national health systems, promoting gender equality, ensuring universal access to sexual and reproductive health care and reproductive rights, including family planning services and information (United Nations Population Fund, 2018.[42]

The right to family planning endorses women's recognition, as it guarantees that a woman has the conditions for freely exercise her sexual and reproductive choices, being also well informed about it.

6.4.7 The Right to Development

In 1986, the United Nations General Assembly issued the Declaration on the Right to Development:

> Article 1
>
> 1. The right to development is an inalienable human right by virtue of which every human person and all peoples are entitled to participate in, contribute to, and enjoy economic, social, cultural and political development, in which all human rights and fundamental freedoms can be fully realized.
> 2. The human right to development also implies the full realization of the right of peoples to self-determination, which includes, subject to the relevant provisions of both International Covenants on Human Rights, the exercise of their inalienable right to full sovereignty over all their natural wealth and resources.[43]

The document clarifies that development should have the human person as the central subject, whereas she is not just the addressee of human rights, but also individually and collectively responsible for development, considering the need

[42] United Nations Population Found. Family planning is a human right. Message for World Population Day by Dr. Natalia Kanem, Executive Director. 11 July 2018. 06 Jul 2018. Available at https://www.unfpa.org/press/family-planning-human-right. Access on 12.04.2022.

[43] United Nations Population Found. Declaration on the Right to Development. Adopted by General Assembly resolution 41/128 of 4 December 1986. Available at https://www.ohchr.org/sites/default/files/rtd.pdf. Access on 14.04.2022.

for full respect for their human rights, fundamental freedoms, and duties to the community. (Declaration on the Right to Development 1986, article 2).[44]

I understand that the right to development is a right to women's recognition, because it aims to guarantee the basic resources to women, allowing them to develop their identity within all the patterns of recognition.

Article 8 of the Declaration on the Right to Development clearly relates the right to development to the situation of women:

> Article 8 1. States should undertake, at the national level, all necessary measures for the realization of the right to development and shall ensure, inter alia , equality of opportunity for all in their access to basic resources, education, health services, food, housing, employment and the fair distribution of income. Effective measures should be undertaken to ensure that women have an active role in the development process. Appropriate economic and social reforms should be carried out with a view to eradicating all social injustices.[45]

Nancy Fraser, for instance, holds that recognition regards to redistribution, whereas the fulfillment of economic conditions is necessary for the achievement of recognition.[46]

6.5 Conclusion of Chap. 6

If I take into consideration the pattern of law and the normative reconstruction, I can understand that rights may have a legal or a moral form, but their relevance for the achievement of recognition is unquestionable.

Recognition is universal, all human beings share instances of recognition and must be able to be agents of struggles. Struggles for recognition are historical, continuous, and dynamic. From the perspective of law, human rights are the institutes more related to the nature of struggles for recognition, as they are also historical, continuous, and dynamic. There are legal and moral human rights, as well as human rights continually in construction. In conclusion, struggles for human rights are necessary for the achievement of women's recognition.

---

[44] United Nations Population Found. Declaration on the Right to Development. Adopted by General Assembly resolution 41/128 of 4 December 1986. Available at https://www.ohchr.org/sites/default/files/rtd.pdf. Access on 14.04.2022.

[45] United Nations Population Found. Declaration on the Right to Development. Adopted by General Assembly resolution 41/128 of 4 December 1986. Available at https://www.ohchr.org/sites/default/files/rtd.pdf. Access on 14.04.2022.

[46] Fraser 2003b, 12.

In this context, I have suggested a shortlist of human rights that relate to women's recognition, namely *the right to recognition; the right to freedom of movement and residence; the right to marry and to found a family; the right to freedom of thought, conscience and religion; the right to freedom of opinion and expression; the right to family planning*; and *the right to development.*

The struggles for the human rights above are possible in different private and social contexts, and individuals themselves may take the accountability of struggling for them. Over time, rights to women's recognition would have an effect on legal or moral instances of societies, being effective and continuously discussed within public and private lives. Until it happens, there are actual struggles ready to be started.

7 Struggles for Recognition in the Pattern of Solidarity

Article 29 of the Universal Declaration states that "*1. Everyone has duties to the community in which alone the free and full development of his personality is possible [...]*"[1]. The obligation to care about one's community relates to the Honnethian notion of solidarity. In the pattern of solidarity, the individual realizes that he has worth, when he commits to the values of his community. This obligation has a moral nature coming from an ethics of recognition, which presupposes feelings such as care, empathy, and affection.

The pattern of solidarity has a particular role for recognition because it is the one that make the relation between private and public life.

This chapter proposes different forms of struggling for recognition in the pattern of solidarity.

I have already concluded that Honnethian solidarity embraces a variety of elements, such as empathy, caring, compassion, loyalty, respect, toleration, and equality. To investigate which are the universal premises of solidarity in order to understand how to struggle inside this pattern, I will make a historical study of the institute, as it was born before Honneth's theory of recognition.

Furthermore, I will clarify the vital relationship between the pattern of love and solidarity.

---

[1] United Nations, 1948, Universal Declaration of Human Rights.

C. Diamantino Esser Santana, *Recognized Women:*, Juridicum – Schriften zur Rechtsphilosophie, https://doi.org/10.1007/978-3-658-46849-1_7

7.1 The Role of Solidarity in Love

Usually, infringements of recognition occur in the sphere of love, as it represents relationships experienced in private life, when individuals are vulnerable and exposed, without protection.

I have already mentioned that in a case of misrecognition, one alternative to the one affected is to appeal in the pattern of law, making a claim for legal support and sanctions against the perpetrator. Nevertheless, depending on the community where the victim is, she may not have a proper protective system of rights. It may also be that she does not want to bring the situation to the sphere of law.

Independently of the inclusion of the situation in the pattern of law, I advocate that a case of disrespect in the pattern of love should be considered under the sphere of solidarity. If there is a situation of misrecognition in the pattern of love, the first attitude for the one affected and eventual witnesses is to bring this situation into the dimensions of solidarity.

Take, for instance, the example of spousal abuse. If the wife does not bring it to the court—which can be very common in some communities, she can count on the support of close friends or relatives. She may remain married to the perpetrator, but at least she will have a voice, she will have people by her side, comforting her, sharing her suffering with her. This relationship, between this woman and the ones who help her, turns into a relationship of solidarity.

I am arguing that solidarity has two dimensions: one private and one public. Usually, authors focus on the public dimension of solidarity, from a political and social perspective. I recognize the importance of solidarity in public spaces, but it is also important to interpret it from a more individual and private perspective. Either from public or private views, solidarity is the opposite of indifference, culminating in the recovery of recognition.

In an ideal model of struggle, this transition of the pattern of love to the pattern of solidarity will arrive, in the end, at the sphere of law. Of course, some societies do not have a proper pattern of law, and even when private disrespect reaches the courts or instances such as the police, the victim can, again, suffer from indifference. There are cases of abuses against women, which are not taken into consideration by Moroccan and Chinese police, for instance. The police refuse to register the report.

Nevertheless, I think that the process of transition of disrespect coming from the pattern of love and reaching the pattern of law takes time and varies from society to society. In any case, what is essential at least is the transition from love to solidarity. If someone somehow helps a victim of disrespect in the sphere of love, it represents an act of solidarity and culminates necessarily in an increase of self-esteem and respect for the one being affected.

7.2 Solidarity as Feeling and Behavior

I have already seen that Honnethian solidarity has influences from Hegel, Dewey, Lukàcs, and Heidegger. Although these scholars have adequately defined the institute from a theoretical perspective, I understand that only Lukàcs and Dewey tried to comprehend it from a more practical and realistic perspective, which could culminate in struggles[2]. In the end, I will conclude that solidarity is a feeling and a behavior.

Rebecca Todd Peters clarifies that, in the beginning, solidarity was related to the idea of fraternity and brotherhood. The first Christian communities endorsed this conception, and it gained traction in the Middle Ages, when specifically men began to form professional social identities and ties—I can mention, for instance, the artisans[3]. People involved in such solidarity groups were considered part of a brotherhood.

At that time, the ones who practice solidarity were people with particular conditions, and there is no regard for the ones outside the group's context. There is any active solidarity as a behavior of caring for someone. Privileged participants of specific social groups exclusively enjoy this form of solidarity.

Max Pensky states that nowadays, there are still interpretations of solidarity as a brotherhood, friendship, and affection. Nevertheless, he considers it inadequate, because solidarity is only seen as a feeling of belonging to some group, as a result of social norms, which obliges people to join some social conformations.

After the Middle Ages, solidarity had migrated from a religious conception of fraternity to a political meaning, representing the individual feeling of a person to be part of a community:"*[...] solidarity is a concept that attempts to balance the individual and the community and to live into the tension between an increasing focus on individual rights and liberty and traditional concerns for the common or*

---

[2] Richard Rorty does not understand solidarity coming from an ethics of care and recognition: "This tradition dreams of an ultimate community which will have transcended the distinction between the natural and the social, which will exhibit a solidarity that is not parochial because it is the expression of an ahistorical human nature. Much of the rethoric of contemporary intellectual life takes for granted that the goal of scientific inquiry into man is to understand "underlying structures", or, "culturally invariant factors", or "biologically determined patterns."(Rorty 1989, 168)

[3] Peters 2014, 18.

collective good"[4]. Solidarity, then, involves two elements: social integration and bonding[5].

Now, the government should protect and promote solidarity. For Comte, "*government must act deliberately to facilitate the development of a feeling of solidarity among its citizens*"[6]. Taking solidarity as a political institute, it tends to signify *integration*: the inclusion of new members inside institutions, allowed by different means of participation—for instance, periodic elections[7]. This inclusion is still not very open, people to be included must follow certain premises to be accepted in the communities of solidarity.

From Durkheim, firstly, there was mechanical solidarity, meaning the bonds that hold people together, from their sharing of life experiences and worldviews, culture, rituals[8]. Here, solidarity comes from a cultural identification, being static. Afterward, mechanical solidarity was replaced by a notion of organic solidarity.

Organic solidarity is focused on the performance of individuals in the labor dynamic. Each person is responsible for the whole group, acting as an organ in the body: "*Thus, like the organs in the body that perform specialized functions but depend upon the healthy functioning of the whole in order to survive, the solidarity that is present in modern (industrial) societies is an organic solidarity.*"[9] It seems that organic solidarity gives the individual a more active role in her community[10]. Nevertheless, it comes much more from a mechanism of market and labor

---

[4] Peters 2014, 20.

[5] Pensky 2011, 128.

[6] Comte *apud* Peters 2014, 20.

[7] "Integration is thus a function of inclusion, and inclusion implies the production of individuals with the aptitudes, orientations and desires appropriate for a given institution's purposes and function. For instance, insofar as modern democratic governance entails periodic elections, solidarity refers to the successful integration of new individuals into the existing institutions of electoral politics, such that they have the competences, aptitudes, and—crucially—values requisite for such institutions to remain functional. Citizenship, broadly construed, is a range of institutions whose continued existence requires solidarity—here taken only as the ongoing production and inclusion of new members." (Pensky 2011, 128)

[8] Peters 2014, 21.

[9] Pensky 2011, 129. See also: "Persons were capable of recognising one another as co-members of the same social project precisely insofar as the differences between them arising from the division of labour could be construed as integrated parts of a single social whole." (Pensky 2011, 129).

[10] "Karl Marx also approaches two kinds of solidarity, considering the labor dynamic. Firstly, representing relationships and bonds between members of the working class due to their common struggle against oppression under capitalism. Secondly, the utopian version of solidarity that Marx sees within communist societies" (Peters 2014, 23).

dynamics, than from the individual's conscience. Solidarity is not an intentional human behavior yet.

Max Weber was the one responsible for showing that solidarity can be different between groups, promoting the identification of each different community. From Weber, solidarity begins to be analyzed not just from the perspective of people inside the same group, but also between different communities, a perspective of extragroup solidarity.[11]

Richard Rorty does not agree with the idea of an extragroup solidarity, because for him there is no relationship between solidarity and an ethics of care and recognition. In his words:

> I have been arguing that we pragmatists should grasp the ethnocentric horn of this dilemma. We should say that we must, in practice, privilege our own group, even though there can be no noncircular justification for doing so. We must insist that the fact that nothing is immune from criticism does not mean that we have a duty to justify everything. We Western liberal intellectuals should accept the fact that we have to start from where we are, and that this means there are lots of views we simply cannot take seriously.[12]

Considering all these interpretations of solidarity, including the one made by Honneth and explained in Chap. 1, I understand that solidarity is a feeling and behavior.

Solidarity must contain more than just observers, but rather participants. Furthermore, solidarity should be applicable not just intragroup, but also extragroup, and interculturally. In the end, I am arguing that in order to attain recognition, the struggles must count on an engaged, active, and intercultural solidarity.

As already mentioned above, a situation of solidarity can be analyzed between two persons: the addressee—the one receiving practices of solidarity—and the agent—the one who acts. Both have feelings of solidarity. Honneth's theory mostly focuses on the addressee—the one who deserves self-esteem and social-esteem. Nevertheless, if recognition presupposes struggle, then it is also essential to focus on the one who struggles, on the agent of solidarity.

The agent of solidarity does not need to previously know the victim, the one suffering disrespect. Acts of solidarity should be practiced to the benefit of anyone, from inside or outside the group. It does not matter if the agent knows the victim of disrespect.

---

[11] Peters 2014, 21.

[12] Rorty 1989, 176.

Jürgen Habermas has touched on the necessity to expand solidarity beyond cultural borders:

> These problems can be solved only within a framework that, from the perspective of egalitarian universalism, disconnects the mobilization of civic solidarity from ethnic nationality and radicalizes it toward a solidarity among "others". In binding itself to universalistic constitutional principles and to "human" rights, the sovereign will-formation of democratic citizens is only acting according to the necessary presuppositions of a legitimate legal institutionalization of its own practice.[13]

I do not agree on the necessity to link the solidarity among "others" with a sphere of legalized democracy. Some communities do not have enough democratic structures in their public sphere. Nevertheless, they are still able to practice and to receive solidarity.

The struggles for the other[14], for people whom the agent does not know, come from her consciousness and morality as a human being, and recognition as an ethics of care. Considering that, solidarity should not be imposed by the state or by the law, but rather be understood as a feeling to be shared between people, such as a moral value for human beings. Habermas recognizes it when discussing Erhard Denninger's triad of diversity, security, and solidarity:

> Solidarity among citizens who expect one another to take responsibility for each other, even though they are strangers, is artificial insofar as it is produced by means of the law. To be sure, a liberal political culture is required so that the abstract principle of the constitution can take root in the minds and motivations of the citizens.[15]

Pensky goes straight to the point when discussing the pattern of solidarity in Honneth's theory of recognition:

---

[13] Habermas 2005, 3. Tod Petter calls such actions as "countercultural":

"In a world that values and promotes unmitigated consumerism and wealth creation, practicing an ethic of solidarity requires first-world citizens to think and act in countercultural ways." (Peters 2014, 8).

[14] "The postmodern project undercuts every sort of common identity and standard behavior: it makes for a society in which the plural pronouns "us" and "them" (and even the mixed pronouns "us" and "me") have no fixed reference; it points to the very perfection of individual liberty. The Bulgarian-French writer Julia Kristeva has been one of the more interesting theoretical defenders of this project; she urges us to recognize a world of strangers ("for only strangeness is universal") and to acknowledge the stranger in ourselves". (Walzer 1997, 88)

[15] Habermas 2000, 524.

> Would a third option between liberal and communitarian theories find some mediating position between them and thereby counteract the weaknesses of each? This is precisely what Honneth's account of solidarity as a sphere of recognition in modern societies attempt.[16]

Honneth does not believe that solidarity should come from some institutional normativity, for instance, from the rule of law or governmental incentives. Nevertheless, if solidarity should be a result of an individual's choice and morality, how do you define it for different people? Pensky calls such a situation "the Goldilocks problem."

From one side, social norms regarding solidarity should be universal, or individuals should be capable of including struggles for solidarity in their self-realization. Pensky calls the Goldilocks problem the fact that social norms cannot be somewhat universal, if a person is also entitled to sustain a self-realizing project[17].

> If the former scenario holds, and if Honneth is correct that esteem for our projects from others is a necessary albeit insufficient condition for our success, then it is not at all clear why we are entitled to differential solidarity amongst social members – we would in fact have an obligation to esteem one another just the same insofar as our self-realising projects (mergers and acquisitions or Oxfam, triathlons or slacking, SUV's or Earth First, death metal or Mozart) conform to the principles of modern justice, or at least do not harm them.[18]

Whether solidarity comes from social norms and, as a consequence, as an ethical requirement, then Honneth should consider a social consensus on this topic. However, Honneth did not make it. For Pensky, such cultural consensus would be related to the Honnethian notions of honor or 'standing,' in a way that being solidary would contribute to the practical realization of society's abstractly defined goals.[19]

---

[16] Pensky 2011, 137.

[17] Pensky 2011, 151.

[18] Pensky 2011, 151.

[19] "As a kind of grandchild of the premodern notion of honour or 'standing', esteem-through-difference 'signifies only the degree of social recognition the individual earns for his or her form of self-realization by thus contributing, to a certain extent, to the practical realization of society's abstractly defined goals.' In this sense, for Honneth social solidarity retains a distinctly premodern, even nostalgic tinge. Unlike legal respect, with its levelling of differences and its flat ascription of equal status, solidarity still seems to require the very substantive value consensus to whose absence the modern regime of legal rights attests so powerfully". (Pensky 2011, 142)

> The individualisation of bases for esteem, the universalisation of norms of recognition, and the emptying of substantive cultural consensuses on shared social goals in the wake of the bourgeois revolutions of the eighteenth century all made it increasingly difficult for modern societies to find a way to recognise individuals as valued social members *on the basis of their differences*—on the basis of their differentiated social roles.[20]

Furthermore, solidarity as a social norm would presuppose a broad conception of the good life. In that case, it could lead to an individual's commitments to procedures and forms of reason[21], which would not differentiate Honneth from the tradition which preceded him—think about Kant, Rawls, or Habermas -, and which he has criticized[22].

I understand that the so-called "Goldilocks problem" is solved when we understand recognition as an ethics of care. Caring for someone has a nature of humankind and morality. Solidarity, then, becomes a moral virtue and a feeling to be shared between individuals.

Pensky also investigates Honneth's solidarity from the individual's perspective, with regard to self-realization. According to him:

> Honneth's own definition of "formal ethical life" is simply that set of structural conditions in which people are capable of achieving that degree of recognition necessary for them to pursue their projects of self-realisation, a definition that remains neutral on what such projects might be.[23]

Honneth, then, also does not define human beings' projects of self-realization. It makes sense in his theory, as, since the beginning, he assumes that recognition

[20] Pensky 2011, 141.

[21] "How, for example, can the evangelical Christian Midwesterners and the urban lesbian mums *esteem* each other's projects of self-realisation, rather than simply find a *modus vivendi* or, better, a common ground to settle their inevitable legal and economic struggle? Would solidarity here be anything other than the purely negative ability to refrain from denigrating one another? And if so, is that really the same as the bonding effects of solidary relationships? Would a shared conception of the good life broad enough to allow such different secondary interpretations even to contest each other be anything other than the broadest commitments to procedures and forms of reason?" (Pensky 2011, 148)

[22] "For Honneth, it is thus precisely the modern solidarity problem that the natural law tradition from Kant through Rawls, and indeed through Habermas as well, cannot resolve." (Pensky 2011, 140)

[23] Pensky 2011, 151.

and its patterns can change according to the community and, naturally, the individual. The variety of self-realization's projects of life is what makes solidarity a struggle:

> Individualised solidarity still retains a strongly corporatist dimension in the individual's capacity to expect and receive symmetrical esteem from co-members, on the basis of shared traits that are definitive for membership. […] Given a hazy and insubstantial set of ethical values, an agonistic field of civil society in which the practical meaning of those values is constantly contested, and persons whose projects of individual self-realisation depend in large measure on winning the esteem of others, then, solidarity is indeed a struggle, with constantly shifting goalposts, rules, players and umpires.[24]

Solidarity as a struggle, from Pensky's perspective, occurs because people are trying to be esteemed by their communities and partners.

My concept of solidarity as a struggle is different from Pensky's, because, in my model, individuals have a minimum of ethical principles and human rights. They do not engage in solidarity to obtain the esteem of others. On the contrary, they are caring and compassionate about others.

If I adopt the ethical principles of recognition and also the fundamental human rights, then I would eliminate the problem highlighted by Pensky, "*Individuals and groups could thus be mistaken in their beliefs that their modes of self-realisation warrant the esteem of their fellow citizens, if those modes conflict with principles of justice.*"[25]

From this context, struggles for recognition through solidarity would contribute not just for a private reaching of respect and autonomy, but also for a global solidarity. Hauke Brunkhorst highlights the role of democracy in theses struggles, as without democracy in, between, and beyond states, there is no global solidarity, and it is difficult to imagine a solution to the problems of inclusion that follow all modernization path.[26]

It is relevant, then, to present some examples of how to struggle for recognition through solidarity.

---

[24] Pensky 2011, 145.

[25] Pensky 2011, 151.

[26] Brunkhorst 2016, 203.

7.3 Struggles against the Social Pathology of "Indifference"

In Chap. 4, I have seen that indifference can be seen as an emotion and behavior, affecting the three patterns of recognition.

In Chap. 5, I have seen how struggles can confront indifference as an emotion.

Now, in this chapter, I will show how indifference as a general behavior should be confronted. When indifference as behavior is shared in a public space, compromising all the struggles there, then it starts to transform into a social pathology damaging the pattern of solidarity.

It is important to analyze how Honneth defines social pathology[27]. Honneth, following the tradition of Critical Theory, clarifies that social pathology is everything that damages social cooperation. The symptoms of social pathology affect the individual and society, and a social pathology necessarily represents Honnethian disrespect.

I have seen that the pattern of solidarity relates to social relationships, which can be experienced privately or publicly. Indifference as a social pathology is a social problem which affects engagement in solidary acts. When people are ignored and made invisible, the social pattern of solidarity is damaged.

In case an act of disrespect happens in the public space of solidarity, people around will witness the situation. After witnessing such a situation of disrespect, it is necessary, according to Honneth, to struggle for recognition. In these cases, struggle means confronting the social pathology of indifference.

7.4 Struggles for Metanoia, the Honor of Difference, Accountability, and Action

Rebeca Todd Peters advocates that first-world citizens should act for the benefit of unprivileged people. For her, it is necessary to create a theo-ethic of solidarity[28], coming from the lessons of Jesus and adapting solidarity to the current world.

---

[27] For a full definition of Honnethian social pathology, see Chap. 2.

[28] "[…] a Christian ethic of solidarity will negotiate the delicate territory between pragmatism and prophetic vision. From a pragmatic perspective, it is true that a shift from neoliberal capitalism to a more just economic model of society appears to be a utopian vision, an impossibility given the political-economic structures of our present-day world. However, prophetic vision plays an important role in society by allowing people to imagine what the world could be like. […] Shaped by realism, any justice ethic must recognize and acknowledge the devastation and destruction that humans have waged on one another." (Peters 2014, 50).

I do not agree on an essential relationship of solidarity with religion, because it can easily be misunderstood if used by orthodox religious practices or traditional and patriarchal cultures. Nevertheless, I think that the theory of Peters contributes to the Honnethian perspective on solidarity, as it goes further and proposes real practices and actions, which should be taken by individuals to promote solidarity.

Peters' ethics of solidarity is transformative because first-world citizens are called to action through transforming their lifestyles in their private life, as well as working on economic and political structures, which cause inequality and injustice[29].

According to Peters, first-world citizens are in a privileged position, and they are responsible for creating situations of solidarity, for creating better conditions of life for disadvantaged people.

I argue that in the majority of communities normally there are people in a more privileged situation than others. Usually, a society has people with good standards of life (wealth, high level of health care and education, leisure). Nevertheless, not all of them mobilize their efforts to improve the social conditions of their community. When Peters speaks about first-world people, I could expand it to privileged people in general.

To promote conditions for the development of solidarity, privileged people should take three premises into consideration:

> There are three key points that are foundational for first-world people who wish to develop an ethic of solidarity: 1) Understanding social location and personal privilege 2) Building relationships with people across lines of difference 3) Engaging in structural change.[30]

First of all, the agent of solidarity understands social location when she is aware of the context where she is, her race, gender, ethnicity, culture, sexual orientation, and class. All these aspects interfere in her relationship with other persons[31].

Secondly, the agent of solidarity must build relationships with people across lines of difference. It means that she must abandon the notion that solidarity is just attaining to charity or isolate situations of helping disadvantaged people. It is necessary that privileged people develop personal relationships with people in need, creating bonds of solidarity and understanding. Peters understands that

[29] Peters 2014, 2.

[30] Peters 2014, 10.

[31] Peters 2014, 10.

"the poor," or, as Honneth would say, "the other," is also someone for building real relationships, with whom people from the first-world should share life experiences and worldviews[32].

Lastly, engaging in structural change means going further than the practice of charity. People in need are open to receive food or shelter, but at the same time, it is essential to consider how to guarantee justice for them, changing the direction of the world[33].

If the subject is capable of complying with the three premises above, then she could act solidary by employing four different tools, namely, metanoia, honoring difference, accountability, and action.

"*While metanoia is most often translated in the New Testament as "repentance," it is more accurately understood as a total personal transformation that is reflected in both thought and behavior. Metanoia is a radical transformation of heart, mind, and soul that literally makes one a new person.*"[34] The author argues that human beings should be open to transform their behavior and lifestyle, as the world's sustainability and human beings' social justice require it. It relates to my argument that the most crucial struggle for recognition nowadays is against indifference. Exercising *metanoia* is a form of being active; it changes the agent's position from observer to the one who participates in the process of change. In the end, active practices of solidarity are struggles for recognition.

Furthermore, Peters calls people to honor differences, as this is a characteristic of all communities. The agent of solidarity must presuppose that people are not the same, and any tendency towards uniform cultures makes people lose their identity and the possibility of enrichment of society[35].

Nevertheless, I have argued above that respect and tolerance for different individuals and communities must consider the limits of the human rights listed in this present work. The difference must be respected and celebrated, as soon as human beings keep having their autonomy and free will, and recognition is guaranteed.

Regarding accountability, "*Beverly Harrison argued that solidarity required genuine accountability, describing it as concrete answerability to oppressed people. Understood in Harrison's terms, solidarity has to be more than a sympathetic gesture in support of a cause or the pain and suffering of others.*"[36] What makes

[32] Peters 2014, 11.

[33] Peters 2014, 11.

[34] Peters 2014, 60.

[35] Peters 2014, 62.

[36] Peters 2014, 64.

solidarity different from sympathy and empathy is the element of action. When the agent acts to the benefit of the addressee, he begins to participate, to engage in the struggle for recognition, being much more than just someone who suffers observing the pain of another individual[37].

Peters suggests that the "doing for" should be substituted by "working with." Instead of doing something for a person in a situation of disrespect, the agent should also include the affected victim in the struggle, literally acting side-by-side with her. It is called "mutuality"[38].

Peters criticizes contemporary interpretations of solidarity, especially the fact that it relates to the moral intuitions of the individual. Peters analyses three intuitions, namely sympathy, responsibility, and mutuality, but she highlights that all of them are in danger, because they can be easily manipulated[39]. I have already mentioned the social pathology of alienation, which interferes in an individual's life. The three moral intuitions relate to solidarity and would be useful in the confrontation of indifference. I understand that sympathy, responsibility, and mutuality, if not intuitive, should be morally required.

The human moral intuition of sympathy makes a person compassionate with the others, caring about them and desiring to help them in some way. "*Primarily,*

---

[37] "I researched, the more I realized that these well-intentioned structures of benevolence and charity inevitably contribute to the creation of imbalanced relationships. These relationships allow first-world Christians to feel good about ourselves because we "helped," without ultimately requiring us to change anything about our own personal habits and behaviors or the social and economic structures that shape our societies in patterns of wealth and poverty, have and have-not, deserving and undeserving". (Peters 2014, 99).

[38] Peters 2014, 45. See also: "Solidarity, as defined here, is fundamentally both a theory and an action. From a theoretical perspective, solidarity describes a state of being in which two or more distinct communities or groups of people develop a bond or a relationship based on a shared interest, value, or goal. When we talk about solidarity as an organizing model for changing the direction of globalization in our world, we are talking about the praxis aspect of solidarity: developing a new model for working across chasms of difference toward a common goal. Developing a deep understanding of what solidarity has to offer as a new model of thinking about and living in the world requires both theory and action. It is both a noun and a verb, a way of understanding how we can live in the world and a concrete way of living in the world. Solidarity is the expression of support and partnership between these two people or groups of people. It is the enactment of justice in society as a foundation for building a peace between nations and peoples that recognizes our common humanity and our common origin as beings created in God's image". (Peters 2014, 51)

[39] "Because moral intuitions represent visceral reactions rather than thoughtful reflection and analysis, they are also subject to manipulation by media outlets, politicians, or unscrupulous corporations seeking to exploit guilt and prejudices in order to further their own agendas." (Peters 2014, 42)

people who respond from a moral intuition of sympathy are motivated either by feelings of pity and sorrow for the misfortunes of others, or by the guilt they feel when they judge that their lives are "better" than the lives of those they reach out to help."[40]

Secondly, the moral intuition of responsibility occurs when the agent of solidarity recognizes that he is privileged, and then, he should help others, especially those that are less fortunate.[41]

Finally, actions from mutuality come from the understanding that an individual's practices build up the community, and the well-being of all depends on everyone. In this case, the agent of solidarity should build partnerships and cooperation.[42]

Sympathy, responsibility, and mutuality are elements of a solidary act. Although Peters understands that institutions can easily manipulate these elements, I understand that human beings are capable of acting solidary from an autonomous perspective free from alienation, preserving their sympathy, responsibility, and mutuality.

Pensky reiterates that Honneth has mentioned other challenges for solidarity. These challenges are social integration, cultural pluralism, social complexity, and individualism.[43] There is also the principle of achievement, which affects solidarity negatively: "*It is the hegemonic function of the achievement principle, Honneth suggests, that tends to withdraw esteem-recognition from all those projects of individual self-realisation that do not conform to it.*"[44]

Besides the difficulties that solidarity finds nowadays, I understand that Honneth mentions some possible solutions for increasing solidarity and, as a consequence, recognition.

---

[40] Peters 2014, 36.

[41] Peters 2014, 38.

[42] Peters 2014, 40.

[43] "Whether in terms of Hegel's vision of subjective and objective freedom mutually fulfilling one another only in the form of a state institution that supersedes that of civil society, or Durkheim's conception of a fundamental replacement of mechanical solidarity for organic solidarity based on differences via the division of labour, or Habermas' notion of civil society institutions conveying communicative bonds into the political system via deliberative institutions, the specifically modern form of social solidarity has to be explained in terms of the basic features of social modernity: the collapse of traditional resources for social integration, and the corresponding rise of cultural pluralism, social complexity and individualism." (Pensky 2011, 136)

[44] Pensky 2011, 147.

7.5 Struggles for Honnethian Voluntary Practices

In "*Freedom's Right*", Honneth endorses the necessity of voluntary practices in the public sphere:

> Therefore, in order to be able to share the freedom of democratic self-legislation at all, citizens must do more than merely switch back and forth between speaker and listener, author and reader. It is crucial that they also be willing to resist the dissolution of the public sphere by dividing up the necessary voluntary services needed for the material preparation and execution of actual events.[45]

Honneth also recognizes the role of non-governmental organizations, and the use of the internet as tools to increase recognition.[46] The non-governmental organizations that have proliferated since the 1990s, have formed globally connected alliances, addressing problems, emergencies and injustices.[47] Furthermore, although one may argue that the politically active use of the internet and the multiplying webs of communication are not sufficient empirical certain yet, they also transcend national borders and endorse transnational over national processes of will-formation.[48]

They all represent acts of solidarity, struggles for recognition. I understand that these Honnethian proposals relate to a social space, which stimulates people's participation. I have already mentioned that not all societies have public spaces that endorse solidarity, debate, and freedom. For Honneth, it relates to his notion of democracy, as I will further see.

7.6 Struggles for Honnethian Democracy

Axel Honneth understands that democracy should be seen as more than just a political regime, but first and foremost as a social ideal[49]. He recognizes the importance of public manifestations, such as voting and public discussions, but he advocates that more than that, democracy should be exercised in the everyday

---

[45] Honneth 2014a, 292.
[46] Honneth 2014a, 300.
[47] Honneth 2014a, 300.
[48] Honneth 2014a, 300.
[49] Honneth 1998, 780.

habits of individuals, through democratic principles. The democratic principles become moral ones, preserving respect and equality between individuals[50].

Honneth defends that in the school, for instance, children would have the chance to begin their processes of becoming a citizen, exercising democratic attitudes and learning to have voice and to give voice to the other ones (*demokratische Erziehung*).[51] Nevertheless, Honneth highlights that, nowadays, these practices of democracy are undermined by many factors. First of all, the economic system compromises social freedom. In this system, people do not exercise role obligations from a mutual and relational perspective[52], but instead as isolated subjects competing against each other.

Furthermore, Honneth clarifies that individuals are not focused on the sphere of democratic will-formation, because usually, people do not believe in the freedom guaranteed by institutions. Dewey call this "apathy"—similar definitions are

---

[50] See the interview of Honneth in 2012: "RW: A leading concept in your new book is democratic ethical life (demokratische Sittlichkeit). Can you explain what you mean by this concept?

AH: This concept, which after all is the subtitle of the book, is one of the theoretical tools I use to try and revitalize Hegel's thought. As is well known, Hegel believed that the social integration of modern societies requires more than legal rules and procedural mechanisms; it needs the development of everyday habits in which the moral principles of modern constitutions are anchored. If we apply this concept to the present, we face the necessity of making the stability and vitality of our democracy dependent on whether the moral attitudes of equality and respect have also taken hold in our everyday practices. My book represents an attempt to examine how far along Western democracies are in this process of anchoring democratic principles in the everyday habits and customs of its citizens." (Honneth; Willig 146, 2012c)

[51] "Die Idee der demokratischen Erziehung, an die ich mit meinem Vortrag erinnern wollte, hält für den ersten, methodischen Teil dieser Frage bereits die Antwort bereit: Je weniger der Schüler oder die Schülerin im Unterricht als ein isoliertes, leistungserbringendes Subjekt adressiert, je stärker er oder sie mithin als Mitglied einer lernenden Kooperationsgemeinschaft behandelt wird, desto eher dürften sich unter ihnen Kommunikationsformen einstellen, in denen kulturelle Differenzen nicht nur spielerisch akzeptiert, sondern als Chancen der wechselseitigen Bereicherung begriffen werden können." (Honneth 2020, 206)

[52] Honneth states that: "At any rate, there can be no doubt that the current economic system in the developed countries of the West in no way represents a 'relational' institution and is thus not a sphere of social freedom. It lacks all the necessary characteristics of such a sphere: It is not anchored in role obligations to which all could agree, and which interweave with each other in a way that would enable subjects to view each other's freedom as the condition of their own freedom; it therefore lacks an antecedent relation of mutual recognition from which the corresponding role obligations could draw any validity or persuasive power." (Honneth 2014a, 176).

"privatization" and "depoliticization"[53]. People do not trust the institutions and do not believe in public support for increasing democracy.

Besides the interpretation of democracy as an ideal and attitude, Honneth also understands it as a political regime. For him and many other scholars of political philosophy, democracy is a premise for the achievement of justice.

In the article "*Democracy as Reflexive Cooperation*" (1998), he endorses Dewey's model of democracy, as a good alternative between republican and proceduralist models. He clarifies that, in republicanism, people are seen as citizens who intersubjectively negotiate everyday affairs[54]. Here, the law expresses the solidary citizenry.[55]

In proceduralism, on the other hand, citizens are not the essential element of democracy—self-governing political community. Instead, the most important element of democracy is the morally justified procedure[56]. Here, law is a state-sanctioned tool, which has the function of protecting democratic procedure[57].

The proceduralist model of democracy comes from Jürgen Habermas. He proposes this model in the substitution of republican and liberal models of democracy. According to Habermas, in the republican model, politics is:

> [...] the reflective form of substantial ethical life, namely as the medium in which the members of somehow solitary communities become aware of their dependence on one another and, acting with full deliberation as citizens, further shape and develop existing relations of reciprocal recognition into an association of free and equal consociates under law. [...][58]

---

[53] According to Honneth: "Whereas we always seek involvement in the other two spheres of social freedom, because our 'natural' desires or objective constraints of survival compel us to, we must first resolve to engage in the sphere of democratic will-formation. Therefore, it is only in this last step of our normative reconstruction that a problem arises that we could not have been faced with before: the sheer disinterest in institutionally promised freedoms. The concept Dewey used to describe this threat is 'apathy'; other terms depicting similar phenomena include 'privatization' or 'depoliticization'.

We will repeatedly encounter these concepts in our account of the development of the democratic public up into the present." (Honneth 2014a, 278).

[54] Honneth 1998, 763.

[55] Honneth 1998, 764.

[56] Honneth 1998, 763.

[57] Honneth 1998, 764.

[58] Habermas 1994a, 1.

That means, in republican democracy, solidarity comes together with administrative power and individual personal interests. Here, society has a political nature[59]. In republican democracy, For Habermas, democratic will-formation comes from a culturally established background consensus, in the form of an ethical-political discourse[60]. Furthermore, in republicanism, human rights are secondary, as popular sovereignty comes first[61]. For Habermas, human rights promote popular sovereignty and should come as a premise and a factor of motivation in such a dynamic.[62]

Whereas republican democracy has political rights, on the other hand, liberal democracy is characterized by the negative rights of citizens, as they are protected from the government, and free to enjoy their private life[63]. Citizens are free and equal to reach an understanding:

> According to the liberal view, the democratic process takes place exclusively in the form of compromises between competing interests. Fairness is supposed to be granted by the general and equal right to vote, the representative composition of parliamentary bodies, by decision rules, and so on. Such rules are ultimately justified in terms of liberal basic rights.[64]

Liberal democracy, for Kymlicka, is not just guaranteed by an election system, but also by a system of equal representation.[65] It should acknowledge solidarity as

---

[59] Habermas 1994a, 6.

[60] Habermas 1994a, 6.

[61] Habermas 1994b, 6.

[62] According to Habermas: "The internal connection between popular sovereignty and human rights that we are looking for consists in the fact that human rights state precisely the conditions under which the various forms of communication necessary for politically autonomous law-making can be legally institutionalized. These conditions are no longer constraints, but enabling conditions for the exercise of popular sovereignty. […] The normative intuitions we associate with human rights and popular sovereignty only achieve their full articulation in the system of negative and private rights if we assume that negative liberties and private autonomy may neither be imposed as a moral right in a way that constrains political legislation, nor instrumentalized just as a functional requisite for the democratic process. Private and public autonomy are co-original and of equal weight." (Habermas 1994b, 13)

[63] Habermas 1994a, 1.

[64] Habermas 1994a, 6.

[65] "Or, put another way, a group of citizens is represented in a legislature if one or more of the members of the assembly are the same sort of people as the citizens. This contrasts with the more familiar idea in democratic theory which defines representation in terms of the procedure by which office-holders are elected, rather than their personal attributes. On this traditional view, a group of citizens is represented in the legislature if they participated

a strong sense of common identity[66] and an openness to dialogue and peaceful negotiation between people (Kymlicka is discussing specifically the majorities and minorities)[67].

Coming from these two perspectives—liberal or republican, Habermas proposes a proceduralist model of democracy. He defends deliberative politics, in which the discourse is no more political, but pragmatic, ethical, and moral. The discourse, now, is represented in different communicative procedures[68].

In proceduralist democracy, the state is no more the center of society, but rather the formation of the public understanding by individuals: "*Discourse theory has the success of deliberative politics depend not on a collectively acting citizenry but on the institutionalization of the corresponding procedures and conditions of communication.*"[69]

Habermas argues that proceduralist democracy brings solidarity together with money and administrative power—the three elements of society's integration:

> The normative implications are obvious: the integrative force of "solidarity", which can no longer be drawn solely from sources of communicative action, should develop through widely expanded and differentiated public spheres as well as through legally institutionalized procedures of democratic deliberation and decision-making.[70]

The difference of proceduralism from republicanism and liberalism is that politics has other subsystems, which exist together, and promote the opportunity for individuals to exercise their communication:

> In this regards the discourse-theoretic reading of democracy has a point of contact with a detached sociological approach that considers the political system neither the peak nor the center, nor even the formative model of society in general, but just one

---

in the election of one or more members of the assembly, even if the elected members are very different in their personal characteristics. Why are the personal characteristics of representatives so important? There is surprisingly little written about the competing conceptions of representation which underlie recent proposals for group representation." (Kymlicka 1995, 138).

66 "The sort of solidarity essential for a welfare state requires that citizens have a strong sense of common identity and common membership, so that they will make sacrifices for each other, and this common identity is assumed to require (or at least be facilitated by) a common language and history." (Kymlicka 1995, 77).

67 Kymlicka 1995, 167.

68 Habermas 1994a, 5.

69 Habermas 1994a, 7.

70 Habermas 1994a, 8.

> action system among others. On the other hand, politics must still be able to communicate, through the medium of law, with all the other legitimately ordered spheres of action, however these happen to be structured and steered.[71]

Considering that Honneth endorses Dewey's model of democracy, Dewey does not adopt either republican, liberal, or proceduralist models of democracy. For him, the institute of social cooperation is the key to the development of democracy.[72]

Dewey believes in democracy as a social organism, in which people exercise their activities and functions, contributing to the maintenance of their society[73]. Coming from this model, Honneth argues for a review of it, considering that the capitalist labor market has been changing the *work society* and, as a consequence, the way people work and cooperate.[74]

Honneth seems to be more attached to Dewey's model of democracy as a political regime, as he understands that cooperation is a crucial element for recognition, for the individual's identity development, coming from private to the public life. In any case, what is critical for Honneth is the element of solidarity, which is present in the three democratic models—republican, liberal, and proceduralist, in different forms. Struggling for a minimum of democratic ideals is a way to struggle for recognition.

I have shown that struggles for recognition—and, then, recognition itself—presuppose minimal democratic conformations—at least, democracy as a principle, an ideal, an attitude -. Considering that, now I should see how to increase the conditions of democracy in societies with a low level of democracy or in non-democratic societies.

First of all, for Honneth, the public patterns of politics and law should not be considered as the ones to guarantee social freedom. Such a paradigm nowadays does not work anymore, and the institutional spheres begin to have a secondary role:

> The motor and the medium of the historical process of realizing institutionalized principles of freedom is not the law, at least not in the first instance, but social struggles over the appropriate understanding of these principles and the resulting changes of behaviour. Therefore, the fact that contemporary theories of justice are guided almost exclusively by the legal paradigm is a theoretical folly. We must instead take account

[71] Habermas 1994a, 10.

[72] Honneth 1998, 764.

[73] Honneth 1998, 767.

[74] Honneth 1998, 780.

> of sociology and historiography, as these disciplines are inherently more sensitive to changes in everyday moral behaviour.[75]

For Honneth, the spheres of personal relationships (love) and the economic market are the ones to include processes that are more democratic.[76] As already mentioned, the sphere of love is the one more appropriate to hold such practices.

To allow the theory of recognition to be effective, I advocate that democracy should be seen more as an ideal than as a form of the investiture of public agents at public administration. Democracy should be interpreted from the Honnethian perspective of an ideal, embracing different dimensions of an individual's life.

Honneth, in "*The Political Identity of the Green Movement in Germany: Social-Philosophical Reflections*", has recognized that civic engagement presupposes certain political conditions.[77] The so-called "pre-political" situation makes it possible for the individual to comprehend democratic attitudes and necessities.

Coming from this discussion, I should also reiterate Kymlicka's point of view. The multiculturalism scholar understands that the liberal approach has levels, and an illiberal community has the potential to be liberal[78] and should be slowly transformed into a liberal one, utilizing individuals' actions—individuals outside of that context or even the ones inside the illiberal community. From Honnethian theory, it would be represented by struggles for recognition:

> Liberals have a right, and a responsibility, to speak out against such injustice. Hence liberal reformers inside the culture should seek to promote their liberal principles,

---

[75] Honneth 2014a, 329.

[76] Honneth 2014a, 330.

[77] "The exclusive emphasis on the civil sphere, in which the citizens' engagement takes place, makes them overlook the fact that a range of social and economic enabling preconditions are required for individuals to participate freely and without shame in active public engagement. The idea of "civil society" tends to overlook the importance of these pre-political conditions of civic activities because they can only be granted through social and political rights guaranteed by a state whose bureaucratic power is precisely to be curbed. On this point again, it is not the place to go into the political-conceptual background that would explain how such a blind spot could have arisen in the conception of "civil society". For me, what is decisive here is that due to the neglect of social-economic claims this leading concept refers only one-sidedly to the civil sphere of citizens' engagement and consequently cannot provide a bridge that would link up with the two other key themes." (Honneth 2010b, 11).

[78] "The aim of liberals should not be to dissolve non-liberal nations, but rather to seek to liberalize them. This may not always be possible. But it is worth remembering that all existing liberal nations had illiberal pasts, and their liberalization required a prolonged process of institutional reform. To assume that any culture is inherently illiberal, and incapable of reform, is ethnocentric and ahistorical". (Kymlicka 1995, 94).

> through reason or example, and liberals outside should lend their support to any efforts the group makes to liberalize their culture.[79]

Making an analogy with Kymlicka, who argues that non-liberal states always have the potential to increase their liberal ideals, I endorse that, in general, societies have the potential to increase their democratic ideals, step-by-step, without necessarily confronting government and law. There are countries where processes of democratization are either happening very slowly or not happening at all. Nevertheless, the use of the critical ideas of democracy is necessary to allow people in such societies to struggle for recognition.

My argument could be endorsed by Kymlicka, who holds that without an individual consciousness with regard to democracy—democratic ideal -, even the political democracy would not work. For him, many classical liberals believed that a liberal democracy could be made secure, even in the absence of an especially virtuous citizenry, through institutional and procedural devices such as the separation of powers, a bicameral legislature, and federalism.[80] Kant, for instance, affirmed that the problem of good government 'can be solved even for a race of devils'.[81] Nevertheless, for Kymlicka, procedural-institutional mechanisms to balance self-interest are not enough, and some level of civic virtue and public-spiritedness is required.[82]

The solution, from my point of view, is at least to foster democracy as an ideal, in public and private dimensions of an individual's life. First of all, I propose an extension of Walzer's concept of toleration[83] for the private life of individuals—the pattern of love. The author defines tolerance from an extragroup perspective, in the discussion of cultural majorities and minorities. Tolerance, for him, is related to democracy and, through a democratic education, people would be able to develop not just a critical thought, but rather to develop the virtue of tolerance and associational life.[84]

Nevertheless, toleration should include not just the respect to different cultures—extragroup toleration—, but also the respect to differences inside the same community—intragroup tolerance—. Especially inside the family context, one

[79] Kymlicka 1995, 168.

[80] Kymlicka 1995, 175.

[81] Kymlicka 1995, 175.

[82] Kymlicka 1995, 175.

[83] "We might think of these two forms of toleration—individual assimilation and group recognition—as the central projects of modern democratic politics". (Walzer 1997, 84)

[84] Walzer 1997, 110.

may act according to the *right of freedom of thought, conscience, and religion*, and choose to not comply with their own culture. Someone should be authorized to not comply with cultural traditions, usually transmitted by family generations. It is a form of promoting difference, debate, and democratic attitudes in an individual's private life.

It is relevant to highlight that I endorse toleration, whether it has limitations imposed by human rights and the elements of recognition. Some cultural practices should not be tolerated at all, in case they infringe on recognition and human rights.

The endorsement of toleration and other democratic attitudes could be done by education[85], in the way proposed by Okin:

> But it seems not at all unreasonable, within the context of a liberal state, that values its citizens' capacity to make informed decisions about whether to lead autonomous or nonautonomous lives as adults, to require both that children's education – including their religious education – be nonsexist, and that all children be thoroughly exposed to and taught about other religious as well as secular beliefs held by people around the world. Indeed, without this, it would be difficult to claim that their adhering to their parents' religion was voluntary at all.[86]

The feminist author is arguing that education has a crucial role in promoting individual autonomy in a cultural context, letting them decide about their religion and culture. It is a form of guaranteeing the democratic ideal[87]. For Walzer, the school is just one of a variety of places where democracy can be discussed:

---

[85] "Article 26:

1. Everyone has the right to education. Education shall be free, at least in the elementary and fundamental stages. Elementary education shall be compulsory. Technical and professional education shall be made generally available and higher education shall be equally accessible to all on the basis of merit.
2. Education shall be directed to the full development of the human personality and to the strengthening of respect for human rights and fundamental freedoms. It shall promote understanding, tolerance and friendship among all nations, racial or religious groups, and shall further the activities of the United Nations for the maintenance of peace.
3. Parents have a prior right to choose the kind of education that shall be given to their children." (United Nations, 1948, Universal Declaration of Human Rights)

[86] Okin 1999, 122.

[87] Kymlicka and Raz also foster the role of education. See: "Among typical general measures we could mention providing schooling enabling members of cultural communities to learn their own cultures, languages, or religions, supporting cultural institutions, requiring

> These conversations should take place everywhere, but perhaps especially in the public schools (and in public and private colleges and universities), which have historically been marked, at least in the major immigrant centers, by an integrative mode of association. Public schools bring together the children of parents committed to different religious and ethnic communities—as well as the children of parents who have escaped or are in the process of escaping from such commitments.[88]

I understand that in cases where public discussions are not permitted, the family context, again, is an instance where people should be able to discuss, to adopt different forms of life and belief.

Additionally, liberals such as Kymlicka and Okin endorse the importance of the majorities' struggle for the minorities in need.

Okin agrees with Kymlicka when he states that multiculturalism and feminism are related struggles: "*Both seek the recognition of difference in the context of norms that are universal in theory, but not in practice.*"[89]. Nevertheless, she argues that the theorists of multiculturalism should highlight gender equality in the context of intragroup inequalities, for guaranteeing moral equality[90].

For her, the majority is responsible for the minority groups:

> [...] whose oppression it may promote or exacerbate by granting group rights without careful consideration of intragroup inequalities. As Tamir points out, the leaders of most groups are motivated to put forth their group's interests as those of a unified agent, and therefore "to foster unanimity, or at least an appearance of unanimity, even at the cost of internal oppression".[91]

Walzer, on his part, incentivizes the associational ties in the societies.[92] This may occur through government policies creating jobs and sponsoring the unionization on the job.[93] It would contribute for grounding democratic politics and improving

employers to allow employees time off if this is needed for religious or other cultural purposes, and, most important, enhancing an understanding and acceptance of cultural diversity in the population at large, replacing the attitude of a majority that agrees to tolerate minorities with one of coexistence of various groups within the general framework of one civic and political culture". (Raz 1999, 89).

88 Walzer 1997, 109.

89 Okin 1999, 123.

90 Okin 1999, 123.

91 Okin 1999, 112.

92 Walzer 1997, 105.

93 Walzer 1997, 105.

economic, solidary, and mutual aid.[94] Furthermore, Walzer endorses programs for the strength of family life, in any forms that support stable relationships and networks.[95] He highlights the cultural associations, and the fact that nowadays they are not sufficiently strong to represent a distinctive working class culture.[96] If they are not sufficiently strong, then they may turn labor into radicalism.[97] For Walzer, the associational ties may be represented through language, memory, familiar rituals, and different forms of common practices.[98] From Walzer: "*So we need more cultural associations, not fewer, and more powerful and cohesive ones, too, with a wider range of responsibilities.*"[99]

The existence of such associational ties would increase democratic discussions, contributing to recognition. For instance, Honneth, in the recent work "*Democracy and Fair Labor Conditions*" (2023)[100], states that the associational ties promoted by fair labour conditions would endorse the reaching of recognition, especially through democracy. He has discussed the fundamental importance of fair labour conditions for the reaching of recognition.

Hegel, Durkheim, and Cole have somehow discussed the important role of fair conditions within the social division of labour and its regards to public deliberation and consensus-building.[101] Hegel, for instance, stated that the member of civil society is somebody through his competence and regular income and means of support, being honored and recognized as the representative of a trade or profession.[102] Nevertheless, Honneth holds that their theories fail not to satisfactorily consider the importance of a fairly and properly constituted world of labour in enabling successful democratic participation. Working conditions

---

[94] Walzer 1997, 105.

[95] Walzer 1997, 105.

[96] Walzer 1997, 105.

[97] Walzer 1997, 105.

[98] Walzer 1997, 105.

[99] Walzer 1997, 105.

[100] Honneth, A. Democracy and Fair Labor Conditions. Journal of Business Ethics. 2023. Springer.

[101] Honneth 2023, 4.

[102] Honneth 2023, 2. See also: "In Hegel (2018) [1807] the Lockean conception resurfaces as an essential element of his philosophy of spirit: labour, he maintains, has a formative function for self-consciousness, because labour is a means by which a subject objectifies himself in an external thing and thereby has his own powers and capacities reflected back to him." (Honneth 2022a, 153).

must have normative rules that allow the persons to use their right of political co-determination.[103]

Furthermore, for Honneth, the discussions on the role of democracy and the moral foundations of the modern constitutional state lack on considering a kind of principle of empowerment, not just a traditional principle of equality.[104] In other words, when the employee is located at the workplace, she has firstly an individual perspective of empowerment, detached of a supposedly relation to the others. Just in a second moment of recognition, this person will then comprehend herself in an equal fair condition with others.

For Honneth, then, it is relevant for a theory of recognition to look at forms of social disadvantage that do not allow a singular participant to participate in democratic practices at all.[105] For instance, some kinds of work do not allow the individual to reflect on political matters or engagement. "*All these forms of injury and impairment consist in a deprivation of the minimum necessary capacities required for democratic participation*"[106]. From this individual perspective, unfair labour conditions impair the participation in processes of democratic decision-making, damaging the reaching of self-confidence and autonomy.[107]

For Honneth, if someone is not respected within the work environment, then this person is not able to build other necessary nuances of recognition[108]. The disrespect in the workplace may be represented not just by unfair and unequal conditions within the workplace itself, but also through high levels of unemployment and unequal conditions for even having the chance to have a job vacancy[109].

Actually, social labour has been gradually embracing different kinds of activities, not just relating to the production of physical objects, but also other performances[110]. In terms of the theory of recognition, Honneth argues that social labour today should embrace producing useful commodities; interacting with other persons for the purpose of care-giving, consultancy, and teaching; and operating with symbols with the aim of processing data beneficial to the

[103] Honneth 2023, 4.
[104] Honneth 2023, 4.
[105] Honneth 2023, 4.
[106] Honneth 2023, 5.
[107] Honneth 2023, 5.
[108] Honneth 2023, 5.
[109] Honneth 2023, 5.
[110] Honneth 2022a, 150.

administration of social and economic processes.[111] As a consequence, cooking or childcare, typical activities performed by women, do contribute for the community as much as paid employment in a factory or office.[112]

For Honneth, the capacities for democratic participation is endorsed through different facets: economic, temporal, psychological, social, and intellectual.[113] The psychological harm may come, for instance, from the one's labor being held in a low esteem by the community.[114] "*When a form of labor enjoys no social recognition, its practitioners will struggle to understand themselves as suited to participation in democratic decision-making [...]*"[115] In this context, for Honneth, cultural value systems are historically emerging broadly shared beliefs, which can be broken only through long-term processes of education and discovery, which may happen under fair labour conditions.[116]

7.7 Conclusion of Chap. 7

Chapter 7 has brought forms of increasing recognition within Honnethian solidarity. To confront infringements on recognition, the pattern of solidarity should be seen as the one for recovering self-confidence in love relationships. Whereas the dimension of love is the one more important regarding the infringements on recognition—namely disrespect, the dimension of solidarity is the one more important regarding the struggles for recognition.

Chapter 7 has shown that solidarity has dimensions of brotherhood and social integration, which are relevant to this day. Honneth, from my point of view, is proposing participative solidarity, which is an emotion as well as a behavior. Solidary acts should be seen from an emotional and affective perspective, morally required.

First of all, the chapter has proposed the struggle against indifference located in the pattern of solidarity. There, indifference becomes a social pathology and must be confronted by solidary acts.

Coming from the Honnethian understanding of solidarity, I have argued that solidarity should also be applicable interculturally. In this topic, I have adopted

111 Honneth 2022a, 161.

112 Honneth 2022a, 164.

113 Honneth 2023, 5.

114 Honneth 2023, 5.

115 Honneth 2023, 9.

116 Honneth 2023, 9.

the theo-ethic of solidarity proposed by Peters, as she argues that nowadays it is necessary that privileged people engage as agents of solidarity, respecting its four dimensions. Firstly, people should be open to experiencing metanoia, to change their lifestyles for the benefit of society—this reminds me of Dewey's understanding of democracy as based on cooperation. Secondly, when they encounter social differences, people should honor them, comprehending that social and cultural differences are part of human nature. Thirdly, agents of solidarity have accountability; they are responsible for changing from the position of observers to the position of participants. Finally, solidarity is an action.

For Honneth, voluntary practices endorsed by the current use of social media, internet, as well as non-profit organizations are all useful for the achievement of solidarity. More than that, he advocates for a democratic model of society which comes from Dewey and promotes the participation of people in all instances of recognition. If people understand democracy as an ideal and a set of attitudes, also seeing solidarity as a necessary moral obligation, then the struggles for recognition are possible.

Authors such as Honneth, Okin, Kymlicka, Raz, and Walzer recognize the relevance of education for the emancipation of democratic principles. Furthermore, Walzer highlights the relevance of associational ties as well. In 2023, Honneth has endorsed that associational and fair practices, within the context of labour, benefit the reaching of recognition through the guarantee of democratic participation.

Considering all these proposals for struggles in the pattern of solidarity, the work will now relate this and the other above discussions on the theory of recognition with the reality of women and the achievement of women's recognition.

Part III

Case Studies

From the Hegelian Notion of Recognition to Contemporary Case Studies on the Legal Recognition of Women

8

8.1 Hegel and Recognition

Chapters 5, 6, and 7 have discussed how struggles for recognition may happen within Honneth's three patterns of recognition. It was possible to comprehend how love, law, and solidarity relate to each other and any struggle for recognition influences building a person's identity as a whole.

I understand that legal recognition is the key to achieving women's recognition. In cases of disrespect, the recovery of recognition comes firstly from legal recognition. Struggles for recognition within this pattern do not just endorse an expansion of rights, but also the transformation of rights, according to new individual and social claims.

Honneth states that to deny someone the capacity to be a legally responsible subject does not mean questioning their capacity for moral self-determination, but also deeming them incapable of making veridical reports of states of affairs.[1] The relevance of legal recognition may be endorsed, especially if I study the origins of the Honnethian model of recognition, which rests mainly in the work of G.W.F. Hegel. Whereas Honneth conceives recognition from the patterns of love, rights, and solidarity, Hegel conceives ethical life from family, civil society, and state perspectives.

For Hegel, ethical life (*Sittlichkeit*) is the concrete identity of the good with the subjective will, an identity that is, therefore, the truth of them[2]. Ethical life is preceded by the abstract right, which also represents the basis for morality. For Hegel, "*At the moral standpoint, the abstract determinacy of the will in the sphere of*

[1] Honneth 2022b, 24.

[2] Hegel 2008, 152, pp. 141.

C. Diamantino Esser Santana, *Recognized Women:*, Juridicum – Schriften zur Rechtsphilosophie, https://doi.org/10.1007/978-3-658-46849-1_8

right has been so far overcome that this contingency itself is, as reflected into itself and self-identical, the infinite inward contingency of the will, i.e. its subjectivity".[3] The abstract right and morality, then, need the support of ethics:

> 141. [...] Addition: [...] The spheres of right and morality cannot exist independently [*für sich*]; they must have the ethical as their support and foundation, for right lacks the moment of subjectivity, while morality in turn alone possesses that moment, and consequently both right and morality lack actuality by themselves. Only the infinite, the Idea, is actual. Right exists only as a branch of a whole or like the plant which twines itself round a tree that is firmly rooted in and for itself.[4]

The Hegelian ethical life is the concept of freedom developed into the existing world[5]. For Hegel, the role of the philosophy of law rests on the abandonment of an atomized individual—who believes in her subjective freedom—replacing it with a complex interaction between autonomous individuals and shared social practices[6]. Hegel rejects the social contract currently adopted by modern philosophical thought, abandoning the idea of isolated individuals' hypothetical "natural state"[7]. Honneth holds that, for Hegel, the "you" not only contains an attribution of moral autonomy, but also at the same time it refers to the commonalities we possess as members of one and the same moral community.[8]

Hegel studies the relationship between the singular and the universal when conceiving recognition. Honneth, on the other hand, has reinterpreted the Hegelian theory of intersubjectivity, not in metaphysical terms, but empirically, from the social psychology of Mead[9].

The ethical life of Hegel understands property and law, together with the modern political economy, as forms of social existence[10]. This combination of ethical life and economic processes is the basis of civil society[11]. Civil society relates to family and state, so that particularity goes and universality comes.[12]

[3] Hegel 2008, 108 pp. 104.

[4] Hegel 2008, 153, pp. 141.

[5] Hegel 2008, 154, pp. 142.

[6] Sinnerbrink 2017, 51.

[7] Sinnerbrink 2017, 166.

[8] Honneth 2021b, 585.

[9] Sinnerbrink 2017, 165.

[10] Sinnerbrink 2017, 167.

[11] Sinnerbrink 2017, 167.

[12] Hegel 2008, 179, pp. 181.

The individuals interact with others, and these social relationships turn into legal relationships. The social relationships, then, are seen by Hegel as intersubjective normative relationships.[13] Honneth holds that, for Hegel, "recognition" is more than merely the reciprocal ascription of a normative status that obligates one to correct inferences and authorities the judgement of inferences carried out by other members of the community.[14] Rather, through recognitive processes, we reciprocally generate ourselves as subjects who possess duties to restrict ourselves out of "moral" consideration for our fellow subjects.[15] In this sense, "recognition" for Hegel is not merely "ascription", a bestowal of epistemic authority, but thereby at the same time the collective constitution of a moral world.[16]

This comprehension of intersubjective normative relationships endorses the argument of this work, which advocates that women's recognition presupposes first and foremost legal recognition. If I choose for instance, the recognition in the pattern of love, despite the Honnethian understanding of recognition in the pattern of love as a precondition for participation in public life—love seems to be a first experience of expecting to be part of ethical life, Hegel does not focus on the pattern of family in the same way as Honneth focuses on the pattern of love[17].

Regarding family, Hegel conceives the individual as a member of her family, belonging to it without independence[18]. The family includes three phases, namely marriage; family property and assets; and the education of children—which culminate in the dissolution of the family, preparing for the transition to civil society.[19]

---

[13] Sinnerbrink 2017, 167.

[14] Honneth 2021a, 720.

[15] Honneth 2021a, 720.

[16] Honneth 2021a, 720.

[17] Sinnerbrink 2017, 170.

[18] "158. […] Hence in a family, one's disposition is to have self-consciousness of one's individuality within this unity as the essentiality that has being in and for itself, with the result that one is in it not as an independent person but as a *member*." (Hegel 2008, 162, pp. 158).

[19] "160. The Family is completed in these three phases:

(a) marriage, the form assumed by the concept of the family in its immediate phase;
(b) family property and assets (the external existence of the concept) and attention to these;
(c) the education of children and the dissolution of the family." (Hegel 2008, 163, pp. 160).

Marriage, for Hegel, relates not just to love as a purely subjective instance but also as a rightfully ethical love.[20] Through this interpretation, Hegel understands that although marriage may be subject to dissolution, legislators must make it as difficult as possible.[21]

Love, for Hegel, turns out to be a feeling that will disappear in civil society when individuals are conscious of unity as law[22]. I understand that Honneth expands this notion of love, conceiving it not just as a feeling, but also as an essential pattern of recognition that endorses recognition as a whole. When individuals experience the patterns of law or solidarity, love still exists and sustains feelings of respect, confidence, and esteem.

After being a member of the family, the individual, then, is part of civil society. As a third step, she reaches the state. For Hegel, the state "[...] exists immediately in *custom [Sitte]*, mediately in individual *self-consciousness*, knowledge, and activity, while self-consciousness in virtue of its disposition finds in the state, as its essence and the end and product of its activity, its substantial freedom"[23].

From Hegel, then, recognition is not just about recognizing ourselves, but actually recognizing others in the same manner as ourselves.[24] Honneth comprehends it as an educative process, beginning with subjects learning to perceive their closest attachment figures as human beings, whose specific needs and desires demand a certain care and consideration.[25]

In the context of gender equality, it is then necessary to conceive struggles for the recognition of women coming not just from the women victims of disrespect or advocates for gender equality. Men are also part of the struggles for recognition

---

[20] "161 [...] Addition: [...] Marriage, therefore, is to be more precisely characterized as rightfully ethical [*rechtlich sittliche*] love, and this eliminates from marriage the transient, fickle, and purely subjective aspects of love." (Hegel 2008, 164, pp. 161).

[21] "163. [...] Addition: [...] Since marriage has feeling for one of its moments, it is not absolute but subject to fluctuations and potentially dissoluble. Legislators, however, must make its dissolution as difficult as possible and uphold the right of the ethical order against caprice." (Hegel 2008, 166, pp. 163).

[22] "158. [...] Addition: [...] Love, however, is feeling, i.e. ethical life in the form of something natural. In the state, feeling disappears; there we are conscious of unity as law; there the content must be rational and known to us." (Hegel 2008, 162, pp. 158).

[23] Hegel 2008, 228, pp. 257.

[24] Sinnerbrink 2017, 169. See Hegel 2008, 188, pp. 192: "[...] When needs and means become abstract in quality (see pp. 191), abstraction also becomes a determination of the reciprocal relation of individuals to one another. This universality, as the quality of *being recognized*, is the moment which makes *concrete* and *social* the isolated and abstract needs and their ways and means of satisfaction."

[25] Honneth 2022b, 23.

of women; all people are part of the struggles for recognition of women. The person or the community, disregarding the gender, which does not fully recognize a woman, is not identifying themselves as persons or members of a community.

Women's recognition may happen if they share conditions of recognition with all other persons, endorsed either through coherent legal norms or—in cases where it is not yet reached—through a minimum of coherent moral norms of recognition.

I have already studied in Chap. 1 that Honneth tries not to state that recognition is an ethical model. Still, I understand that he understands recognition as ethics in different moments. Recognition, according to Honneth, has normative ethical principles, such as the already discussed principles of love, law, and merit—all of them mentioned in Chap. 1.

If I take Honneth's theory and perform the interpretations and changes proposed in this work, then struggles for the recognition of women are possible. Law is not just a pattern of recognition responsible for achieving recognition in the whole model of recognition, but also a very relevant form of struggling for it.

According to Hegel, the processes of struggling for recognition comprehend the dialectic between the enslaved person and the master. Whereas the slave renounces his independence and submits himself to the master, the master is also dependent on the slave, as the slave works to satisfy the necessities of the master. The slave, in the end, will reach the comprehension of real freedom, from the connection between dependency and independence[26]. This parable means, in the end, the union of the unity-in-the-difference of the Spirit:

> The truth of the independent consciousness is accordingly the servile consciousness. This servile consciousness does indeed appear initially outside of itself and not as the truth of self-consciousness. But just as lordship showed that its essence is the inverse of what it wants to be, so too servitude in its consummation will really turn into the contrary of what it immediately is; as a consciousness driven back into itself, it will withdraw into itself and be converted into true independence.[27]

The intersubjective nature is the realization of freedom[28]. For Hegel, "*Spirit is the ethical life of a people insofar as spirit is the immediate truth; the individual that is a world. Spirit must advance to the consciousness of what it immediately is,*

[26] Sinnerbrink 2017, 36.

[27] Hegel 2018, 81, pp. 193.

[28] Sinnerbrink 2017, 39.

must sublate the beautiful ethical life, and by way of a series of shapes attain to knowledge of itself."[29]

I have seen that, according to Honneth, the law represents a struggle, especially if I understand the struggles practiced by institutions, as agents of struggles—for instance, legal security, state authority, and civil support[30].

In the next two Chapters (Chap. 10 and Chap. 11) I will approach case studies on women's recognition and how struggles for the recovery of their respect would be possible. It will illustrate how the conceptions of *struggles* for Honneth and Hegel allow different practices and actions in the direction of promoting recognition within gender equality.

Law as recognition and *law as a struggle* should also be related to the Hegelian notion of history. From Hegel, the rationality of a historical community is appreciated if I focus on its development of the idea of freedom[31].

For Hegel, the individuals and the social experiences are historically situated; they are formed through the history which they are part of. History, for him, is not just a chronology of events and struggles, but also rational progress[32]. This understanding of the role of history in forming an individual's identity relates directly with the recognition of women, as their identity is formed through the struggles they are part of.

Not just Hegelian recognition has influenced the studies of Honneth, but also all the historical facts that culminated in the formation of the so-called Critical Theory.

8.2 Critical Theory and Recognition

The years preceding 1848 characterized a double revolution: the industrial transformation, which occurred in England, and the political transformation, caused by the French Revolution[33]. For Eric Hobsbawn, from 1848 on, wars and facts no longer brought the traditional heroism, but started to legitimize themselves from aspects arising from capitalism[34]. The "Springtime of the peoples", which took

---

[29] Hegel 2018, 175, pp. 441.

[30] Honneth 2014a, 61.

[31] Sinnerbrink 2017, 47.

[32] Sinnerbrink 2017, 46.

[33] Hobsbawn 2011a, 24.

[34] Hobsbawn 2011a, 24.

place in 1848, had the ability to spread into different places like no other revolution up to that time. Proclaimed in February, it won Germany by early March; Vienna, Hungary, and Italy by mid-March[35].

Nevertheless, it turned out that also in a short period of time, with the exception of France, all the regimes overthrown by the revolution were retaken[36]. In any case, the "Springtime of the peoples" demonstrated to the conservatism of the time that the people were no longer quietly submissive to their orders. The revolutions of 1848 stated that the middle class, liberalism, political democracy, nationalism, and the working classes would be present on the political scene from that moment on[37].

The second half of the 19th century was also affected by the migration movements, which contributed to the formation of a mass of workers in industry. In view of this, since 1866, industrial and union movements began to emerge in some countries, guided by Karl Marx's First International.[38] In 1875, the Social Democratic Party of Germany was formed, which functioned as an independent working class movement. Strikes began and new trade unions sprang up.[39]

Marx, after a few years of leading the First International, felt unable to remain in control and moved to New York. Still, his ideas triumphed[40]. Some thinkers, called Marxists, began to propagate his ideas—albeit in an adapted way—from 1870 onward.[41] The Paris Commune, in 1871, was an important symbol of workers' insurrection, requiring autonomous cooperatives or corporate units of producers, from a radical and systematic government intervention.

From this context, the 20th century, for Hobsbawn (2011), can be interpreted from the beginning of World War I until the end of the Union of Soviet Socialist Republics (USSR). The context that permeated the First World War was composed of a civilization that was capitalist in its economy, liberal in its legal and constitutional structure, bourgeois in the image of its characteristic hegemonic class, and exultant with the advances of science and reason, and it was certain that Europe was considered the cradle of the arts, politics, and economics.[42]

---

[35] Hobsbawn 2011a, 32.

[36] Hobsbawn 2011a, 51.

[37] Hobsbawn 2011a, 56.

[38] Hobsbawn 2011a, 56.

[39] Hobsbawn 2011a, 56.

[40] Hobsbawn 2011a, 57.

[41] Hobsbawn 2011a, 57.

[42] Hobsbawn 2011a, 57.

In Germany, the First World War culminated in the Weimar Republic and the establishment of economic chaos. Although the American support guaranteed to Germany[43], with the First World War and its effects, all these traces of a prosperous civilization were left behind. For Delacampagne[44], the malaise caused by the First World War was mostly reflected in German philosophy.

Before 1914, Europe was cheering Kant's studies and new languages about the human being and the world. With the defeat in the First World War, Germany constituted an anguished collective identity, still based on a recent national unity and extremist movements with popular support[45]. In this scenario, *Critical Theory* emerged in the post-First World War climate.[46] Their scholars promoted the defense of the so-called "Critical Theory", to the detriment of Traditional Theory. They witnessed the Bolshevik Revolution in 1917, the proclamations of the German republic in 1918 and 1923, and the workers' uprisings in Poland and other countries. In this context, its thinkers intended to reflect on the power structures dominant at the time, with a methodology that intended to transform theoretical studies into social practice[47].

In September 1922, Felix Weil wrote a "Memorandum on the Creation of an Institute for Social Research" addressed to the curator of the University of Frankfurt. In this document, it was stated as the proposed goal of the Institute the "knowledge and understanding of social life in its totality," from the economic base to the institutional and ideational superstructure.[48] It turned out that Weil and the other members who inaugurated the School—Max Horkheimer and Friedrich Pollock—did not have the higher professorship, a necessary title to occupy the directorship of the institute. Therefore, they invited Carl Gründberg, an internationally renowned Marxist historian, to become the first director of the Institute[49]. Gründberg made it clear in his inaugural class that the scientific method to be adopted by the School would follow that laid out by Marxism.

In 1923, Gründberg inaugurated, as the first director, the work of the Institute for Social Research, academically affiliated to the University of Frankfurt.

---

[43] Slater 1978, 37.

[44] Delacampagne 1997, 69.

[45] Delacampagne 1997, 72.

[46] Reale and Antiseri 2006, 470.

[47] Horkheimer 1980, 137.

[48] Slater 1978, 16.

[49] Slater 1978, 16.

Sequentially, the rise of Nazism, World War II, the postwar "economic miracle" and Stalinism were the factors that marked the *Critical Theory of Society*[50].

On the eve of World War II, the Jewish community in Germany was quite developed in the cultural and social spheres. German philosophers of Jewish origin had a strong presence in the first third of the 20th century[51]. Because of this, with the beginning of World War II, many of these thinkers were forced to take refuge in exile, among them the members of the first generation of the Frankfurt School. With the National Socialists taking power in 1933, the institute created groups in Paris and New York.

With the end of World War II, preceded by Walter Benjamin's suicide in 1940, when the institute reopened in 1950 in Frankfurt, the work was restarted without reference to its past.

Along these lines, for Honneth, Critical Theory studies encompass an economic analysis of post-liberal capitalism, the socio-psychological investigation of societal integration and the cultural-theoretical analysis of mass culture[52]. Nevertheless, for Honneth, Frankfurt School lost its internal connection after the end of World War II and, as a result, began to disintegrate[53]. However, it is understood that their thinkers kept alive the reflection on society that developed from there, among them Honneth himself. In this sense, the theory of recognition of Honneth not just is influenced by the work of Hegel, but also it has a variety of influences coming from the Critical Theory.[54]

Additionally, according to Honneth, if one makes a history of the European idea of recognition, his theory is mostly adherent to the German tradition influenced by Hegel, but he was also influenced by some discussions developed by the French scholars.[55]

---

[50] Matos 1993, 6.

[51] Delacampagne 1997, 135.

[52] Honneth 1999, 514.

[53] Honneth 1999, 536.

[54] Honneth has approached the Marxist theory and pointed out some mistakes, which made him not completely attached to the thinking of Marx. For instance, see: "Der Fehler von Marx bestand vielmehr darin, nicht gesehen zu haben, dass derselbe Prozess an jeder seiner Stationen wie durch undurchsichtige Fäden an die institutionellen Verhältnisse der Gesellschaft gebunden bleibt, die je nach ihrem moralischen Klima, ihrer rechtlichen Organisation und ihrer politischen Konstellation seinen Verlauf beeinflussen können: Die kapitalistische Akkumulation wird in ihrem jeweiligen Charakter durch die politische, rechtliche und moralische Verfasstheit der Gesellschaft bestimmt—und nicht umgekehrt, wie Marx es in seiner reifen Theorie des Kapitalismus zu glauben schien." (Honneth 2020, 138).

[55] Honneth, A.; Bankovsky, M. 2021c.

From the French theories of recognition, Honneth has been influenced by discussions on the negative impact of denigration on existential recognition (from Jean-Paul Sartre); the understanding of recognition as an ideology and its regulative power (from Michel Foucault); the need for recognition of our own particular needs, through the care of others who love us (from Emmanuel Levinas and Jacques Derrida, for instance); and the particular makeup of institutions in our social world in which implicit normative claims to recognition are located (particularly from Pierre Bourdieu and Luc Boltanski).[56]

If I focus specifically on women's recognition theories, it is necessary to comprehend that recognition of women relates to the role of woman in labour. The struggles for recognition of women began within the context of work. Honneth holds that, in the beginning of 20th century, the marginalization of personal services has influenced female formation of recognition. Women were active in all areas of economic life, but the majority of them were employed at the private houses of the wealthy bourgeoisie.[57] Women were not just domestics, but also female secretaries and sales clerks. In all these activities, they were underpaid, explored, and invisible[58]. Their work used to have no economic significance. Women were experiencing daily denigration, authoritarian paternalism, unwanted sexual attention and personal harassment.[59]

From Honneth, the reflections developed by John Locke, Adam Smith, Hegel, and Marx culminated in Hanna Arendt's analysis of the gradual dominance of labour over communicative action.[60] All these contributions were willing for taking personal service work from the marginalization. Furthermore, coming back to the First World War, Honneth holds that the care provided by thousands of female nurses to wounded soldiers was also responsible for empowering some kinds of female work[61]. Nevertheless, it was not sufficient and female workforce kept being continuously disrespected. For instance, it turns that female domestic labour endorsed the prevailing ideology of the patriarchal age: whereas man and woman complement one another, woman naturally suited to household and man has naturally a place in the public political and commercial spheres.[62]

---

[56] Honneth, A.; Bankovsky, M. 2021c.

[57] Honneth 2022a, 158.

[58] HOnneth 2022a, 157.

[59] Honneth 2022a, 157.

[60] Honneth 2022a, 157.

[61] Honneth 2022a, 158.

[62] Honneth 2022a, 159.

Unpaid labour performed by the housewife, including cooking, cleaning and child-rearing remained in the shadow of the traditional conception of labour.[63] Within this scenario, the first representatives of the women's movement began to demand that domestic labour be assigned to better conditions[64].

Nevertheless, it took around 50 years until the topic gained attention in the public political domain and imply on a transformation of the concept of socially necessary labour.[65] In the 1970 s, the feminist campaign for paid housework designed the gender-specific assignment regarding private domestic labour.[66] At that time, the social necessity of work was reflected not just through labour market demands.[67] In other words, the feminist campaign stated that the countless necessary tasks performed in private households without any compensation in the form of wages were actually a form of contributing to maintaining the universally favored components of a given lifeform in the sense of socially essential activities.[68]

Although some studies on the conditions of women, Honneth does not interpret his theory of recognition from the perspective of the recognition of women. In 2022, for instance, he has stated that the material from which he has developed his concept of social disrespect are historical studies that show how workers have been regarded by the bourgeoisie as morally unreliable and cognitively deficient.[69] This is justified by his influences from the Critical Theory. Honneth, nevertheless, admits the importance of comprehending a theory of recognition of women, for instance through the study of Miranda Fricker, who, by contrast, deals with an epistemic injustice based on socially disrespected and humiliated experiences of women, to whom men, in their everyday interactions with the opposite sex, assign a smaller measure of cognitive credibility.[70]

It is relevant, then, to advance the studies on Honneth's recognition, taking all his influences in consideration and embracing discussions on the condition of women.

---

[63] Honneth 2022a, 160.
[64] Honneth 2022a, 160.
[65] Honneth 2022a, 160.
[66] Honneth 2022a, 160.
[67] Honneth 2022a, 160.
[68] Honneth 2022a, 162.
[69] Honneth 2022b, 13.
[70] Honneth 2022b, 13.

8.3 Legal Recognition of Women

The comprehension of women's recognition requires an illustration of the elements and conditions for recognition, which are shared not just in positive rights, but also in a shared ethics. The adoption of case studies is helpful to illustrate how different forms of disrespect and lack of recognition exist within women's different contexts of life, affecting not just women themselves but all members of their community—including men.

Taking formal legal rights into consideration, there are international treaties on women's rights. I have already seen that Article 6 of the Universal Declaration of Human Rights introduces the universal right to recognition. I have related it to Kirste's interpretation of a right to rights, coming from Hannah Arendt[71].

The right to recognition stated in the Universal Declaration is also a right to women's recognition, allowing all women to be the addressees of rights and duties. Nevertheless, other international conventions regarding women's rights are adopted by the countries I will take as my object of study.

The adopted case studies from China and Morocco illustrate different forms of disrespect and unfavorable conditions for the recognition of women. They demonstrate how practices of struggling for recognition are challenging to be reached within these communities, especially the ones usually related to democracy.

China ratified the Convention on the Elimination of All Forms of Discrimination against Women in 1980. In 1995, Beijing hosted the Fourth World Conference on Women, with the publication of the Beijing Declaration and Platform for Action. Furthermore, in 2003, the country ratified the United Nations Convention against Transnational Organized Crime, which introduces dispositions regarding women. Nevertheless, the Chinese government did not sign the Protocol to Prevent, Suppress and Punish Trafficking in Persons, Especially Women and Children, supplementing the United Nations Convention against Transnational Organized Crime (University of Minnesota Human Rights Library, 2022).[72]

Morocco accessed to the Convention on the Elimination of All Forms of Discrimination against Women in 1993 and the United Nations Convention against Transnational Organized Crime in 2022. Nevertheless, in the same way as China, Morocco did not sign the Protocol to Prevent, Suppress and Punish Trafficking in Persons, Especially Women and Children, supplementing the United Nations

---

[71] Kirste 2019, 34.

[72] University of Minnesota Human Rights Library, 2022. Ratification of International Human Rights Treaties—China. Available at hrlibrary.umn.edu/research/ratification-china.html, access on 01.08.2022.

Convention against Transnational Organized Crime (University of Minnesota Human Rights Library, 2022)[73]

China and Morocco have not just the positive human rights treaties aforementioned, but they also have federal legislation regarding women and gender equality. Nevertheless, I will see in the following chapters that it is insufficient. Women need not just positive rights of recognition, but also a shared ethics of recognition, allowing them to build their identity freely. I question, then, how could a woman be fully recognized under Honneth's ethics of recognition—and based on Hegelian influences?

8.4 Case Studies of Legal and Ethical (Mis)recognition of Women

Honneth states that: "*Women in particular have sought in their decades-long struggles within the private sphere to assert their own, structurally disadvantaged needs within established practices in order to change the rules to their own advantage.*"[74] I understand that the struggles for women's recognition may exist in the recognition's patterns, namely love, law, and solidarity.

The dissertation questions why Axel Honneth's theory of recognition is not reasonable for women's recognition? Coming from this inquiry, the chapters have been studying the theory of recognition and relating it to the reality of women. The intent is to clarify how to modify Honneth's theory to include the recognition of women.

I understand that legal recognition is the most critical pattern of recognition, able to fulfill the conditions for achieving respect and freedom for women. Since Hegel, the role of law—not just as a pattern of recognition but also as a representation of the struggle itself—has required an extension of its meaning for the theory of recognition. Considering gender equality, it has become even more necessary.

Liberal democracy endorses the reaching of recognition. Nevertheless, this political regime does not exist in various countries, interfering in the conformation of legal rights and especially in the rise of universal human rights related to recognition. It is relevant, then, to interpret the (mis)recognition of women

[73] University of Minnesota Human Rights Library, 2022. Ratification of International Human Rights Treaties—China. Available at hrlibrary.umn.edu/research/ratification-china.html, access on 01.08.2022.

[74] Honneth 2014a, 133.

from the perspective of non-democratic countries and, even more, of non-Western countries, as Honneth and other authors from the legal theory of philosophy of law usually adopt Western contexts into their studies.

I adopt, then, case studies from two different countries: China and Morocco. In the Asiatic context, China is a significant player, not just from a legal perspective but also because it represents an economic power. In the North African context, Morocco is the most advanced country with regard to the evolution of legislation, being also an important player in political and economic aspects. Both countries share similarities in the (mis)recognition of women. They are experiencing several reforms in their legal rights related to gender equality, but it seems that they keep experiencing a shared ethics based on patriarchalism, hierarchy, and different forms of violence against women pulverized in social and cultural practices.

Furthermore, case studies from China and Morocco contribute to the dissertation, because there is limited access to sources on these countries, especially concerning the offenses to human rights and rights to the recognition of women. Both share grave violations to freedom of expression and freedom of the press, as well as several others. Nevertheless, the author of the dissertation has lived in both countries and performed on-site investigations, making the case studies richer for the studies of the recognition of women. Both countries will be analyzed in the next chapters.

8.5 Conclusion of Chap. 8

Honneth's theory of recognition has fundamental influences coming from Hegel. Furthermore, discussions on recognition from the French scholars, and relevant debates from the Critical Theory all contributed for the formation of Honneth's thought. The chapter has approached these interpretations on recognition. All of these influences endorse the necessity to comprehend a theory of recognition from a practical social perspective of the society itself.

Despite the theoretical comprehension of recognition, Chap. 8 has then inquired how to adopt the theory on the reality of women's recognition. To provide an attempt to study recognition taking the condition of women in consideration, the further chapters will perform case studies. The following chapters focus on case studies related to the (mis)recognition women suffer within specific contexts.

Taking the relevance of embracing social contexts not sufficiently explored by Honneth, I adopt China and Morocco as my countries of study. The adoption of these countries will be further justified.

(Mis)recognition of Chinese Women 9

Following the methodology of Critical theorists, in this Chapter and in the next chapter, the theory of Honneth will be illustrated in the reality of Chinese and Moroccan women. Whereas the pattern of love is located in the private sphere of a woman, such as her family, her friendships, and her neighborhood, which makes her more vulnerable to suffering situations of disrespect, in the dimensions of law and of solidarity, I will also encounter offenses against women. In any case, whether in China or in Morocco, offenses to recognition are complex and, in the end, affect the formation and development of women's identity.

To provide an overview of misrecognition of women in this Chapter and in the next chapter—women located in China and in Morocco—, this dissertation draws on data from statistics issued by international organizations through institutional reports, such as World Bank Group; United States Department Of State; United Nations Children's Fund; United Nations Development Programme; United Nations Entity For Gender Equality And The Empowerment Of Women; United Nations Population Fund; United Nations Woman; Réseau National des Centres d'Ecoute des Femmes Victimes de Violences; International Monetary Fund; Human Rights Watch; Global Human Rights Defense; European Institute of the Mediterranean; Amnesty International and others.

Existing literature is also drawn on not just to help interpret the statistical evidence, but also to illustrate the situation of women from the eyes of Chinese and Moroccan authors. Additionally, this dissertation contemplates legal norms and the constitutions of China and Morocco.

Finally, to support some arguments sustained through the secondary literature above, I also bring some collected data by myself in both countries—China and Morocco—, through my research and interviews performed with Chinese and Moroccan people there. Whereas I was living in China and Morocco, it was not

C. Diamantino Esser Santana, *Recognized Women:*, Juridicum – Schriften zur Rechtsphilosophie, https://doi.org/10.1007/978-3-658-46849-1_9

my intention to collect this information through sophisticated statistical methods. For that reason, information collected through interviews are used to supplement the collected data carefully provided.

This Chap. 9 analyses the situation of Chinese women in each different pattern of recognition. In other words, I inquire how each sphere of recognition has been offended within the female Chinese population.

9.1 Offenses to the Sphere of Love of Chinese Women

Chinese women are affected in their pattern of love by a patriarchalist tradition.

I will see that Chinese are still exposed to arranged marriage and to an intense pressure to get married generally before the age of 30. Honneth argues that arranged marriage interferes in the emotional harmony and individual happiness of individuals[1].

Furthermore, in the pattern of love, Chinese women can experience domestic violence, gender inequality during processes of divorce, and practices of conjugal infidelity.

In rural areas, there is still marriage with female minors.

This section also highlights the Chinese tradition of female infanticide, a practice which leaves its deep scars in Chinese society to this day.

9.1.1 Patriarchalism

Patriarchalism is a millenary Chinese characteristic. Confucius, for instance, had stated a supposed equality, which happens just between male members of a specific status. He had 3,000 male pupils, without any woman.[2] On Confucius' most important work, the *Analects* (*Lunyu*), King Wu spoke: "*'I have ten human beings [shi ren] who are able ministers.' [...] Confucius said: [...] There was a woman [furen] among them, so there were only nine human beings [jiu ren]. [...].*"[3]

The relationship between yin (the female principle) and yang (the male principle) can be seen as a relationship of hierarchical dependency, in which the woman

---

[1] Honneth 2014a, 142.

[2] Von Senger 1993, 294.

[3] Von Senger 1993, 294. See also: "A further revealing Confucius quotation in this context reads: The Master said: 'Of all people, girls (nüzi) and servants (xiaoren) are the most difficult to behave to. If you are familiar with them, they lose their humility. If you maintain a reserve towards them, they are discontent.'" (Von Senger 1993, 294).

(yin) occupies a lower position in comparison with the man (yang). The woman is the fragile side, and the man the stronger one. Yin-yang are two cosmic forces, and as the female wife (yin) receives semen from her husband (yang), the earth (yin) receives rain from heaven (yang). "*This produced the associations: heaven/husband, earth/wife and—applying these ideas to the state—heaven/ruler (called the "Son of Heaven" already in pre-imperial China), earth/subject.*"[4]

However, the most potent symbol of Chinese patriarchalism regards the preference for Chinese boys. From 1979, China began the one-child policy, and the government restricted the rights of parents to choose the number of children they may have, limiting them to have just one child. Since that time, practices of infanticide against female babies were recurrent.[5]

In 2001, the Chinese Marriage Law (first promulgated in 1980) was amended, and it stipulates in Article 20 that: "*[...] Infanticide by drowning, abandonment of infants and all other acts causing serious harm to infants shall be prohibited.*"[6] Furthermore, discrimination against and maltreatment of women who give birth to baby girls or who have infertility were also prohibited by the above law[7].

Despite the legal reform, Xinran explains that in the last decade Chinese social norms were still prejudiced against women who do not give birth to baby boys: "*However, a 'good woman' must give birth to a boy [...]*".[8] Furthermore, although the new Chinese Civil Law (2020) generally prohibits desertion and maltreatment, this legislation does not stipulate any article regarding infanticide and discrimination specifically against women who give birth to baby girls or who have infertility.[9]

The one-child policy lasted until 2016, and during this time women were usually subjected to various abuses, such as mandatory birth control, forced abortion, forced sterilization, mandatory state penalties, and authoritarian administrative punishments.[10] More than that, government officials used to apply

---

[4] Von Senger 1993, 300. See also Von Senger, 301.

[5] United States Department of State 2015, 53.

[6] Marriage Law of the People's Republic Of China 2001, National People's Congress.

[7] Xinran 2011, 13.

[8] Xinran 2011, 13.

[9] "Arranged marriages, mercenary marriages, and other acts interfering with the freedom of marriage are prohibited. The exaction of money or other property by way of marriage is prohibited. Bigamy is prohibited. No one who has a spouse may cohabit with another person. Domestic violence is prohibited. Maltreatment or desertion of family members is prohibited." (Article 1042, Civil Code of the People's Republic of China, 2020).

[10] United States Department of State 2015, 54.

"social compensation fees" for families, which did not comply with the rules of the policy.[11]

Furthermore, the culture of abandonment or infanticide of baby girls in China intensified during the one-child policy. For Xinran, the policy is not the sole reason, but also the fact that Chinese farming cultures were usually occupied mostly by men, in a way that girls were seen as less useful in agricultural production. Additionally, Chinese have been used to not having sex education and, through ignorance, women got pregnant and then the couple intended to abort. Furthermore, for Xinran the economic boom also caused the necessity for Chinese to abort or abandon, as one more family member would incur more expenses[12].

The preference for boys in the farming cultures was inevitable. Men used to have physical advantage and preference in the ancient system of land distribution in China.[13]

The work of Xinran called "*Message from an Unknown Chinese Mother: Stories of Loss and Love*" describes real cases of killed or abandoned female children. For instance, when doing field research, the Chinese author has witnessed the infanticide of a baby girl:

> 'Doing a baby girl is not a big thing around here. You city folk are shocked the first time you see it, right?' the older woman said comfortingly, obviously seeing how shocked I was. 'That's a living child!' I said in a shaking voice, pointing at the slops pail. I was still so shocked, I didn't dare to move. 'It's not a child,' she corrected me.
>
> 'What do you mean, it's not a child? I saw it.' I could scarcely believe that she could tell me such a blatant lie!
>
> 'It's not a child. If it was, we'd be looking after it, wouldn't we?' she interrupted. 'It's a girl baby, and we can't keep it.' 'A girl baby isn't a child, and you can't keep it?' I repeated uncomprehendingly. 'Around these parts, you can't get by without a son. You have no one to burn incense at the ancestors' shrine. But it's not just that.
>
> You don't get the extra land given to you either. If your children just eat, and don't earn, and you have no land and no grain, then you might as well starve!' She looked at me and added: 'You city folk get food from the government. We get our grain ration according to the number of people in the family. Girl babies don't count.

---

[11] United States Department of State 2015, 54.

[12] Xinran 2011, 12.

[13] Xinran 2011, 12. See also: "And so dynasties have come and gone through Chinese history, but the ways in which land is apportioned has never really changed, and the basic inequality between men and women has became a deeply entrenched tradition. In the villages, boy children not only carried on the family line and inherited the clan name, they were the source of the family property and the creator of its wealth." (Xinran 2011, 13).

> The officials in charge don't give us any extra land when a girl is born, and there's so little arable land that the girls will starve to death anyway.'[14]

Such practices are a result of not just the one-child policy, but also of the Chinese patriarchal tradition and the lack of information of the Chinese population regarding sex education, as I will further see.

It is necessary to clarify that I am not questioning the one-child policy as a demographic policy in a country like China. The demographic policy is necessary and can be adopted by governmental policies to avoid an oversized population and all the social problems it may cause. Nevertheless, it must be accompanied by other governmental policies for guaranteeing sex education and a minimum of decent living conditions for the families. During almost four decades of the one-child policy, the Chinese government did not work satisfactorily on sex education of the population, regarding contraceptive methods and birth control. On the contrary, the Chinese government has focused on strict sanctions and restrictions[15].

In 2013, the Chinese government revised the National Population and Family Planning Policy, allowing families to have two children. The new policy officially began on January 1, 2016 and it represented the end of the one-child policy.[16]

Nevertheless, in the census of 2021, the Chinese government was surprised by the lowest number of births in China recorded since the 1960s (BBC News, 2021[17]). As a result of this decrease, the Standing Committee of China's National People's Congress (NPC) decided to amend the 2015 Population and Family Planning Law to allow married couples in the country to have three children, as well as to exclude the sanctions for couples who exceeded the birth limit under the previous law (Library of Congress, 2021[18]).

[14] Xinran 2011, 55. The book brings other testimonies, see Xinran 2011, 61.

[15] "In contrast, in eastern China's urban areas, enforcement was and is draconian. Almost everyone lived within the state-planned economy up until the beginning of the 1990 s. So having more than one child meant losing your job, your home (which was allocated by your employer), your entitlement to food and clothing rations, your child's entitlement to schooling and medical care, and even your chance of finding other work, as no one would dare employ you". (Xinran 2011, 18)

[16] United States Department of State 2015, 53.

[17] BBC News. Mcdonell, S. 2021. China allows three children in major policy shift. Available at https://www.bbc.com/news/world-asia-china-57303592. 31.05.2021. Access on 24.04.2022.

[18] Library of Congress. 2021. China: Three-Child Policy Becomes Law, Social Maintenance Fee Abolished. Available at https://www.loc.gov/item/global-legal-monitor/2021-09-23/china-three-child-policy-becomes-law-social-maintenance-fee-abolished/. Access on 24.04.2022.

The three-child policy includes other measures to boost childbirths, for example, extended maternity leave and other social welfare benefits for couples (Library of Congress, 2021[19]). Nevertheless, there are still further regulations to be either abolished or amended, to reflect China's new family planning policy (Library of Congress, 2021[20]). Despite the one-child policy ending in 2013, it created different social problems for Chinese women. In September 2015, a Chinese woman in Yunnan Province complained on social media that local officials threatened to fire her husband, if she refused to abort their second child.[21]

According to Lake, "*Between 2001 and 2010 alone, an average of 1.3 million more boys than girls were born in China each year, indicating that sex-selective abortions are still occurring and continuing to upset the laws of nature*".[22]

Furthermore, in 2015, the United States Department of State stated that at that time, it was still illegal in almost all provinces of China for a single woman to have a child[23], and family-planning bureaus have conducted pregnancy tests on married women as well.[24] Local officials, who have restricted Chinese women through control of birth, have received job promotions and honors.[25]

---

[19] Library of Congress. 2021. China: Three-Child Policy Becomes Law, Social Maintenance Fee Abolished. Available at https://www.loc.gov/item/global-legal-monitor/2021-09-23/china-three-child-policy-becomes-law-social-maintenance-fee-abolished/. Access on 24.04.2022.

[20] Library of Congress. 2021. China: Three-Child Policy Becomes Law, Social Maintenance Fee Abolished. Available at https://www.loc.gov/item/global-legal-monitor/2021-09-23/china-three-child-policy-becomes-law-social-maintenance-fee-abolished/. Access on 24.04.2022.

[21] United States Department of State 2015, 55.

[22] Lake 2018, 27.

[23] "Cultural beliefs of familism may bring special implications to the single mothers. Under patriarchal Confucian ethics, the males have decision-making authority in their families. According to the Three Obediences (san cong), a wife was expected to "follow" her husband after marriage (chu jia cong fu). Hence, single-motherhood (particularly divorce) may imply the failure of maintaining family solidarity. Furthermore, the concept of familism develops along the male lineage in the Chinese culture (i.e., family members are expected to bring glory to their paternal family lineage; Ting & Chiu, 2002). This brings ambivalence to single mothers, as they no longer belong to their ex-spouses' family lineages." (Leung 2017, 769).

[24] United States Department of State 2015, 55.

[25] United States Department of State 2015, 55.

Another consequence of the one-child policy was the demographic masculinization of the Chinese population. Chinese male population became oversized[26] in the decades after the one-child policy. Men used to have difficulties in finding wives, especially men with low education and living in rural spaces: "*While men with secondary or higher education are almost universally married by age 40, 10% of those with a primary education level are still unmarried; this percentage even reaches 40% for those with no schooling [...]*".[27]

In 2020, statistics showed that the male population has become almost the same as the female population, and the demographic masculinization seemed to be decreased[28]. Nevertheless, still in 2019, reports state that Burmese women were captured as 'brides,' to marry and become pregnant for Chinese men.[29]

The preference for Chinese boys was a fact with several consequences for Chinese society to this day. Additionally, there is the other current stigma in Chinese society: single mothers. They used to be stigmatized by their own Chinese family, as I can see from the real story told by Xinran:

> 'One day, my mother made me a sort of "deathbed" speech. "All our lives," she said, "your father and I have fought to present a united front to everyone so that no one could say bad things about us when we were dead and gone. But if our only child lives as a single mother, how can your father and I go home to Shanghai? Never mind about passing our last years in peace and comfort, we simply couldn't face our friends and family. I didn't force you to have an abortion because I'm a mother, and I felt it wouldn't have been fair on a living creature to get rid of it like that, but we're just not brave enough to face the kind of life that you and your baby will bring us![30]

---

[26] Attané; Gu 2014, 4.

[27] Lu; Wang 2014, 41.

[28] "In gender terms, the male population was 723.11 million, and the female population was 689.49 million." (China Macro Economy. Mullen, A. 2022. China population: is a demographic turning point just around the corner as births drop again? 06.02.2022. Available at https://www.scmp.com/economy/economic-indicators/article/3165798/china-population-demographic-turning-point-just-around. Access on 30.07.2022.)

[29] 'Young Burmese women are being trafficked to China as 'brides' then locked in rooms and raped until they become pregnant, says a chilling new report by Human Rights Watch released on Thursday. The 112-page report, "Give Us a Baby and We'll Let You Go," reveals that vulnerable young women from Burma's conflict-ridden northern Kachin and Shan states are being tricked into forced marriages in China where the earlier "one-child policy" and preference for sons has created a huge gender gap.' (The Telegraph. Smith N. 2019. Burmese women trafficked into sexual slavery in China, says new report. 21.03.2019. Available at https://www.telegraph.co.uk/global-health/terror-and-security/burmese-women-trafficked-sexual-slavery-china-says-new-report/. Access on 05.08.2022).

[30] Xinran 2011, 180.

More than a patriarchal tradition, which is reflected in China to this day, the situation of Chinese women is also influenced by the Chinese notion of *autonomy*.

9.1.2 Autonomy

The comprehension of autonomy in China is different from the Western paradigm. I have seen that Honneth comes from a Western tradition of scholars: "*As far back as Kant, and probably ever since Rousseau, we have defined 'autonomy' as a certain type of individual relation-to-self that allows us to be confident of our needs and beliefs, and to value our own capacities.*"[31] For this tradition, autonomy is related to free capacity of the individual to develop his own identity, taking into consideration his free-will and needs, feeling that he is respected, recognized, and included in his society. Furthermore, this subject is also able to appreciate the subjects who share with him the same community, understanding that everybody should be equally recognized.[32]

Chinese conception of the formation of the identity and authenticity of individuals are different from traditional Western philosophy. The Chinese notion of autonomy does not rely on the existence of the subject by herself, but rather on the connection of the individual with her community, regarding her role in public obligations.[33]

According to Mcleod, what differentiates the Confucian notion from the Enlightenment notion is the basis of personhood. For the former, personhood is based on the relationships of community, whereas for the latter, personhood is based on rationality and autonomy[34].

> Confucius recognized that relationships are close to the center of human life, and that our ultimate happiness and thriving depends on being part of harmonious and life-affirming communities. Social harmony, Confucius taught, is thus the key to human

[31] Honneth 2012b, 41.

[32] "Autonomy is a relational, intersubjective entity, not a monological achievement. What helps us to acquire autonomy is not cut out of the same cloth as a good that can be distributed; it is fashioned out of living relations of reciprocal recognition that are just to the degree that they allow us to reciprocally value our needs, beliefs and abilities." (Honneth 2012b, 41).

[33] "It is important to see that this assumption that one gains full personhood through rationality is not obviously true. Confucius and others had a very different picture of what makes one a full person. This might entail that children are not full persons, because they do not play a full role in the community in the sense that they do not yet have a profession, or a spouse and children of their own." (Mcleod 2014, 16).

[34] Mcleod 2014, 16.

> thriving. Individuals cannot successfully make their way through the world or attain happiness by themselves, abstracted from the context of the most central human communities, such as the family and the village.[35]

Furthermore, Chinese philosophy adopts the notion of nothingness or emptiness, meaning that the individuals do not reflect on their existence and capacity to measure the circumstances around them. On the contrary, they should interpret the world and all the facts and situations as reflections of a natural emptiness. This notion comes from Buddhism, Daoism, and Hinduism.[36]

Von Senger explains that in Confucianism, there is no notion of autonomous, abstract, self-determined, and non-gender-specific human beings. Actually, for Confucius, human beings have specific roles within a collective context: father, son, wife, ruler, subject, friend[37].

I can mention, for instance, "Chinese familism": a Chinese person must adhere to a complex system of social attitudes, coming from her family and related to family affairs[38]. The elements of Chinese familism are family obligations, maintenance of social bonds, conformity to rules, respect of seniors and parents, and family reputation[39]. As a consequence, in China the individualistic orientation is substituted by a collective orientation focused on family[40].

In imperial times, Chinese family-consciousness was stronger than individual identity.[41] It justifies a strong belief of Chinese people, and especially women, in some social roles, which should be respected without further reflections. McLeod clarifies it: "*Ethics deals with the broadest questions of how the individual or community should live. [...] Especially for Confucius and the authors of the Bhagavad*

---

[35] "Chinese culture revolves around the family and clan system, and traditional culture privileges collective rights and interests over individual and personal rights". (Liu; Hu; Liao 2009, 530).

[36] 'In Buddhism, the notion of emptiness signifies the underlying nature of the process of change in the impermanent world and the ultimate truth about our transient existence. In Daoism, it is suggested that the word "wu ([...], nothing or nonbeing)" may best characterize the origin of the entire cosmological order as well as the ontological grounding of our existence. In Hinduism, the ultimate and unitary nature of reality was often described negatively, as "not this and not that" with respect to all the differentiated phenomena that we could speak about, and yet as their shared innermost essence.' (Liu; Berger 2014, p.xi).

[37] Von Senger 1993, 295.

[38] Yang *apud* Leung 2017, 768.

[39] King&Bond *apud* Leung 2017, 768.

[40] Yeh&Yang *apud* Leung 2017, 768.

[41] Von Senger 1993, 304.

Gita, the questions of the ideal individual life are inseparable from those of the ideal communal life."[42]

Chinese autonomy is influenced not just by patriarchalism and familism, but also by a strong sense of *hierarchy*. *Hierarchy* exists in Chinese family relations:

> In China, parent–child relationships represent a clear example of relationships of inequality. Family relationships are traditional and a general pattern of obedience and respect of the child for the parents is maintained throughout life. This is expressed in the concept of filial piety that is the predominant norm in China. Ho (1996) argued that authoritarian moralism is a central characteristic of the Chinese pattern of socialization guided by filial piety. The emphasis is on obedience, indebtedness to parents and on moral correctness, not on self-fulfillment or psychological sensitivity.[43]

A Chinese woman should respect parents' decisions related to studying, finding a job, getting married, and giving birth. To this day, especially in rural areas, Chinese women feel that they should comply with decisions made by their parents.

Besides the fact that this dissertation is focused on women, I am aware that such negative aspects affect the young Chinese generation as a whole, including Chinese boys and men. I have been at the weekly wedding-market in Shanghai's People's Square, where Chinese parents show their children's data—containing a name, age, height, weight, job, salary, studies, and international experience[44]. They are offering their children for marriage. Young women and men are being traded in the marriage market.

---

[42] Mcleod 2014, 4. See also: "It is important to highlight that religions in Asia are not always concerned with transcendent divinities and there is no clear division between religion and philosophical theory" (Mcleod 2014, 5). When we questioned some Chinese about their religion, many Chinese answer that they do not have religion, that Confucianism and other theories are "just philosophy".

[43] Keller et al. 2005, 5.

[44] 'Traditionally, parents in China have played a major role in their children's married lives, even seeking potential partners at marriage markets. Every weekend, parents from the outskirts of Shanghai gather at the People's Park and post brief ads for their single children. The ads, written in Chinese, are typically straightforward — *Good cook. Likes to read. Age: 29.* Missing from those ads were any sentiments of a deeper connection, Ms. Lech said, noting that the market felt more like a business exchange than a path to a romantic partnership. "What they need is love, and their experience is that love is not really something you talk about in China," she said. "You talk about having a responsible husband."' (The New York Times. Richardson, W. 2015. China, Single Women Live by Their Own Rules. 14.08.2015. Available on https://lens.blogs.nytimes.com/2015/08/14/in-china-the-single-ladies-push-back/. Access on 05.04.2019.)

The tradition also happens in Beijing, according to Lake (Lake 2018, 38).

I should also mention a traditional Chinese proverb, which, to this day, interferes in the dynamic of women in Chinese society. The proverb *diu mianzi* (lose face) is very usual in Chinese daily life. Traditional Chinese families use the feeling of shame, to threaten the young who do not act according to the social rules. There are many ways to be ashamed. One of them is the non-practice of honor regarding her family, her country, her culture. According to Mcleod, this is also an influence of Confucianism:

> If you guide them using institutions, and order them using punishments, the people will avoid disorder but will be without a sense of shame. If you guide them using virtue, and order them using ritual, they will have a sense of shame, and moreover will have a standard.[45]

Mencius, a Chinese Confucian philosopher, has also considered shame as one of the aspects of the Chinese sense of duty.[46] I have seen that, for Honneth, feelings of social shame are a kind of disrespect, and they damage recognition.

Based on these considerations, the aspects that Chinese women experience nowadays are influenced by traditions of patriarchalism, familism, hierarchy, and a distinct sense of autonomy dependent on social roles to be performed by women and threated by the risk to *diu mianzi* (lose face).

Now, in the next section, I will highlight other aspects of Chinese society, which affect women's private pattern of love.

9.1.3 Marriage

Article 1041 of the Chinese Civil Law promulgated in 2020 stipulates that: "*Marriage and family are protected by the State. A marriage system based on freedom of marriage, monogamy, and equality between men and women is implemented.*"[47] Article 1042 defines that arranged marriages, mercenary marriages,

---

[45] Mcleod 2014, 40.

[46] "[…] without the feeling of commiseration, there is no human being; without the feeling of shame and dislike, there is no human being; without the feeling of modesty and complaisance, there is no human being; without the feeling of right and wrong, there is no human being. The feeling of commiseration is the disposition to altruity. The feeling of shame and dislike is the disposition to a sense of duty; the feeling of modesty and complaisance is the disposition to propriety; the feeling of right and wrong is the disposition to wisdom. All human beings are endowed with these four dispositions, just as they have their four limbs." (Mencius *apud* Von Senger 1993, 294).

[47] Civil Code of the People's Republic of China, 2020.

and other acts interfering with the freedom of marriage are prohibited, as well as domestic violence, and maltreatment or desertion of family members (Article 1042, Chinese Civil Law, 2020). The Chinese Civil Law brings other articles regarding this topic, such as article 1046 that states that man and woman shall enter into marriage freely and voluntarily. Neither party may compel the other party to enter into marriage against his will, and no organization or individual may interfere with the freedom of marriage (Article 1046, Chinese Civil Law, 2020). Article 1052 states that "*If a marriage is entered into as a result of coercion, the coerced party may apply to the people's court to annul the marriage*" (Article 1052, Chinese Civil Law, 2020).

In spite of such legal dispositions, I have already mentioned that there are still practices of arranged marriage in China. For a long time, marriage has been seen as a contract, a union of interests between two families, disregarding love and willingness of the couple.

Nowadays, Chinese marriage represents a paradox. On the one hand, in the countryside and in traditional urban families, marriage is still a formal tradition, representing parent's aspirations.[48] On the other hand, urban China holds a young generation of women who are not interested in getting married anymore and aspire to attain the status of being a single and independent woman.[49]

In the first case, Chinese families still pressure women to get married: '*"I don't mean to stress you, but I simply cannot relax until you are married," Christy's mom recently said to her. "You're thirty-four already. How can you be sure you're still ovulating?"*'.[50] As soon as a Chinese woman gets married, there is then the obligation to get pregnant.

---

[48] "Despite the seemingly common trends of women's decreasing marriage rate and improved educational and labour market performance in China and western developed countries, factors driving these trends differ because of substantial differences in gender ideology. Patriarchy still appears to prevail in China. Given the deteriorating gender inequality in the labour market and state-endorsed revival of traditional ideology, it is highly likely that urban Chinese women find themselves facing an agonizing dilemma: to lower their expectations of education and labour market outcomes to fit the traditional wifely role, or to persevere in their educational and career pursuit." (You;Yi; Chen. 2016. Love, Life, and "Leftover Ladies" in Urban China. Available at https://mpra.ub.uni-muenchen.de/70494/1/MPRA_paper_70494.pdf. Access on 09.05.2023.)

[49] "The Chinese urban society in recent years has shown rising age at first marriage and declining marriage rates, especially among professional females with at least college degrees in their late 20 s or their 30 s." (You;Yi; Chen. 2016. Love, Life, and "Leftover Ladies" in Urban China. Available at https://mpra.ub.uni-muenchen.de/70494/1/MPRA_paper_70494.pdf. Access on 09.05.2023.)

[50] Lake 2018, 144.

When the Chinese woman finally gives birth, it will be probably required that she integrates her husband's family into the routine of childcare.

From Chinese tradition, the parents of the husband are responsible for raising the grandsons[51], and their son has the responsibility to take care of his parents, in a way that the majority of married couples live together with or next to the husband's family:

> According to Chinese tradition, a son was expected to return to his parents' house with his wife after he married; a son would forever have a home in the village where he was born. Daughters, once grown, would never return home to live—until they married, they didn't belong anywhere.[52]

This tradition is endorsed by the Chinese Civil Law, which stipulates at Article 1050 that: "*After a marriage has been registered, by mutual consent, the woman may become a member of the man's family or vice versa*"[53]. Although the law allows that the couple negotiate which parents-in-law they are going to take care of, in China, several couples stay closer to the husband's family. The relationship of a woman with her parents-in-law can be very problematic.[54]

---

[51] "According to divorce lawyers, the in-law relationship is a major cause for the high divorce rate of the post-1980 generation. Last year, 1.96 million couples applied for divorce, and the divorce rate has risen by an average of 7.6 percent a year since 2003, figures released by the Ministry of Civil Affairs show. [...]Traditionally, after a woman married, she became part of the husband's family and lived with them. Men did not leave their parents' home, so a bride lived with her parents-in-law and even grandparents-in-law. "Influenced by the feudal ethical code, a daughter-in-law always had a subordinate status in a Chinese family," said Gu Xiuqin, secretary-general of the China Association of Social Workers' marriage and family affairs committee." (China Daily. Wenting Z. 2011. The mother-in-law of all family battles. 22.04.2011. Available on www.chinadaily.com.cn/china/2011-04/22/content_12373683.htm. Access on 06.05.2019.)

[52] Chang 2008, 57.

[53] Civil Code of the People's Republic of China, 2020.

[54] "Whether or not this was true, Kumei continued to slave away for her parents-in-law at home. They, on the other hand, did not stick up for their daughter-in-law, and even went around telling everyone that their son had found himself a big-hipped woman who had given them a grandson, while Kumei stayed at home eating up their insufficient grain rations!" (Xinran 2011, 90). See also Xinran 2011, 104.

Additionally, the Chinese system of *hukou*[55] sometimes does not allow those women to bring their children to the big cities. Many of these women leave their children in the countryside with their parents-in-law, and then go alone to the big cities to work there. Even if a woman can stay in the countryside with her baby, her husband may get a job in big cities, and then she will raise her child together with her parents-in-law. "*In 2010 the ACWF estimated that 40 million children under the age of 14 were left behind by their migrant-worker parents in rural areas*".[56]

On the other hand, if the women get an appropriate *hukou*, the big Chinese cities promote the chance for Chinese women to build their lives far from their hometowns, thus achieving financial independence. In these cases, Chinese women endorse their autonomy and freedom.[57]

Not just married women with children face challenges in the big Chinese cities, but also the ones who decide to not get married. Independently of the social status and the location, usually, the ones who do not get married before their 30 s, are called "*shengnu*", the "leftover women":

> The prefix "sheng" is the same as in sheng cai, or "leftover food"—hardly a palatable association. In more rural areas, this term may be applied as early as age twenty-five, whereas in larger cities, it kicks in closer to thirty, or what is generally considered the last stop before spinsterhood.[58]

Getting married in China has sometimes put women into paradoxical stigmas. On the one hand, there used to be an expectation of getting married and giving birth. However, on the other hand, there was a time in the country when some

---

[55] Most migrants cannot change their rural *hukou* to an urban one, thus losing a major avenue for social mobility (Treiman and Zhang 2011; Chan 2012a). Even more restrictive to their social mobility is that by law, *hukou* status is hereditary, which basically shuts off intergenerational social mobility. (Chan 2018, 11)

[56] United States Department of State 2015, 60.

[57] 'Zhu Chi, a 34-year-old television host, told Ms. Lech that she didn't want to compromise on a husband less successful than she was. Zhu Meiting, 29, an English teacher in Beijing, said she often lied to her family members about her dating life so they would stop setting her up on blind dates. Sabrina Wei, a 36-year-old entrepreneur, told Ms. Lech that she dated only foreign men who wouldn't judge her because of her age. "They go out, they eat dinner with friends, they do yoga, they even travel abroad," Ms. Lech said. "They have their lifestyle, so they don't really need to marry into this."' (The New York Times. Richardson, W. 2015. China, Single Women Live by Their Own Rules. 14.08.2015. Available on https://lens.blogs.nytimes.com/2015/08/14/in-china-the-single-ladies-push-back/. Access on 05.04.2019.)

[58] Lake 2018, 29.

universities forbade Chinese married women or Chinese mothers from studying on their campuses. After protests by NGOs, the Ministry of Education changed such rules and nowadays, the reproductive rights and freedom of Chinese women are protected.[59]

If a Chinese woman gets married, she can be exposed to different forms of offenses to the pattern of love. For instance, the next section will study the practices of marital infidelity in China.

9.1.3.1 Conjugal Infidelity

Chinese emperors were allowed to have many concubines. These women used to have a considerable social status—for example, the last Chinese empress Tseu-Hi was a concubine before getting married to the emperor. When she was a concubine, she enjoyed high cultural and political education, being able to develop her strategy to become empress.[60]

From 1950, polygamy was extinguished from China, and Article 1042 of the Chinese Civil Law stipulates that *"[...] Bigamy is prohibited.[...]"*[61].

Nevertheless, according to Lake, there is still male conjugal infidelity in China, and some Chinese wives seem not to worry about that, they allow it and understand marriage as a contract and an institution, more than a private relationship based on love, trustfulness, and monogamy. Having a mistress can be seen as normal behavior for men.[62] More than offending the respect and fidelity to wives, I understand that the practices of conjugal infidelity in China also represent inequality between the spouses, as commonly women are not supposed to have extramarital affairs. If wives begin to have lovers with the same frequency and the same exposition as their husbands, probably these women will be much more judged by Chinese society than men.

This gender inequality inside Chinese relationships also happens in the case of divorce, as I will see in the next section.

---

[59] Liu; Hu; Liao 2009, 542.

[60] Buck 2013.

[61] Marriage Law of the People's Republic Of China 2001.

[62] "For a Chinese man of Dr. X's standing—well off, well connected, well educated, and well into his fifties—a mistress (or two, or three) is practically a requirement. But when I first met him—still only in my salad days of understanding the dynamics of extramarital relations in China—his ideas and observations seemed extraordinary, if not completely farfetched. 'If a man in China doesn't have a mistress, it's because his economic situation doesn't allow for it,' he announced, as casually and assuredly as if he were reporting the latest figures for China's GDP. 'And if a very successful man doesn't have a mistress, his wife will be puzzled as to why he doesn't.'" (Lake 2018, 59). See also Lake 2018, 71.

9.1.3.2 Divorce

Whereas in the Chinese Marriage Law divorce would be granted if husband and wife both desire it (Article 31, Chinese Marriage Law, 2001), the new Chinese Civil Law stipulates in Article 1079 that husband or wife may unilaterally petition for divorce directly with the people's court[63]. In this case, a relevant organization may offer mediation. The article states that "*(...) The people's court shall, during the divorce trial, offer mediation, and grant divorce if mutual affection no longer exists between the two parties and mediation fails.*"[64]

Chinese legal norms authorize divorce for women and men, theoretically granting them the same and equal conditions. For instance, according to the Chinese Civil Law:

> Article 1087: Upon divorce, the community property of the spouses shall be partitioned by them through agreement, or, where no such an agreement is reached, adjudicated by the people's court in light of the actual state of the property and in compliance with the principle of favoring the rights and interests of their children, the wife, and the no-fault party.
>
> The rights and interests of the husband or wife arising from the contractual management of land based on the household shall be protected in accordance with law.[65]

Nevertheless, the consequences of Chinese divorce for women are an example of the expression *youfa buyi:* having laws, but not complying with them accordingly[66]. Wong and Phillips (2009) quote some Chinese proverbs: "if a woman marries a chicken, she should follow the chicken; if she marries a dog, she should follow the dog" (*jia ji sui ji, jia gou sui gou*).[67]

Usually, a Chinese divorced woman will be undermined in the division of the properties and goods. In rural China, in 2015, the divorced wives were more likely to receive less than an equal share of common property and lose their common residence to their ex-husbands[68].

---

[63] Civil Code of the People's Republic of China, 2020.

[64] Civil Code of the People's Republic of China, 2020.

[65] Civil Code of the People's Republic of China, 2020.

[66] Zhu 2013, 215.

[67] Zeng, 2000 *apud* Wong; Phillips, 2009, 656.

[68] Zhang, 2006 *apud* Wong; Phillips, 2009, 656.

> A 2011 Supreme People's Court decision exacerbated the gender wealth gap by stating that after divorce marital property belongs solely to the person registered as the homeowner in mortgage and registration documents--in most cases the husband.[69]

To this day, there is still gender inequality regarding the division of property in divorce.[70]

Regarding child custody, Article 1084 of the Chinese Civil Law states that a mother shall have physical custody of her child under the age of two.[71]

The next section explains another aspect related to Chinese children: marriage with minors.

9.1.3.3 Marriage with Minors

Article 6 of the Chinese Marriage Law has stated: "*No marriage may be contracted before the man has reached 22 years of age and the woman 20 years of age. Late marriage and late childbirth shall be encouraged.*"[72] The new Chinese Civil Law reiterates it in Article 1047.[73] Nevertheless, I found some reports addressing the sale of babies to be future brides in 2015[74] and the sale of women and girls in 2022.[75]

Despite these reports, the protection of Chinese girls by the legal norms and authorities seem to be increasing. The new Chinese Civil Law states in Article

---

69 United States Department of State 2015, 57. See also Liu; Hu; Liao 2009, 538.

70 "The value of property is usually determined by bidding—whoever bids highest can buy out the other party—while child custody is often decided by earning capacity. In both cases, women are usually in the weaker financial position. And for child custody, the men often insist on having the child, especially male children because they want an heir." (He X. The University of Hong Kong Bulletin. 2022. Men Win out in Divorce in China. Available at https://bulletin.hku.hk/research/men-win-out-in-divorce-in-china/, access on 30.07.2022.)

71 Article 1084, Civil Code of the People's Republic of China, 2020.

72 Marriage Law of the People's Republic Of China 2001.

73 Civil Code of the People's Republic of China, 2020.

74 United States Department of State 2015, 59.

75 "Human Rights Watch investigated bride trafficking to China from northern Myanmar, where women and girls are vulnerable to trafficking due to abuses by the Myanmar government. Once purchased they were held prisoner, in sexual slavery, and pressured to produce babies as quickly as possible." (Human Rights Watch. Barr; Wang. Chained Woman has become the face of bride trafficking in China. 07.06.2022. Available at https://www.hrw.org/news/2022/06/07/chained-woman-has-become-face-bride-trafficking-china. Access on 30.07.2022.)

1055 that "*The lawful rights and interests of women, minors, the elderly, and persons with disabilities are protected.*"[76]

Besides the legislation already analyzed, now I will further consider the Chinese sphere of law. I will understand how Chinese legislation and legal practices also influence the pattern of love of Chinese women, especially with regard to domestic violence in the private life of a Chinese woman.

9.2 Offenses to the Sphere of Law of Chinese Women

Since the beginning of the twenty-first century, China has been revising or amending existing laws and regulations on women, for example the Chinese Law on Women's Rights and Interests (2005), the Chinese Regulations on Labor Protection for Female Employees (2009), the third amendment of the Chinese Marriage Law (introduced in 2011), and the Chinese Domestic Violence Prevention Act (introduced in 2012, adopted in 2015) (Yifei 2016, 12). More recently, in 2020, the first Civil Law was promulgated in China, thus replacing the Chinese Marriage Law[77]. These pieces of legislation are also accompanied by governmental programs that also affect women's situation, as I will further see.

The analysis of the role of women in Chinese society must consider the historical change in Chinese legal norms and its consequences on law and social conformations.

Before the Chinese legal reforms as from 1949, Chinese law was primarily penal law.[78]

After that, statutory law was promulgated to structure and organize the imperial bureaucracy. Statutory law means almost administrative law. At that time, '*Legislative power was concentrated in the hands of the Emperor. To the extent that the Emperor was above statutory law, one cannot actually speak in terms of the "rule of law" in ancient China, but rather of "rule by law".*'[79]

At that time, people did not understand the statutory law as a representation of their subjective rights, but actually as a way to serve the interests of the authorities.

---

[76] Civil Code of the People's Republic of China, 2020.

[77] Civil Code of the People's Republic of China, 2020.

[78] Von Senger 1993, 302.

[79] Von Senger 1993, 302.

Although the concept of "subjective right" came from 1850, rendered with the Chinese word "*quanli*" "*(which originally meant "power and material benefit")*"[80], I have already studied that the notions of subjectivity, individuality, and autonomy in China are constantly substituted by collectivism.

For instance, the Chinese Constitution details citizens' obligations, but not their rights within a coherent legal protection, "*This adheres to China's legal tradition, under which such rights are not derived from the "inherent dignity" of being human or from "natural rights", but are granted from the political authority as "legal rights", or as "discretionary entitlements.*"[81] Von Senger argues that: "*The Chinese reject the theory of pre-governmental, supertemporal human rights founded on natural law or, even, by reference to God*"[82]. China has relied on governmental rules, and individual rights have come late in Chinese society.[83]

In the last amendment to the Chinese Constitution in 2018, Article 24 of the Constitution was reformed and stipulates:

> The state shall champion core socialist values; advocate the civic virtues of love for the motherland, for the people, for work, for science and for socialism; educate the people in patriotism and collectivism, in internationalism and communism, and in dialectical and historical materialism; and combat capitalist, feudal and other forms of decadent thought.[84]

Collectivism and other related values such as patriotism were, again, reiterated in the Chinese Constitution.

The word for "human rights" had been introduced in China in the 19th century as well, but it was inserted in the Chinese Constitution only in 2004.[85]

In the past, Chinese people were not used to understanding the statutory law critically, to comprehend how to interpret it, and to apply it to their benefit. Over three thousand years, jurisprudence in China was not properly developed. The practices of logic, rhetoric, and methods were rudimentarily used[86]. The Chinese statutory law was mainly casuistic and not written. At the end of the imperial period, from 1911, Chinese law started to become more consistent[87].

---

[80] Von Senger 1993, 303.

[81] Zhu 2013, 217.

[82] Von Senger 1993, 307.

[83] Von Senger 1993, 301.

[84] Amendment to the Chinese Constitution, article 39, 2018.

[85] Von Senger 1993, 303.

[86] Von Senger 1993, 303.

[87] Von Senger 1993, 304.

From the late Qing dynasty, China had three legal reforms.[88] The first one happened during this dynasty, and it made a separation between civil and criminal law[89]. At that time, women began to have more legal rights, and theoretically, they should not be treated as inferior to men anymore. More than that, practices of corporal punishment were prohibited[90]. Nevertheless, the constitutions since the late Qing dynasty were mostly ignored, and their fundamental political and legal rights were not sufficient[91].

As already mentioned, the most important Chinese legal reforms began in 1949, when, on October 1, the People's Republic of China (PRC) was officially founded[92].

Thirty-three years after the foundation of the republic, the current Chinese Constitution was adopted. The document declares in its first article that China is a socialist state under the people's democratic dictatorship[93].

This document has influenced Chinese society in varied forms. Politically, it has formalized bureaucratic and segmented political instances, and each administrative division has freedom to practice the law according to their interests.[94]

Most recently, in the amendment to the Chinese Constitution in 2018, the government created Commissions of Supervision, another instance of supervisory organs of the state.[95]

I understand that this structure contributes to a high level of bureaucracy, increases corruption opportunities among public employees, and provokes a distance between the local population and the central government, as people always have local authorities as intermediaries and sometimes some important local issue does not reach higher instances of discussion. Furthermore, the regional administrative instances have different approaches to the law, and people from specific regions may have better governmental assistance than others. For instance, police protection and attendance may vary in each different district.

---

[88] Li; Fang 2013, 13.

[89] Li; Fang 2013, 13.

[90] Li; Fang 2013, 13.

[91] Li; Fang 2013, 13.

[92] Jianmin 2014, 15.

[93] Jianmin 2014, 15.

[94] For instance, see articles 4 and 30 of the Chinese Constitution, 2018.

[95] Amendment to the Chinese Constitution, Article 52, 2018. The 8th section related to the Commissions of Supervision begins at Article 128 of the amended Chinese Constitution.

Court decisions and lawyers' performance do not always properly follow the Chinese Constitution and legislation, and sometimes corruption and political lobbies damage the law.[96]

In 1996, Chinese criminal justice procedures were reformed, and only in that year, did Chinese lawyers get their right to represent their clients fully and not to represent the state exclusively[97]. Before that time, lawyers were supposed to submit to the state, being state workers and not private attorneys.

Sequentially, in 2004, the Chinese Constitution underwent the most important amendments—the Chinese Constitution, first published in 1982, has been amended in 1988, 1993, 1999, 2004[98] and most recently in 2018.

Article 33 stipulates that "*The state respects and guarantees human rights*"[99]. It was the first mention of human rights in the Chinese Constitution[100]. At that time, the *Law on National Regional Autonomy*, the *General Principles of the Civil Law*, the *Education Law*, and the *Labor Law* were also adopted[101].

Nevertheless, it is public and widely known that, notwithstading Article 33 of the Chinese Constitution, China still disrespects human rights. In April 2022, Human Rights Watch published a manifesto signed by several institutions such as Amnesty International and Human Rights Foundation, addressed to the United Nations High Commissioner for Human Rights. The document comes in the context of a planned visit of the High Commissioner to China, to take place in 2022.

The manifesto demands that the High Commissioner be more transparent and accurate regarding the several violations of human rights in China, especially regarding Xinjiang (the Uyghur region)[102]. The manifesto urges the High Commissioner to conduct safe meetings with independent civil society organizations, human rights defenders and victims from, or working in relation to, China,

---

[96] Li; Fang 2013, 70.

[97] Li; Fang 2013, xxiii.

[98] Jianmin 2014, 17.

[99] Von Senger 1993, 297.

[100] Von Senger 1993, 297.

[101] Von Senger 1993, 297.

[102] "Human rights groups believe China has detained more than one million Uyghurs against their will over the past few years in a large network of what the state calls "re-education camps", and sentenced hundreds of thousands to prison terms. [...] There are about 12 million Uyghurs, mostly Muslim, living in Xinjiang, which is officially known as the Xinjiang Uyghur Autonomous Region (XUAR)." (BBC News, 2022. Who are the Uyghurs and why is China being accused of genocide? 24.05.2022. Available at https://www.bbc.com/news/world-asia-china-22278037. Access on 08.08.2022.)

including groups in the diaspora. Such meetings should be confidential and unsupervised. Furthermore, the document requires more transparency and diplomatic reassurances.[103]

The manifesto from the Human Rights Watch calls attention to violations of human rights that have always been happening in China. Coming from a historical context, there are two Chinese expressions for the severe problems with regard to Chinese law: the already mentioned *youfa buyi* (that means, having laws but not complying with them accordingly); and the *zhifa buyan*, which means inadequate law enforcement[104].

The *youfa buyi* happens, for instance, when the authorities sometimes do not follow due legal process, and they withhold access to due process from the defendant and the defense attorney. Despite the authorization granted to the lawyers to represent their clients, from 1996 to now[105], in 2013 the defense attorneys still did not have full access to case information in comparison with the access guaranteed to the prosecutors and the police in criminal cases[106].

According to the United States Department of State, the Chinese judiciary does not independently exercise judicial power. The government and the party regularly influence court decisions, "*The CCP Politics and Law Committee has the authority to review and influence court operations at all levels of the judiciary.*"[107]

The situation has been worse since November 2015, when new legislation began to influence the actions of lawyers in China. Attorneys' actions that "*insult, defame or threaten judicial officers,*" "do *not heed the court's admonition,*" or "*severely disrupt courtroom order*" are criminalized.[108]

If I consider the history of the Chinese Constitution, I have seen that the mention of "human rights" was only introduced in 2004[109]. Although the current 1982 Chinese Constitution stipulates a range of rights and freedoms, its main goal still is the modernization of the country. Moreover, all amendments have maintained the market-oriented economic approach[110].

---

[103] Human Rights Watch, 2022. UN High Commissioner must uphold principled and coherent response to China's human rights crisis. 19.04.2022. Available at https://www.hrw.org/node/381788/printable/print. Access on 24.04.2022.

[104] Zhu 2013, 215.

[105] Li; Fang, 2013, P.xxiii.

[106] Zhu 2013, 218.

[107] United States Department of State 2015, 14.

[108] United States Department of State 2015, 15.

[109] Li; Fang, 2013, xxvi.

[110] Zhu 2013, 216.

Zhu clarifies the prominent problems of the current Chinese Constitution:

> [...] there is no provision to guarantee political and civil rights, and there exist very few restrictions on the state's arbitrary power. No real political structural change has been made as far as the constitution is concerned. Thus, the current constitution, including its amendments, has some intrinsic deficiencies. For example, the scale of human rights protection is still limited.[111]

Furthermore, there are no legal remedies for citizens whose constitutional rights and freedoms are violated. More than that, there is no human rights ombudsman or human rights commission in China[112].

One of the main problems of Chinese law, especially in relation to human rights, is the belief that China is a peculiar country, with a supposed "special system" of government and rights, as well as a particular culture, which supposedly allow them to relativize the observance of human rights:

> The government maintained that each country's economic, social, cultural, and historical conditions determined its approach to human rights. The government claimed that its treatment of suspects, considered to be victims of human rights abuses by the international community, was in accordance with national law.[113]

The argument used by some Chinese is that China's overall human rights policy has been *developmentalist*, in the sense that it is a country still in a low stage of development, which cannot "afford the luxury" of fully implementing universal human rights[114].

There are two main distinctions in the human rights theories: cultural relativism and universalism. According to Michael Sullivan and Peter Van Ness (*apud* Moore, 2001), in China there is a third theoretical distinction: the developmentalist theory. From Chinese developmentalists, the universalism of human rights is desirable, but it is achievable by only developed countries[115]. Countries in development, such as China, do not have the conditions to secure universal human rights for their whole population.

I disagree with this argument, whereas the high level of economic and political organization in China proves that the country is ready to adopt universal human

[111] Zhu 2013, 217.

[112] United States Department of State 2015, 50.

[113] United States Department of State 2015, 50.

[114] Moore 2001, 24.

[115] Moore 2001, 24.

rights. The reason not to do that is related to the authoritarian government and the risk of losing its power and control over the population.

Unfortunately, the influences of the party on the law are getting stronger, especially in relation to some universal human rights guaranteed by the United Nations. Such restrictions directly influence Chinese women, damaging the freedom of marriage—and the related equal rights before and during the marriage, as well as in cases of divorce; freedom of thought and conscience; and freedom of opinion and expression.

Freedom of speech is also limited by the Chinese Constitution.[116]

According to Li; Fang, whereas formerly the government used to refute the criticism against the freedoms of speech and assembly, nowadays they admit their practice of restriction and justify it based on the thesis of the developmentalist theory of human rights:

> [...] Beijing has acknowledged that the country has significant problems in the area of political rights and civil liberties protection. Nevertheless, the Chinese government also argues that these issues can be addressed through the current political system, insisting that it takes time, since any push for fundamental change brings the risk of instability and a breakdown of economic development.[117]

Furthermore, in China, the press is also controlled.[118] The restrictions on the press damage any attempt to denounce abuses against women and to promote gender

[116] „In the existing laws, the restrictions on freedom of speech primarily include three main parts. First, article 51 of the constitution stipulates, "Citizens of the People's Republic of China, in exercising their freedom and rights, may not infringe on the interests of the state, of society, or of the collective, or on the lawful freedoms and rights of other citizens." Second, speech may be judged according to the provisions of Criminal Law, such as crimes of antirevolutionary propaganda, insults, slander, and false witness. Third, similar restrictions on speech can be found in civil and administrative law. Thus, the Chinese government can easily restrict freedom of speech and the press wherever it wants to link them to the jeopardy of national, social, and collective interests." (Li; Fang 2013, 95).

[117] Li; Fang 2013, 97.

[118] "What is especially crucial is government control of the mass media, which ensures critical of the state will not be heard, and authorities have organized powerful institutions and related networks charged with specific duties, such as monitoring speeches, to attain this goal. A censorship system has been adopted for news of great importance, which must be issued by appointed authoritative bodies, but not by private media outlets. Controversial political topics may be discussed individually, or in small groups, but if a speech that includes controversial material is made in public or disseminated to overseas audiences, those involved may be, and often are, punished." (Li; Fang 2013, 97).

equality. According to the United States Department of State, the government frequently impedes the work of the press, foreign and Chinese journalists:

> Journalists reported being subjected to physical attack, harassment, and intimidation when reporting on sensitive topics. Government officials used criminal prosecution, civil lawsuits, and other punishments, including violence, detention, and other forms of harassment, to intimidate authors and journalists and to prevent the dissemination of controversial writings. A domestic journalist could face demotion or job loss for publishing views that challenged the government.[119]

Regarding *zhifa buyan*, China's law system also has inadequate law enforcement, for instance, the restrictions of freedom of expression. Since 2010, the Chinese government has access to "illegal text messages" and "unhealthy content." The cellphone service companies automatically scan text messages to find keywords and send related messages to the police[120].

The United States Department of State states that: "*Authorities continued to censor and tightly control public discourse on the internet and in print and other media.*"[121]. It happens through control of telephone calls, text messages, faxes, e-mail, instant messaging, and other digital communications, including domestic and international mail[122].

When people use the internet to access some international social media and platforms, I have experienced, during the years living in China, restrictions on the use of Google, Facebook, Instagram, Skype, and WhatsApp. Usually, foreign people, living in China and wanting to access such platforms, buy a virtual private network (VPN) to access the internet via an international provider which is not Chinese. The government does not allow such practice, but it has not made any sanction until now.

Most recently, during the pandemic, some big Chinese cities have experienced massive violations of the human rights to privacy, freedom of movement[123], and

---

[119] United States Department of State 2015, 24.

[120] Li; Fang 2013, xxix.

[121] United States Department of State 2015, 1.

[122] United States Department of State 2015, 20.

[123] 'There have been many videos of incidents of resistance to the draconian policies, which are probably just the tip of the iceberg. In one video, nearly 20 officials in "white suits" (police and other government officials in PPE) storm the door of an apartment complex to take away a woman and place her in quarantine, and one of the officials is heard yelling "you are not allowed to film". In another, a "white suit" police officer breaks down a woman's door to take her into quarantine and tells her to stop filming. In another video, four white suits try to capture two elderly women with a long metal

many others. Shanghai, for instance, was under a very strict lockdown under the so-called "Zero Covid" policy. Families were subjected to several visits and compulsory Covid-tests performed by Chinese police, as well as separation from their children if they tested positive[124]. People were not allowed to go out, to buy their own food or supplies, and the exceptions in cases of high-risk diseases requiring immediate treatment were not duly respected. Some residents have been ordered to leave their keys with a community volunteer, so that he could arbitrarily get into their places without prior consent to disinfect it.[125] There were denounces of shortages of food and other daily necessities.[126]

After the general description of Chinese law and how state power limits it, I will now turn to the situation of Chinese law regarding women. The offenses, which occur mostly in the domestic environment, are part of the pattern of love of Chinese women. Nevertheless, for the sake of clarity, I opt to study this legislation in this section, after realizing the above contextualization of Chinese law.

9.2.1 Chinese Domestic Violence

In the context of marriage, Chinese women are exposed to violence. Recently, some legislation regarding domestic violence and women's rights was passed in China, as I will further analyze.

The United States Department of State states that in 2015 25% of Chinese families suffer from domestic violence, and 85% of the victims were women[127].

---

rods with tongs at the end. Eventually the women escape control as onlookers can be heard cheering their bravery.' (Chinese Human Rights Defenders. 2022. 05.05.22. Available at https://www.nchrd.org/2022/05/urgent-life-threatening-conditions-in-lockdown-shanghai-demand-prompt-investigation/. Access on 30.07.2022).

[124] "If your kid is sick, she is sent to a quarantine center. If you test positive, too, you can join her. If you have pets at home, they will be left to starve." (Inside Sources. Rapoza, K. Shanghai's COVID Lockdown Is a Human Rights Atrocity. 19.04.2022. Available at https://insidesources.com/shanghais-covid-lockdown-is-a-human-rights-atrocity/. Access on 30.07.2022)

[125] NPR. Shanghai maintains 'zero-COVID' policy but the U.N. says it is not sustainable. 11.05.2022. Available on https://www.npr.org/2022/05/11/1098150456/shanghai-maintains-zero-covid-policy-but-the-u-n-says-it-is-not-sustainable?t=1659161763653. Access on 30.07.2022.

[126] NPR. Shanghai maintains 'zero-COVID' policy but the U.N. says it is not sustainable. 11.05.2022. Available on https://www.npr.org/2022/05/11/1098150456/shanghai-maintains-zero-covid-policy-but-the-u-n-says-it-is-not-sustainable?t=1659161763653. Access on 30.07.2022.

[127] United States Department of State 2015, 51.

Furthermore, at least 40% of Chinese women had experienced physical or sexual abuse, in the context of a relationship or marriage.[128]

A recently published report reveals that, nationwide, court statistics provide findings suggesting that family violence has not been given enough attention by the Chinese criminal justice system.[129] As with court case statistics, empirical research on family violence published in the Chinese language is also limited.[130]

This phenomenon occurs more in rural areas, but the highly educated urban population also experiences domestic violence. In 2015, the All China Women's Federation reported that approximately 25% of the divorces registered per year were a result of family violence[131]. In 2019, I talked with Chinese activists engaged in support of women victims of violence, and they stated that commonly the cases involving episodes of violence in Shanghai happen within high-class families.[132]

In 2021, the All-China Women's Federation and the China Population and Development Research Center have validated that it is common for women to experience gender-based violence.[133] Nearly half of the men surveyed reported committing physical or sexual violence against their partners or non-partner female.[134]

During the pandemic, China has also seen an increase in domestic violence rates. In the Hubei province alone (the epicenter of the outbreak), the number of domestic abuse cases surged, tripling the level.[135]

I understand that practices of violence against women are a consequence of the cultural and traditional ethical values of the country. According to Wong and Phillips, domestic violence in China is endorsed by Chinese tradition and patriarchalism.[136]

---

[128] United States Department of State 2015, 51.

[129] Kuo; Zhang; Zhao 2021, 637.

[130] Kuo; Zhang; Zhao, 2021, 637.

[131] United States Department of State 2015, 52.

[132] E.S.L., Chinese Activist interviewed by Carolina Esser. 22.10.2019, Shanghai. See the full interview transcript in the Appendix of this dissertation.

[133] Global Human Rights Defense, 2021. Focus on Domestic Violence in China. November 2010.

[134] Global Human Rights Defense, 2021. Focus on Domestic Violence in China. November 2010.

[135] Global Human Rights Defense, 2021. Focus on Domestic Violence in China. November 2010.

[136] Wong; Phillips 2009, 649.

First of all, Chinese police are the first to be called in a case of domestic violence, and usually, police are oriented to find an agreement between victim and perpetrator, trying to mediate. It may happen that the police do not strictly apply the legislation and do not arrest the perpetrator of violence. Usually, they relativize the situations of abuse and orient the victim to peacefully make an agreement with the perpetrator and find family harmony and unity.

Recently, Global Human Rights Defense published that research into the attitudes of police officers towards intervention in cases of domestic abuse showed that police officers remain reluctant to interfere in domestic violence cases.[137]

The Chinese National Law on Domestic Violence was published by the National People's Congress of China in 2015 (here mentioned as "Chinese Anti-Domestic Violence Law").[138] This document was a result of intensive lobbying by women's rights groups and the official All-China Women's Federation ("Women's Federation").[139]

The document defines domestic violence as *"the inflicting of physical, psychological or other harm by a family member on another by beating, trussing, injury, restraint and forcible limits on personal freedom, recurring verbal abuse, threats and other means"*.[140]

The definition of violence—including physical and mental abuse—does not mention other types of domestic violence, mainly economic and sexual ones. Furthermore, homosexual couples[141] are not included in such legislation.[142]

If I take into consideration the Chinese Penal Law, it also does not have sufficient clarifications regarding violence inside the family. Clause 1 of Article 260, for instance, applies to cases involving non-fatal or less severe injuries.[143] This article requires the abuse to be "egregious," but does not define such conduct.[144] Furthermore, *China's Standards for Forensic Examination of Personal Injuries* (2014), defines "light injuries" as the one "causing medium level harm to human health," such as facial lacerations of more than 6 centimeters, skull

---

[137] Global Human Rights Defense, 2021. Focus on Domestic Violence in China. November 2010.

[138] United States Department of State 2015, 52.

[139] Han 2017, 2.

[140] Anti-domestic Violence Law of the People's Republic of China. 2016. Available at http://www.ilo.org/dyn/natlex/natlex4.detail?p_lang=en&p_isn=103955&p_count=1&p_classification=01.04. Access on 23.04.2019.

[141] United States Department of State 2015, 67.

[142] United States Department of State 2015, 52.

[143] Han 2017, 7.

[144] Han 2017, 7.

fractures, and broken ribs.[145] Such requirements and vague descriptions result in few arrests in cases of domestic violence in China.[146]

In the same year of the promulgation of the Chinese Anti-Domestic Violence Law, China's Central judicial organs issued an *Opinion on the Handling of Criminal Domestic Violence Cases in Accordance with Law*, in recognition of the need to strengthen criminal justice response[147]. The document was an attempt to clarify the situations and procedures related to domestic violence in China, for instance, police actions. But:

> The difficulty in enforcing general penal statutes against crimes of domestic abuse underscores a fundamental weakness in China's overall legal approach to domestic violence. By failing to criminalize domestic violence, the DV Law relies heavily on police discretion in applying the appropriate civil, administrative and criminal responses.[148]

The Chinese Anti-Domestic Violence Law elevates "family harmony" and "social stability".[149] As an example, I can mention Article 16:

> Article 16 Where the domestic violence is not serious enough for public security administration punishment in accordance with the law, the public security organ shall criticize and educate the inflicter or issue a caution letter.
>
> The caution letter shall cover the inflicter's identity information, statements of facts of domestic violence, and content of prohibiting the inflicter from committing domestic violence, among others.[150]

The article is proposing a mere caution letter to be sent by the authorities to the perpetrator of violence, after a violent act. It demonstrates that the legislation relativizes practices of violence, in the name of a supposed harmony. Receiving a caution letter from the police hardly stops the perpetrator from committing new acts of violence, and he is not sanctioned at all. The victim, on the other hand, may continue to be without public protection and protective measures.

---

145 Han 2017, 7.

146 Han 2017, 7.

147 Han 2017, 7.

148 Han 2017, 8.

149 Han 2017, 3.

150 Anti-domestic Violence Law of the People's Republic of China. 2016.

In China, harmony is part of their shared ethics, and it influences the way conflicts and acts of violence against women are interpreted. According to Li[151], Confucian *harmony* has five characteristics.

Firstly, *heterogeneity*, meaning that *harmony* exists between two or more different subjects. Secondly, *tension*, which comes from the relationship between the various subjects, who will not think and act in the same way. The third element is *coordination and cooperation*, meaning that the two various parties will try to preserve their connection, making concessions, and exercising cooperation and coordination. After that, *harmony* holds the fourth element: *transformation and growth*, which means, the initial tension is transformed, and the conflict is reconciled. In the end, the last component of *harmony* appears: *renewal. Harmony*, in the end, is an ongoing process.

Chinese will usually try to engage in a harmonious relationship, avoiding conflict and making concessions between each other. Violence turns out to be something negotiable.

Most recently, in October, 2021, accusations of rape were exposed in the Chinese technology giant Alibaba, and led to discussions about the work culture of pressuring employees to drink during work meetings, a violent practice that normally has no consequences for the perpetrators.[152]

According to a female employee at Alibaba, called Mingxi, the drinking nights were organized every two weeks, and she must join it. During these meetings, she has been forced to smile and toast drinks with clients. She describes herself as being pressured to attend such events and not to refuse drinking when the supervisor asks for it.[153]

The Chinese Anti-Domestic Violence Law stipulates in Article 4 that "*Anti-domestic violence work shall observe the principles of putting prevention first and combining education, correction and punishment. [...]*". Furthermore:

> Article 6 The state will carry out family virtues publicity and education, and popularize knowledge of anti-domestic violence, so as to enhance the citizens' anti-domestic violence awareness.
>
> Trade unions, communist youth leagues, women's federations, disabled persons' federations shall, within the scope of their work, organize publicity and education on family virtues and anti-domestic violence.

[151] Li 2014, 9.

[152] Global Human Rights Defense, 2021. Report Focus on Domestic Violence in China. November 2010.

[153] Global Human Rights Defense, 2021. Report Focus on Domestic Violence in China. November 2010.

> Radios, televisions, newspapers, and the Internet, among others, shall conduct publicity on family virtues and anti-domestic violence.
>
> Schools and kindergartens shall conduct education on family virtues and anti-domestic violence.[154]

In spite of the legal dispositions above, Chinese society usually does not have enough campaigns and public incentives to denounce practices of violence, for instance, sexual harassment.[155]

It can also be exemplified by the insignificant penalty for "violations not serious enough to constitute a crime," according to the Chinese Anti-Domestic Violence Law:

> Article 34 Where the respondent's violation of the personal safety protective order constitutes a crime, the respondent shall be subject to criminal liability in accordance with the law; and if the violation is not serious enough to constitute a crime, the people's court shall reprimand the respondent, and may, according to the seriousness of circumstances, fine the respondent not more than 1,000 yuan or detain the respondent for not more than 15 days.

The sanctions and features contained in the law do not have enough strength:

> Two of the DV Law's most prominent features, written police warnings and court protective orders, are both civil remedies strong enough to deter minor offenders but have no real teeth to stop violence. Written police warnings amount to neither civil nor criminal sanctions, nor do violators face penalties. Once issued, they function as a trigger to monitoring obligations of police and community organizations and can be used as evidence in subsequent court proceedings involving domestic violence, but do not shield victims from further abuse.[156]

In addition to the lack of engagement of Chinese police, the second agent that influences the situation of women is the Chinese court. If a woman opts to file a lawsuit, then probably she will, again, be pressured to reconcile with the perpetrator[157].

The Chinese government is also an agent with influences in the maintenance of a low level of support of women victims of violence. Article 18 of the Chinese Anti-Domestic Violence Law stipulates that "*The people's governments at the level*

---

[154] Anti-domestic Violence Law of the People's Republic of China. 2016.

[155] United States Department of State 2015, 53.

[156] Han 2017, 5.

[157] Han 2017, 3.

of county or districted city may, on their own or by relying on relief management institutions, set up temporary shelters to provide temporary living assistance for domestic violence victims."[158]

Nevertheless, in 2019, I have talked to unofficial and undercover activists in Shanghai, who have told me that at some Chinese cities there are shelters out of work. Government has built them, but not further put them into operation.[159] The situation was similar in 2015, according to the United States Department of State.[160]

Chinese activists have informed that they are almost the only organization in Shanghai for the support of women victims of violence, and the government has been monitoring and suspending different initiatives for the support of women. Furthermore, one of their difficulties relates to the segmented administrative structure in the city because each administrative region supports or does not support the female victims in a different form. According to them, the majority of the public officials working at these instances are not sufficiently engaged, and there are not any formal and standardized activities from the state authorities in cases of violence.[161]

Recently, the new Chinese Civil Law introduces dispositions regarding sexual harassment:

> Article 1010 A person who has been sexually harassed against his will by another person through oral words, written language, images, physical acts, or the like, has the right to request the actor to bear civil liability in accordance with law. The State organs, enterprises, schools, and other organizations shall take reasonable precautions, accept and hear complaints, investigate and handle cases, and take other like measures to prevent and stop sexual harassment conducted by a person through taking advantage of his position and power or a superior-subordinate relationship, and the like.[162]

This recent legislation is an important step in confronting domestic violence in China. The Chinese Anti-Domestic Violence Law was also an important step in China in confronting domestic violence. Nevertheless, the document does not comprehend different kinds of violence as crimes, and the sanctions are feeble.

---

[158] Anti-domestic Violence Law of the People's Republic of China, 2016.

[159] E.S.L., Chinese Activist interviewed by Carolina Esser. 22.10.2019, Shanghai. See the full interview transcript in the Appendix of this dissertation.

[160] United States Department of State 2015, 51.

[161] E.S.L., Chinese Activist interviewed by Carolina Esser. 22.10.2019, Shanghai. See the full interview transcript in the Appendix of this dissertation.

[162] Civil Code of the People's Republic of China, 2020.

In a country with significant levels of violence against women, mere conciliation between the parties is not enough. Domestic violence is a considerable disrespect against a woman's identity and freedom. It influences not just her life, but also her children and relatives. Furthermore, several cases can result in death.

In general, the Chinese Anti-Domestic Violence Law does have important articles, for instance Article 43, which stipulates the right to request help from the neighborhood committee, villagers committee, or the unit which the victim belongs to[163]. Nevertheless, these articles should be complied with and the Chinese population and authorities should be aware of the relevance of the topic. I understand that a change of mentality is necessary in China, using political campaigns and stronger sanctions against perpetrators of violence against women.

In 2018, almost three years after the promulgation of the Chinese Anti-Domestic Violence Law, China passed an amendment to the Chinese Law on the Protection of Women's Rights and Interests.

The objective of this legislation is "*to protect women's lawful rights and interests, promote the equality between men and women and allow full play to women's role in socialist modernization*"[164].

Article 5 of the Chinese Law on the Protection of Women's Rights and Interests holds that the State shall encourage women to cultivate "*a sense of self-respect, self-confidence, self-reliance and self-strengthening, and to safeguard their own lawful rights and interests by utilizing law.*" Nevertheless, at the same time, "*[…] Women shall abide by the laws of the state, respect social morality and*

[163] "Article 43 Where a person indulges in family violence or maltreats a family member, the victim shall have the right to advance a request; the neighborhood committee, villagers committee or the unit where they belong to, shall persuade the person to stop doing it and conduct mediation. Where a person is committing family violence, the victim shall have the right to advance a request; the neighborhood committee or the villagers committee shall persuade the person to stop doing it; the public security organ shall stop such violence." (Marriage Law of the People's Republic Of China, 2001).

[164] Article 1, Law of the People's Republic of China on the Protection of Women's Rights and Interests, 2018. See also: "Article 2 Women shall enjoy equal rights with men in all aspects of political, economic, cultural, social and family life. It is a basic state policy to realize equality between men and women. The state shall take necessary measures to gradually improve various systems for the protection of the rights and interests of women and to eliminate all kinds of discrimination against women. The state shall protect the special rights and interests enjoyed by the women under the law. It is prohibited to discriminate against, ill-treat, abandon or cruelly kill the women."

perform their obligations prescribed by law."[165] The Chinese Law on the Protection of Women's Rights and Interests does not define social morality. As a consequence, female attitudes on their own benefit could be misinterpreted and considered a supposed infringement of Chinese social morality.

The Chinese Law on the Protection of Women's Rights and Interests endorses the activities of the *All-China Women's Federation* and the women's federations[166]. Nevertheless, I have met with several activists and workers engaged in women's rights issues in Shanghai, and all of them have said that the Chinese government controls the activities of this federation, which is, in the end, part of the government[167].

Nonetheless, the law introduces some crucial articles for gender equality in China, for instance with regard to property rights in marriage, personal freedom, and health[168]. Over time, this legislation may become more effective.

On the other hand, the document gives discretion to each province, autonomous region or municipality, to formulate measures for the implementation of the law. Article 60 of the Law on the Protection of Women's Rights and Interests relativizes its legal dispositions, and it can result in arbitrariness from the local authorities[169], a problem that already exists in China.

I understand that it is necessary for the Chinese legislation to be more transparent regarding acts of violence and injury against women, as well as the sanctions. Sanctions against acts of disrespect and violence are non-negotiable, and China still gives the authorities vast discretion in dealing with these cases.

Now, I will see how Chinese women experience the pattern of solidarity.

---

[165] Article 5 of the Law of the People's Republic of China on the Protection of Women's Rights and Interests, 2018.

[166] Article 13 The All-China Women Federation and the women's federations shall, on behalf of the women, actively participate in the democratic decision-making, management and supervision of the state and social affairs. Women's federations at various levels and their member organizations may recommend female cadres to state organs, public organizations, enterprises or institutions. (Law of the People's Republic of China on the Protection of Women's Rights and Interests, 2018)

[167] For instance, E.S.L., Chinese Activist interviewed by Carolina Esser. 22.10.2019, Shanghai. See the full interview transcript in the Appendix of this dissertation.

[168] For instance, Articles 31, 32, 36, 37, 38 of the Law of the People's Republic of China on the Protection of Women's Rights and Interests, 2018.

[169] Article 60, Law of the People's Republic of China on the Protection of Women's Rights and Interests, 2018.

9.3 Offenses to the Sphere of Solidarity of Chinese Women

The main characteristics, which affect Chinese women in the public dimension of solidarity, are social inequality and gender inequality in labor and education.

9.3.1 Inequality and Poverty

According to the World Bank Group: "*Within 35 years, China has transformed itself from an impoverished and mostly agrarian economy to an increasingly wealthy, internationalized, and urban economy*"[170]. There was an intense migration from the labor in agriculture to manufacturing and services, and this transformation was accompanied by rapid urbanization, increased labor productivity, higher living standards, and a significant boost in incomes. "*China's poverty rate fell from 88.3 percent in 1981 to 1.9 percent in 2013, an achievement that is unprecedented in scope and scale.*"[171]

Nevertheless, China keeps experiencing problems related to poverty in urban and rural areas. According to a research performed in 2017, there was around 25.2 million (2013, PPP US$1.90 per day poverty line) to 43.4 million (end of 2016, national poverty line) impoverished people in Chinese rural area[172]. This situation is a challenge for the Chinese government because usually Chinese impoverished rural population is located in regions with poor access, without transportation connections. In 2014, the government created a "*poverty alleviation database of the rural poor to improve the targeting of poverty reduction programs*".[173]

In early 2021, the government of China announced the elimination of poverty in rural areas, as measured using the official poverty standard, equivalent to $2.30/ day (2011 purchasing power parity). Nevertheless, using a higher poverty line, typical of upper-middle income economies such as China, in 2019 15.9 percent of the population was still living below $5.50/day.[174]

---

[170] World Bank Group 2017, 1.

[171] World Bank Group 2017, 1.

[172] World Bank Group 2017, VII.

[173] World Bank Group 2017, VII.

[174] World Bank Group 2022. Poverty & Equity Brief China East Asia & Pacific. April 2022. World Bank Group Poverty & Equity. Available at https://databank.worldbank.org/data/download/poverty/987B9C90-CB9F-4D93-AE8C-750588BF00QA/current/Global_POVEQ_CHN.pdf. Access on 30.07.2022.

Income inequality in China calls for further relaxation of the hukou system, progressive taxation and a strengthened social protection system.[175]

Urban context also represents a challenge for the Chinese government. Unfortunately, there are no official urban estimates of urban poverty. Since 2012, China's National Bureau of Statistics started to work on such data, to provide an up-to-date view of the situation of China.[176]

> The problems of imputed rents, differential cost-of-living, migration, and changes in rural and urban definition of counties are challenges to properly analyzing poverty, inequality, and shared prosperity in coming years. The integrated household surveys, as well as new administrative data from antipoverty programs, could be used to improve the impact evaluation of China's poverty reduction strategy and programs.[177]

During my years living in Shanghai, it was astonishing how some neighborhoods have social inequality regarding housing. In one block, I see high tech buildings, surrounded by high-class shopping malls. Walking to the other block, I find Chinese slums, with people living in old small houses, usually without any heating. In Beijing, I have seen beggars and the homeless sleeping on the streets—including during the cold winter.

Peng; Ding argue that China holds, in urban areas, the so-called 'Three-no category': "*Usually, they formed part of the 'Three-No' category—people who have no working ability, or no stable income, or no dependable providers—consisting largely of the childless elderly, disabled people and orphans*".[178]

All these economic factors affect genders in China:

> Difference in treatment of men and women are visible in many areas of society. In China, gender inequalities are prevalent not only in access to education, employment and health, but also in the rules of inheritance, wages, political representation and decision-making within the family.[179]

---

[175] World Bank Group 2022. Poverty & Equity Brief China East Asia & Pacific. April 2022. World Bank Group Poverty & Equity. Available at https://databank.worldbank.org/data/download/poverty/987B9C90-CB9F-4D93-AE8C-750588BF00QA/current/Global_POVEQ_CHN.pdf. Access on 30.07.2022.

[176] World Bank Group 2017, XI.

[177] World Bank Group 2017, XI. See also World Bank Group 2017, 26.

[178] Peng; Ding, 2012, 262.

[179] Bossen 2007; Tan 2006 *apud* Attané 2014, 98.

Although the Chinese Constitution holds that "*women enjoy equal rights with men in all spheres of life.*"[180], China still has considerable gender inequality.[181]

Until 2019, China's Human Development Index (HDI) value increased.[182] During this time, much progress has been made on gender equality and women's empowerment in China.[183] The United Nations Development Programme (UNDP) also understands that important achievements have been made in legislation, policy, and other key areas in China. In 2021, China voluntarily joined the 2021–2023 Round of Gender Equality Seal Certification.[184] It is expected that by the end of 2022, at least 70 percent of project funding will promote gender equality and women's empowerment.[185]

The next section will deal with the situation of Chinese women with regard to labor.

9.3.2 Labor

Considering the history of China, during the 90 s, the country rejected universal standards of labor based on the *developmentalist theory*—already explained in the previous sections.[186] In 2004, the situation was improved, and the *Labor Law* was passed, and it has introduced essential dispositions regarding Chinese women workers.[187]

Despite a considerable change in the access of women to the labor market after market openness in China, women continue to experience gender inequality regarding their salaries, their participation in informal or unpaid work, being subjected to miserable work conditions, and the restrictions regarding any labor mobilization for better conditions.

---

[180] United States Department of State 2015, 57.

[181] United Nations System in China 2015, 09.

[182] UNDP China, 2022. Gender Equality and Women's Empowerment in China. Available on https://www.undp.org/china/gender. Access on 30.07.2022.

[183] UNDP China, 2022. Gender Equality and Women's Empowerment in China. Available on https://www.undp.org/china/gender. Access on 30.07.2022.

[184] UNDP China, 2022. Gender Equality and Women's Empowerment in China. Available on https://www.undp.org/china/gender. Access on 30.07.2022.

[185] UNDP China, 2022. Gender Equality and Women's Empowerment in China. Available on https://www.undp.org/china/gender. Access on 30.07.2022.

[186] Moore 2001, 27.

[187] Li; Fang 2013, 143.

Another problem around female labor in China touches the migrants. Women who come from the countryside and try to find a job in big cities can be exploited in different ways:

> The city does not offer them an easy living. The pay for hard labor is low—often lower than the official minimum wage, which ranges between fifty and eighty dollars a month. Work hours frequently stretch beyond the legal limit of forty-nine hours per week. Get hurt, sick, or pregnant, and you're on your own. Local governments have little incentive to protect workers; their job is to keep the factory owners happy, which will bring in more investment and tax revenue.[188]

Regarding the relationship between labor and education, I will see in the next section that Chinese women have made considerable advancements in education, but it was not sufficient to diminish the gender gap in the labor market.[189] It can be exemplified by the low participation of women in Chinese politics:

> While the government placed no special restrictions on the participation of women or minority groups in the political process, women held few positions of significant influence in the CCP or government structure. Among the 2,987 delegates of the 12th NPC (term 2013-18), 699 (23.4 percent) were women. Following the 18th Party Congress in 2013, two women were members of the CCP's 25-member Politburo. There were no women in the Politburo Standing Committee.[190]

Another social problem is female unpaid work, a universal phenomenon that also affects China. All women's efforts dedicated to housework and caring for the family[191] do not have significance for the market economy. Women are marginalized in working on these functions and do not enter the formal labor market.[192]

---

[188] Chang 2008, 11.

[189] United Nations System in China 2015, 06.

[190] United States Department of State 2015, 46.

[191] For instance, Chinese women are normally the ones responsible for caring for the elderly relatives:

"In other countries, such as China and Singapore, legislation has been put in place to stipulate the obligation of adult children to provide care for their elderly parents by threat of jail or fines. […] A recent survey of long-term care arrangements in China, Mexico, Nigeria and Peru found that the principal caregivers of care-dependent older people with dementia were mostly women—daughters or daughters-in-law as well as spouses—and that many of them had cut back on paid work in order to provide unpaid care and domestic […]." (United Nations Entity For Gender Equality And The Empowerment Of Women 2015, 125)

[192] United Nations System in China 2015, 06.

According to the National Bureau of Statistics, women do almost three times the unpaid work done by men, every week.[193] On the other hand, even in paid work, Chinese women still do not have many opportunities to engage in associations and movements to require better work conditions. When they do have, normally workers themselves organize thestrikes in China, instead of through labor unions.[194] In recent years, although more laws regarding work conditions were promulgated, more riots mount.[195] It may be justified by the lack of support and mediation from labour unions.[196]

The gender gap in labor force participation between men and women nearly doubled over the last two decades, and while many countries have moved closer to parity, China now ranks 106th in the global gender gap rankings among 153 countries slipping from 63rd position in 2006, according to the World Economic Forum (2019) report.[197] The COVID-19 pandemic is having a disproportionate impact on women and their employment opportunities in China. "*Existing gender gaps are likely to widen due to the elevated risk of job losses in affected sectors and the significantly higher family and childcare burden faced by women.*"[198]

UNDP argues that gender equality needs to be further promoted in China specifically regarding equal pay and employment, women's representation in the green economy and tech sectors, addressing COVID-19's economic impact on women, equal access to productive resources and services, women's participation in climate action and local governance, and equal distribution of caring responsibilities and social norms on gender roles.[199]

Coming from this context, the next section will analyze the situation of Chinese women regarding education.

[193] United Nations System in China 2015, 06.

[194] Li; Fang 2013, 122.

[195] Li; Fang 2013, 122.

[196] Li; Fang 2013, 122.

[197] International Monetary Fund 2021, 1.

[198] International Monetary Fund 2021, 1.

[199] UNDP China, 2022. Gender Equality and Women's Empowerment in China. Available on https://www.undp.org/china/gender. Access on 30.07.2022.

9.3.3 Education

In 1998, China began a massive reform in education, expanding the vocational and technical colleges, and developing Chinese universities.[200] If one visits Chinese public universities nowadays, their size, structure, and technology are impressive. World Bank Group argues that China achieved considerable progress in universalization of fundamental education and is now focusing on the universalization of the secondary school.[201]

Despite such a noticeable increase in Chinese education, the situation of women is not sufficiently favorable. For instance, there are reports, which prove that access to higher education for women has been more difficult than for men. Women needed to obtain a higher required score in the National Higher Entrance Examination[202]. More than that, for the women accepted at the universities, they would probably suffer discrimination when they finish university and enter the job market.[203]

Education for Chinese women is also influenced by where the woman is—rural or urban area. As already mentioned in the above sections, the situation of the rural population is usually worse than the urban population[204].

In 2017, the Chinese government approved the "*13th Five-Year Plan for Poverty Alleviation through Education*", to improve the situation of Chinese education in rural and poor areas.[205]

Another challenge to be overcome is the situation of Chinese migrant children. Children who accompany their mothers to the big cities, because of the *hukou* system, are denied access to schooling:

> The government reported that nearly 20 million children of migrant laborers followed their parents to urban areas. Denied access to state-run schools, most children of migrant workers who attended school did so at unlicensed and poorly equipped schools.[206]

[200] Ren; Zhu 2014, 54.

[201] World Bank Group 2017, 35.

[202] United States Department of State 2015, 58.

[203] United States Department of State 2015, 58.

[204] World Bank Group 2017, IX.

[205] World Bank Group 2017, IX.

[206] United States Department of State 2015, 59. See also:
"What is unique about migration in China is that the two aspects of internal migration — movement and citizenship — are often at odds with each other: i.e. one may move to a new

I also need to highlight the situation of Chinese children who were not registered in the past, because of the one-child policy and the tradition of female infanticide. Many families have hidden their second child, or their female children, not registering them. There is a Chinese expression called "extra-birth guerrilla troops" for the families who have gone on the run to hide their second children:

> As they wander from place to place, they grumble and squabble with each other. The sketch took the government line in its depiction of the harm done by 'extra' births, butit also showed how hard the life of this 'floating' population was. After that, the media gave the name of 'extra-birth guerrilla troops' to couples who did a runner and went anywhere in China, often by train when they could, or even abroad so the woman could get pregnant and give birth away from their registered residence.[207]

Unregistered children cannot access public services in China. In 2010, an official census estimated 13 million people without official documentation.[208]

The education of Chinese women also has other harmful aspects. The totality of the Chinese population does not receive sufficient sex education. It results in a lack of knowledge of Chinese population regarding pregnancy, contraception, and the risks of sexual disease. Indeed, according to the Chinese author Xinran, the gap in sex education in China has come since the'90 s.[209]

This situation has been influenced since Mao Zedong's leadership, who suppressed individuality and sexuality[210]. Romance and personal interests were shameful topics because they represent individualist practices, and the state incentivizes collectivism[211]. Therefore, at that time, the de-feminization of women and gender neutrality were promoted[212].

place but may at the same time be permanently denied access to community-membership-based services and welfare. Those who have moved to a new place but do not possess local citizenship (*hukou*) are referred to as the non-*hukou* population." (Chan 2018, 6).

[207] Xinran 2011, 114.

[208] United States Department of State 2015, 58.

[209] Xinran 2011, 20. One of the testimonies in Xinran's book is about a young pregnant Chinese girl: "[...] two months later, she went home for the Chinese New Year holiday, her period hadn't come. She didn't know what this meant—her parents had not allowed her to have any sex education as she grew up. For as long as she could remember, the only way they loved her, the only thing they wanted from her, was that she should study." (Xinran 2011, 36)

[210] Steinhauer 2016, 6.

[211] Steinhauer 2016, 6.

[212] Steinhauer 2016, 6.

Steinhauer provides a description of the situation of sex education in China. According to the author, it is either almost nonexistent, or heavily restrained[213]. Chinese school system approaches it very little and most of the parents finds the subject too embarrassing[214]. The lessons about puberty normally occur in the secondary school and are brief and gender segregated[215]. Into high school, it comes on the form of basic biology of human reproduction.[216] If I consider Chinese rural areas, the sexual education is nonexistent.[217]

Whereas in China abortion is legal in line with some specific criteria, Chinese women are exposed to sexual relationships without acquiring basic knowledge on that, and sometimes they are victims of sexual diseases, as I will now analyze. "*A 2013 survey published by the China World Contraception Day Organization showed that more than 68 percent of women were confused about contraceptive methods.*"[218] Abortion usually occurs among women between 15 and 24 years old[219], and almost half of the abortions every year occurs among college students[220]. General information regarding abortion, such as advertisements, is commonly shared among Chinese women[221]. On the other hand, there is insufficient information about contraception and sexual diseases.[222]

There are reports about the imposition of abortion by authorities in some Chinese provinces, although the birth-approval requirement before a first child is no longer applicable. Some provinces continue requiring Chinese families to present the birth-approval, and abortions are still being imposed on single mothers[223].

More than that, whereas the use of birth control pills is usually discouraged because of the unhealthy side effects, information regarding the use of condoms is also considered to be embarrassing and inappropriate to teach unmarried individuals[224]. As a result, in 2016 there was an increase in HIV in China[225].

---

213 Steinhauer 2016, 7.

214 Steinhauer 2016, 7.

215 Steinhauer 2016, 7.

216 Steinhauer 2016, 7.

217 Steinhauer 2016, 7.

218 United States Department of State 2015, 56.

219 United States Department of State 2015, 56.

220 Jiang 2016 *apud* Steinhauer 2016, 24.

221 Steinhauer 2016, 24.

222 United States Department of State 2015, 55.

223 United States Department of State 2015, 56.

224 Steinhauser 2016, 22.

225 Steinhauser 2016, 22.

In 2020, Chinese government promulgated the *China National Program for Women's Development*, with the aim of presenting the achievements in gender equality in China, including health.[226]

The document is based on the Chinese Constitution, the stipulations of the Chinese Law on the Protection of Rights and Interests of Women and other related laws, the purposes of the UN Convention on the Elimination of All Forms of Discrimination Against Women, the Beijing Declaration and Platform for Action adopted at the Fourth World Conference on Women, and other international conventions and documents, the general objectives and requirements of economic and social development, and the actual situation concerning women's development and gender equality in China (China National Program for Women's Development, 2020).[227]

Within the strategies and methods of the program, the Chinese government intends to provide a standard reproductive health care service for women at adolescence, at child-bearing age, pregnancy and delivery, menopause, and old age.[228]. Furthermore, it intends to ensure women's access to quality family planning services, such as conducting research and popularizing safe, effective and appropriate new contraception and birth-control technologies and methods. The document aims to raise women's self-protection awareness and improve their ability to choose scientific and rational contraceptive methods, and prevent and control unwanted pregnancies and induced abortions.[229]

---

[226] China News, 2020. China National Program for Women's Development (2011–2020). 16.11.2020. Available at http://news.cri.cn/20201116/d094f49f-aab7-2895-3600-b04fead5f1db.html#:~:text=National%20Program%20for%20Women's%20Development%20(2011%2D2020)%20has%20been,and%20other%20related%20laws%2C%20the. Access on 25.04.2022.

[227] China News, 2020. China National Program for Women's Development (2011–2020). 2020. 16.11.2020. Available at http://news.cri.cn/20201116/d094f49f-aab7-2895-3600-b04fead5f1db.html#:~:text=National%20Program%20for%20Women's%20Development%20(2011%2D2020)%20has%20been,and%20other%20related%20laws%2C%20the. Access on 25.04.2022.

[228] China News, 2020. China National Program for Women's Development (2011–2020). 2020. 16.11.2020. Available at http://news.cri.cn/20201116/d094f49f-aab7-2895-3600-b04fead5f1db.html#:~:text=National%20Program%20for%20Women's%20Development%20(2011%2D2020)%20has%20been,and%20other%20related%20laws%2C%20the. Access on 25.04.2022.

[229] China News, 2020. China National Program for Women's Development (2011–2020). 2020. 16.11.2020. Available at http://news.cri.cn/20201116/d094f49f-aab7-2895-3600-b04fead5f1db.html#:~:text=National%20Program%20for%20Women's%20Development%20(2011%2D2020)%20has%20been,and%20other%20related%20laws%2C%20the. Access on 25.04.2022.

It is relevant to highlight that the China National Program for Women's Development mentions the importance of strengthening not just women, but also men, regarding their awareness of common responsibilities with regard to contraception and birth control, research and development of male contraceptives and birth-control products. Men should be encouraged to adopt birth-control measures to increase the proportion of male contraception.[230] In addition to the lack of sex education, all the issues described in this chapter have been affecting the development of Chinese female identity. In the past, it has resulted in female mental disorders, some of them resulting in suicide.

9.3.4 Suicide

The above sections have shown that Chinese women still face many social problems. Their access to education and labor is competitive and sometimes unfair and unequal in comparison with men, and they suffer from the pressure of a collectivistic and paternalistic culture. More than that, generations of women in China have been growing with the fear of not having a baby boy or the need to avoid a second—prohibited—child in the past. These situations left a deep scar on Chinese women. According to Xinran:

> Countless numbers of country women in China commit suicide by swallowing pesticides. In a 2002 United Nations report, China came top of the list for female suicides, and pesticide was the favourite method. China is one of the few countries where more women than men commit suicide.[231]

Wong; Phillips state that at the beginning of this century, China occupied the third place in the world's annual suicides and, unlike the majority of countries, more women than men commit suicide in China. The leading cause of death among rural women between 13 and 35 years, at that time, was suicide.[232]

The aforementioned authors highlight the fact that, for Chinese culture, suicide used to be an acceptable manner:

---

[230] China News, 2020. China National Program for Women's Development (2011–2020). 2020. 16.11.2020. Available at http://news.cri.cn/20201116/d094f49f-aab7-2895-3600-b04fead5f1db.html#:~:text=National%20Program%20for%20Women's%20Development%20(2011%2D2020)%20has%20been,and%20other%20related%20laws%2C%20the. Access on 25.04.2022.

[231] Xinran 2011, 113.

[232] Wong; Phillips 2009, 648.

> [...] to handle stresses and to punish and blame others for their wrongdoings (Colucci & Martin, 2007; Pearson & Liu 2002). Suicide is stigmatic and socially damaging to others (Li, Phillips, Wang, Liang, Wang, & Lee, 2004), possibly giving a woman more power in death than in life over the people who have wronged her (Pearson & Liu, 2002).[233]

The United States Department of State has updated the suicide rate for Chinese women. From 1990 to 2013—reported from the Chinese Center for Disease Control and Prevention, female suicides in rural areas have diminished significantly. The researchers understand that it is a result of better work conditions and the limitation of access to toxic pesticides usually used for suicide. *The Economist*, in June 2015, stated that although the suicide rate was still high in the rural Chinese female population, it has decreased because of the migration to urban areas.[234]

9.4 Conclusion of Chap. 9

Although China has been increasing its economic ties, the Chinese government has been more restricted with regard to the freedom of thought and conscience, and well as freedom of opinion and expression. It affects different dimensions of Chinese struggles for women's recognition, as people usually are afraid to engage in social or private movements to demand changes.

More than that, Chinese women are affected by a patriarchalist tradition, which comes from Confucianism. In the sphere of love, they are supposed to marry and give birth to a boy. Before the one-child policy, the preference for baby boys already existed, and to this day, in Chinese rural areas the preference for boys may still exist.

[233] Wong; Phillips 2009, 649. See also:

"Finally, female suicide in Chinese history has carried positive overtones of virtuosity and selflessness (Carlitz, 1994), and thus maybe a demonstrative act to prove innocence and integrity, repudiating any suspicions that the woman was not a dutiful wife or that she was deserving of abuse. Cultural acceptability of suicide and internalization of positive conceptions of suicide can serve to lower abused women's threshold to engage in suicidal behaviors and confounds assessment of impulsivity and suicidal intent in suicidal behavior". (Wong; Phillips 2009, 650)

[234] United States Department of State 2015, 58.

This social practice has resulted in a vast number of abortions and infanticide of baby girls during Chinese history. Coming from this scenario, some Chinese women obligated to abandon or even kill their baby girls had committed suicide, making China one of the first countries in the world in numbers of female suicides in 2009.

In the context of marriage, I have seen that, in general, Chinese women are called "leftover" if they do not marry by the age of 30. If they get married, probably they will live together with or close to their parents-in-law, a situation which may cause suffering from other kinds of oppression, such as the imposition of a time to be pregnant or how to raise their children. There is also data confirming that there are still Chinese wives accepting practices of conjugal infidelity, as a cultural tradition.

Regarding divorce, Chinese women usually are not equally treated in comparison with men.

I had also studied Chinese legislation regarding women. Chinese pattern of law has been modified over time, but there is gender inequality when courts, police, and lawyers act in individual cases. The Chinese Anti-Domestic Violence Law promulgated in 2015, for instance, endorses family harmony and social stability, in such a way that some practices of violence against women stay unpunished. I also confirmed that domestic violence is a reality of Chinese women to this day. Furthermore, the recent Chinese Law on the Protection of Women's Rights and Interests published in 2018 has given discretion to the authorities and local administrations.

Regarding human rights, I have criticized the developmentalist theory, which argues that China is a country with unique characteristics, permitting a relativization or even a non application of human rights. Indeed, the term "human rights" was inserted in the Chinese Constitution only in 2004.

Sequentially, the chapter has analyzed the female Chinese pattern of solidarity. I have demonstrated that women are subjected to social and gender inequality, which influences their situation in education and labor. There is a gap between rural and urban areas, and the *hukou* system makes the segregation stronger. Migrant women, for instance, may have problems accessing public services in the urban areas if they do not get the proper *hukou* registration, and their children may not be allowed to attend public school and use public health system. More than that, Chinese women can suffer from denigrated conditions in the labor market, sometimes taking up informal work. Furthermore, they are also burdened with unpaid work at home.

In conclusion, it was possible to demonstrate that China is a socialist state under a "people's democratic dictatorship," but there is not enough independence for the people to exercise democratic attitudes. Furthermore, Chinese Judiciary are also subject to control from the government.

Additionally, in the private pattern of recognition, there are strong patriarchal traditions, influencing the development of a woman's identity, and personal projects of self-realization.

The next Chapter will evaluate the situation of Moroccan women.

(Mis)recognition of Moroccan Women 10

This chapter analyses the situation of Moroccan women in each different pattern of recognition. In other words, I inquire how each sphere of recognition has been violated within the Moroccan female population.

My study is based on documentary bibliography, on my personal experience as a volunteer at Centre Batha[1]—a center for the assistance of women victims of gender-based violence in the city of Fès, Morocco, as well as on my time living there as a woman.

In Fès, the occurrence of disrespect and violence against women is significant. Research on the victims of marital violence, conducted by the *Initiative pour la protection des droits des femmes* (IPDF) in 2011, has shown that 7 in 10 women have suffered violence. The types of violence are varied: psychological violence (66,4%), physical violence (49,5%), sexual violence (26,7%), and material violence (16,7%).[2]

In 2022, a report published by the European Institute of the Mediterranean stated that within the 52.6% of forms of violence against women taking place in domestic contexts, 55% were spousal violence.[3] Furthermore, "*Within the 47.4% of violent incidences that took place outside the domestic contexts, 32.9% occurred*

[1] Centre Batha is a multifunctional center for the empowerment of women victims of violence based on gender in the city of Fès. Unesco sponsors the center and it is considered a model for other civil societies and NGOs in Morocco. The author of the present dissertation has done a volunteered internship at the center in June 2018.

[2] "La violence basée sur le genre au niveau de la région de Fès est un phénomène d'envergure." (Asociation Iniciatives pour la protection des droits des femmes 2011, 25.)

[3] European Institute of the Mediterranean 2022, 10.

C. Diamantino Esser Santana, *Recognized Women:*, Juridicum – Schriften zur Rechtsphilosophie, https://doi.org/10.1007/978-3-658-46849-1_10

in public spaces, 24.2% occurred in educational facilities, and 16% occurred in workplaces."[4]

Now, I will inquire how this violence happens.

10.1 Offenses to the Sphere of Love of Moroccan Women

The sphere of love of Moroccan women is influenced by different aspects of Moroccan culture and religion, for instance, by patriarchalism. In this section, I will understand various aspects of love, namely marriage, polygamy, domestic violence, and the stigma of the Moroccan single mother.

10.1.1 Patriarchalism

Islamic culture is patriarchal, affecting Moroccan women's private relationships, especially in the family context. The culture has strong traces of hierarchy, which exists between man and woman, parents and children, older generations and younger generations.

When a woman is living in Morocco, she should consider the traditions of Islamic culture and religion and respect to those superior in the hierarchy. Usually, the superiors are men:

> The established order within the Arabian peninsula at the time of the revelation was patriarchal: a 'culture built on a structure of domination and subordination …' which 'demands hierarchy'. It was a culture with an androcentric bias, one where the male and the male experience are looked upon as the norm. (With such a bias, statements like 'All men are created equal', are left to individual whoms which can interpret the term 'men' as human beings including women, or as exclusive to male humans.)[5]

Moroccan women should always honor their families. "*The concept of honour plays a crucial role in the lives of both men and women in Morocco*"[6]. Honor is the opposite of causing shame in her own family. She needs to honor her family and their shared religion.

---

[4] European Institute of the Mediterranean 2022, 10.

[5] Wadud 1999, 80.

[6] Zerrifi 2001, 59.

Women are the ones to feel ashamed if they do not follow family and social expectations. *Hchouma* is the word for shame, and it permeates the world of female sexuality, in a way that Moroccan women take mostly of their decisions based on the threat of shame[7]. It is one of the key values in Moroccan society, placing women in a position to fear of the opinion of her community.[8] Moroccan men, on the other hand, do not need to concern about shame.[9]

I understand that patriarchalism is a value directly endorsed by the Islamic religion and culture. The Qur'an does have patriarchal verses, which consider men superior to women. I disagree with the authors who understand that patriarchalism in Morocco comes from patriarchal readings of the Qur'an, from a misinterpretation of the religion[10]. Although some interpretations can be very conservative and patriarchal, there are patriarchal verses in the Qur'an, which declare that women are supposed to obey men without any need for an interpretation. The verses are literal.

According to Barlas[11], the fact that the Qur'an defines God as a male figure is general for most religions, and it should not be seen as a necessarily patriarchal aspect. I disagree, firstly, because other male chiefs accompany the figure of a male God (the Father) in Islamic culture: the male *imam* (the leader at the mosques), the father, and the husband at home. They are all the chiefs and leaders, representations that influence Muslim mentality.

Furthermore, one could argue that monotheistic religions are all organized based on the same patriarchal structure[12]. I understand that although many monotheistic religions have a patriarchal system, it does not mean they should not be confronted regarding this topic, including the Islamic faith. On the contrary,

---

7 Barlas 2002, 5.

8 Barlas 2002, 5.

9 Zerrifi 2001, 60.

10 "Moreover, patriarchal readings of Islam collapse the Qur'an with its exegesis (Divine Discourse with "its earthly realization"); God with the languages used to speak about God (the Signified with the signifier); and normative Islam with historical Islam. Thus, Islam and Muslims are confused on the one hand, and texts, cultures, and histories are collapsed on the other." (Barlas 2002, 5)

11 Barlas 2002, 93.

12 "The misogyny and sexism of Arab culture, especially at the time of the Qur'ān's revelation, have been well documented by Muslims themselves (Ahmed 1992; Bouhdiba 1985; Malti-Douglas 1991). However, the Arabs did not invent sexual inequality or discrimination; no society in the seventh century was egalitarian since no society at that time recognized women as full human beings, or as moral agents, or as independent legal persons." (Barlas 2002, 169)

if all monotheistic religions share this same characteristic, then they all need to take gender equality into consideration, including Islam.

One of the examples of patriarchalism in the private sphere of love in Morocco is how marriage happens there. I will analyze Moroccan marriage, one of the social obligations of Moroccan women.

10.1.2 Marriage

The Qur'an endorses marriage as a necessary act for Muslims. Marriage is a powerful institution in Moroccan society.[13] Being a wife is not just a life dedicated to the husband's rules but also submission to family regulations, coming from parents and parents-in-law. The process of finding a husband and celebrating the wedding is something crucial for a Moroccan family, and the bride is prepared for it: "*As a very docile body, the bride's becomes like a doll in the hands of the neggafa, who dresses her and arranges her costumes and hair, as if she is preparing the bride psychologically to give up her volition to her groom*".[14]

For Zerrifi, marriage in Morocco is a way to guarantee a woman's virginity, honor her family, and avoid the shame of not respecting this social taboo.[15] Virginity is indeed endorsed in the Moroccan Penal Law and also in the Qur'an:

> Art. 490 of Dahir n ° 1-59-413 approving the text of the Criminal Code (the Criminal Code): It is illegal for a man and a woman to have sexual relations outside of wedlock, under penalty of imprisonment of one month to one year. […]
>
> Qur'an 17:32: Nor come nigh to fornication/adultery: for it is a shameful (deed) and an evil, opening the road (to other evils).
>
> Qur'an 24:2: The woman and the man guilty of fornication,- flog each of them with a hundred stripes: Let not compassion move you in their case, in a matter prescribed by

[13] "[…] the Qur'an prefers that men and women marry (4:25). Within marriage, there should be harmony (4:128) mutually built with love and mercy (30:21). The marriage tie is considered a protection for both the male and the female: 'They (feminine plural) are raiment for you (masculine plural) and you are raiment for them.' (2:187). However, the Qur'an does not rule out the possibility of difficulty, which it suggests can be resolved. If all else fails, it also permits equitable divorce." (Wadud 1999, 78).

[14] Zerrifi 2001, 219.

[15] "The Moroccan female body is overprotected by the family, especially by the mother who looks after her daughter's virginity and, thus, preserves her from any sexual relationship before marriage. Virginity is an obsession for Moroccan girls; for the Moroccan man still thinks that virginity is the symbol of his wife's chastity and purity. This satisfies his crave to be first male in her life." (Zerrifi 2001, 80).

> Allah, if ye believe in Allah and the Last Day: and let a party of the Believers witness their punishment.
>
> [...] Book 17, Hadith 4191: 'Ubada b. as-Samit reported: Allah's Messenger as saying: Receive (teaching) from me, receive (teaching) from me. Allah has ordained a way for those (women). When an unmarried male commits adultery with an unmarried female, (they should receive) one hundred lashes and banishment for one year.
>
> And in case of married male committing adultery with a married female, they shall receive one hundred lashes and be stoned to death.[16]

Regarding Article 490 of the Moroccan Penal Law[17], Amnesty International states that, in 2015, the Moroccan government discussed the possibility of decriminalizing consensual sexual relations outside marriage, as it compels women victims of rape—in a relationship outside marriage—not to file complaints, including adultery situations. Amnesty International also argues that such criminalization violates women's rights to privacy and free expression[18]. Nevertheless, the aforementioned article has not been reformed yet.

Additionally, regarding marriage, some couples still experience arranged marriage, especially in small rural villages. Parents exercise a significant power of decision in the marriage of their children, and in traditional families, the couple usually does not question the decisions made by their parents.

According to Wadud, a misinterpretation of the Qur'an has turned marriage into a kind of oppression in Morocco:

> However, some interpretations of the rights and responsibilities between the married couple have so severely restricted woman that marriage becomes an institution of oppression for her. If marriage is the means by which a woman is stripped of her individuality and her self-respect as a human equal in humanity and in spiritual capacity to any man, then this is clearly against the Qur'anic intent for a just and moral social order that encourages the doing of good and forbids the doing of evil. It is necessary to resolve this flaw of interpretation.[19]

The discussion of whether the oppressive practices in the Islamic religion come from the Qur'an or misinterpretations should be overlooked, and scholars should

---

[16] Southern African Aids Trust et al., 3.

[17] "Article 490: Sont punies de l'emprisonnement d'un mois à un an, toutes personnes de sexe différent qui, n'étant pas unies par les liens du mariage, ont entre elles des relations sexuelles." (Moroccan Criminal Code, 2016).

[18] Amnesty International 2016, 8.

[19] Wadud 1999, 103.

focus on the consequences on the Moroccan reality and on the possible solutions to the social problems caused by an oppressive interpretation of marriage.

In the case of divorces, Moroccan law has been improving the conditions for gender equality. The verbal divorce initiated by men was made illegal by the Moroccan Family Law enacted in 2004 (European Institute of the Mediterranean 2022, 12). Furthermore, the divorce becomes valid only when approved by a judge (European Institute of the Mediterranean 2022, 12). Regarding women, they acquired equal rights to initiate a judicial divorce and continued custody of their children in case of their remarriage (European Institute of the Mediterranean 2022, 12). Nevertheless, many women still face social prejudice if they get divorced, and economic gender inequality, due to the inefficiency and inefficacy of the reformed legislation. This will be further explored in the following sections.

Moroccan marriage involves other kinds of offenses against women. I will analyze marriage with girls under 18 years old. Furthermore, I will highlight the Moroccan stigma against single mothers, pregnant women without being married. Next, I will study the Moroccan practices of polygamy. Finally, I will catalog the high level of marital domestic violence in this country.

10.1.2.1 Marriage with Minors

According to the Moroccan Family Law, matrimonial capacity is acquired at eighteen years of Gregorian age. [20]Nevertheless, a family court judge may authorize marriage before the age of matrimonial capacity by reasoned decision, specifying the interest and the reasons justifying such marriage.[21]

---

[20] Moroccan Family Code (Moudawana) 2004, Article 19.

[21] "Article 19: La capacité matrimoniale s'acquiert, pour le garçon et la fille, jouissant de leurs facultés mentales, à dix huit années grégoriennes révolues.

Parmi les nouveaux principes prévus par le code de la famille figure l'égalité du garçon et de la fille quant à l'âge de mariage fixé à dix-huit années grégoriennes révolues. L'âge devient ainsi unifié aussi bien pour le garçon que pour la fille. La capacité au mariage ne s'acquiert pas seulement lorsque le garçon et la fille atteignent cet âge, mais chacun d'eux doit jouir de toutes ses facultés mentales.

Article 20: Le juge de la famille chargé du mariage peut autoriser le mariage du garçon et de la fille avant l'âge de la capacité prévu à l'article 19 ci- dessus, par décision motivée précisant l'intérêt et les motifs justifiant ce mariage, après avoir entendu les parents du mineur ou son représentant légal, et après avoir eu recours à une expertise médicale ou procédé à une enquête sociale.

La décision du juge autorisant le mariage d'un mineur n'est susceptible d'aucun recours." (Moroccan Family Code Moudawana, 2004).

Article 19 of the Moroccan Family Law was reformed in 2004 to make marriage with minors an exception in Moroccan society. Nevertheless, jurisprudence has been discretionarily authorizing it to this day. The European Institute of the Mediterranean, in 2022, published that the courts approved 85.2% of requests of marriage with minors, often based on families' claims of poverty and how these marriages help alleviate economic hardships for the family. (European Institute of the Mediterranean 2022, 17). Moroccan judges keep allowing marriage with minors, employing a discretionary observation of the girl's physical and mental development.[22] Furthermore, early marriage would be criminalized only when the minor files a complaint (European Institute of the Mediterranean 2022, 17).

Indeed, some Moroccan judges do not take into consideration the international human rights conventions to which Morocco is a signatory[23]. Furthermore, there are reports from NGOs denouncing judges who do not apply even the reformed Moroccan Family Law.[24]

In 2014, Article 475 of the Moroccan Penal Law was reformed. Before the reform, the second paragraph of Article 475 had provided that anyone who abducts or deceives a minor without violence, threat or fraud could not be arrested if he marries the victim without some annulment request from relatives. In 2014, this paragraph was eliminated from the Moroccan Penal Law. Nevertheless:

> Reforms did not offer minor victims of rape any services or solutions to address problems of social stigma, family pressure, threats of prosecution for illicit sexual relations, unwed motherhood, continuing education, or psychological and health care. Initial reports from local NGOs indicate that in the absence of any alternatives, minor victims of rape and their families still view marriage to the rapist as a "solution."[25]

---

[22] "In practice, judges often issue authorization to marry minors based on their own cursory visual examination of the minor girl's physical appearance and determination that she is capable of assuming "marital responsibilities," rather than resorting to the required expertise. Reasons advanced by judges for authorizing underage marriage include saving family honor, avoiding scandal, protecting the girl's chastity and preventing her from debauchery. Some cite marriage as a solution to poverty. At times judges do not even substantiate their decisions in writing. Corruption among public actors and the ease by which medical certificates attesting to the minor girl's "maturity" can be obtained are also factors allowing circumvention of the law." (The Advocates for Human Rights et al. 2015, 13.)

[23] Schlumpf 2016, 25.

[24] "Other reports by local NGOs reveal a more negative picture of the judiciary stating that in practice they often do not apply the relevant laws.222 So far, there is no reporting mechanism for judicial decision, which means there is little control over the decisions taken by the judges." (Schlumpf 2016, 24).

[25] The Advocates for Human Rights et al. 2015, 13.

Two years after this reform, in 2016, the Moroccan Penal Law was amended again, to legalize abortion in cases of rape, and increase penalties for sexual harassment and rape of minors (Euromed Rights, 2015 *apud* European Institute for the Mediterranean 2022, 13).

Nevertheless, Moroccan girls are still victims of patriarchal legislation and judicial practices. In spite of the international conventions and the reforms of Moroccan law, a lot of improvement is still required. Next, I will see how Moroccan women experience single motherhood.

10.1.2.2 Moroccan Single Mother

"*Stigmatization has far-reaching consequences for the realization of economic and social rights: it renders the needs of certain groups and individuals invisible, pushes them to the margins of society and excludes them from access to resources and services [...]*"[26]. One of the strongest stigmas in Morocco affects the single mother: getting pregnant before marriage.

For Moroccan society, the pregnancy coming from a couple that is not married means that the woman has had sexual relations without respecting the religious, social, and legal dispositions concerning virginity. "*Single mother is one of the biggest social problems and stigmas in Morocco,*" is a phrase commonly heard from the workers of Centre Batha.

The center supports women and their children victims of domestic and family violence, in different forms—such as physical, economic, psychic, and legal; women and their children victims of sexual abuse inside the private sphere (conjugal rape, incest, etc.), as well as in public spaces (sexual harassment, rape, legal discrimination, forced prostitution, etc.).[27]

Considering my time working at Centre Batha, in a range of testimonials and consultations in which I took part in the center, one of the gravest situations of violence I witnessed was related to a single mother.

It was a typical day in the center. As usual, the social assistants were attending the women victims of violence, and the other workers were doing their administrative work.

Suddenly, the worker responsible for taking care of the users who live in the shelter[28] came to our office. Something was wrong.

---

[26] United Nations Entity For Gender Equality And The Empowerment Of Women 2015, 50.

[27] Association Initiatives pour la protection des droits des femmes 2011, 104.

[28] Shelter is a place inside the center, where some female users can stay for a certain period of time. Normally, they stay there in cases of abandonment by their husband, ex-husband, and/or relatives.

I went out of our office, and then I noticed that one of the women users of the center was lying on the floor, very ill and weak.

After a while, I noticed that she was firmly holding something besides the heavy coughs and blood. Coming closer, I saw that she was holding her baby.

This woman had arrived at the center a month and a half before this day, accompanied by her baby, then aged seven months. The mother already had cancer when she arrived.

Making a retrospective, after having a sexual relationship without being married, the baby's father abandoned this woman and her child, and all her relatives—father, mother, and uncles—left her as well. In a situation of homelessness and unemployment, she came to the Centre Batha.

During her time in the center, her cancer got worse, and on this day, the disease became aggravated. It was time to go to the hospital and alleviate her pain and discomfort, waiting for the time to pass away.

Indeed, she knows, at that moment, her child's destiny. After living with him for eight months—one and a half in the center, now she would need to go alone to the hospital and, her child, would be sent to a center for abandoned children.

At that moment, all of us were devastated. The scene of this mother hugging her child, struggling not to let him go, represented one of the main problems of Moroccan women: being a single mother.

After accompanying this woman to a public hospital—which, by the way, did not accept her promptly, as they did not have the proper equipment to care for her—the social assistants made contact with her parents, uncles, and other relatives. As expected, no one accepted her baby.

He was, then, driven to a Moroccan center for abandoned children. According to Centre Batha's workers, centers for abandoned children are quite poor in Morocco, and children stay together with disabled persons and the elderly, without any personal support. This afternoon, we all were in mourning, not just for the mother, but for her child's destiny.

The personal testimonial described above is used here to exemplify the high level of stigmatization experienced by single mothers in Morocco.

A single mother does not have protection from Moroccan law, neither does her child. According to Schlumpf[29], in Morocco and other Middle Eastern and North African states, there are two categories of children: legitimate and illegitimate. The first are the ones born from married parents. In contrast, children born out of wedlock are illegitimate, proving that extramarital sexual intercourse is considered a sin and a criminal offense, under the Moroccan Penal Law.

---

29 Schlumpf 2016, 2.

Article 152 of the Moroccan Family Law states that paternity comes from the marital bed, from an acknowledgment, or from sexual intercourse by error—cases when the couple did not know that they were not living in a marriage regime. Because of that, no filiation comes from an illegitimate child; there is no way to determine this filiation[30].

Therefore, the mother is the only person financially responsible for the child, and the father will not have any legal obligation if he does not accept the paternity of this child[31]. Secondly, the child will have neither the rights of inheritance, nor the right to use the surname of his/her biological father[32].

A single mother has to deal with stigmatization, and she will be obligated to solely support the child financially, a quite difficult requirement for many Moroccan women, who normally experience unemployment[33].

In conclusion, if Moroccan legislation maintains the concept of the illegitimate child, the country will not be able to guarantee gender equality and respect for women's and children's rights. Now, I will analyze another aspect of Moroccan marriage: polygamy.

10.1.2.3 Moroccan Polygamy

After the reform of the Moroccan Family Law, polygamy continues to exist, despite some limitations. Now, polygamy is possible if the first wife permits it by not including a monogamy clause in her marriage contract. Besides that, the husband should also file a petition to the judge, to prove that he wants to practice polygamy for a very exceptional reason and that he has sufficient resources to support both families.[34]

---

[30] Schlumpf 2016, 7.

[31] "A mother cannot deny her child and, as art. 146 *Moudawana* states, filiation to the mother has the same effects whether the child was the result of a legitimate or illegitimate relationship. On the other hand, the parentage to the father ('filiation paternelle' or 'nasab') can only be established for a legitimate child". (Schlumpf 2016, 6)

[32] Schlumpf 2016, 6.

[33] "As long as children born out of wedlock are treated differently than children born to a married couple and as long as sexual relationships outside of marriage remain a criminal offence, these children will be stigmatized and cannot be granted full legal rights. In the end, it is not a problem of religion or legislation but of the mentality. Morocco still has a lot of work to do—legally, socially, culturally and economically—in order to acknowledge illegitimate children and related issues. However, the developments of the past years have shown that Morocco is willing to do so and that it is on the right path". (Schlumpf 2016, 26)

[34] The Advocates for Human Rights et al. 2015, 14.

After this phase, the judge will then notify the first wife to obtain her consent for the second marriage. On the other hand, the second wife will also be notified; she will be formally advised that the husband already has one wife.

According to the Advocates for Human Rights:

> However, the approval rate of petitions for authorization to take another wife is high and increasing; 43.41% of petitions for polygamy authorizations were granted in 2010, up from 40.36% in 2009. NGO reports describe how rather than requiring the petitioner husband to prove an exceptional and objective reason, judges tend to grant authorizations based on his financial situation alone.[35]

Polygamy is a form of legal violence, and between its grave consequences to the children, I should mention the damage to the psychological health of the woman, who feels herself rejected and undesirable, being treated as an object[36]. Polygamy is an example of the current discrimination against women in Morocco. A husband who decides to have a second wife is attesting that he is not satisfied with the first wife, and, by objectifying women, he will have another one. In the end, both women will be damaged, and the children will be witnesses of this violence.

Furthermore, wives are not allowed to practice polygamy, only husbands, thus endorsing gender inequality.

Marriage in Morocco involves other forms of violence against women, especially domestic violence, as described below.

10.1.2.4 Domestic Violence

Moroccan women experience domestic violence not just coming from their husbands, but also from other persons related to the conjugal environment, such as the family of the husband or ex-husband.[37] The conjugal domicile becomes a place of deprivation of dignity:

> According to the statistics above, it can be said that the marital home is a place of torture, deprivation and violation of the dignity of the woman. This thesis is corroborated by the overall number of cases of violence in all its forms that have been committed within the marital home, that is to say 3851 acts of aggression. This is also confirmed by the rate of abusive husbands (76.0%). Where are we now with this literature which

[35] The Advocates for Human Rights et al. 2015, 14.

[36] Réseau National des Centres d'Ecoute des Femmes Victimes de Violences 2007, 61.

[37] Réseau National des Centres d'Ecoute des Femmes Victimes de Violences 2007, 15.

> describes the marital home as a place for love, affection and intimacy? How come that this literature characterizes the marital home as the kingdom of the woman?[38]

In 2022, the European Institute of the Mediterranean statues that "*In spatial terms, the domestic context (spousal and non-spousal) reflected the highest rates [of violence against women]*" (European Institute of the Mediterranean 2022, 10).

The situation is grave, first, because over a long period of time Morocco did not have specific legislation concerning domestic violence[39]. Most recently, in 2018, Law 103.03 on the Elimination of Violence against Women (mentioned here as "*Moroccan Law on the Elimination of Violence against Women*") was enacted. Although it does not clarify exactly what domestic violence means, the legislation introduces the definition of *violence against women*, as well as its categories, namely physical, sexual, psychological, and economic violence.[40] Furthermore, this legislation amends punitive provisions for the perpetrator of

[38] Our translation from: "Selon les statistiques ci-dessus, on peut affirmer que le domicile conjugal est un lieu de torture, de privation et d'atteinte à la dignité de la femme. Cette thèse est corroborée par le nombre global des cas de violence sous toutes ses formes qui ont été exercés au sein du foyer conjugal, soit 3851 actes d'agression. Ceci est confirmé également par le taux des maris agresseurs (76,0%). Où on en est alors de cette littérature qui décrit le foyer conjugal comme un lieu pour l'amour, l'affection et l'intimité? où on en aussi de cette littérature qui qualifie le domicile conjugal de royaume de la femme?" (Réseau National des Centres d'Ecoute des Femmes Victimes de Violences 2007, 52).

[39] UNICEF 2011, 2.

[40] "*Violence against women*: Any material or moral act or omission thereof based on gender discrimination that results in physical, psychological, sexual, or economic harm to a woman; *Physical violence*: Any act or omission thereof that affects or may affect the physical safety of a woman, regardless of the aggressor, aggressor's means or place of perpetration; *Sexual violence*: Any statement, act or exploitation that may affects the inviolability of the woman's body, whether such statement, act or exploitation is for sexual or business purposes, and regardless of the means thereto; *Psychological violence*: any verbal assault, coercion, threat, negligence or deprivation, in the intent (i) to affect the dignity, liberty or serenity of a woman; or (ii) to threat or intimidate her; *Economic violence*: Any act or omission thereof, regardless of its financial or economic nature, that causes or may cause prejudice to the economic or social rights of a woman." (Moroccan Law 103.03 on the Elimination of Violence against Women, 2018, article 1)

violence against women[41], sexual exploitation and youth corruption[42], procedural provisions[43], support mechanisms for women victims of violence[44], and measures and initiatives to prevent violence[45].

Article 5 of the Moroccan Law on the Elimination of Violence against Women has amended Article 88–1 of the Moroccan Penal Law regarding sexual violence[46]. Nevertheless, the new Article 88–1, in section 1, allows a reconciliation between husband and wife after a crime of harassment, assault, sexual abuse, mistreatment or violence against women, allowing the perpetrator to contact the victim again.[47] This disposition is an example of relativization of the violence against women, endorsing supposed family harmony at the expense of women's dignity.

These problems related to the current legislation in Morocco may be justified based on the judicial procedures in the country. Moroccan law is based on *Sharia* law as rooted in the legal system of Sunni Muslims (the people of the tradition) (Konrad-Adenauer-Stiftung e.V. 2020, 4), specifically following the teachings of the Maliki school of thought (Konrad-Adenauer-Stiftung e.V. 2020, 4). *Sharia* law is guaranteed by the Moroccan Constitution, as the King is the Commander of the Faithful, ensuring respect for Islam throughout the legal system (Konrad-Adenauer-Stiftung e.V. 2020, 4).

---

[41] Moroccan Law 103.03 on the Elimination of Violence against Women, 2018, Part two, articles 2 and 3.

[42] Moroccan Law 103.03 on the Elimination of Violence against Women, 2018, Part two, section seven, articles 4 and 5.

[43] Moroccan Law 103.03 on the Elimination of Violence against Women, 2018, Part three, articles 6 to 8.

[44] Moroccan Law 103.03 on the Elimination of Violence against Women, 2018, Part Law 103–13 2018, Part four, articles 9 to 16.

[45] Moroccan Law 103.03 on the Elimination of Violence against Women, 2018, Part five, article 17.

[46] Moroccan Law 103.03 on the Elimination of Violence against Women, 2018, article 5.

[47] "Article 88–1: If a person is convicted for a crime of harassment, assault, sexual abuse, mistreatment or violence against women or minors, regardless of the nature of the act or the perpetrator thereof, the court may adjudicate the following: 1—Prohibit the convict from contacting the victim, approaching victim's whereabouts, communicating with the victim by any means whatsoever for a period no longer than five years as of the date of his release, or as of the date of the judicial decision in case of a suspended sentence, fine or alternative punishment; Reconciliation between the spouses shall terminate the prohibition against contact with the victim; […]" (Moroccan Law 103.03 on the Elimination of Violence against Women, 2018, article 5.)

The influences of Sharia law are endorsed throughout the segmented judicial system. Besides the formal judicial courts based on codified laws and regulations, Morocco has an informal justice system based on customs (Konrad-Adenauer-Stiftung e.V. 2020, 4). The necessity to integrate and reconcile both systems is very relevant for achieving gender equality, but it is still far from being reached in Morocco[48]. Despite the relevance of informal justice for the development and evolution of the Moroccan legal system (Konrad-Adenauer-Stiftung e.V. 2020, 4)—as people theoretically would have an easier and faster solution to their judicial claims, this dual system produces uncertainty for Moroccans, especially for women. For instance, in *Amazigh* communities in the rural regions of Morocco, the tribal judges tend to be conservative and patriarchal in their application of the law, prejudicing equality for women (Konrad-Adenauer-Stiftung e.V. 2020, 5).

For instance, regarding the violence against women, a literal reading of the Qur'an says:

> Men are the protectors
>
> And maintainers of women,
>
> Because God has given
>
> The one more (*strength*)
>
> Than the other, and because
>
> They support them
>
> From their means.
>
> Therefore the righteous women
>
> Are devoutly *obedient*, and guard
>
> In (the husband's) absence

[48] "In 1974, the Moroccan Government attempted to integrate tribal laws into the formal justice reforms by recognising the inclusion of tribal law through the appointment of rural commune traditional judges, known as *Hakim*, as state mediators. The Government initiated an election process for these traditional judges at the level of each rural commune, but the attempt failed because of disagreement between the Moroccan Government and the rural communes on financial compensation for such roles. Following this failed attempt, the Moroccan legislature did not reattempt to set a policy towards codifying, controlling, or containing the work of informal justice, until the adoption of the 2004 *Moudawana*; whereby unregistered tribal marriage, known as *Zawaj bil- Fatiha*, can be formalised in the Family Court through the application of Article 16 of the *Moudawana*, which registers the marriage retroactively." (Konrad-Adenauer-Stiftung e.V. 2020, 6)

What God would have them guard.
As to those women
On whose part ye fear
Disloyalty and ill-conduct,
Admonish them (first),
(Next), refuse to share their beds,
(And last) beat them (lightly);
But if they return to obedience,
Seek not against them
Means (of annoyance).[49]

The literal interpretation of this Qur'anic passage mentions violent acts against women. The verses states that women should obey men, and, if they do not, men are allowed to beat women.

There are authors, such as Barlas[50] or Wadud[51], who understand that these verses and other passages of the Qur'an should be interpreted considering all the philosophies of the Qur'an, which advocate for the harmony of marriage and gender equality. They argue that the words used in the Qur'an are mere metaphors.

---

[49] The Qur'ān, 4:34; in Ali, 190 *apud* Barlas 2002, 182, emphasis by Barlas.

[50] "Perhaps the only teaching of the Qur'ān that shows a measure of inequality is the yah on confining the wife ("wife beating"), since it does not give the wife comparable rights. However, if Hassan's (1999) reading is accurate that such a confinement is only to be effected in the face of a mass revolt by women against childbearing—a function only women can perform (at least, thus far)—then, such an eventuality seems remote and, to that extent, the yah also becomes peripheral to understanding the Qur'ān's view of spousal relationships. What this yah does reveal, however, as do others, is that the Qur'ān recognizes that men have the power and authority in patriarchies. However, this does not mean that it either condones patriarchies, or that it is itself a patriarchal text." (Barlas 2002, 198)

[51] "Is this Qur'anic prohibition applied only to women because they were specifically addressed—implying therefore that it is all right for men to practise it? This is clearly not so. Because women were mentioned consequently in a verse, it is no indication that the verse must be restricted in its application to only that gender. All who wish to attain moral excellence in the Qur'anic world-view of social behaviour must strive to avoid going out of the house with the express purpose of wanton display. Such a gender-constraint on the understanding and application of the verse is unnecessary. Rather, the women are used to state a general social principle." (Wadud 1999, 98)

I do not agree with these authors. The Qur'anic passage above is clear, direct, and does not require a very complex semantic interpretation. The reading is literal.

When I was living in the city of Fès, I talked with native people, and many persons have said that Islamic religion should not be confused with Islamic culture, even the non-orthodox Muslims. The culture of Islam usually comes from the misinterpretations of the Qur'an and the Islamic religion. In the same direction, there is a vast literature discussing interpretations of the Qur'an and defending the Islamic religion, some of them arguing that Islam promotes equality between men and women, and respect for human rights.

Nevertheless, this work comes from the presupposition that the misinterpretations or general interpretations of a religion or a sacred text are part of the culture, and have effects on the daily life of people, stimulating their behavior. I contend that Islamic culture, including the religion itself and its interpretations or misinterpretations, should be reflected and reviewed—especially regarding respect to fundamental human rights -.

Such a transformation of Islamic culture should be discussed by Muslims, the Moroccan population, and implemented by them. People themselves should understand that there are some human rights—including women's rights, to be universally respected and practiced. People should be aware of the importance of gender equality.

Unfortunately, I do think that misinterpretations of Islam stimulate inequality between men and women. The way the religion is being practiced in Morocco nowadays is still traditional, and there are many persons—especially women—suffering consequences. In a country where Islam is part of the state and the culture, it begins to affect every aspect of a person's life, such as their daily experience in family, educational, work, and social environments, from private and public perspectives. The fact that Moroccan legislation and the Constitution are tied to Islam is a reason, in our opinion, which affects the real development of human rights in Morocco, especially with regard to women's rights.

The exercise of religion is the right of all populations. Nevertheless, if it implies misogynistic practices and compromises fundamental human rights—in the case of Morocco, women's rights, then the culture of this religion should be transformed.

I am not advocating the abandonment or extinction of Islamic religion and culture in Morocco. On the contrary, I comprehend the transformation of cultures over time. I endorse the necessity of interpreting the Qur'an and the religion from a balanced perspective regarding men and women, respecting gender equality.

Coming from the data presented in this work, as well as from our personal experience in Morocco, different kinds of violence against women are justified by Moroccans' thinking that men are superior to women and that they should exercise this power over them. Our argument is endorsed by civil organizations, NGOs, and scholars. The *Réseau National des Centres d'Ecoute des Femmes Victimes de Violences*, for instance, argues:

> This aggressive behavior against women can be attributed to this still prevalent idea that the husband can educate his wife. Certain husbands consider this as their legitimate right, arguing for the relationship of dependence and submission that binds the wife to her husband. This so-called right finds its justification in the cultural roots of the man-woman relationship.[52]

I can see that, in the sphere of love, Moroccan women are exposed to different forms of disrespect. First of all, before getting married, she is under a patriarchal education inside her family. She must honor her family and avoid feelings of shame. Furthermore, she should preserve her virginity until she gets married.

If a Moroccan woman gets pregnant without being married, then she will be exclusively responsible for the financial support of the child, and her child is considered illegitimate, not holding any right related to the father—such as inheritance.

On the other hand, if the Moroccan woman decides to get married, she may be exposed to different forms of disrespect, such as polygamy and domestic violence. Child marriage is also practiced in Morocco.

After analyzing these aspects of Moroccan female private life, I will now study how women are treated in the sphere of law.

10.2 Offenses to the Sphere of Law of Moroccan Women

First of all, this section will analyze the most recent reforms in Moroccan law concerning Moroccan women.

---

[52] Our translation from: "Ce comportement agressif contre la femme peut être attribué à cette idée toujours répandue, selon laquelle le mari peut éduquer sa femme. Certains maris considèrent cecci comme leur droit légitime, en faisant valoir le rapport de dépendance et de soumission qui lie la femme à son mari. Ce soit disant droit trouve sa justification dans les racines culturelles de la relation homme-femme." (Réseau National des Centres d'Ecoute des Femmes Victimes de Violences 2007, 20)

Nowadays, Morocco is considered one of the most advanced Islamic countries, with legislation called "modern." It is a result of reforms made in the last 25 years.

Firstly, as I will see, in the last decades Morocco has become a signatory to international conventions on human rights. Secondly, in 2004, the Moroccan Family Law (in Arabic, the *Moudawana*) was reformed. Thirdly, the Moroccan Constitution was amended in 2011. Finally, in 2018, the passage of the Moroccan Law on the Elimination of Violence against Women amended the Moroccan Penal Law.

In the course of the explanation, I will notice that, despite legal changes in articles, sanctions, and legal procedures, unfortunately, Morocco does not have satisfactory gender equality. The legislation still contains inconsistencies. Furthermore, either legal decisions sometimes ignore the reformed legislation, considering just the traditional and conservative system; or, in the case of judges, do recognize the improved law, but have difficulties in applying it. Sometimes, they opt to maintain a traditional position instead of creating new precedents and using their discretion to defend gender equality[53].

The Moroccan Family Law was first established in 1958, two years after Morocco's independence from France. At that time, this code represented almost a transcription of the classical Islamic family law[54].

In 1962, the Moroccan Constitution was voted on, and at that time, it settled equal political rights for males and females. Nevertheless, the general legislation of Morocco and the *Moudawana* have continued to treat women unequally[55].

Only in 2004 did the Moroccan legislation have the first significant reform regarding women—which, as I will further see, is not sufficient. The Moroccan Family Law was reformed in that year. It introduces many dispositions related to gender equality, such as inheritance, marriage, divorce, and child custody[56].

[53] Indeed, there are Moroccan NGOs, which consider Moroccan jurisprudence an example of institutional violence: "On entend plutôt par ceci que les femmes victimes de ces formes de violence, avant de recourir aux centres d'écoute, se sont adressés aux institutions de l'Etat: police, gendarmerie, tribunaux… Cependant, elles n'ont pas été satisfaites, en raison soit de la lenteur des procédures ou atermoiement, soit des difficultés dans l'exécution des jugements rendus, voire leur inexécution, ou encore en raison de "inacceptation du dispositif du jugement". (Réseau National des Centres d'Ecoute des Femmes Victimes de Violences, 2007, 32).

[54] Schlumpf 2016, 3.

[55] Schlumpf 2016, 3.

[56] UNICEF 2011, 1.

The time that preceded the reform of the Moroccan Family Law was quite hectic. Public opinion in Morocco was divided. Firstly, there were anti-reform protesters:

> The half million Islamists, veiled women (on the right of the picture below) and bearded men (on the left), marched in separate male and female columns (see the image of the right) in Casablanca on 12th March 2000—which was an utter surprise, never mentioned before—to demonstrate against the 'Integration Plan' and against the government's proposals to ban polygamy, raise the legal age for marriage from 14 to 18 and reform divorce laws. The anti-reform protesters—as they define themselves—denounced the reforms as Western-inspired, and alien to Islamic religion and Moroccan traditions.[57]

On the other hand, there were also many civil society organizations and women's rights movements, which endorse the reform of *Moudawana*. Fortunately, in 2004, the new *Moudawana* was enacted. According to UNICEF, "*new Moudawana is considered one of the most progressive in the Arab world*"[58], and the United Nations states that this legal reform represented progress in women's rights in Morocco[59]. Additionally, in 2004, a new labor code was enacted in Morocco, guaranteeing the right to maternity leave for Moroccan women[60].

Seven years after the passage of the new Moroccan Family Law, in 2011, the Moroccan Constitution was also amended, in line with the government's objective to adapt the legislation of the country to a modern and progressive vision of the law.[61]

The preamble of the Moroccan Constitution defends moderation, tolerance, and dialogue with other cultures and world civilizations. Furthermore, the Moroccan Constitution endorses international conventions, human rights, and the fight against all kinds of discrimination[62].

---

[57] Zerrifi 2001, 22.

[58] UNICEF 2011, 1

[59] United Nations Entity For Gender Equality And The Empowerment Of Women, 2015, 232.

[60] United Nations Entity For Gender Equality And The Empowerment Of Women, 2015, 232.

[61] "In 2011, the country passed a new constitution guaranteeing gender equality in civil, political, economic, social, cultural and environmental rights. In the same year, Morocco removed several of its reservations to CEDAW, in relation to women's rights to nationality and to rights within marriage and the family." (United Nations Entity For Gender Equality And The Empowerment Of Women 2015, 232).

[62] Morocco's Constitution, Preamble, 2011.

Article 19 of the Moroccan constitution stipulates gender equality in civil, political, economic, social, cultural, and environmental rights and freedoms[63].

Nevertheless, according to the United States Department of State, in 2017, the defense of human rights and equality in Moroccan courts was still not sufficient:

> Although individuals have access to civil courts for lawsuits relating to human rights violations and have filed lawsuits, such lawsuits were frequently unsuccessful due to the courts' lack of independence on politically sensitive cases, or lack of impartiality stemming from extrajudicial influence and corruption. The newly created Supreme Judicial Council is tasked with ensuring ethical behavior by judicial personnel (see section 4). There are administrative as well as judicial remedies for alleged wrongs. Authorities sometimes failed to respect court orders in a timely manner.[64]

Actually, the Moroccan government limits the activities of some NGOs in Morocco, including the ones related to human rights. The Moroccan government does not recognize the NGOs that may threaten Islam, state religion, legitimacy of monarchy, or Morocco's territorial integrity[65].

The problem is intensified if one analyzes Moroccan constitutional freedoms. The Moroccan Constitution guarantees freedom of opinion, expression, and thinking (article 25)[66], as well as freedom of the press (article 28)[67].

Nevertheless, these rights are not duly respected in Morocco. They are restricted in some situations. Moroccan people are not allowed to criticize Islam,

---

[63] "Article 19: L'homme et la femme jouissent, à égalité, des droits et libertés à caractère civil, politique, économique, social, culturel et environnemental, énoncés dans le présent Titre et dans les autres dispositions de la Constitution, ainsi que dans les conventions et pactes internationaux dûment ratifiés par le Maroc et ce, dans le respect des dispositions de la Constitution, des constantes du Royaume et de ses lois. L'Etat oeuvre à la réalisation de la parité entre les hommes et les femmes. Il est créé, à cet effet, une Autorité pour la parité et la lutte contre toutes formes de discrimination." (Morocco's Constitution, 2011)

[64] United States Department of State 2017, 13.

[65] United States Department of State 2017, 19.

[66] "Article 25: Sont garanties les libertés de pensée, d'opinion et d'expression sous toutes leurs formes.

Sont garanties les libertés de création, de publication et d'exposition en matière littéraire et artistique et de recherche scientifique et technique." (Morocco's Constitution, 2011)

[67] "Article 28: La liberté de la presse est garantie et ne peut être limitée par aucune forme de censure préalable. Tous ont le droit d'exprimer et de diffuser librement et dans les seules limites expressément prévues par la loi, des informations, des idées et des opinions. [...] La loi fixe les règles d'organisation et de contrôle des moyens publics de communication. Elle garantit l'accès à ces moyens dans le respect du pluralisme linguistique, culturel et politique de la société marocaine. [...]" (Morocco's Constitution, 2011)

the institution of the monarchy, and the government's position regarding territorial integrity and Western Sahara. Such criticism may provoke prosecutions and punishments. Although the 2016 press code guarantees freedom of expression, the document applies only to journalists accredited by the Ministry of Communication.[68]

The prohibited themes, which the population is not allowed to discuss, are contradictorily described in the Moroccan Constitution. For instance, the same constitutional fundamental article, which restricts any change related to fundamental rights and freedoms in Morocco, simultaneously restricts any change related to the Islamic religion[69]. Therefore, one may ask: if there were something in the Islamic religion in opposition to fundamental rights and freedoms, would it be maintained in the Moroccan Constitution? The answer is yes. In the end, respect for the Islamic religion prevails over respect for fundamental rights and freedoms.

Despite the reforms of the Family Law and the Constitution, Morocco still has a long way to go to respect women's rights and achieve gender equality. Only legal norms are not sufficient to guarantee gender equality. Moroccan legislation has clear statements regarding gender equality, especially in the Moroccan Constitution. Nevertheless, the law is also related to the efficiency and efficacy of its application. Furthermore, the legal norms should also be understood by societies through social norms, as shared values accepted, understood, and practiced by individuals.

17 years after the reform of the Moroccan Constitution, the Moroccan Law on the Elimination of Violence against Women amended the Moroccan Penal Law. Nevertheless, the structure of the Moroccan Penal Law needs to be revised to minimize the conflict between old and new laws (European Institute of the Mediterranean 2022, 22). Additionally, the public instances and bodies whose mandate includes reporting and fighting violence against women are still in need of additional training and resources (European Institute of the Mediterranean 2022, 22). Morocco also needs a central national body with the authority to enforce compliance and fight against violence against women (European Institute of the Mediterranean 2022, 22).

Next, I will analyze how Moroccan women experience disrespect in the pattern of solidarity.

---

[68] United States Department of State 2017, 14.

[69] "Article 175: Aucune révision ne peut porter sur les dispositions relatives à la religion musulmane, sur la forme monarchique de l'Etat, sur le choix démocratique de la Nation ou sur les acquis en matière de libertés et de droits fondamentaux inscrits dans la présente Constitution". (Morocco's Constitution, 2011)

10.3 Offenses to the Sphere of Solidarity of Moroccan Women

According to Honneth, the pattern of solidarity is the one where a person feels self- and social-esteem, when she realizes that she has appreciation from her community and a role in the social dynamic.

Considering the situation of Morocco, the public role of women in society is oppressed, and it affects different public instances, such as labor, education, and politics.

10.3.1 Moroccan Public Spaces

> The female enters the public (masculine) space, as Barbara Brook (1999) adequately argues: as a potentially disruptive, transgressive body and it is her position as spectacle (making a spectacle of herself) under the view of the masculine eye, that disciplines her back into line, returns her into a docile body (p:112).[70]

The dynamic of men and women in Moroccan public spaces is different. Usually, public locations are mostly frequented by men. Barlas interprets what "public spaces" mean for Islamic culture and the West. For Westerners, the public sphere is where I can exercise our freedom, politics, and culture. Historically, these spaces are mostly frequented by men[71]. The private sphere, by contrast, is where we experience necessity and not freedom; nature, and not culture[72]. The private space holds the family, not the political state[73]. Although private spaces relate to women, the king of the house is still the man.[74]

Barlas argues that the division between private and public is different for the Western theory, and for the Qur'an. Nevertheless, I understand that such interpretation of public and private worlds are part of Islamic culture as well as some Western cultures. It is widespread in Islamic countries, such as Morocco, that public spaces are reserved for politics and social traditions, and mainly occupied

[70] Zerrifi, 2001, 85.

[71] Barlas 2002, 171.

[72] Barlas 2002, 171.

[73] Barlas 2002, 171.

[74] "While men may move freely between both spheres, women are confined to the private. The family and marriage, then, also fall into a private, nonpolitical domain, and it is this location, argue many feminists, that accounts for the history of sexual inequality and oppression in Western societies" (Barlas 2002, 171).

by men. Private spaces, on the other hand, although linked to the presence of women, are typically dominated by men. Women in private space are seen as an accessory. It is exemplified by the *Mahjouba*, a traditional Muslim term for the woman who was allowed to go outside the home just for three reasons:

> This has encouraged Muslim traditionalists to advocate the harem and forbid women the public space. The term *Mahjouba*—the hidden—the invisible from the male's gaze is concurrent with this. *Mahjouba* is not allowed to go out except to three places; the *Hammam* (the public hot steam, bath) to purify her body, to her husband's house as a new bride, and to the grave when she dies.[75]

Although nowadays these restrictions of movement are usually practiced only by orthodox Muslims, the tradition and power of this expression still influence the dynamic of Moroccan women.

One of the most discussed examples of women's limitations in Moroccan public spaces relates to the way they dress themselves, the use of the veil. There are vast discussions in the literature, whether the use of the veil relates directly or not to Islamic restrictions on women in public spaces.

I understand that veiling is just one element of Islamic culture, which derives from an original idea of modesty of a woman, who should not show herself, respecting Islamic commandments. She needs to dress according to Islam. She needs to respect the limits of dressing required by religion. It is important to mention that it is not just related to veiling, but also with the outfit of women in general.

Islamic culture and religion endorse the modesty and discretion of women in public spaces[76]. They should avoid attracting attention outside the home, trying to be almost invisible when they are occupying public spaces. The use of the veil could be a way to discipline women's authenticity.

On the other hand, some authors understand veiling as a practice related to the history of Moroccan culture, even before Islam. From this perspective, women who still veil are not necessarily endorsing Islam, endorsing practices that minimize the right of a woman to show her beauty as well as exercise her freedom

---

[75] Zerrifi 2001, 43.

[76] "The reasons that explain woman's silence are various and rooted in the socialization process, starting from the upbringing and the education the little girl receives within her family, following the androcentric textbooks and methods she learns in schools, and experiencing subordination at work outside home. All these constraints oblige her to "turn her tongue seven times before speaking", especially when she leaves, her own private world to enter the public, that is, the male world". (Zerrifi, 2001, 107)

of expression, freedom of movement, and the right to dress the way she wants. Actually, they are practicing their historical culture as Berbers or Arabs.

There are also authors arguing that the use of the veil is resistance, which is a way to disconnect themselves from beauty standards. They hold that not veiling will attract the attention of men to their female attributes, and it damages their rights to have a voice, without a male judgment. Using the veil is a way to become invisible:

> As a free comment to the last open-ended question of the questionnaire, many veiled respondents write: "with the hijab men do not harass us in the streets, and our fathers, brothers, and husbands do not annoy us and do respect us". [...] They passionately continued, "We want to stop men from treating us like sex objects, as they have always done. We want them to ignore our appearance and to be attentive to our personalities and minds. We want them to take us seriously and treat us as equals and not just chase us around for our bodies and physical looks." A Muslim woman who covers her head is making a statement about her identity.[77]

Despite these views on veiling, I understand that the use of the veil mainly represents the obligations of female Muslims, who should avoid showing themselves in public spaces. Evidently, some women veil because they want it as a personal and authentic decision, and they feel comfortable. Nevertheless, these women are not the majority.

The discussion relates not just to the use of veil; women can also be restricted in other ways of dressing, such as avoiding wearing tight clothes or short skirts. I advocate that the use of the veil and all other aspects related to the way women dress in public spaces is a question of women's rights to movement and freedom of expression. All restrictions which are imposed by religion or culture, and disrespect the freedom of movement and freedom of expression of women should be reviewed.

I contend that Muslims should be equally free to decide the way they dress. If a Moroccan woman has this freedom to choose, the freedom to opt for using the veil in public spaces, according to a choice made uniquely by her, then it is her choice to veil. Nevertheless, when this behavior comes uniquely from the pressure of religion or culture, then it violates women's rights.

---

[77] Zerrifi 2001, 87. See also:

"Due to cultural pressures to dress "decently," even women who do not believe in the justification behind the veil feel compelled to wear one. This social practice reinforces the perception of women as purely sexual beings who need to be controlled, as it is proved by the findings of the analysis of questionnaire in the next chapter". (Zerrifi, 2001, 62)

In our opinion, beauty should not be understood just from an aesthetic perspective. This work argues that beauty is a form of freedom. It definitely is not related to standards introduced by the market and cultures. Being beautiful does not mean wearing and showing herself in the way that external institutions impose, such as the market, a culture, or a religion. Being beautiful is related to the freedom to exercise practices of enjoyment with oneself, to dress, and to adorn oneself in the way the woman wants to. Beauty is not interpreted as a state, but as a process, an exercise, the right to display the beauty, to enjoy the beauty:

> Beautiful things cause pleasure, and this pleasure can be more or less intense and perceived in different ways. This idea is not new: As Otto (1993) states, from Plato and Aristotle, to the early British empiricists aestheticians and on to Kant, Hegel, Schopenhauer and very recent authors, it is considered that pleasure is a central element of aesthetic experience (cf. Otto, 1993, p. 113).[78]

Islamic religion and culture allow a limited women's beauty as an exercise just inside her private family circle, in intimacy, especially with her husband, inside the pattern of love: "*The domestic space allows Moroccans, especially females, to present themselves in a way distinct from the ways women portray themselves in public through their public personas.*"[79]

Muslim women are not encouraged to enjoy their beauty outside of the home. They must avoid showing themselves, avoiding highlighting their female characteristics and body forms. The Qur'an encourages "modesty." Women's bodies are seen as sacred and should be kept in privacy.

The beauty standards of a Moroccan woman are imposed from the outside; women are encouraged to see beauty as something that does not come from the inside, beauty is not seen as a decision, as a free exercise[80]. Beauty becomes a burden for these women, and they should use it only when the social norms allow them, when their husbands, their bosses, their family allow it. Beauty is not something to be enjoyed, to be pleased with, and to be shared according to their self-determination.

Notwithstanding the general description of the limitations for Moroccan women in public spaces, when I was living in Fès, either on the university campus or in the medina, I noticed that not all Moroccan women veil themselves anymore. I can see both people without veil, and people dressing in the most

[78] Delle 2010, 89.

[79] Euler 2013, 19.

[80] "Moroccan women, therefore, have no right over their bodies and are prohibited from even thinking that they are their own." (Zerrifi 2001, 60)

orthodox Islamic clothes. There are new interpretations of Islamic culture and religion that acknowledge the freedom of women to emancipate the way they dress. I hope that, during this time, the notions of freedom of expression and movement related to beauty will be expanded.

Additionally, taking into consideration the pattern of solidarity in Morocco, public spaces can be stages of violence such as sexual violence and harassment[81]. For instance, I can mention the Moroccan episodes of sexual rape and harassment, which occurred on public transportation or on Moroccan streets. These facts resulted in United Nations campaigns:

> There is hardly a woman or a girl in urban and rural areas alike "who has not experienced sexual harassment or the threat of sexual violence in public spaces. Unwanted sexual remarks and jokes, groping, indecent exposure and many other forms of sexual harassment are often trivialized and rarely legislated. As women's voices around the world rise in protest, UN Women's Safe City programme in Marrakech has engaged people from all walks of life — from bus and taxi drivers to journalists — to prevent and respond to sexual harassment.[82]

These kinds of violence can also happen within women's workplaces.

10.3.2 Labor

Moroccan women represent just 25,7% of the labor force[83]. Nevertheless, these are data regarding formal cataloged work. Several Moroccan women occupy informal workplaces, with no labor rights and legal guarantees. Besides the fact that Moroccan women occupy informal work, they also practice unpaid work,

---

[81] "Dès que la femme quitte l'espace privé et se trouve dans l'espace public (le quartier, la rue, le lieu de travail, l'école...), elle devient proie facile aux violences sexuelles sous ses formes les plus abjectes: le viol et le harcèlement sexuel. D'aprés le tableau ci-dessus, le viol est le type d'agression le plus usité, soit plus de la moitié des cas de violences sexuelles. Non loin, on trouve le harcèlement sexuel (42,3%)". (Réseau National des Centres d'Ecoute des Femmes Victimes de Violences, 2007, 36)

[82] United Nations Women, 2015. Bringing bus drivers on board against sexual harassment in Marrakesh. Available at http://www.unwomen.org/en/news/stories/2015/6/bringing-buses-on-board-against-sexual-harassment-in-marrakesh. Access on 04.04.2018.

[83] The World Bank 2022. Labor force, female (% of total labor force)—Morocco. Available at https://data.worldbank.org/indicator/SL.TLF.TOTL.FE.ZS?locations=MA, access on 02.08.2022.

which means they work in either a family business, producing goods or services for sale, or producing services or products for self-consumption[84]. In 2018, women and girls aged 15 and above spend 20.8% of their time on unpaid care and domestic work, whereas men spend just 3% of their time (UN Women 2021, 1).[85]

This data is better understood if I consider the vast economic gap between the rural and urban populations in Morocco. It reflects in women's lives. The participation of women in Morocco's economy is among the lowest in the world. In 2015, in the urban regions, women's labor force participation was just 19%, against 71% for men. In rural areas, women represent 37% of labor and men 82%.[86]

1.6 million Moroccans live in poverty (out of 37 million inhabitants), and one in eight Moroccans are economically vulnerable (Oxfam 2019 *apud* BTI Transformation Index 2022). In 2018, Morocco's Gini coefficient (a statistical measure for quantifying inequality) was the highest in North Africa, at 0.403 (BTI Transformation Index 2022).

During our time living in Fès and working at Centre Batha, it was possible to attest that the tourism market—guides, sellers, producers—is mostly occupied by men. Most of the female victims the center attended to did not have a job and were illiterate. The educational system does not contribute to women's achievement of high education, and for the ones who can attain high educational standards—for example, female university students -, the city of Fès does not have enough and adequate job vacancies for them.

I personally developed a project for Centre Batha called "*Art of the feminine*". The main objective of our campaign was to encourage sellers and producers from the tourism industry to employ women in their labor force. If they do so, then their business would have a certificate attesting "gender equality practices". The tourists who visit Morocco, on the other hand, would also be integrated into the campaign, being encouraged to buy products and hire services from companies and local sellers, which recruit the female workforce. In 2018, I introduced the project to Centre Batha, but I did not have enough time in the city to introduce

---

[84] [...] While unpaid work in family businesses is routinely included in calculations of gross domestic product (GDP), unpaid care and domestic work, as defined in this report, is rarely included in what is known as the System of National Accounts (SNA) production boundary. [...] (United Nations Entity For Gender Equality And The Empowerment Of Women 2015, 83)

[85] UN Women 2021. Country Fact Sheet Morocco, available at https://data.unwomen.org/country/morocco, access on 02.08.2022.

[86] World Bank Group 2015, xiv.

the project to other partner institutions yet—for instance, the University of Fès and the local government.

10.3.3 Education

Regarding education, Morocco has significant gender gaps in primary completion rates, which is much broader in that country than in other lower and middle-income countries. Female adult literacy is 64.6%, whereas male adult literacy is 83.3% (World Bank Group *apud* BTI Transformation Index 2022, 26). In Centre Batha, the presence of illiterate women victims of violence was widespread.

According to the director of Centre Batha, *"One of the key problems we deal with in Moroccan society is the fact of the economic dependency of women, caused mainly by the fact that they do not study and are illiterate. If a woman is victim of violence caused by her husband, how could she divorce him, if she does not have any educational background and work?"* The majority of Moroccan women leave school at a younger age than do male students (World Bank Group *apud* BTI Transformation Index 2022, 26).

Children have the right to primary school guaranteed by the Moroccan Constitution: "*Article 32 [...] L'enseignement fondamental est un droit de l'enfant et une obligation de la famille et de l'Etat. [...]*"[87]. Nevertheless, Morocco does not have all children at school, especially in rural areas.[88]

Girls in rural areas are even more damaged, as some families do not allow them to stay in school when they become teenagers. "*It is dangerous to walk to school and, then, they prefer to keep the girls at home and to find a husband for them*", says a worker of Centre Batha. These girls may probably become victims of violence if they keep walking to school and being in public spaces. As a solution, their families prefer marriage and remaning at home.

> There is a large gap between rural and urban areas. Literacy rates in rural areas are lower. The average years of education is 2.2 years in rural areas, compared to 6.1 years in urban areas, according to the National Observatory for Human Development (2018).[89]

[87] Morocco's Constitution, 2011.

[88] "While the gross enrollment ratio is 114.8 in primary, 81.2 in secondary and 38.5 in tertiary education, the female-to-male enrollment ratio is 1.0 at the primary level, 0.9 at the secondary level and 1.0 at the tertiary level." (BTI Transformation Index 2022, 26).

[89] BTI Transformation Index 2022, 29.

Concerning sex education, schools do not have this subject in their curriculum. Because of the religion and culture of Islam, people usually do not discuss these themes in a family context or at school.

Sexuality is a taboo in Morocco. It is easily demonstrated, for instance, by the use of contraceptives by Moroccan women. Unfortunately, "*Sex is only socially approved for married women, so unmarried women have a hard time accessing contraception.*" (Chtatou 2022)[90]. Sexual activities for non-married people is not allowed by Moroccan legislation, so an unmarried woman using contraception would make it obvious that she is having a forbidden sexual life (Chtatou, 2022).[91] Unfortunately, the strong cultural ideal against women having a free right to sex regardless of their relationship status stigmatized extramarital pregnancy and birth control methods (Chtatou, 2022)[92]. This leaves a woman with the option of abstinence, or, necessarily, abortion (Chtatou, 2022).[93]

As already mentioned in this work, in 2016 the Moroccan Penal Law was reformed to allow abortion in cases of rape. Theoretically, it includes non-married women as well.

If a Moroccan woman is married, she is allowed to abort if her health is threatened, and if she has the authorization of the spouse[94]. In case the situation is grave, and there is no authorization from the spouse, Moroccan Penal Law allows authorization coming from the head medical doctor of the prefecture or province[95]. "*In practice, the legal requirements are applied relatively strictly; to the knowledge of local counsel it is rare for illegal abortions to be performed.*"[96]

After describing the labor and education of women in Morocco, I will now study another aspect: the role of women in Moroccan politics.

---

[90] Chtatou, 2022. Reflecting on women issues in Morocco. 19.01.2022. The Times of Israel. Available at https://blogs.timesofisrael.com/reflecting-on-women-issues-in-morocco/. Access on 03.08.2022.

[91] Chtatou, 2022. Reflecting on women issues in Morocco. 19.01.2022. The Times of Israel. Available at https://blogs.timesofisrael.com/reflecting-on-women-issues-in-morocco/. Access on 03.08.2022.

[92] Chtatou, 2022. Reflecting on women issues in Morocco. 19.01.2022. The Times of Israel. Available at https://blogs.timesofisrael.com/reflecting-on-women-issues-in-morocco/. Access on 03.08.2022.

[93] Chtatou, 2022. Reflecting on women issues in Morocco. 19.01.2022. The Times of Israel. Available at https://blogs.timesofisrael.com/reflecting-on-women-issues-in-morocco/. Access on 03.08.2022.

[94] Art. 453, Moroccan Criminal Code, 2016.

[95] Southern African Aids Trust et al. _, 11.

[96] Southern African Aids Trust et al. _, 11.

10.3.4 Politics

King Mohamed VI has been in power since 1999, and his dynasty has been in control since 1666[97]. There are elections for the assembly of representatives by direct universal suffrage and elections for the assembly of councilors by indirect universal suffrage. The king is head of state and head of government, being also the leader of the faithful, the one who represents Islam in Morocco.

In 1963, women received the right to vote and stand for election in Morocco. Thirty years after, in 1993, the first woman was elected to parliament. Afterward, a quota system was implemented, to increase women's representation in the lower house of parliament.[98]

Nevertheless, in 2021, only 20,5% of seats in parliament were held by women (UN Women 2021, 1)[99]. Considering this scenario, besides the fact that in comparison with other Middle Eastern and North African countries, King Mohamed VI is considered progressive and modern, his advances in Moroccan legislation were not sufficient to improve the situation of women in the country.

Female representation in politics is still low, and according to the World Bank Group, *"[...] family, religion, and work are the three most important things for the population in Morocco. Politics is the least important."*.[100]

10.4 Conclusion of Chap. 10

Taking the situation of Moroccan women into consideration, I have studied it from the perspectives of love, law, and solidarity.

Patriarchal culture and religion influence the Moroccan pattern of love. The idea that the woman is the one to feel ashamed, if she does not comply with

[97] "On the contrary, Islam in Morocco is State religion, for in the Constitution, Morocco is an Islamic monarchy. This is symbolised in the king's status as both the head of the executive power and the Commander of the Believers." (Zerrifi 2001, 21)

[98] "[...] following the 2007 national election, women now occupy 34 out of the 325 seats in the lower house of parliament, the Majlissannouwab, (10 per cent of the seats). After the 2007 election, there was also a significant increase of female ministers and of women in other key positions. In the 2009 local elections, a 12 per cent quota was applied which significantly increased women's political representation (following the 2003 local elections women filled less than 1 per cent of the contested posts)." (UNICEF 2011, 3).

[99] UN Women 2021, 1. Country Fact Sheet Morocco. Available at https://data.unwomen.org/country/morocco. Access on 03.08.2022.

[100] World Bank Group 2015, 10.

social and religious norms is an example of the role of the woman in Moroccan society.

According to Moroccan culture, women are supposed to remain chaste until marriage. When they get married, they may suffer from offenses to recognition, for instance, experience polygamy or domestic violence. More than that, women are subject to worse conditions during divorce, as they need their husbands' approval to get a divorce, whereas men do not need any approval at all.

Women who get pregnant without being married, the single mothers, are subjected to intense stigma in Moroccan society.

Regarding Moroccan law, there were significant changes in the legislation over the years, and nowadays, the Moroccan Constitution and Moroccan Family Law are considered one of the most advanced in the Islamic world. Nevertheless, I have seen that despite the legal changes, legislation still does not tackle some critical issues affecting women. Furthermore, the courts and judges sometimes do not apply the new legislation and the international conventions to which Morocco is a signatory, maintaining surpassed and overdue decisions.

Press and social media in Morocco may have their freedom of opinion and expression limited, and the activities of NGOs and associations are also under the state's control.

If I take into consideration the pattern of solidarity, I have seen that, first of all, Moroccan women suffer a significant separation between their private and public spaces. At home, the woman may be allowed by her husband to display her beauty, to adorn herself. In public spaces, there are still many Moroccan families requiring the use of veil and endorsing Quranic modesty, which requires women to be modest and not show themselves.

The situation of female education also needs to improve a lot. Illiterate women in Morocco comprise a significant percentage of the population, and they usually either perform informal work or engage in unpaid work at home. Education in rural areas is worse than in the cities, and the level of poverty in Morocco is still high.

Furthermore, Moroccan women do not have sex education at all.

Into politics, the right to vote only came in 1963, and in 1993, the first Moroccan woman entered parliament.

Despite all legal reforms since 2004 (2004: Family Law, Labor Code; 2011: Constitution; 2014, 2016: Penal Law), unfortunately, the country has severe limitations regarding human rights, freedom of expression, and freedom of the press, as well as non-independent and non-impartial court decisions. More than that, the population's consciousness of human rights, especially related to women, is also weak.

It is a result of a dominant patriarchal culture, influenced by the Islamic religion. The institution of marriage and its dimensions related to minors, polygamy, the stigma of single mothers, and the high level of domestic violence against Moroccan women and girls, all exemplify that gender equality is far from being achieved.

This scenario turns out to be worse when I analyze the violence faced by women in public spaces, as well as the situation regarding a woman in the Moroccan economy, education, labor market, health system, and political representation. It is possible to argue that the history of Morocco has always been endorsing gender inequality. In the next chapter, I describe the conditions in which Chinese and Moroccan people engage in struggles for women's recognition.

11 Chinese and Moroccan Struggles for Recognition

"[...] we as human beings have a permanent demand imposed on ourselves, a demand to make things better".[1]

This work has already studied the concept of "struggle" according to Axel Honneth. I have proposed ways of struggling within the patterns of love, law, and solidarity.

Pensky understands that struggles necessarily presuppose a public institutional intervention, and people themselves would not achieve demands for recognition without support from the government or the public instances.

Honneth states that people should have a pre-political situation of democracy, allowing them to struggle for recognition. Societies, for him, should have at least a minimum of normative liberal democratic conditions to begin struggles for recognition.

On the other hand, I have argued that struggles for women's recognition should not be attached to public institutional intervention because some societies do not have such public support. It would be ideal for all communities to have a minimum of democratic freedom. Still, I must reiterate that it is not the reality in several societies, for instance, China and Morocco. Consequently, within the theory of recognition, it was relevant to include struggles exercised by persons, mainly in their private life, without necessary public support.

---

[1] Honneth 2013, 217.

Supplementary Information The online version contains supplementary material available at https://doi.org/10.1007/978-3-658-46849-1_11.

C. Diamantino Esser Santana, *Recognized Women:*, Juridicum – Schriften zur Rechtsphilosophie, https://doi.org/10.1007/978-3-658-46849-1_11

When I have studied the meaning of solidarity, I noticed that it relates to care, practical involvement, and engaged praxis. Care, for instance, involves the ability to listen to someone, to take into consideration the perspective of the other. That means solidary acts endorse the struggles and make people individually or collectively act and strive for recognition.

First, a struggle inside oneself is necessary, inside each individual who is going to engage in an external battle. When the individual abandons an indifferent posture regarding some situation of disrespect and adopts a solidary action for the benefit of the one being disrespected, he is struggling inside himself. Usually, persons remain indifferent when they witness a situation of disrespect. Still, it should be continuously confronted by each individual as a kind of struggle against any feeling of indifference.

This chapter evaluates how the struggles are happening in China and Morocco, especially the ones lacking public support. Whereas the above chapters have shown how the patterns of love, law, and solidarity of women are violated in these countries and how hard it is to begin institutional, official, and public struggles, now it is relevant to evaluate how the Chinese and the Moroccan people have been confronting disrespect through other means.

11.1 Social Struggles in China and Morocco: Going beyond Public Repression

In 2022, Honneth stated that the oppression of women—exemplified by their degradation as mere sexual objects and their political marginalization—represents a violation of women's moral status[2]. Nevertheless, there is also a degradation of the cognitive capacities of a woman, which is perhaps even more oppressive at a personal level.[3]

This work has performed a study on the theory of recognition from Honneth, trying to figure out how to comprehend struggles for recognition that really contribute for the recognition of women. In his most recent writings, Honneth seems to include more analysis of misrecognition related to gender equality, but it is not sufficient yet. He does not face it from the perspective of the struggles, that means, Honneth does not figure out how the struggles for recognition of women are being developed, especially in non-democratic and non-Western contexts.

[2] Honneth 2022b, 30.

[3] Honneth 2022b, 30.

In the above chapters, I have clarified how a concept of recognition is sustained through ethical principles, conditions, and premises. Furthermore, it was demonstrated how the lack of recognition results in disrespect, a situation related to a variety of social denigrations—such as injustice and indifference -. Sequentially, the theoretical aspects of recognition and misrecognition were analysed from the perspective of case studies related to the recognition of women in China and Morocco.

Chapter 1 has stated that recognition represents not just moral acts and feelings, but also comprehends an ethical process with principles and premises. Case studies on women's recognition in China and Morocco have described how significant conditions of recognition are neglected. For instance, the Chinese Anti-Domestic Violence Law and the Chinese Law on the Protection of Women's Rights and Interests both hold that acts of violence against a woman may be surpassed through the maintenance of family stability and harmony. In other words, although a woman suffers different forms of violence in the familiar context, it may be that she will be oriented by the authorities to accept it and to dismiss that she was actually a victim of a crime. In such cases, the building of self-confidence, self-esteem, and self-respect of this woman is denigrated and she will not reach recognition at all.

Sequentially, Chap. 2 has studied how to comprehend the disrespect, the offenses against recognition, whereas Chap. 3 has explained the concept of struggles for recognition. The analysed case studies described several situations of disrespect and misrecognition of Chinese and Moroccan women, as well as how their conditions for struggling for recognition are poor. For instance, it is very unusual to find in China cases of deliberative democratic spaces, either through small individual circles in the family, friendship, or neighborhood, or through official public debates. Actually, public, democratic, equal, and free debates in China do not exist at all. In Morocco, there are already more opportunities for public discussions regarding gender equality, and there were recent changes in the legislation to include better conditions for gender equality. Nevertheless, the roles of religion and culture still strongly affect the effectiveness of equal conditions of recognition for men and women in Moroccan society.

The struggles for the emancipation of a family member and for the open revisability of a culture as described in Chap. 5 are also difficult to reach in Chinese and Moroccan contexts, as the influence of patriarchalism and all cultural nuances—characterized through the case studies—impair the debates in private and familiar contexts of a woman's life. It also happens regarding the struggles for democracy through education, labour, and through an ethics of solidarity and care. In Morocco, for instance, women still hold a high level of illiteracy and their access to education at all is limited. NGOs in both countries are subjected to government control. From these characteristics, it is possible to conclude that the struggles proposed in Chap. 7 are also very impared in both countries.

Additionally, human rights in China and Morocco are still under construction and face complex challenges. In China, for instance, the developmentalist theory tries to place China out of the obligation to comply with human rights.

Considering that, I understand that a very relevant struggle to be stated in China and Morocco relates to the confrontation of indifference. This is the first step to implement better conditions for the reaching of gender equality. The struggle against indifference is sustained mainly through the pattern of law, whereas a previous moment of legal recognition would allow that an individual realizes herself as an addressee and author of rights, being able to begin struggles for better conditions of recognition.

Legal recognition is reachable especially through human rights. I have studied in Chap. 6 that struggles for recognition and human rights share similar characteristics regarding their theoretical description. Furthermore, human rights either in a moral or legal form carry a moment of recognition, as they guarantee conditions for a person's autonomy through respect and dignity.

This work has shown that China and Morocco have to make significant improvements in gender equality. Generally, Chinese and Moroccan women still do not have their rights respected in the same way as men, and they keep experiencing a patriarchal and repressive culture.

In the case of China, the Chinese state is authoritarian, and it is forbidden to discuss or even talk about topics considered "sensitive" by the government. There are illegal detentions, harassment, and disappearances involving lawyers, activists, and journalists. They need to act with caution[4].

---

[4] "As in previous years, citizens did not have the right to change their government and had limited forms of redress against official abuse. Other human rights abuses during the year included alleged extrajudicial killings; executions without due process; prolonged illegal detentions at unofficial holding facilities known as "black jails"; torture and coerced confessions of prisoners; detention and harassment of lawyers who took on "sensitive" cases, journalists, writers, bloggers, dissidents, petitioners, and others whose actions the authorities deemed unacceptable; lack of due process in judicial proceedings; political control of courts and judges; closed trials; the use of administrative detention; failure to protect refugees and asylum seekers; extrajudicial disappearances of Chinese and foreign citizens; restrictions on nongovernmental organizations (NGOs); discrimination against women, minorities, and persons with disabilities; a coercive birth-limitation policy that, despite the lifting of one-child-per-family restrictions, in some cases resulted in forced abortion (sometimes at advanced stages of pregnancy); and trafficking in persons." (United States Department of State 2015, 2)

Social mobilizations, such as protests, are not desirable:

> In China, on the other hand, both the political culture and the current political system are not conducive to the development of effective social movements. While the government is sometimes responsive to crises fueled by public concern over the effects of natural disasters or the health implications of pollutants, officials work hard to put barriers in the way of efforts to instigate effective social movements to address societal concerns.[5]

The testimonial of a Chinese feminist exemplifies how brutal governmental repression can be in China. Lü Pin is the founder of the Chinese magazine *Feminist Voices*, which was founded in 2011.

More than a magazine, *Feminist Voices* has become a promoter of social movements for the benefit of gender equality in China. For instance, on Valentine's Day in 2012, for the first time, the new generation of Chinese feminists took to the streets in Beijing, calling for the approval of the anti-domestic violence laws[6]. In June of the same year, a feminist group in Shanghai protested against a public advertisement posted in the Shanghai Metro, which required all passengers to "*dress appropriately to avoid harassment*"[7].

The achievements of the feminist groups in China were very significant from 2012 to 2015. The Chinese government has made some positive changes in legislation: "*In May 2013, for instance, the Ministry of Education announced that universities cannot set separate test score cutoffs for applicants of different genders, or establish gender ratios for admission [...]*"[8].

Nevertheless, since the election of the current Chinese president Xi Jinping, who has lifetime tenure, the repression against the feminist movement became stronger. All online speech in China is now actively controlled, and "*Afterwards, the Internet would no longer be a so-called "free zone," but would become an important site of authoritarian governance*"[9].

In 2015, the so-called "Feminist Five" (five young feminists) were arrested by the government in different Chinese cities: '*For the first time in its history, the*

[5] Guttman et al. 2015, 170.

[6] China File. Pin, L. 2019. Finding a Voice. March 28, 2019. http://www.chinafile.com/reporting-opinion/viewpoint/finding-voice. 25.10.2019.

[7] China File. Pin, L. 2019. Finding a Voice. March 28, 2019. http://www.chinafile.com/reporting-opinion/viewpoint/finding-voice. 25.10.2019.

[8] China File. Pin, L. 2019. Finding a Voice. March 28, 2019. http://www.chinafile.com/reporting-opinion/viewpoint/finding-voice. 25.10.2019.

[9] China File. Pin, L. 2019. Finding a Voice. March 28, 2019. http://www.chinafile.com/reporting-opinion/viewpoint/finding-voice. 25.10.2019.

Chinese Communist Party publicly suppressed a feminist action. Feminist activity was criminalized in a country where the constitution guarantees "equality between men and women."'[10].

However, the most significant change happened in 2017, when the public institution the *All-China Women's Federation* declared that feminists are spreading wrong Western ideas. The All-China Women's Federation is the unique official women's rights organization in China, and they have an official influence within the Chinese Communist Party[11].

Also, in 2017, not just the associations related to women's rights, but all the NGOs in China had their activities restricted. In January 2017, new legislation regarding NGOs in China was passed. Even the NGOs already based in China have had their activities limited by the government. Now, they are supposed to be contributive to the Chinese government. Even before the passage of the new legislation, the United States Department of State confirmed that the Chinese government maintains control over civil society groups, on the emergence of independent NGOs, and prevents the "westernization" of the country. In China, "*the large NGOs were quasi-governmental, and government agencies had to sponsor all official NGOs*"[12].

Against this backdrop, the magazine and movement *Feminist Voices* were banned by the Chinese government. All their posts on social media were blocked and deleted, and it was declared that they are a movement related to prostitution and crime.

---

[10] China File. Pin, L. 2019. Finding a Voice. March 28, 2019. http://www.chinafile.com/reporting-opinion/viewpoint/finding-voice. 25.10.2019.

[11] China File. Pin, L. 2019. Finding a Voice. March 28, 2019. http://www.chinafile.com/reporting-opinion/viewpoint/finding-voice. 25.10.2019.

[12] United States Department of State 2015, 49. See also:

"Currently, China's social organizations are restricted by administrative concerns. First, many of them are either divided from the government internally or directly "organized by the government" itself (i.e. government organized, non-governmental organization "GONGO"). These organizations are born out of governmental agencies, lack independence and autonomy, and are operated and organized bureaucratically. Second, the government has strict supervision and management over social organizations. The registration management system, as part of the general system governing social organization management, is relevant at the stage that determines which organizations are under direct registration management and which are under dual management. Many social organizations receive their income from government allocations and subsidies. This indicates that they lack sustainable operating income and reinforces their dependency on the government. Third, the senior management positions of social organizations are often occupied by retired cadres, given their governmental affiliation and ability to obtain resources." (UNDP 2016, 17)

Regarding Morocco, the situation of the Moroccan NGOs is not very different. Although Moroccan legislation has been modified to promote more private and public donations to NGOs, the government figures as one of the main donors, thus allowing it to increase control and power within the organizations[13].

Furthermore, since 2015 the Moroccan government has been more aggressive regarding public demonstrations, "*The so-called 'Makhzen' authorities have returned to the old practices of electoral manipulation and other realpolitik constraints on freedom of protest and freedom of expression*"[14]. For instance, in 2016, there were protests in different cities of Morocco, demanding better socio-economic conditions. The response from the government was excessively repressive, with massive arrests of citizens[15].

It happens, for instance, when Moroccan women try to assemble together. According to Euromed Rights (2013), Moroccan Family Law does not formally impairs women's freedom of assembly, but actually cultural and religious considerations impair it, especially concerning the exercise of this right in public spaces.[16] There are certain common law from Moroccan "tribes" that prevent women from taking part in collective discussions, decisions, and management of collective grounds.[17] "*The strength of this common law and the ignorance of positive laws protecting their rights are a barrier to the organisation and defence of their interests for these women, who are afraid to demonstrate and to organise to plead their cause.*"[18]

[13] Atia and Harrold calls it patronage: "In both cases, as a result of patronage, NGOs witnessed rapid professionalization, experienced increased regulation and surveillance and were held accountable to donors instead of communities. We refer to these as technologies of governing and demonstrate how they led to the depoliticization of the NGO sectors and to crises of sustainability and legitimacy. After patronage, NGOs felt restrained by what they could say and do politically and were reticent to engage in contentious collective action. Rather than providing the bedrock for a citizen-owned, change-oriented civil society, patron-driven NGO sectors became tools of their donors". (Atia; Herrold 2018, 4)

[14] Masbah 2018, 05. See also:

"It is also important to note that freedom of expression, hence indirectly freedom of association and assembly, are bound by intangible and non-written "red lines" that punish speeches or writings which openly criticize the King, his family or authority, the Islamic nature of the State or Islam as such, and Morocco's "territorial integrity"—i.e. Morocco's claimed sovereignty over Western Sahara". (Euromed Rights 2013, 02)

[15] Masbah 2018, 05.

[16] Euromed Rights 2013, 10.

[17] Euromed Rights 2013, 10.

[18] Euromed Rights 2013, 10.

Most recently, in July 2021, several global media firms reported that the Moroccan government has been using a powerful spyware to infiltrate the smartphones of many individuals in Morocco, accessing contact lists, reading emails and text messages, tracking calls, collecting passwords, mobile phone tracking, and hijacking the target device's microphone and video camera to turn it into a surveillance device.[19] Moroccan journalists and people who speak out on social media have been prosecuted under the penal code for their critical speech, although nonviolent.[20]

Despite the difficulties related above, Moroccan society still tries to struggle in different forms. I can mention the Moroccan 'Arab Spring.' In 2011, thousands of protesters demonstrated for social justice and political reform. At that time, the monarchy had proposed political reforms in order to respond to society's claims[21].

Moroccan movements have their origin from the revolutionary social movements of 1970.[22] At that time, students and intellectuals were inspired by the French uprisings in 1968, the revolutionary movements in Vietnam and China, and the spread of Marxism in the Arab[23]. In Morocco, the New Left has come as an alternative to the traditional Communist parties and the nationalist movement[24]. It was calling for a revolution of workers and peasants, confronting the Moroccan monarchy.[25] Nowadays, such demonstrations would be more restricted

[19] Human Rights Watch. 2022. World Report 2022: Morocco and Western Sahara 01/08/2022. Human Rights Watch. Available at https://www.hrw.org/world-report/2022/country-chapters/morocco/western-sahara 3/9 Access on 17.08.22.

[20] Human Rights Watch. 2022. World Report 2022: Morocco and Western Sahara 01/08/2022. Human Rights Watch. Available at https://www.hrw.org/world-report/2022/country-chapters/morocco/western-sahara 3/9 Access on 17.08.22.

[21] Masbah 2018, 05.

[22] Verso. Koumiya, G. 2018. Post-68 student uprisings and the rise of the Moroccan Marxist Leninist movement. May 25, 2018. https://www.versobooks.com/blogs/3838-post-68-student-uprisings-and-the-rise-of-the-moroccan-marxist-leninist-movement. 25.10.2019.

[23] Verso. Koumiya, G. 2018. Post-68 student uprisings and the rise of the Moroccan Marxist Leninist movement. May 25, 2018. https://www.versobooks.com/blogs/3838-post-68-student-uprisings-and-the-rise-of-the-moroccan-marxist-leninist-movement. 25.10.2019.

[24] Verso. Koumiya, G. 2018. Post-68 student uprisings and the rise of the Moroccan Marxist Leninist movement. May 25, 2018. https://www.versobooks.com/blogs/3838-post-68-student-uprisings-and-the-rise-of-the-moroccan-marxist-leninist-movement. 25.10.2019.

[25] Verso. Koumiya, G. 2018. Post-68 student uprisings and the rise of the Moroccan Marxist Leninist movement. May 25, 2018. https://www.versobooks.com/blogs/3838-post-68-student-uprisings-and-the-rise-of-the-moroccan-marxist-leninist-movement. 25.10.2019.

in the country, but the population has still been creating different forms of struggle, as I will further see.

11.2 Private Struggles in China and Morocco

In 2022, Honneth stated that depending on historical and socioeconomic circumstances, the struggles for recognition generally begin in small-scale domains, such as in private households, places of work, on public transport, or in administrative offices, places where isolated individuals contend with representatives of power holders over the meaning and normative horizon of established recognitional norms.[26] Nevertheless, these struggles must be somehow recognized as a collective shared rebellion. In the past, it was translatable under general concepts such as 'exploitation', 'unpaid domestic labour', or inspired statements like 'I have a dream'. Nowadays, in the internet age, abbreviations and slogans like *#MeToo* or *#BlackLivesMatter* are signs of an arena of struggles.[27]

It is relevant to comprehend how struggles for the recognition of women are spreading in China and Morocco. Individual engagement for better condition of life, if exercised inside the context of the home, family, and private relationships, may face challenges in China and Morocco.

In Chinese territory, the control of private life is stronger than in Morocco. I have seen that there are restrictions of freedom of thought and conscience, opinion and expression, speech, and belief. In Morocco, I understand that the limitations relate more to the right to freedom of thought, conscience, and religion.

In both countries, social media and internet are platforms where persons can, individually, demonstrate and engage in struggles for recognition. Nevertheless, in both countries the government controls the virtual space as well.

If I focus on the Chinese context, the state limitations result in a lack of reaction from Chinese people, when they face a situation of disrespect: "*I can only rely on myself*" (Xinran 2011, 404). More than that, some theorists argue that the Chinese act indifferent because of the Chinese traditions of collectivism. For von Senger, the history of Chinese law makes the population suffer from a collective egoism and a latent individualism.[28]

[26] Honneth 2022b, 29.

[27] Honneth 2022b, 29.

[28] "The result was a common destiny shared with such reference persons for better (career advancement, etc.) or for worse (collective punishment). The bond to persons and not to abstract legal norms favoured a certain tendency towards lawlessness or "collective egoism" (the propensity to preserve the interests of one's own "clique", of compatriots from one's own

In the same direction, research developed by Michael Shengtao Wu *et al.* has measured how sensitive Chinese, Germans, and Russians are to justice issues. According to them:

> Justice sensitivity (JS) includes a low perceptual threshold for incidents of injustice, strong emotional responses to injustice (anger, outrage, and guilt), the tendency to ruminate about injustice, and the motivation to reestablish justice (Schmitt, 1996; Schmitt & Mohiyeddini, 1996; Schmitt, Neumann, & Montada, 1995).[29]

Justice sensitivity was analyzed from four perspectives. Firstly, it considers the *victim*, who suffers the injustice. Secondly, from the *perpetrator*'s perspective, the one who provokes the injustice. Thirdly, from the perspective of someone, who has witnessed an injustice, but it does not affect his life: the *observer* perspective. Finally, justice was analyzed from the perspective of the *beneficiary*, the one who receives some profit coming from an injustice committed against another person.[30]

Regarding China, the study demonstrates that although Chinese are more beneficiary sensitive to justice—compared to individualistic societies, they are less observer sensitive to justice.[31]

The Chinese low level of observer justice sensitivity shows some indifference in Chinese society. Feelings of empathy, assertiveness, and autonomy to help each other in situations of injustice can be rare in China. It could be a result of the ethics of collectivism, which ensures that people are not concerned about the individuality of each other, but only the offenses against the group and if there is a public rule or determination to help the one being disrespected.

Chinese do not feel comfortable to engage in any demonstration demanding social changes in China. If someone witnesses a situation of disrespect, it is better to keep oneself out of the conflict and to avoid some state repression or even social repression. The Chinese author Xinran presents an example of Chinese indifference when describing a situation of an abandoned Chinese baby girl in a public place:

---

region, etc.). This was supplemented by a latent individualism, i.e. the extremely strong sense of self-esteem which existed among the Chinese, but which also took the form of blatant egoism (although this was always suppressed officially)." (Von Senger 1993, 305).

[29] Wu; Schmitt et al. 2014, 232.

[30] Wu; Schmitt et al. 2014, 234.

[31] Wu; Schmitt et al. 2014, 239.

"'Hey, look, it's still moving!' The shout went up from the bystanders, but no one picked the baby up. I do not know how long it had been lying there, but judging by the size of the crowd and how cold they looked, it must have been quite a long time. Why? Were these people so lacking in humanity that they could watch an infant freeze to death in front of them without lifting a finger to help? I just shoved my bicycle at someone in the crowd, made a dive for the baby, picked her up and tucked her inside the front of my leather coat. There was uproar. 'What is she doing?' 'Is she going to take the baby away with her?' 'Does she know what she's doing? What an idiot. You can't go doing things like that!' I rushed into the hospital Emergency Department, and straight to the Registration window. The Registration nurse stopped me: 'Excuse me, is this your baby? Do you have its birth permit? Without the birth permit, we can't treat it.'"[32]

I already saw that the abandonment of Chinese baby girls was a recurrent phenomenon in China's past, and this practice, as well as infanticide and abortion, became common. These social practices were a result of different factors, for instance, the one-child policy. Nevertheless, it seems that the Chinese population, at that time, got used to these practices. Seeing an abandoned baby or killing a baby just after her birth became acceptable practices within a context where people had no choice[33]. Considering these traditions, the Chinese may have less tendency to struggle against indifference.

Besides such Chinese practices, which occurred in the past, Zhou Wenting, in an article in China Daily, analyzes the current context of Chinese society, and he sees that the one-child policy has resulted in other characteristics of the Chinese related to indifference: the low level of social skills:

Experts in family affairs said the young generation should not suffer all the blame, for they were educated only to achieve success, not to give care and manage relationships. "The only-child generation is exempted from all the housework by parents so that they can grab every minute to study and stand out in the fierce competition for schools and jobs," Gu, of the social workers group, said. "It is understandable that they are weak in living habits and handling relationships."[34]

---

[32] Xinran 2011, 69.

[33] Xinran's book "Message from an Unknown Chinese Mother: Stories of Loss and Love" precisely describes this situation.

[34] China Daily. Wenting Z. 2011. The mother-in-law off all family battles. 22.04.2011. Available on www.chinadaily.com.cn/china/2011-04/22/content_12373683.htm. Access on 06.05.2019.

Additionally, Chen holds that: "*For many Chinese, social justice might be an ideal concept, rather than a motivation or belief*"[35]. It is not common for the Chinese people to reflect on the real implementation of justice for all. Citizens do not understand themselves as part of a democratic process of achieving recognition and justice.

Regarding the Chinese individual's behavior, instead of going to an argumentative process of defense of someone being a victim of a misrecognition, the Chinese would prefer to stay quiet and let *harmony* be restored. Gao, Bian, Liu, He and Oei confirm the hypothesis that the Chinese try to avoid conflict, using non-confrontation strategies like compliance and withdrawal.[36]

Furthermore, I also need to highlight the stigmatization of Chinese minorities. Many Chinese are proud to say that they are "Han people"[37]. According to United States Department of State, in China, minority groups in borders and other regions may have less access to education, to the job market, and also to government programs and economic growth than Han Chinese[38]. Unfortunately, in the name of a "harmonious society" and social stability, Chinese government downplays racism and institutional discrimination against minorities.[39]

The veneration of personal ethnicity can provoke in Chinese the stigmatization of "the others." It also happens between different provinces, or with the Chinese migrant-workers[40]. As a result, people usually do not engage in struggles for the ones considered different.

[35] Chen 2016, 255. See also: "In future work, scholars could investigate social justice across cultures, particularly examining Chinese context-sensitive understanding and conceptualization of social justice, and explain the extent to which Chinese possess knowledge about social justice. At the same time, scholars could also explore whether social justice is neglected in other systems (e.g., education) of China." (Chen 2016, 255)

[36] Chen, 2015, *apud* Gao; Bian; Liu; He; Oei, 2017, 10.

[37] We have also observed that in Morocco, regarding the separation between "Berbers" and "Arabs".

[38] United States Department of State 2015, 63.

[39] United States Department of State 2015, 63.

[40] We have seen that *hukou* influences Chinese women in many aspects. We already mentioned the common situation of women leaving their children with parents-in-law, to work in big cities, where they can not afford to live with their children; there is no vacancy in urban schools for children born in the countryside; between other social problems and stigmatization. "*In China, for example, rural-urban migration of working age adults has resulted in a large left-behind population: a full 28 per cent of rural children live with only one parent, grandparents or other relatives*". (United Nations Entity For Gender Equality And The Empowerment Of Women 2015, 125)

The Sunflower Women Workers Centre interviewed women victims of sexual harassment at the workplace, and they were questioned: "*What assistance do you think the victims of sexual harassment need?*"[41]

Some women said that they do not have any idea about how to solve the problem, and "*The factory wouldn't care and the police simply do not have the time for it.*"[42]. More than 25% have answered that victims should have comfort, psychological counseling, and guidance from family and friends[43], showing that they focus on the private dimension of life to find support. They do not expect public institutional support coming from police, for instance.

The research carried out by the Sunflower Women Workers Centre has shown how the Chinese female population usually does not have an idea about how to struggle for recognition. All the political and cultural conditions which Chinese female generations have been dealing with made them alienated. For them, it is hard to demand social justice and gender equality.

On the other hand, the UNDP has stated that:

> The idea of charity has a long history in Chinese thought. China's ancient philosophers and schools of thought all had their own views on what charity is and what it means in practice. Their views laid the philosophical basis for the development of today's modern charity industry. For example, the Confucian school promoted the idea of "benevolence and humanity"; the Taoist school advocated "treating others kindly, regardless of reciprocity"; the Mohist school emphasized "universal love" and "indiscriminate love"; and the Buddhist school believed in "karma" and "infinite compassion and mercy".[44]

Nevertheless, nowadays I do not see the practices of charity in China as a spontaneous and individual manifestation but rather as a practice that must be required by authorities.

Regarding Morocco, when questioned "*Pensez-vous que au Maroc existe la indifference?*" ("Do you think that there is indifference in Morocco?"), the coordinator of Centre Batha Souabni Hanane answered:

> We need to remember that some people are "indifferent" in Morocco because they do not have enough conditions to mobilize themselves. For example, witnesses, who do

[41] Sunflower Women Workers Centre 2013, 5.

[42] Sunflower Women Workers Centre 2013, 5.

[43] Sunflower Women Workers Centre 2013, 5.

[44] UNDP 2016, 11.

> not cooperate in legal cases regarding violence against women, are afraid of retaliation. They are not protected enough by the system.[45]

If I take into consideration the situation of Moroccan women and their engagement in private struggles for recognition, in 2009, 25% of women trying to exercise their rights under the Family Code have suffered violence from their families and another 17% violence from their husbands or husband's families. Overall, 19% of urban and 15% of rural women were victims of violence when trying to exercise their rights.[46]

Whether in Morocco or in China, the most feasible struggles for women's recognition are located in the private lives of individuals. It is crucial to study Chinese and Moroccan private spheres of an individual's life, to evaluate how family and friends deal with practices of violence, and how they could engage in individual manifestations of recognition. The work on the consciousness of the individual's role in the processes of recognition would be the first step for these societies.

Furthermore, there are other possibilities of struggles located in the context of labour. This work has above clarified that, for Marx and the critical theorists, *social labour* is an institute that carries demands and social insurgencies for better living conditions. Honneth has delved into the topic of labour as well[47], as an attempt to comprehend his theory from the current demands for recognition.

The challenges of female workforce during the time and from different cultural perspectives illustrate how women may be recognized or, on the other hand, disrespected, from a variety of forms. Chinese and Moroccan female fair labor conditions have been neglected not just from a cultural perspective coming from inside home—for instance, in the control and authority exercised by their family encounters regarding their free access to work places; or in the absence of recognition of domestic labour[48] —, but also from the public access to job opportunities in general and having gender equality.

The female role within the labour instances represents, on the one hand, the meeting with recognitional fundamental nuances. On the other hand, if it is not dully respected, it also holds the different forms of denials of recognition. Labour

[45] Appendix, Interview I, Hanane, 2018.

[46] World Bank Group 2015, 74.

[47] Honneth, A. 'Labour', a Brief History of a Modern Concept. 2022a. Cambridge University Press. 17.02.2022. Translated by Alex Englander.

[48] "Cultural distinctions between necessary labour and purely personal pursuits are in fact always fairly fluid, subject as they are to the vicissitudes of continual contests over the interpretation of the 'socially valuable'." (Honneth 2022a, 164).

relates not just with a private instance of recognition, whereas a woman face daily developments of her self-confidence whereas performing, but also public instances through the enjoyment of her self-respect and self and social-esteem within her community.

Either performing domestic labour or producing commodities, female workforce has been facing different kinds of disrespect and misrecognition. It may come as a structural lack of working conditions for women, caused by cultural and economic obstacles, which results in their unemployment; or in the lack of equal and healthy work environments, whereas women may be submitted to silent forms of oppressive violence, for instance moral harassment.

Within the pattern of love, women perform domestic work in her daily support of the administration, cleaning, cooking, childrearing, and other forms. She meets her self-confidence as soon as this work is recognized by her family encounters, having value for them and for their community. Legally, women is recognized through work by means of normative legal conditions and requisites. On the pattern of solidarity, woman is recognized through work when her self- and social esteem come from the respect that she has from her community, which recognizes all her performances—either in the traditional form of commodities production or through general care giving, or administration of social and economic processes.

For Honneth, *work* has been gradually liberated from the personal dependency in legal terms, beginning to signify a free decision, as a precondition of one's independence.[49] In this sense, being recognized within *work* is not just a legal recognition, but also a recognition in the patterns of love—that is individual and private—and solidarity.

The struggles in China and Morocco may occur mainly in the daily private dimensions of life including labour, through the confrontation of practices of indifference. People themselves are the agents for increasing recognition, and it can be useful if the population becomes conscious of their role in the process of achieving more autonomy and human rights.

Furthermore, the struggles for the emancipation of the family members, as well as for the open revisability of culture could all contribute to a change in the scenario of women's recognition in these countries.

To develop this consciousness in these societies, it would be ideal to get some social and public support from institutions, for instance NGOs and other civil organizations, through campaigns and public debates. It is necessary to make compassion, care, affection, and accountability social norms in China and Morocco.

---

[49] Honneth 2022a, 149.

I am aware that this process takes time and a change in life's perspective. Even so, taking into consideration all the characteristics already discussed, the struggles I have proposed are a crucial step to promote recognition in the daily life of women in China and Morocco.

It is necessary for these countries to review their public ethics—in China, for instance, a review of Chinese collectivistic values[50].

Although Chinese and Moroccan cultures still have patriarchal and hierarchical cultures, they are already signatories of international treaties, which stipulate human rights related to the recognition of women. It represents a favorable context for changes, but people themselves should begin to discuss and understand the importance of struggle.

11.3 Real Cases of Struggle in China and Morocco

Despite all public restrictions on the social movements in China, the feminist Lü Pin clarifies that there are still several groups struggling for the recognition of women in the country. One example is the global movement #MeToo, which has also reached China: '*In fact, some people online used emoji to avoid censorship. Instead of posting "#MeToo," they used the emoji for a bowl of rice (mi) and a rabbit (tu), which together sound the same as "me too."*'[51].

I have personally met two Chinese activists in Shanghai, who support women victims of violence—see the interview with one of the activists in the Appendix in the electronic supplementary material. The work of these activists is an example of struggles without any governmental support. On the contrary, these people confront their government and put their lives at risk in order to struggle for gender equality. They are effectively struggling for recognition.

---

[50] "We speculate that individuals from more individualistic cultures may not restrain themselves from exhibiting disrespectful behaviors as much as individuals from more collectivistic cultures, and would also openly discuss or confront perceived disrespectful behaviors directed towards themselves from others. Indeed, those from individualistic cultures may expect others to confront perceived injustices, and assume that lack of protest signals acceptance of such intrusion. If so, the stage is set for difficult relationships between roommates from collective and individualistic cultures". (Tam; Bond 2002, 71)

[51] China File. Pin, L. 2019. Finding a Voice. March 28, 2019. http://www.chinafile.com/reporting-opinion/viewpoint/finding-voice. 25.10.2019.

The *Sunflower Women Workers Centre* is another example of struggle in China. Sunflower Centre is located in Hong Kong[52], which facilitates their work[53]. The center is focused on the collective action and solidarity.[54] For instance, they coach Chinese female workers to participate more in the management of the factories were they are located.[55] Although the majority of Chinese female workers prefer to remain silent, sociologist Wang Lie holds that "*If leaving, remitting, and returning are the three key words that define the old generation, then leaving, searching, and becoming are the main themes for the new generation.*"[56] While the Sunflower Centre works with employees, other organizations such as the Business for Social Responsibility (BSR) works with employers, to encourage communication with their workers.[57]

In Shanghai, I have tried to find NGOs that deal specifically with the situation of women. I have talked with several people engaged in different non-profit organizations, but I have found just the two aforementioned activists working specifically with women and able to talk openly with me. These activists work on supporting Chinese women victims of violence. They are informed by Chinese citizens about some situations of violence, and then they support the victim by telephone or personally, and in some cases, they accompany the victims to the police department to guarantee that they are making the legal accusation at the police. According to them, police officers in China may still be indifferent to a

[52] Despite the better conditions for freedom in Hong Kong in comparison with mainland China, since June 2019 Hong Kong has been experiencing repression from the Chinese government and limitations in several freedoms, such as the freedom of expression. The conflicts started as Hong Kong's government was debating an extradition law, which could extradite people from Hong Kong to mainland China.

[53] China Labour Bulletin. Cheung, J. 2013. Young women workers in China: Seeking a better life. https://clb.org.hk/en/content/young-women-workers-china-seeking-better-life. 19.04.2019.

[54] China Labour Bulletin. Cheung, J. 2013. Young women workers in China: Seeking a better life. https://clb.org.hk/en/content/young-women-workers-china-seeking-better-life. 19.04.2019.

[55] China Labour Bulletin. Cheung, J. 2013. Young women workers in China: Seeking a better life. https://clb.org.hk/en/content/young-women-workers-china-seeking-better-life. 19.04.2019.

[56] China Labour Bulletin. Cheung, J. 2013. Young women workers in China: Seeking a better life. https://clb.org.hk/en/content/young-women-workers-china-seeking-better-life. 19.04.2019.

[57] China Labour Bulletin. Cheung, J. 2013. Young women workers in China: Seeking a better life. https://clb.org.hk/en/content/young-women-workers-china-seeking-better-life. 19.04.2019.

situation of violence, and then the activists need to intervene and insist that the police accepts the accusation.

At the police districts, to protect their identity, these two women identify themselves as friends or acquaintances of the victims. The police cannot know that they are activists struggling for the recognition of Chinese women.

I have also had the chance to attend a lecture by Corinne Hua, the founder of *Stepping Stones*, an organization with the mission to improve the education and general welfare of disadvantaged children in China. During 2018, Stepping Stones coordinated more than 1,500 volunteers who provided English classes at more than 45 sites in Shanghai and 9 other provinces[58].

According to her testimony, she, as a foreigner, needed to struggle for several years to get her NGO's registration in China. Stepping Stones was registered in 2013 as a private non-enterprise organization[59], as a "*youth development center*," and the Chinese police must be notified in advance of activities of the association. The case of Hua illustrates the fact that Chinese government controls the activities of the NGOs and their owners do not have sufficient freedom to comply with the social demands of the country. Section 11.1 already described that since 2017, all the NGOs in China had their activities restricted by the government. Even before that time, the United States Department of State confirmed that the Chinese government maintains control over civil society groups, on the emergence of independent NGOs.

Hua states that, for her, a hope of improvement rests on the Chinese population. Every year she gets surprised by some significant Chinese donations to her NGO. In 2016, a Charity Policy Law was passed in China. After this time, people in China began to donate more to charity. Nevertheless, it seems that their actions are still based on a utilitarian perspective. Hua has stated that several Chinese and foreign companies are interested in taking part in her project, just in order to use it as a promotion of themselves, as engaged and sensitive employers.

Even before 2016, 2008 was considered the "first year of charity" in China, because of the Wenchuan earthquake and the Beijing Olympics, which influenced Chinese people to volunteer.[60]

Nevertheless, research conducted in 2017 placed China in the 134th position in a ranking of 139 countries that have volunteer services.[61]

---

[58] Stepping Stones 2018, 8.

[59] Stepping Stones 2018, 8.

[60] UNDP 2016, 07.

[61] UNDP 2016, 10.

Morocco also has different forms of struggles, despite government restrictions. According to Masbah, new forms of resistance had developed in Morocco[62]. Masbah has used Assef Bayat's concept of 'social nonmovements' to describe the new generation of social movements in the Middle East, which also relates to regions such as Morocco:

> What he has termed as 'social nonmovements' refer to how ordinary individuals in the Middle East who are not members of the elite are able to change politics through their simple daily routines that take the form of a negative protest against situations and grievances.[63]

In Morocco, there are also different NGOs and associations such as Centre Batha. According to the coordinator of the center:

> The Centre Batha is an example of struggles for recognition. Furthermore, there are movements of coalition, in order to promote modifications to the norms of Morocco, for example, discriminatory norms. One example is the movement called "Printemps de la dignité" which has 24 associations as members. There is coordination between these associations, and it is an example of mobilization.[64]

Despite the limitations related to struggles for recognition in these countries, while at a slow pace, Chinese and Moroccan governments have created some policies as forms of pretending to be more open and democratic. Despite the utilitarian intention behind it, these policies, in the end, have supported the conditions for struggles.

In China, I have already mentioned, as an example, the changes in the *hukou* system, to improve the conditions of Chinese migrants. More than that, I can also mention the creation of circuit courts, to supposedly promote the dialogue and control of local officials and local judiciary, avoiding arbitrary decisions and actions:

> China started establishing circuit courts in January 2015. This could potentially help address collusion between local officials and local judiciary. It could, along with the proposal to develop a mechanism to keep records of officials who interfere in judicial cases, potentially limit local governments' influence in legal affairs and increase the independence of the local judiciary and allow it to more effectively be a check on the local government's exercise of power. The proposed regional courts could

[62] Masbah 2018, 05.

[63] Masbah 2018, 03.

[64] Appendix, Interview I, Hanane, 2018.

> limit the possibilities for local officials to bypass rules and legislation and strengthen supervision over them.[65]

Despite governmental policies, there are other organizations in Morocco that contribute to the achievement of human rights and women's rights. For instance, I can mention the work of Euromed Rights:

> At policy level, EuroMed Rights' credibility and good relationship with members of the European Parliament's Committee on Women's Rights and Gender Equality (FEMM) yielded results. EuroMed Rights was invited by FEMM to share its expertise during a hearing on "Women as agents of change in the Southern Partnership". Subsequently, Ms Marie Arena, member of the European Parliament and appointed rapporteur for a report on the situation of women in the Southern Neighbourhood asked EuroMed Rights and its Moroccan members to organise a series of meetings between her and women's rights organisations in Morocco.[66]

In 2018, the Moroccan government and the EU Delegation agreed to meet with Moroccan civil society to discuss the opportunities for entering into cooperation[67]. This is a significant step for Moroccan society.

11.4 Conclusion of Chap. 11

Chapter 11 has presented examples of struggles for the recognition of women in China and Morocco. Both countries share challenges regarding gender equality, and it seems that, over time, political interference make it even more difficult. Nevertheless, there are still struggles for recognition practiced individually and also through institutional support, such as the ones supported by NGOs. Honneth's processes of struggle are dynamic and dialectical. China and Morocco have a long path of struggles already started, to achieve better conditions of recognition for women.

I comprehend that without struggles against indifference, it is not possible for Chinese and Moroccan women to be fully respected. I understand that potentially trivial actions in daily life—such as debates between relatives regarding women's situation, or the support of people in need—could open members of society to more sensitive and emotional behavior toward each other.

---

[65] World Bank Group 2017, 57.

[66] Euromed Rights 2019, 21.

[67] Euromed Rights 2019, 21.

All these private struggles for recognition would result in Honnethian self-aware democratic citizenship and emancipated family members, as I explained in the chapters above. I have also listed methods for increasing democratic attitudes in the private life of individuals, such as the teaching of tolerance in schools or inside the family.

Furthermore, Moroccans and Chinese need to guarantee a minimum of human rights for their population. The debate about human rights does not necessarily need to count on public instances, and it can be developed by private institutions or inside the family. The most important thing is to demonstrate to the people the significance of being respected in the pattern of law, and the relevance of creating new social norms and values, which can guide them toward achieving future legislated and effective human rights in the countries.

All these struggles relate to the open revisability of a culture. I have noticed that, in China and Morocco, some cultural values and social norms may reduce people's engagement, especially for women whom they do not know at all. It is fundamental, then, to revise their cultures to satisfactorily respect gender equality.

General Conclusion

The work has presented the theoretical framework of Axel Honneth's theory of recognition. The stated problems were:

a) Why is Axel Honneth's theory of recognition not reasonable for women's recognition?
b) How can his theory be modified to fully include the recognition of women?

The analysis was divided into two parts. The first part of the work includes Chaps. 1 to 7. From Chaps. 1 to 3, I performed a theoretical study of Honneth's definitions of recognition, disrespect, and struggles. From Chaps. 4 to 7, I presented our proposals for struggles for recognition of women.

Following Critical Theory methodology, after the theoretical approach, the second part of the dissertation, including Chaps. 8 to 11, illustrated the theory of recognition in the contexts of Chinese and Moroccan women.

In Chap. 1, I have studied the book *Struggle for recognition,* where Honneth states an interpretation of recognition from three perspectives: love, rights (law), and solidarity. This categorization is helpful because it clarifies how individuals experience recognition in their private and public lives.

For Honneth, the pattern of love is represented by an individual's private life. It begins when she is born and enjoys the symbiotic relationship with her mother and the care and love from her caregivers. When the person grows, during her childhood and youth, she makes friends and enjoys relationships with her relatives. These experiences allow the person to attain self-confidence. She has individual freedom and self-determination to choose her project of life, being

C. Diamantino Esser Santana, *Recognized Women:*, Juridicum – Schriften zur Rechtsphilosophie, https://doi.org/10.1007/978-3-658-46849-1

respected by the ones who share these moments of her life with her. For Honneth, an individual has self-realization and authenticity inside the pattern of love.

Indeed, in 2004, when proposing principles of recognition, Honneth submitted them to a criterion of progress. To follow the criterion of progress, the pattern of love should expand its forms of relationship, involving different and new possibilities for persons to experience love, thus freeing them from stereotypes.

Regarding the recognition of women, I understand that the pattern of love is the one more exposed to offenses against recognition because of its privacy. Women are fragile and exposed to different forms of offenses when experiencing love. It is then necessary to understand how she could be protected and supported by the second pattern of recognition, the pattern of rights (law).

The work studied the pattern of recognition of law. According to Honneth, when the individual reaches adulthood and realizes her accountability in obeying the legal norms and her rights to claim justice, she will feel self-respected.

Honneth has reviewed his studies on the law by publishing *Freedom's right* and *Die Armut unserer Freiheit*. Now, Honneth advocates for a normative reconstruction of ethical life, including aspects of sociology and social theory. For Honneth, to guarantee the reach of freedom, individuals should, firstly, enjoy their freedom and autonomy to make choices in their lives. Secondly, they should adopt democratic attitudes concerning their public space through civil cooperation and responsibility. Honnethian democratic attitudes could also be adopted in the private dimensions of life, mainly because women need to have a voice and democratic opportunities within their family and personal contexts of life.

Within the pattern of law, the work studied the Habermasian approach. For Habermas, law represents a public dimension, in which *Lebenswelt* and *Systemwelt* can be reconciled. He advocates for democratic structures in the public dimensions, making it possible for individuals to reach an understanding. The theory of Habermas is helpful for a theory of recognition because the author explains the dynamics of speech and language and their integration from a public perspective. On the other hand, Honneth's theory of recognition comes from the other direction, proposing the development of a person's identity from a private and individual perspective. I had suggested that the theory of recognition could adopt some Habermasian discussions on public debate and democracy but inserting them into the individual's perspective. Communicative action and deliberation, for instance, could also be exercised in private life.

I understand that the pattern of law is essential for achieving women's recognition, as they need to be addressees and authors of rights. Law promotes all other patterns of recognition and protects the individuals in cases of offense and disrespect.

After discussing love and law, the work studied the pattern of solidarity. From the publication of the book *Freedom's Right*, Honneth has given a unique role to solidarity.

It has a significant role in Honneth's theory, because it relates to social freedom. The pattern of solidarity makes law and love relational. Cooperative practices inside communities endorse self-confidence, self-respect, and self-esteem. Solidarity has intentionality, emotional attachment, and a genuine appreciation of others. In different moments of his work, Honneth has argued that in the pattern of solidarity, individuals achieve self-esteem, social-esteem, and self-worth.

Regarding solidarity, Honneth is influenced by Dewey's practical involvement, Lukács'engaged praxis, and Heidegger's care, as I have explained in the above chapters. When employing solidarity, the individual interacts with her world, giving to it a qualitative significance, and actively engaging in practices of solidarity as a participant, more than just as a mere observer.

The work has detailed how scholars discuss the concept of solidarity. It came from ideas of social integration and brotherhood. Over time, the institute has been modified, and nowadays, according to Honneth, solidarity relates to participation and engagement. It is the seed for the individual to struggle for recognition, abandon an indifferent attitude, and engage in struggles for better conditions of respect and equality.

For instance, I studied the theo-ethic of solidarity from Peters, who argues that nowadays it is necessary, for the agents of solidarity, to implement metanoia, the honor of difference, accountability, and the vision of solidarity as an action. In general, they involve openness to difference, and the acceptance of self-determination.

Despite the relevance of his theory of recognition, our work has shown that some theorists have criticized Honneth. Pensky argues that the theory of recognition leads to relativism, as far as Honneth supposedly advocates for liberalization of cultural models. The work has demonstrated that, although Honneth respects cultural differences, his theory has principles, criteria and limits. Nevertheless, to minimize the risks of relativism, I proposed modifications to Honneth's theory, to guarantee its universalism and applicability.

Our proposals were also valuable for arguing against the critique made by Van den Brink. The author argues that Honneth has not clarified how to solve possible conflicts between the patterns of recognition. For me, my proposals guarantee a joined dynamic and coherence between the patterns of women's recognition.

Mark criticized Honneth, regarding conflicts between individuals. The author accuses Honneth of considering only extragroup possibilities of conflict, forgetting that intragroup individuals, people from the same community, tend to compete. For Mark, Honneth does not consider the comparative dimension of honor, and the competition among people to hold more honor than the others interferes with recognition. Considering our proposals, it was clear that the theory of recognition is incompatible with presumptions of competition. Recognition presupposes individuals' cooperation and solidarity, and then the critique of Mark has lost its foundation.

Additionally, I have seen that Nancy Fraser criticizes Honnethian solidarity. For her, it is necessary to think recognition disregards redistribution. For instance, she does not comprehend that capitalism has influences on recognition and on individuals' morals. I disagree with her and, following Honneth, I advocated for a recognition encompassing different aspects of an individual's life, including economic ones.

Capitalism influences recognition, for instance, when Honneth deals with social pathologies. The work has demonstrated that he follows the tradition of Critical Theory and the analysis of social pathologies serves to identify the necessities of a specific community, and how recognition has been violated. Social pathologies are forms of disrespect and moral injustice.

All the patterns of recognition—love, rights, and solidarity—suffer offenses during an individual's life. In Chap. 2, the work explained that the offenses against recognition are called *disrespect*. I studied the elements and premises for disrespect and disagreed with Honneth's affirmation that moral injury presupposes an individual's consciousness. In other words, for Honneth, the individual must be aware of her vulnerability. On the contrary, people's unawareness is already a form of disrespect, for instance when the woman is already alienated. Social pathologies, such as alienation, damage the individual's capacity to form her consciousness and to be aware of the offenses committed against her.

The study of disrespect within its different forms demonstrated the relevance of protecting the patterns of recognition, to make possible the achievement of self-confidence, self-esteem, and self-respect for individuals. I argued that recognition is a moral act based on the ethical principles of recognition: love, law, and merit. The principles of recognition must follow the criterion of progress and support individuals' struggles. They are parameters for an individual's ethical life. In a situation of disrespect, people should then struggle.

Chapter 3 clarified the concept of *struggles*. Struggles are, first of all, a form of recovering violated patterns of recognition. For Honneth, struggles for recognition guarantee social justice, by protecting integrity, cultural pluralism, and concerning future generations.

Although Honneth argues that social justice is not just positive rights but also individual's behavioral routines, within his theory, the struggles with institutional and public support are mainly discussed. Nevertheless, any action trying to recover a pattern of recognition, supporting the victims of disrespect, is considered a necessary struggle, and may be private or public.

I argue that, within the context of women's recognition, it is relevant for the theory of recognition to comprehend law as the pattern able to implement effective struggles for the recognition of women. It is possible to engage in struggles for legal recognition in the private dimension of love, and any interpretation of struggles as exclusively public should be reviewed.

Struggles in the pattern of love can recover the self-confidence of a person. There are communities—for instance, authoritarian states, in which Honnethian recognition is not achievable for all the dimensions of love, law, and solidarity. I understand that, whether at least the pattern of love is recovered through the support of legal recognition, this would be the first step for a recovery of all recognition.

More than that, I have also endorsed that struggles for recognition should be performed not just by the victim of disrespect or her acquaintances or relatives, but actually for all people who witness a situation of disrespect. Recognition relates not just to acknowledging one's identity, but also in seeing respect and dignity in the other.

Chapter 3 also studied the foremost critics of the concept of *struggle* in Honneth's theory. Pensky argues that recovery of patterns of recognition necessarily presupposes the presence of public institutions. It was shown that public institutions are not fundamental, especially when individuals begin to struggle against indifference. Private actions for recognition can solve disrespect, at least in the pattern of love.

Rancière criticizes the objective of struggles, arguing that struggles do not pretend to achieve recognition, but they lay claims on identity and other dimensions of an individual's life. All the dimensions mentioned by Rancière are elements of recognition and, in the end, they contribute to the achievement of recognition itself.

Mark inquires about the reasons for making individuals struggle for recognition and why people would struggle for different persons from different social categories. I understand that struggles are mainly justified by solidarity and cooperation. Our modifications to the theory of Honneth had clarified that, in the end, struggling becomes a moral obligation.

Coming from these discussions in the first three chapters, Chap. 4 then details our first proposal of a struggle for recognition related to women. The individuals must struggle against their own indifference, comprehending indifference as an intentional and negative institute. The chapter studied the various comprehensions of the institute and how Honneth has interpreted it throughout his work.

I understand that many practices of indifference occur inside private relationships, such as marriage or friendship. Individuals frequently witness, hear, or see a situation of disrespect, but they do not act to recover the recognition of the victim. More than that, they do not conceive that a disrespect located in a private dimension also influences the community as a whole. The misrecognition is not just from the victim, but also the whole community.

Indifference can also happen within public spaces. When it is shared and collectively practiced, I comprehend it as a social pathology. In any form of indifference, it should be confronted through struggles for recognition.

In Chap. 5, I proposed specific struggles in the pattern of love. The offenses against the pattern of love are more than physical abuses. I could mention, for instance, the classification of violence against women made by the Réseau National des Centre d'Ecoute des Femmes Victimes de Violences in Morocco, namely legal violence, physical violence, psychological violence, sexual violence, and economic violence.

In the pattern of love, it is necessary to struggle in the contexts of family and friendship, requiring the emancipation of the family member and the open revisability of one's culture (a concept developed by Will Kymlicka). In *Freedom's Right*, Honneth holds that it is essential for a theory of recognition to have emancipated family members. If a family practices recognition inside the home, respecting and allowing the person to make her own decisions and life projects, the tendency is to emancipate their members, forming a deliberative space for discussions, debate, and tolerance of differences inside the family contexts. It also makes necessary the openness to a revision of a culture, respecting the criteria and principles of recognition.

Chapter 6 introduced the proposals of struggles in the pattern of law. Legal recognition would be possible mainly through adopting human rights related to the recognition of women. These rights may be positive or moral, depending on the society I consider. In any of these forms, the law makes possible the implementation of better conditions for the achievement of gender equality. Coming from the Universal Declaration of Human Rights (United Nations), I argued that there are already some human rights related to the recognition of women: *the right to recognition; the right to freedom of movement and residence; the right to marry and to found a family; the right to freedom of thought, conscience and religion;*

the right to freedom of opinion and expression; the right to family planning; and *the right to development.* These human rights share some characteristics with the struggles for recognition. They are dynamic, historical, in construction. Human rights related to recognition may be legal or moral and they will always be open institutes to be further developed and adopted by different societies. Struggles for women's recognition share these same characteristics, especially in the pattern of law, making legal recognition the key for achieving of respect and dignity for women.

In the context of solidarity, Chap. 7 proposed struggles against indifference as a social pathology. Honneth mentioned some social pathologies related to recognition, namely invisibility, individualization, reification, freezing of society, and autonomization. Nevertheless, I understand that indifference holds characteristics of all of them, and the element of intentionality. Indifference is more than isolation, individualism, helplessness, and a loss of communication. Indifference is an intentional action, when a person decides not to help or to not interfere in a situation of disrespect.

Indifference makes people not engage in struggles, whether in private dimensions or in public ones. Indifference should be confronted using solidarity, and the agent of struggle should somehow support the victim. Engagement against indifference is a moral duty.

Furthermore, I have suggested struggles for metanoia, the honor of difference, accountability, and action, based on the studies of Peters. Honneth also has his own proposals for struggles related to solidarity, namely the voluntary practices and the democratic attitudes and ideal. In *Freedom's Right* and *Die Armut unserer Freiheit,* Honneth advocates for the importance of adopting democratic attitudes to increase the possibilities of recognition and to endorse social freedom. Honneth's analysis of democracy should first be interpreted as an ideal. If I come from this premise, the individual, supported by the moral obligation to struggle, would act through democratic attitudes and based on democratic principles. These sorts of attitudes can exist in private or public dimensions of life. Honneth, for instance, hast highlighted the relevance of reaching democratic practices inside labour. The practices of discussion, debate, and argumentation processes should first occur in the family context, to promote the emancipated family members and self-aware democratic citizens, contributing to the achievement of recognition in the pattern of love. The new generations should be allowed to not comply with all the cultural and family requirements imposed on them. Social practices should constantly be reviewed, taking recognition and self-determination as their main aims.

An extension of Walzer's definition of tolerance in the contexts of private relationships, and not just considering extragroup relations, would also contribute to democratic attitudes. Educational arenas of debate would also allow individuals to practice democratic attitudes at least in schools.

The work demonstrated that Honneth had not extensively written about interculturalism or international relations. I had discussed some elements of political philosophy, which are helpful for a more universal perspective on recognition, for instance, the rational revisability conceptualized by Kymlicka, signifying that a person should have the option of questioning his own culture, being free of blindly following all the imposed cultural rules, for instance, marriage.

After the aforementioned theoretical discussions, Chap. 8 summarized how recognition and especially legal recognition relate to gender equality. It is relevant to comprehend the theory of recognition from the perspective of the social reality, through the analysis of gender equality. The chapter analyzed Hegel's fundamental influence in the theory of Honneth, as well as the role of Critical Theory and related French social theories of recognition for Honneth. From these theoretical studies, I then interpreted current legal recognition of women from the perspective of human rights, either positive rights legalized in international treaties, or moral rights shared within ethical norms. The ethical recognition of women from the standpoint of feelings of self-confidence, self-esteem, and self-respect is also necessary. I had inquired how it would be illustrated in case studies, as Honneth comes from the tradition of Critical theorists, who highlight the importance to take the theoretical studies and to merge them with the reality of life.

Taking China and Morocco into consideration, I saw that a woman considered "recognized," being respected and esteemed by her community, as well as feeling confident, is the one who complies with cultural traditions, such as marriage. This woman has a social obligation to respect her parents' decisions, and she may be subjected to actions which she does not choose by herself. In the end, these women are not recognized from the Honnethian perspective.

Chapters 9 and 10 have described different forms of disrespect that Chinese and Moroccan women experience daily. The influence of patriarchalism in both cultures makes women be respected only when they get married and give birth. There is a low level of freedom for them to decide if they want to marry or be mothers.

I must highlight that my work does not pretend to judge Moroccan and Chinese cultures, generalizing social problems. Our discussions of China and Morocco cover offenses against recognition. That is why the work was very critical when analyzing the countries, as our objective was to demonstrate how the patterns of recognition are violated there.

Taking China into consideration, I had concluded in Chap. 9 that the country has considerable limitations on the right to freedom of thought, conscience, and expression. Freedom of the press is also restricted. This context makes people hesitate to engage in social struggles for recognition. Furthermore, the Chinese experience Confucius' endorsement of harmony, and usually the Chinese avoid conflict and do not confront situations of disrespect.

Up to the present, there is still a preference for male children in China. If I consider Chinese history, the country has a considerable number of abortions or infanticide of girls, which resulted in a lack of recognition of the girls themselves as well as their mothers—many times obligated to kill or abandon their babies in the past -. Especially in rural areas, there are arranged marriages, and mistresses. If a woman chooses not to marry, she is stigmatized as "leftover." If a woman is married and decides to divorce, she may suffer from gender inequality in the division of property.

Into the pattern of law, I have seen that court decisions, police performance, and legislation may still lead to prejudice against women.

More than that, some theorists justify the lack of human rights in China with the country having a particular economic and political development, not being able to comply with all the international legal standards.

Taking the pattern of solidarity into consideration, Chinese women are subjected to gender inequality in labor and education. In spite of the significant improvement in the Chinese educational system, migrant women who experience the *hukou* system, for instance, are not allowed to register their children in all Chinese big cities.

I had concluded that, despite the unquestionable advances in the Chinese economy, the country still needs to significantly increase its practice of democracy, within the private and public spheres. Even exercising of democratic attitudes inside the home, as I am proposing here, should be done with parsimony, because the control of the Chinese government is getting more substantial over time.

Chapter 10 analyzed the reality of a Moroccan woman. I concluded that, politically, it seems that governmental control of the population, concerning freedom of expression and freedom of the press, for instance, is lower than in China. Even so, there is control of press and NGO activities in Morocco.

Furthermore, the Islamic country has other sorts of limitations on the patterns of recognition, which come from its religious tradition. More than that, although Morocco is considerably smaller than China in terms of territory, the economic situation of the Islamic country influences the situation of women in a negative way.

Morocco's pattern of solidarity is influenced by poverty. Female education is not sufficient, and the percentage of illiterate Moroccan women is still high. More than that, there is no sex education, and usually, women do not have information regarding pregnancy and sexual diseases.

Moroccan women also represent a small portion of the labor market. Unfortunately, they usually perform informal or unpaid work.

Considering the pattern of law, Morocco has made notable improvements in its legislation regarding women. Nevertheless, there are still legal norms in need of modification—for instance, the possibility of marriage with minors, and some practices of judges, courts, and police, in general, are still sexist.

A Moroccan woman is expected to keep her virginity until she gets married, and after that, her husband may demand polygamy. If a woman gets pregnant before marriage, she will be subjected to a huge social stigma in Morocco: the single mother.

More than that, I had shown that the country has high levels of domestic violence. I have worked at a Moroccan center for the empowerment of women victims of violence sponsored by Unesco. Our personal experiences at the center are compiled in the work. Centre Batha is an example of a struggle for the recognition of women.

In Chap. 11, the dissertation presented other examples of struggles for recognition in China and Morocco. Morocco seems to have more openness to collective engagement, such as public movements. Nevertheless, both countries still have limitations and control under their governments with regard to social engagement. The chapter presented some examples of struggles, within the private or public spaces. I have concluded that China and Morocco still need to confront several practices of indifference and other forms of disrespect towards women.

The pattern of law and legal recognition of women can suffer from disrespect by deceit, fraud, or legal discrimination. For instance, Morocco and China both experience disrespect in the pattern of law, having discriminatory legislation regarding women, or discriminatory court decisions concerning women.

China and Morocco need to struggle against practices of indifference in the family and private contexts of life, and public life. I advocate that there are always potentially trivial actions, which, in the end, can contribute to the recovery of, at least, the pattern of love. These actions should be based on democracy and solidarity in the way I propose. More than that, the fundamental human rights regarding women's recognition are guidelines in identifying disrespect. Honneth, following Hegel, understands that forming individual's identity comes from the relationships with others. In all patterns of recognition, the struggle for women's recognition should be seen as an individual moral obligation so that everybody sees themselves as agents of solidarity.

The dissertation stated in the introduction that our methodology and objective come from Critical Theory, and I aim to interpret a philosophical theory by applying it to the reality of societies. After developing our proposal to struggles for recognition and the evaluation of Chinese and Moroccan society, I conclude that there are always forms of struggling for recognition.

The dynamic of struggles and recognition does not end, and developing struggles in one pattern of recognition may also contribute to achieving recognition in the other patterns, especially if recognition is guaranteed by the pattern of law. However, some countries may need this process to run for a long time.

Keeping our focus on the situation of women, especially the pattern of law has a crucial role in the formation of recognition. I contend that legal recognition may implement practices of care, solidarity, compassion, and affection. In the end, the achievement of recognition and respect comes from the enjoyment of rights by the person, as addressee and author of rights.

So, in this regard, government has made a lot of progress. Until now, the government is at least having some funding and services. Although it is not perfect, we can say that there is some kind of attention to the issue.

References

Adorno, T. 2008. Minima moralia: reflexões a partir da vida lesada. Translation by Gabriel Cohn. Rio de Janeiro, Beco do Azougue.

Amendment to the Constitution of the People's Republic of China, 2018. Adopted at the First Session of the 13th National People's Congress on March 11, 2018. Available at http://www.npc.gov.cn/englishnpc/constitution2019/201911/36a2566d029c4b39966bd942f82a4305.shtml. Access on 23.08.2022.

Amnesty International. 2016. Morocco: Submission to the United Nations Human Rights Committee. 118th Session, 17 October-14 November 2016. Index: MDE 29/4858/2016. Available at https://www.amnesty.org/download/Documents/MDE2948582016ENGLISH.PDF. Access on 02.06.2018.

Anderson, J. 1995. (Translator's introduction). In *The struggle for recognition: the moral grammar of social conflicts*. A. Honneth. Cambridge, MIT Press.

Anderson, J. 2011. Situating Axel Honneth in the Frankfurt School Tradition. In *Axel Honneth: critical essays: with a reply by Axel Honneth*. Social and Critical Theory: a Critical Horizons Book Series. V.12. Brill, Leiden, Boston.

Anti-domestic Violence Law of the People's Republic of China. Available at http://www.ilo.org/dyn/natlex/natlex4.detail?p_lang=en&p_isn=103955&p_count=1&p_classification=01.04. Access on 23.04.2019.

Araújo, J. 2020. A Política do Reconhecimento: Um Diálogo com Charles Taylor, Axel Honneth e Nancy Fraser. *In* EDUCAmazônia—Educação Sociedade e Meio Ambiente, Humaitá, LAPESAM/GISREA/UFAM/CNPq/EDUA—ISSN 1983-3423. Vol XXV, Num. 2, 2020, 13–30.

Asociation Iniciatives pour la protection des droits des femmes (IPDF) Centre multifonctionnel Batha; UNESCO L'Organisation des Nations Unies pour l'éducation, la science et la culture. 2011. Modélisation du Centre multifonctionnel Batha pour l'autonomisation des femmes victimes de violence basée sur le genre. ISBN: 978-9954-415-0

Atia, M.; Herrold, C. E. 2018. Governing Through Patronage: The Rise of NGOs and the Fall of Civil Society in Palestine and Morocco. This is the author's manuscript of the article published in final edited form as: Atia, M., & Herrold, C. Governing Through Patronage: The Rise of NGOs and the Fall of Civil Society in Palestine and Morocco. In *Voluntas: International Journal of Voluntary and Nonprofit Organizations*. Available at https://doi.org/10.1007/s11266-018-9953-6. Access on 19.03.2019.

C. Diamantino Esser Santana, *Recognized Women:*, Juridicum – Schriften zur Rechtsphilosophie, https://doi.org/10.1007/978-3-658-46849-1

Attané, I. 2014. Being a Woman in China Today: A Demography of Gender. In *Analysing China's Population: social changes in a new demographic era.* Edited by I. Attané, B. Gu. V.3. INED Population Studies, Springer.

Attané, I.; Gu, B. (Editors). 2014. Analysing China's Population: social changes in a new demographic era. V.3. INED Population Studies, Springer.

Aurelius, M. 2013. Marcus Aurelius' Meditations. Tr. Casaubon. V. 8.16, uploaded to www.philaletheians.co.uk, 14 July 2013. Available at https://www.maximusveritas.com/wp-content/uploads/2017/09/Marcus-Aurelius-Meditations.pdf. Access on 08.05.2023.

Barlas, A. 2002. "Believing Women" in Islam: unreading patriarchal interpretations of the Qur'an. Austin, University of Texas Press.

BBC News. 2022. 24.05.2022. Who are the Uyghurs and why is China being accused of genocide? Available at https://www.bbc.com/news/world-asia-china-22278037. Access on 08.08.2022.

BBC News. Mcdonell, S. 2021. China allows three children in major policy shift. Available at https://www.bbc.com/news/world-asia-china-57303592. 31.05.2021. Access on 03.05.2023.

Brincat, S. 2013. The Harm Principle and Recognition Theory: On the Complementarity between Linklater, Honneth and the Project of Emancipation. In *Critical horizons*, vol. 14, issue 2. School of Political Science and International Studies, University of Queensland, Australia, 225–256.

Brugger, W. 2003. Communitarianism as the social and legal theory behind the German Constitution. Oxford University Press and New York University School of Law. I.CON. Volume 2, Number 3, 2004, pp.431–460.

Brunkhorst, H. 2016. Solidarität: von der Bürgerfreundschaft zur globalen Rechtsgenossenschaft. Suhrkamp.

BTI Transformation Index 2022. BTI 2022 Country Report Morocco.

Buck, P. S. 2013. Imperial Woman: The Story of the Last Empress of China (English Edition). Open Road Integrated Media, New York. [Kindle 5.12.2] Retrieved from amazon.de

Chan, K. W. 2018. China's Hukou System at 60: Continuity and Reform. In *'The Chinese Hukou System at 50,' Eurasian Geography and Economics*, 50 (2). University of Washington. Published by Bellwether Publishing, Ltd, with the permission of Taylor & Francis Ltd, 197–221.

Chang, L. T. 2008. Factory Girls: From Village to City in a Changing China. (English Edition). Spiegel& Grau, New York. [Kindle 5.12.2] Retrieved from amazon.de

Chen, K. 2016. Vulnerabilities in China's Legal System. In *Tigers Without Teeth: The Pursuit of Justice in Contemporary China.* S. Wilson. Rowman & Littlefield, Lanham, 2015. Published online: 9 May 2016. Springer Science+Business Media, New York.

China Daily. Wenting, Z. 2011. The mother-in-law of all family battles. China Daily. 22.04.2011. Available on www.chinadaily.com.cn/china/2011-04/22/content_12373683.htm. Access on 06.05.2019.

China File. Pin, L. 2019. Finding a Voice. March 28, 2019. Available at http://www.chinafile.com/reporting-opinion/viewpoint/finding-voice. Access on 25.10.2019.

China Labour Bulletin. Cheung, J. 2013. Young women workers in China: Seeking a better life. Available at https://clb.org.hk/en/content/young-women-workers-china-seeking-better-life. Access on 19.04.2019.

China Macro Economy. Mullen, A. 2022. China population: is a demographic turning point just around the corner as births drop again?. Available at https://www.scmp.com/economy/economic-indicators/article/3165798/china-population-demographic-turning-point-just-around. Access on 30.07.2022.

China News, 2020. China National Program for Women's Development (2011–2020). 16.11.2020. Available at http://news.cri.cn/20201116/d094f49f-aab7-2895-3600-b04fead5f1db.html#:~:text=National%20Program%20for%20Women's%20Development%20(2011%2D2020)%20has%20been,and%20other%20related%20laws%2C%20the. Access on 25.04.2022.

Chinese Human Rights Defenders, 2022. Urgent Life-Threatening Conditions in Lockdown Shanghai Demand Prompt Investigation. 05.05.22. Available at https://www.nchrd.org/2022/05/urgent-life-threatening-conditions-in-lockdown-shanghai-demand-prompt-investigation/. Access on 30.07.2022.

Chtatou, M. 2022. Reflecting on women issues in Morocco. 19.01.2022. The Times of Israel. Available at https://blogs.timesofisrael.com/reflecting-on-women-issues-in-morocco/. Access on 03.08.2022.

Civil Code of the People's Republic of China. Adopted at the Third Session of the Thirteenth National People's Congress on May 28, 2020. Available on http://english.www.gov.cn/archive/lawsregulations/202012/31/content_WS5fedad98c6d0f72576943005.html. Access on 24.08.2022.

Connolly, J. 2010. Love in the private: Axel Honneth, feminism and the politics of recognition. In *Contemporary Political Theory*. Vol. 9, 4. Macmillan Publishers Ltd. 414–433.

Constitution of the People's Republic of China. 2018. Adopted at the Fifth Session of the Fifth National People's Congress and promulgated by the Announcement of the National People's Congress on December 4, 1982; and the Amendment to the Constitution of the People's Republic of China adopted at the First Session of the Thirteenth National People's Congress on March 11, 2018. Available at http://www.npc.gov.cn/englishnpc/constitution2019/201911/1f65146fb6104dd3a2793875d19b5b29.shtml. Access on 07.02.2022.

Criminal Code of Morocco. Promulgated by Dahir No. 1–59–413 of 28 Joumada II 1382 (November 26, 1962), and amended up Law No. 33–18. Available at https://www.imolin.org/doc/amlid/Morocco/Morocco_code_penal_1962.pdf. Access on 29.04.2020.

Delacampagne, C. 1997. História da filosofia no século XX. Translated by Lucy Magalhães. Rio de Janeiro: Jorge Zahar.

Delle, V. 2010. How Can We Explain Beauty? A Psychological Answer to a Philosophical Question. Complutense University of Madrid. Proceedings of the European Society for Aesthetics, vol. 2.

Deranty, J. P. 2011. Reflective Critical Theory: a Systematic Reconstruction of Axel Honneth's Social Philosophy. In *Axel Honneth: critical essays: with a reply by Axel Honneth.* Social and Critical Theory: a Critical Horizons Book Series. V.12. Brill, Leiden, Boston.

Deranty, J.P.; Rancière, J; Honneth, A.; Genel, K; 2016. Recognition or Disagreement: a Critical Encounter on the Politics of Freedom, Equality, and Identity. New Directions in Critical Theory Book 30. (English Edition) New York, Columbia University Press.

Dillon, R. S. 1997. Self-Respect: Moral, Emotional, Political. In *Ethics*, vol. 107 (2) JSTOR, 226–249. Available at www.jstor.org/stable/2381947. Access on 05.01.2018.

Donnelly, J. 2007. The relative universality of human rights. Human Rights Quarterly, Volume 29, Number 2, May 2007, pp. 281–306. The Johns Hopkins University Press.

Dumouchel, P. 2003. Indifference and envy: the anthropological analysis of modern economy. In *Contagion: Journal of Violence, Mimesis, and Culture*. Vol. 10, Published by Michigan State University Press, Spring, 149–160.

Edwards, G. 2004. Habermas and social movements: what's new? In *After Habermas: new perspectives on the public sphere*. N. Crossley; J. Roberts; J. Michael. Malden, Blackwell Publishing Ltd.

Engle, E. 2009. Third Party Effect of Fundamental Rights (Drittwirkung). Hanse Law Review (HanseLR). Vol. 5 Number 2. ISSN 1863–5717.

Eriksen, A. 2009. Universalism and Obligation—Is Ernst Tugendhat's concept of an emotional obligation to universalism defensible? Thesis submitted for the Master of Arts Degree. Department of Philosophy, Classics, History of Arts and Ideas. Available at https://www.duo.uio.no/bitstream/handle/10852/24995/universalismxandxobligation.pdf?sequence=2. Access on 15.03.2018.

Erikson, E. H. 1993. Childhood and society. WW Norton & Company, London.

Euler, K. 2013. The face of Al-Maghreb: how Moroccan are using social networking. University of Pittsburgh, B.Phil.

Euromed Rights. 2013. Region EMHRN201: Freedom of assembly Legislation review. Part of a larger study on Freedom of assembly in the Euro-Mediterranean. Available at https://euromedrights.org/wp-content/uploads/2015/03/FOA2013_EN_MOROCCO1.pdf. Access on 03.05.2023.

Euromed Rights. 2019. Euromed Rights Annual Report 2018. ISBN: 978-87-92990-82-2. Available at https://euromedrights.org/publication/euromed-rights-annual-report-2018/. Access on 14.10.2019.

European Institute of the Mediterranean. Rashed, D.; Allam, R. 2022. Gender-Based Violence in Egypt and Morocco: Politics and Policy-Making. Published by the European Institute of the Mediterranean. Euromesco Paper N.54. March, 2022.

Ferrater Mora, J. 1965. Diccionario de Filosofía. Tomo I. A-K. Montecasino. Editorial Sudamericana Buenos Aires.

Forst, R. 2011. First things first: redistribution, recognition and justification In *Axel Honneth: critical essays: with a reply by Axel Honneth*. Social and Critical Theory: a Critical Horizons Book Series. V.12. Brill, Leiden, Boston.

Fraser, N.; Honneth, A. 2003b. Redistribution Or Recognition? A Political-Philosophical Exchange. London, Verso.

Gao, Q.; Bian, R.; Liu, R.-D.u-De; He, Y.ili; Oei, Tian-Po.-P. 2017. Conflict Resolution in Chinese Adolescents' Friendship: Links with Regulatory Focus and Friendship Satisfaction. In *The Journal of Psychology*, https://doi.org/10.1080/00223980.2016.1270887(2017).

Genel, K; Deranty, J.P.; Rancière, J; Honneth, A.; 2016. Recognition or Disagreement: a Critical Encounter on the Politics of Freedom, Equality, and Identity. New Directions in Critical Theory Book 30. (English Edition) New York, Columbia University Press.

Gilligan, C. 1982. In a Different Voice: Psychological Theory and Women's Development. Harvard University Press.

Gilligan, C. 1985. In a Different Voice: Women's Conceptions of Self and of Morality. In *The Future of Difference*. Edited by H. Eisenstein, A. Jardine. New Brunswick, NJ: Rutgers University Press.

Global Human Rights Defense, 2021. Report Focus on Domestic Violence in China. November 2010.

Guttman, D.; Young, O. R.; Qi, Y. Q.; Bachus, K.; Belis, D.; Cheng, H.; Lin, A.; Schreifels, J.; Van Eynde, S.; Wangd, Y.; Wui, L.; Yan, Y.; Yu, A.; Zaelke, D.; Zhang, B.; Zhang, S.; Zhao, X.; Zhu, X. 2015. Institutionalized governance processes: Comparing environmental problem solving in China and the United States. In *Global Environmental Change* Vol. 31. Elsevier. 163–173.

Habermas, J. 1992a. The Theory of Communicative Action. V. I. Boston: Beacon Press.

Habermas, J. 1992b. The Theory of Communicative Action. V. II. Boston, Beacon Press.

Habermas, J. 1994a. Three normative models of democracy. In *Democratic and Constitutional Theory Today.* Constellations Vol. 1, No 1.

Habermas, J. 1994b. Human rights and popular sovereignty. In *Ratio Juris.* Vol. 7. 1–13.

Habermas, J. 1996. Between facts and norms: contributions to a Discourse Theory of Law and Democracy. Cambridge, MIT Press.

Habermas, J. 2000. Remarks on Erhard Denninger's Triad of Diversity, Security, and Solidarity. In *Constellations,* Vol. 7 (4).

Habermas, J. 2005. Equal Treatment of Cultures and the Limits of Postmodern Liberalism. In *The Journal of Political Philosophy*, Vol. 13 (1). 1–28.

Halley, J. E. 1999. Culture Constrains. In *Is Multiculturalism bad for women? Susan Moller Okin with respondents.* Edited by J. Cohen, M. Howard, M. C. Nussbaum. Princeton University Press, Princeton.

Han, S. Lun Lin. 2017. China's new domestic violence law: keeping victims out of harm's way? Working Paper. Yale Law School. Paul Tsai China Center.

Hegel, G.W. 2018. The Phenomenology of Spirit. Translated with introduction and commentary by Michael Inwood. Oxford: Oxford University Press.

Hegel, G.W. 2008. Outlines of the Philosophy of Right. Oxford World's Classics. Translated by T.M. Knox. Revised, edited, and introduced by Stephen Houlgate. Oxford University Press. 2008.

Heidegger, M. 1962. Being and Time. Translated by John Macquarrie & Edward Robinson. Blackwell Publishers Ltd.

Hobsbawn, E. 2011a. A era do capital: 1848–1875. Translated by Luciano Costa Neto. 15. ed. São Paulo: Paz e Terra.

Hobsbawn, E. 2011b. Era dos extremos: o breve século XX. 1914–1991. Translated by Marcos Santarrita. 2. ed. São Paulo: Companhia das Letras.

Horkheimer, M. 1980. Teoria Crítica e Teoria Tradicional. In Textos Escolhidos: Walter Benjamin, Max Horkheimer, Theodor W. Adorno, Jürgen Habermas. Translated by José Lino Grünnewald et al. São Paulo: Abril Cultural. Os Pensadores.

Honig, B. 1999. My Culture Made Me Do It. In *Is Multiculturalism bad for women? Susan Moller Okin with respondents.* Edited by J. Cohen, M. Howard, M. C. Nussbaum. Princeton University Press, Princeton. [Kindle 5.12.2] Retrieved from amazon.de

Honneth, A. 1995. The struggle for recognition: the moral grammar of social conflicts. Cambridge, MIT Press.

Honneth, A. 1997. Recognition and Moral Obligation. Translated by John Farrell. In *Social Research*, Vol. 64 (1).

Honneth, A. 1998. Democracy as reflexive cooperation: John Dewey and the Theory of Democracy Today. *In Political Theory*, Vol. 26 (6). Published by: Sage Publications, Inc. http://www.jstor.org/stable/. 12/09/2016. 763–783.

Honneth, A. 1999. Teoria Crítica *in* Teoria Social Hoje. GIDDENS, Anthony; TURNER, Jonathan (org.). Translated by Gilson César Cardoso de Sousa. São Paulo: UNESP.

Honneth, A. 2001. Invisibility: on the epistemology of 'Recognition'. In *Aristotelian Society Supplementary Volume*, Vol. 75, Issue 1, July 2001. https://doi.org/10.1111/1467-8349.00081. 111–126.

Honneth, A. 2004a. Organized Self-Realization: Some Paradoxes of Individualization. In *European Journal of Social Theory* 7(4). Sage Publications, London, Thousand Oaks, CA and New Delhi. 463–478.

Honneth, A. 2004b. Recognition and Justice: Outline of a Plural Theory of Justice. In *Acta Sociologica*. Vol. 47 (4). Recognition, Redistribution, and Justice. Published by Sage Publications Ltd. 351–364. http://www.jstor.org/stable/4195049. 12/09/2016.

Honneth, A. 2005. Reification: A Recognition-Theoretical View. In *The Tanner Lectures on Human Values*. Delivered at University of California, Berkeley.

Honneth, A. 2007a. Disrespect: the Normative Foundation of Critical Theory. Cambridge, Polity Press.

Honneth, A. 2007b. Pathologies of Reason: On the legacy of Critical Theory. Translated by James Ingram. New York, Columbia University Press. [Kindle 5.12.2] Retrieved from amazon.de

Honneth, A. 2007c. The Irreducibility of Progress: Kant's Account of the Relationship between Morality and History. In *Critical Horizons: A Journal of Philosophy and Social Theory* 8 (1). Translated by Robert Sinnerbrink and Jean-Philippe Deranty. 1–17.

Honneth, A. 2010b. The Political Identity of the Green Movement in Germany: Social- Philosophical Reflections. [CRIT 11.1 (2010) 5–18] In *Critical Horizons*. ISSN 1568–5160. London, Equinox Publishing Ltd.

Honneth, A. 2012a. Brutalization of the social conflict: struggles for recognition in the early 21st century. Distinktion: Scandinavian Journal of Social Theory, 13:1, 5–19.

Honneth, A. 2012b. The I in We: Studies in the Theory of Recognition. Translated by Joseph Ganahl. Cambridge: Polity Press.

Honneth, A. 2014a. Freedom's right: The Social Foundations of Democratic Life. Translated by Joseph Ganahl. Polity Press, Cambridge.

Honneth, A. 2014b. The normativity of ethical life. In *Philosophy and Social Criticism*. Vol. 40 (8). sagepub.co.uk/journalsPermissions.nav. https://doi.org/10.1177/0191453714541538. Translated by Felix Koch. 817–826.

Honneth, A. 2018. Annerkennung: eine europäische Ideengeschichte. Suhrkamp.

Honneth, A. 2020. Die Armut unserer Freiheit: Aufsätze 2012–2019. Suhrkamp.

Honneth, A. 2021a. Demoralizing Recognition: Comments of R. Brandom, A Spirit of Trust. *In* Philosophy and Phenomenological Research, 103, 714–721.

Honneth, A. 2021b. "You" or "We": The limits of the second-person perspective. European Journal of Philosophy, 29(3), 581–591.

Honneth, A. 2022a. 'Labour', a Brief History of a Modern Concept. Cambridge University Press. 17.02.2022. Translated by Alex Englander.

Honneth, A. 2022b. Two interpretations of social disrespect: a comparison between epistemic and moral recognition. *In* Epistemic Injustice and the Philosophy of Recognition. Giladi, P.; Mcmillan, N. New York: Routledge.

Honneth, A. 2023. Democracy and Fair Labor Conditions. Journal of Business Ethics. Springer.

Honneth, A.; Allen, A.; Cooke, M. 2010a. A conversation between Axel Honneth, Amy Allen and Maeve Cooke. In *Journal of Power*. Vol. 3 (2), Frankfurt am Main. 153–170.

Honneth, A.; Fraser, N. 2003b. Redistribution Or Recognition? A Political-Philosophical Exchange. London, Verso.

Honneth, A.; Bankovsky, M. 2021c. Recognition across French-German divides: the social fabric of freedom in French theory. Critical Horizons, 22:1, 5–28. https://doi.org/10.1080/14409917.2021.1886668

Honneth, A.; Gonçalo, M. 2013. Recognition and Critical Theory today: An interview with Axel Honneth. In *Philosophy and Social Criticism* 39 (2). Universidade NOVA de Lisboa, Lisbon, Portugal. sagepub.co.uk/journalsPermissions.nav. https://doi.org/10.1177/0191453712470361. 209–221.

Honneth, A.; Joas, H. 1988. Social action and human nature. Translated by Raymond Meyer. Cambridge University Press, Cambridge.

Honneth, A.; Willig, R. 2012c. Grammatology of modern recognition orders: an interview with Axel Honneth. Interview. In *Distinktion: Scandinavian Journal of Social Theory*. Vol. 13 (1). 145–149.

Human Rights Watch, 2022. UN High Commissioner must uphold principled and coherent response to China's human rights crisis. 19.04.2022. Available at https://www.hrw.org/node/381788/printable/print. Access on 24.04.2022.

Human Rights Watch. Barr H.; Wang Y. 2022. Chained Woman has become the face of bride trafficking in China. 07.06.2022. Available at https://www.hrw.org/news/2022/06/07/chained-woman-has-become-face-bride-trafficking-china. Access on 30.07.2022.

Huttunen, R. 2011. Hegelians Axel Honneth and Robert Williams on the Development of Human Morality. Springer Science+Business Media B.V. Stud Philos Educ (2012) 31. https://doi.org/10.1007/s11217-011-9278-z. 340–355.

Inside Sources. Rapoza, K. Inside Sources. Shanghai's COVID Lockdown Is a Human Rights Atrocity. 2022. 19.04.2022. Available at https://insidesources.com/shanghais-covid-lockdown-is-a-human-rights-atrocity/. Access on 30.07.2022.

International Monetary Fund. Brussevich; M.; Dabla-Norris, E.; Li, B.G. 2021. IMF Working Paper: China's Rebalancing and Gender Inequality. WP/21/138.

Jianmin, Zhao. 2014. Religion and Law in China. The Netherlands, Kluwer Law International BV.

Keller, M.; Edelstein, W.; Krettenauer, T.; Fu-Xi, F.; Ge, F. 2005. Reasoning about Moral Obligations and Interpersonal Responsibilities in Different Cultural Contexts. In *Morality in context*. W. Edelstein, G. Nunner-Winkler. Amsterdam: Elsevier. 317–337.

Kirste, S. 2010. Autonomie. Literatur Bericht. ARSP (Archiv für Rechts- und Sozialphilosophie), Band 96/4. Stuttgart: Franz Steiner Verlag.

Kirste, S. 2019. The formal and substantive core of human rights. Human(ities) and Rights. Global Network Journal. Vol. 1 (2019) Issue 1.

Kirste, S. 2020. Individualism and collectivism in the foundation of group rights. 2020. Prisma Jurídico, São Paulo, V. 19, n.2, p.347–367, jul./dez. 2020. https://doi.org/10.5585/prismaj.v19n2.18721.

Konrad-Adenauer-Stiftung e.V. 2020. Hanafi, L. The Legal System of Morocco an Overview.

Kuo, S.; Zhang, H.; Zhao, R. Journal of Family Violence (2021). 36:637–641 https://link.springer.com/article/ https://doi.org/10.1007/s10896-021-00295-0. Research on Family Violence in Greater China: Opportunities, Challenges, and Development. Springer.

Kurzban, R.; Leary, M. R. 2001. Evolutionary Origins of Stigmatization: The Functions of Social Exclusion. In *Psychological Bulletin*. Vol. 127 (2). American Psychological Association, Inc. 187–208.

Kymlicka, W. 1995. Multicultural Citizenship: A Liberal Theory of Minority Rights. Clarendon Press, Oxford. [Kindle 5.12.2] Retrieved from amazon.de

Lake, R. 2018. Leftover in China: The Women Shaping the World's Next Superpower (English Edition). W.W. Norton & Company, New York. [Kindle 5.12.2] Retrieved from amazon.de

Law 103-13 on Elimination of Violence Against Women. 2018. Translation MRA Mobilising for Rights Associates. Arabic version published in the Official Gazette at http://www.sgg.gov.ma/Portals/1/BO/2018/BO_6655_Ar.pdf?ver=2018-03-16-133134-870.

Law of the People's Republic of China on the Protection of Women's Rights and Interests. 2018. Available at https://www.justice.gov/sites/default/files/eoir/legacy/2013/11/08/Protection%20of%20Women%27s%20Rights.pdf. Access on 03.04.2019.

Leung, J. T. Y. 2017. Cultural family beliefs, maternal sacrifice, and adolescent psychological competence in Chinese poor single-mother families. In *Social Development*. Vol. 26. wileyonlinelibrary.com/journal/sode VC John Wiley & Sons Ltd. 767–782.

Li, C. 2014. The Confucian Philosophy of Harmony. Oxon, Routledge.

Li, X.; Fang, Q. 2013. Modern Chinese Legal Reform: new perspectives. Lexington, Kentucky: Member of the Association of American University Presses.

Library of Congress. 2021. China: Three-Child Policy Becomes Law, Social Maintenance Fee Abolished. Available at https://www.loc.gov/item/global-legal-monitor/2021-09-23/china-three-child-policy-becomes-law-social-maintenance-fee-abolished/. Access on 24.04.2022.

Lillehammer, H. 2017. The nature and ethics of indifference. In *Journal of Ethics*. Vol. 21 (1). 17–35.

Liu J.; Berger D. L. 2014. Nothingness in Asian Philosophy. New York: Taylor&Francis.

Liu, M; Hu, Y.; Liao, M. 2009. Travelling theory in China: contextualization, compromise and combination. In *Global Networks* 9 (4). ISSN 1470–2266. Blackwell Publishing Ltd & Global Networks Partnership. 529–554.

Lu, J.; Wang, X. 2014. Changing Patterns of Marriage and Divorce in Today's China. In *Analysing China's Population: social changes in a new demographic era*. Attané, I.; Gu, B. INED Population Studies, V.3. Springer.

Marcuse, H. 1972. Novas fontes para a fundamentação do materialismo histórico. In *Ideias sobre uma teoria crítica da sociedade*. Marcuse, H. Rio de Janeiro: Zahar.

Mark, C. 2014. Recognition and Honor: A Critique of Axel Honneth's and Charles Taylor's Histories of Recognition. In *Constellations* Vol. 21 (1) https://doi.org/10.1111/1467-8675.12070.

Markle, G. 2004. Interview with Axel Honneth: From Struggles for Recognition to a Plural Concept of Justice. In *Acta Sociologica*. Vol. 47 (4). https://doi.org/10.1177/0001699304048674. London, Thousand Oaks, CA and New Delhi, Scandinavian Sociological Association and SAGE. 383–391.

Marriage Law of the People's Republic Of China. Adopted at the Third Session of the Fifth National People's Congress on September 10, 1980, and amended according to the Decision on Amending the Marriage Law of the People's Republic of China made at the 21st meeting of the Standing Committee of the Ninth National People's Congress on April 28, 2001. Available at http://www.lawinfochina.com/display.aspx?lib=law&id=1793. Access on 23.08.2019.

Masbah, M. 2018. "Let it Spoil!": Morocco's Boycott and the Empowerment of 'Regular' Citizen. Report of Al Jazeera Centre for Studies. Available at http://studies.aljazeera.net/en/reports/2018/11/181114115931285.html. Access on 06.10.2019.

Matos, O. 1993. A Escola de Frankfurt: luzes e sombras do Iluminismo. São Paulo: Moderna.

Mcleod, A. 2014. Understanding Asian Philosophy. London, Bloomsbury.

Meehan, J. 2011. Recognition and the Dynamics of Intersubjectivity In *Axel Honneth: critical essays: with a reply by Axel Honneth*. Social and Critical Theory: a Critical Horizons Book Series. V.12. Brill, Leiden, Boston.

Moore, Greg. 2001. China's Cautious Participation in the UN Human Rights Regime: a review of China, the United Nations, and Human Rights: The Limits of Compliance, by Ann Kent. In *Human Rights & Human Welfare*. Vol. 1 (1).

Moroccan Family Code. Dahir N°1.04.22 du 12 Hija 1424 (3 Fevrier 2004) Portant Promulgation de la Loi N° 70.03 Portant Code de la Famille. Available at http://www.ilo.org/dyn/natlex/natlex4.detail?p_lang=fr&p_isn=72091&p_classification=01.03. Access on 29.04.2020.

Morocco's Constitution 2011. Dahir no 1-11-91 du 27 chaabane 1432 (29 juillet 2011) portant promulgation du texte de la Constitution. Bulletin officiel no 5964 bis—28 chaabane 1432 (30-7-2011). Available at http://www.maroc.ma/en/content/constitution. Access on 01.07.2018.

NPR. 2022. Shanghai maintains 'zero-COVID' policy but the U.N. says it is not sustainable. 11.05.2022. Available at https://www.npr.org/2022/05/11/1098150456/shanghai-maintains-zero-covid-policy-but-the-u-n-says-it-is-not-sustainable?t=1659161763653. Access on 30.07.2022.

Okin, S. M. 1999. Is Multiculturalism bad for women? In *Susan Moller Okin with respondents*. Edited by J. Cohen, M. Howard, M. C. Nussbaum. Princeton University Press, Princeton. [Kindle 5.12.2] Retrieved from amazon.de

O'Lemmon, M. 2022. The worst mistake 2.0? The digital revolution and the consequences of innovation. Springer-Verlag London Ltd. AI & Society (2022). https://doi.org/10.1007/s00146-022-01599-5. Available at https://link.springer.com/article/ https://doi.org/10.1007/s00146-022-01599-5#citeas. Access on 08.05.2023.

Peng, Z.; Ding, Y. 2012. Tackling urban poverty in China: the Minimum Living Standard Scheme and its limitations. In *China Journal of Poverty and Social Justice*, vol 20 (3). ISSN 1759–8273., 261–76. https://doi.org/10.1332/175982712X657082. The Policy Press.

Pensky, M. 2011. Social Solidarity and Intersubjective Recognition: on Axel Honneth's Struggle for Recognition. In *Axel Honneth: critical essays: with a reply by Axel Honneth.* Social and Critical Theory: a Critical Horizons Book Series. V.12. Brill, Leiden, Boston.

Peters, R. T. 2014. Solidarity Ethics: transforming a globalized world. Fortress Press: Minneapolis. [Kindle 5.12.2] Retrieved from amazon.de

Petherbridge, D. (Editor). 2011. Axel Honneth: critical essays: with a reply by Axel Honneth. Social and Critical Theory: a Critical Horizons Book Series. V.12. Brill: Leiden, Boston.

Rancière, J; Honneth, A.; Genel, K; Deranty, J.P. 2016. Recognition or Disagreement: a Critical Encounter on the Politics of Freedom, Equality, and Identity. New Directions in Critical Theory Book 30. (English Edition) New York, Columbia University Press.

Raz, J. 1999. How Perfect Should One Be? And Whose Culture Is? In *Is Multiculturalism bad for women? Susan Moller Okin with respondents.* Edited by J. Cohen, M. Howard, M. C. Nussbaum. Princeton University Press, Princeton. [Kindle 5.12.2] Retrieved from amazon.de

Reale, G.; Antiseri, D. 2006. História da Filosofia: de Nietzsche à Escola de Frankfurt. V.6. Translated by Ivo Storniolo. São Paulo: Paulus.

Ren, Q.; Zhu, P. 2014. Education in China: Uneven Progress. In *Analysing China's Population: social changes in a new demographic era.* Attané, I.; Gu, B. INED Population Studies, V.3. Springer.

Réseau National des Centres d'Ecoute des Femmes Victimes de Violences. 2007. Les violences fondées sur le genre au Maroc. Deuxième rapport: Analyse des plaintes enregistrées par les centres d'écoute et d'assistance juridique des femmes victimes de violence.

Richardson, W. 2015. China, Single Women Live by Their Own Rules. The New York Times. August 14, 2015. Available on https://lens.blogs.nytimes.com/2015/08/14/in-china-the-single-ladies-push-back/. Access on 05.04.2019.

Rieß, A. Eine Ideengeschichte der Freiheit: Die liberale Idee im Zeichen des theologisch-politischen Problems. 2012. Inaugural-Dissertation zur Erlangung des Doktorgrades der Philosophie an der Ludwig-Maximilians-Universität München. 2012. Available at https://edoc.ub.uni-muenchen.de/15054/1/Riess_Andreas.pdf. Access on 08.05.2023.

Rorty, R. 1989. Solidarity or Objectivity? In *Relativism: Interpretation and Confrontation.* Edited by Krauz, M. Notre Dame, University of Notre Dame Press.

Salonia, M. 2008. Suffering from Exclusion: On the critical impulse of the theory of recognition. In *Civitas Porto Alegre* v. 8 (1). 125–136.

Schlumpf, E. 2016. The Legal Status of Children Born out of Wedlock in Morocco. In *Electronic Journal of Islamic and Middle Eastern Law.* Vol. 4. The Center for Islamic and Middle Eastern Legal Studies, University of Zurich (Switzerland). ISSN 1664–5707. 1–26.

Schmale, W. 1993. Human rights in the intercultural perspective and the reorganization of the international debate. In *Human rights and cultural diversity.* Europe-Arabic-Islamic World-Africa-China. Keip Publishing, Goldbach.

Simmel, G. The Metropolis and Mental Life. 1900.

Sinnerbrink, R. 2011. Power, Recognition, and Care: Honneth's Critique of Poststructuralist Social Philosophy. In *Axel Honneth: critical essays: with a reply by Axel Honneth.* Social and Critical Theory: a Critical Horizons Book Series. V.12. Brill: Leiden, Boston.

Sinnerbrink, R. Hegelianismo. Ed. Vozes. 2017. Translated by Fabio Creder.

Slater, P. 1976. Origem e significado da Escola de Frankfurt: uma perspectiva marxista. Rio de Janeiro: Zahar.

Smith, N. The Telegraph. 2019. 21.03.2019. Burmese women trafficked into sexual slavery in China, says new report. Available at https://www.telegraph.co.uk/global-health/terror-and-security/burmese-women-trafficked-sexual-slavery-china-says-new-report/. Access on 05.08.2022.

Southern African Aids Trust. Porter, A.; Kaye And Scholer Law Firm; Thomson Reuters Foundation. _ Age of consent: legal review Morocco Country Report.

Steinhauer, I. 2016. Sex and Sexual Education in China: Traditional Values and Social Implications. SIT Graduate Institute—Study Abroad. Independent Study Project (ISP) Collection. https://digitalcollections.sit.edu/isp_collection/2291. Spring.

Stepping Stones. 2018. Stepping Stones Annual Report. Available at https://steppingstoneschina.net/who-we-are/stepping-stones-annual-reports/. Access on 25.10.2019.

Stichweh, R. 1997. The stranger—on the sociology of indifference. In *Thesis Eleven* (51). London, SAGE Publications. 1–16.

Sunflower Women Workers Centre. 2013. The sexual harassment of women factory workers in Ghangzhou. A survey by the Sunflower Women Workers Centre. November 25, 2013. Available at https://clb.org.hk/sites/default/files/archive/en/Image/research_report/sexual%20harassment%20survey%20sunflower%20centre.pdf. Access on 31.05.2018.

Tam, B. K. Y.; Bond, M. H. 2002. Interpersonal behaviors and friendship in a Chinese culture. In *Asian Journal of Social Psychology*. Vol. 5. 63–74.

Taylor, C. 1992. Inwardness and the culture of modernity. In Philosophical interventions in the unfinished project of Enlightenment. Edited by A. Honneth, T. McCarthy, C. Offe, and A. Wellmer. Translations by William Rehg. The MIT Press, Cambridge, Massachussets, London, England.

Taylor, C. 1994. A política de reconhecimento. In Multiculturalismo. Taylor, C.; Appiah, K. A.; Habermas, J.; Rockefeller, S. C.; Walzer, M.; Wolf, S. Translated by Maria Machado. Lisboa: Instituto Piaget.

Taylor, C. 2011. A ética da autenticidade. Translated by Talyta Carvalho. São Paulo: Realizações.

The Advocates for Human Rights; MRA Mobilising for Rights Associates. 2015. Morocco: Submission to the Committee on Economic, Social and Cultural Rights. Relating to the ESC Rights of Women. Available at https://www.theadvocatesforhumanrights.org/Res/morocco_esc_shadow_report_august_2015.pdf. Access on 03.05.2023.

The University of Hong Kong Bulletin. He, X. 2022. Men Win out in Divorce in China. The University of Hong Kong Bulletin. Available at https://bulletin.hku.hk/research/men-win-out-in-divorce-in-china/. Access on 30.07.2022.

The World Bank. 2022. Labor force, female (% of total labor force)—Morocco. Available at https://data.worldbank.org/indicator/SL.TLF.TOTL.FE.ZS?locations=MA. Access on 02.08.2022.

UN Women 2021. Country Fact Sheet Morocco. Available at https://data.unwomen.org/country/morocco. Access on 03.08.2022.

UNDP China, 2022. Gender Equality and Women's Empowerment in China. Available on https://www.undp.org/china/gender. Access on 30.07.2022.

United Nations Children's Fund (UNICEF). 2011. Morocco: MENA Gender Equality Profile. Status of Girls and Women in the Middle East and North Africa. Regional Office for the Middle East and North Africa.

United Nations Development Programme (UNDP). 2016. Handbook of Charity Law of the People's Republic of China. Available at https://www.cn.undp.org/content/china/en/home/library/democratic_governance/handbook-of-charity-law-of-the-peoples-republic-of-china.html. Access on 28.04.2019.

United Nations Development Programme China (UNDP China), 2022. Gender Equality and Women's Empowerment in China. Available at https://www.undp.org/china/gender. Access on 30.07.2022.

United Nations Entity For Gender Equality And The Empowerment Of Women (UN WOMEN). 2015. Progress of the world's women 2015–2016: Transforming economies, realizing rights. Available at http://progress.unwomen.org. Access on 03.05.2018.

United Nations Population Fund. Family planning is a human right. Message for World Population Day by Dr. Natalia Kanem, Executive Director. 11 July 2018. 06 Jul 2018. Available at https://www.unfpa.org/press/family-planning-human-right. Access on 12.04.2022.

United Nations System in China. 2015. Gender Equality in China's Economic Transformation. Bohong Liu China Women's University; Ling Li National School of Development, Peking University; Chunyu Yang National School of Development, Peking University.

United Nations Woman. 2015. Bringing bus drivers on board against sexual harassment in Marrakesh. June 11, 2015. Available at http://www.unwomen.org/en/news/stories/2015/6/bringing-buses-on-board-against-sexual-harassment-in-marrakesh. Access on 04.04.2018.

United Nations. 1984. Universal Declaration Of Human Rights. Available at https://www.un.org/en/universal-declaration-human-rights/. Access on 23.09.2017.

United Nations. Declaration on the Right to Development. Adopted by General Assembly resolution 41/128 of 4 December 1986. Available at https://www.ohchr.org/sites/default/files/rtd.pdf. Access on 14.04.2022.

United States Department Of State. 2015. China (Includes Tibet, Hong Kong, And Macau) 2015 Human Rights Report. Country Reports on Human Rights Practices for 2015. Bureau of Democracy, Human Rights and Labor. https://2009-2017.state.gov/documents/organization/252967.pdf. 24.07.2018.

United States Department Of State. 2017. Morocco 2017 Human Rights Report. Country Reports on Human Rights Practices for 2017. Bureau of Democracy, Human Rights and Labor.

University of Minnesota Human Rights Library, 2022. Ratification of International Human Rights Treaties—China. Available at hrlibrary.umn.edu/research/ratification-china.html. Access on 01.08.2022.

University of Minnesota Human Rights Library, 2022. Ratification of International Human Rights Treaties—Morocco. Available at hrlibrary.umn.edu/research/ratification-morocco.html. Access on 01.08.2022.

Van Den Brink, B. 2011. Recognition, pluralism and the expectation of harmony: against the ideal of an ethical life 'free from pain'. In Axel Honneth: critical essays: with a reply by Axel Honneth. Social and Critical Theory: a Critical Horizons Book Series. V.12. Brill: Leiden, Boston.

Verso. Koumiya, G. 2018. Post-68 student uprisings and the rise of the Moroccan Marxist Leninist movement. May 25, 2018. Available at https://www.versobooks.com/blogs/3838-post-68-student-uprisings-and-the-rise-of-the-moroccan-marxist-leninist-movement. Access on 25.10.2019.

Von Senger, H. 1993. Chinese Culture and Human Rights. In *Human rights and cultural diversity.* Europe-Arabic-Islamic World-Africa-China. Keip Publishing: Goldbach.

Wadud, A. 1999. Qu'ran and Woman: rereading the sacred text from a woman's perspective. New York, Oxford.

Walzer, M. 1997. On Toleration. The Castle Lectures in Ethics, Politics, and Economics. Yale University Press. New Haven and London. [Kindle 5.12.2] Retrieved from amazon.de

Wong, S.P.Y.; Phillips, M. R. 2009. Nonfatal Suicidal Behavior Among Chinese Women Who Have Been Physically Abused by Their Male Intimate Partners. In *Suicide and Life-Threatening Behavior 39.* (6) The American Association of Suicidology.

World Bank Group. 2015. Morocco Mind the Gap: Empowering Women for a More Open, Inclusive, and Prosperous Society. Middle East and North Africa. Washington. Available at http://documents.worldbank.org/curated/en/818541468179084318/Morocco-mind-the-gap-empowering-women-for-a-more-open-inclusive-and-prosperous-society. Access on 05.05.2018.

World Bank Group. 2017. China: systematic country diagnostic. Towards a more inclusive and sustainable development. Available at http://documents.worldbank.org/curated/en/147231519162198351/China-Systematic-Country-Diagnostic-towards-a-more-inclusive-and-sustainable-development. Access on 23.07.2018.

World Bank Group. 2022. Poverty & Equity Brief China East Asia & Pacific. April 2022. World Bank Group Poverty & Equity. Available at https://databank.worldbank.org/data/download/poverty/987B9C90-CB9F-4D93-AE8C-750588BF00QA/current/Global_POVEQ_CHN.pdf. Access on 30.07.2022.

Wu, M. S.; Schmitt, M. et al. 2014. Examining Self-Advantage in the Suffering of Others: Cross-Cultural Differences in Beneficiary and Observer Justice Sensitivity Among Chinese, Germans, and Russians. Springer Science+Business Media, New York.

Yifei, S. Feminism in China An Analysis of Advocates, Debates, and Strategies. Friedrich Ebert Stiftung. Available at https://library.fes.de/pdf-files/bueros/china/12947.pdf. Access on 07.12.2022.

You; Yi; Chen. 2016. Love, Life, and "Leftover Ladies" in Urban China. Renmin University of China, Peking University, Shanghai University Available at https://mpra.ub.uni-muenchen.de/70494/1/MPRA_paper_70494.pdf. Access on 09.05.2023.

Xinran, N. H. 2011. Message from an Unknown Chinese Mother: Stories of Loss and Love (English Edition). Translated from Chinese by Nicky Harman. London, Vintage Books. [Kindle 5.12.2] Retrieved from amazon.de

Zerrifi, F. A. 2001. Stripping off the veil: women's performance of the veil from street to stage. University of Surrey. School of Performing Arts. Department of Theatre and Performance Studies.

Zhu, Y. 2013. Legal Institution Building for the Rule of Law and Human Rights. In *Modern Chinese Legal Reform: new perspectives.* Li, X.; Fang, Q. Kentucky: American University Presses.

The manufacturer's authorised representative in the EU is Springer Nature Customer Service Centre GmbH, Europaplatz 3, 69115 Heidelberg, Germany. If you have any concerns regarding our products, please contact ProductSafety@springernature.com

Printed and bound by CPI Group (UK) Ltd, Croydon, CR0 4YY

30/09/2026

02225601-0003